MAN ON FIRE

MAN ON FIRE

John Brown and the Cause of Liberty

JULES ABELS

The Macmillan Company, New York, New York

Collier-Macmillan Limited, London

The Macmillan Company
866 Third Avenue, New York, N.Y. 10022
Collier-Macmillan Canada Ltd., Toronto, Ontario

Library of Congress Catalog Card Number: 72-117961

First Printing

Printed in the United States of America

Acknowledgments

MOST OF THE RESEARCH for this book was done in the Library of Congress in Washington, D.C., and I am grateful for the facilities provided to me. The Library in its Manuscripts Division has papers of Governor Henry A. Wise of Virginia relating to the trial and execution of John Brown.

The Kansas State Historical Society in Topeka, Kansas, has the largest collection of John Brown's letters, books, and articles. I wish to express my thanks to Mr. Joseph W. Snell, Assistant State Archivist, for his help to me in my research in the Library of the Society.

I wish to express my appreciation to Miss Joyce Elizabeth Harman, Manuscripts Specialist of the Ohio Historical Society in Columbus, Ohio, for her aid in my research there. The John Brown, Jr., Collection was rewarding indeed.

My great thanks also to Miss Harman for the interlibrary loan of the Boyd B. Stutler Collection, in microfilm. This amazing assembly of variegated source materials, the largest private collection of John Brown papers, has considerably enriched this book.

The Boston Public Library has the two John Brown notebooks. Its Thomas Wentworth Higginson Collection has valuable papers relating to the relationship of the Boston Abolitionist fraternity with John Brown.

Officials of the United States Park Service in Harper's Ferry, West Virginia, were most helpful in explaining geographical factors involved in the John Brown raid. The map of the town in 1859, which is presented in this book, was drawn by Mr. Eugene V. Tourville of Washington, D.C.

Contents

6 · And the angel of the Lord appeared unto him, and said, the Lord is with thee, thou mighty man of valour.
12 · And the Lord looked down on him, and said, Go in this thy might and thou shalt save Israel from the Midianites, have I not sent thee?
15 · And he said, Oh my Lord, wherewith shall I save Israel? Behold my family is poor in Manasseh and I am the least in my father's house.
16 · And the Lord said unto him, Surely I will be with thee, and thou shalt strike the Midianites as one man.
27 · And so Gideon chose ten of his servants and did as the Lord had commanded him . . . and so it was that he did it by night.

JUDGES 6

He was very pious and had been deeply impressed for years with the story of Gideon, believing that he, with a handful of men, could strike down slavery.

HUGH FORBES,
quoted in the New York Herald,
October 29, 1859

Introduction

AT ELEVEN O'CLOCK on a Sunday night, October 16, 1859, a force of armed men crossed the covered railroad bridge spanning the Potomac River from Maryland and invaded the town of Harper's Ferry in Virginia. They seized the federal armory that was one of the largest in the nation. They had brought along a sizable arsenal of firearms of their own, and hundreds of wooden pikes with spears attached, with which they armed a dozen slaves. They announced that they had come to free the slaves of the South.

The startling news of an insurrection was soon conveyed by telegraph to a nation in which emotions had been already raised to a high pitch on the slavery question. The North quivered with excitement and the South was filled with trembling. The size of the invading "army" had been put in the hundreds, but when Brevet-Colonel Robert E. Lee arrived on the scene on Monday night in command of ninety United States Marines dispatched from Washington, the dimensions of the expeditionary force had been deflated. Its leader was fifty-nine-year-old John Brown, long a fighter against slavery, an outlaw with a price on his head, and notorious for his deeds in Bleeding Kansas as Osawatomie Brown. He commanded in all twenty-one men, five of whom were black.

By daybreak of Tuesday morning, Lee's men had subdued the invaders. The wounded Brown was a captive. Two of his sons who had fought by his side, Oliver, twenty, and Watson, twenty-four, were slain as were eight others of the band. Brown's men had killed five, and the first victim, as fate would have it, had been a free Negro who had a responsible job with the Baltimore and Ohio Railroad.

Brown was taken to nearby Charlestown and his trial began within a week, on October 25. He lay on a pallet throughout, claiming that he was too weak from his wounds to rise. He was sentenced to death on November 2 and executed on December 2. Six of his command followed him to the gallows, two of them having been captured in Pennsylvania and turned over by that state to Virginia for execution. Only five, including Brown's son, Owen, made good their escape.

The invasion, on the first news, had been branded even in northern Abolitionist quarters as the act of a madman. By the time Brown was hanged a great wave of sympathy had been generated in the North for him; bells tolled and mass meetings were held starting at the hour of his death. Much of this sympathy was evoked by the nobility of the statements made by Brown at his trial and in his letters written in prison between his sentence and execution, which were widely published. Their general tenor was that his mission had been in the cause of God and that he was content, nay, even eager "to die for God's eternal truth on the scaffold as in any other way."

Brown had succeeded in clothing what had appeared "mad" with virtue and plausibility, that of self-sacrifice for a cause. There were millions in the United States and in Europe (where it was almost as much a sensation as at home) who believed that Old Brown had been judicially murdered only because slavery had turned the hearts of otherwise decent human beings in the South into stone, and many in the North felt that John Brown had given his life for the Negro race much as Christ had given his for all humanity. In the Civil War, which commenced a year and a half after his futile raid, Brown slept in a fortress which cannon could not shake. Stephen Vincent Benét, in his great poem, *John Brown's Body*, wrote, "His song is alive and throbs in the tramp of the columns,/His song is blown out of the mouth of a cannon. . . ." In later years, the vitality of the John Brown legend gives testimony that his heroism, however foolhardy it might have been, strikes a deep and responsive chord among those who admire individual conviction and the will of the individual to protest to the ultimate degree against what he considers a wrong.

The face of this man, looking more fierce from his upright hair, stares at us from the long-buried past. Was he mad? That Brown was unbalanced and that insanity was rampant on the mother's side of his family was an argument presented by his friends in the Ohio area where he grew up in their frantic attempt to persuade Governor Henry A. Wise of Virginia to spare his life. In later years these "proofs" were used by his detractors to denigrate his memory. This is a topic that shall be explored later in this book.

Terminology in 1859 was nebulous and his friends in their pleas to Governor Wise insisted that Brown was a "monomaniac." Today, we can have no hesitancy in saying that Brown was an "egomaniac." From increasingly deep reading of the Bible he turned drunk on the Old Testament and became convinced that he had been selected by God to break the jaws of the wicked, a belief he maintained through the stark reality of years of disappointment and failure when he was scorned by men and ignored by destiny. Immediately after his capture at Harper's Ferry he informed his interrogators that he had acted as "an instrument of God."

He was unlovely in the flesh. He was crafty if not dishonest in his business dealings before he turned to public affairs and was then deceitful to his associates in his antislavery crusade. That he had a light regard for the truth is an understatement. We have an assessment of Brown, made in 1893, by George B. Gill, who, as we shall see, as a literary youth in his early twenties was a trusted lieutenant and lived cheek by jowl with Brown in 1858–59. He stayed clear of the Virginia foray, but parted from Brown on friendly terms. He found his commander arrogant, vindictive, bloodthirsty, intolerant of weakness. "The angel wings were so dim as to be almost unseen." Gill did not deem Brown insane as no one closely associated with Brown thought him insane; but "very superstitious, very selfish and very intolerant, with great self-esteem. His immense egotism coupled with love of approbation and his god-idea begat in him a feeling that he was the Moses that was to lead the Exodus of the colored people from their Southern taskmasters."

Gill went on. "And yet this very concentration in self commanded the great advance on American slavery," and "vindicated an apparent absurd assault by accelerating the forces which in the end gave success." Thus Brown proved to be indeed "an instrument of God." Although his venture ended only in a "dreamless sleep, yet the wave moved on upon whose bloody crest the slave rode to freedom."

It required a character of enormous drive and force of will, a sense of great purpose that could pay no heed to small morals or men around him, to project this man Brown on the world stage—a man born into a poor and lowly family, with very little education, of mediocre talent, who started out with nothing and accumulated nothing along the way.

However unlovely his personal characteristics, he was lifted above the herd because he was inspired, he felt passionately about the curse of slavery and was willing to endure suffering and risk death fighting it. That is the total involvement, the fire in the bosom that transfigures you and me.

During his lifetime there were many who knew him who were strongly reminded of the stern stuff of Oliver Cromwell, and his daughter Ruth said that her father's favorite book after the Bible was a biography of Cromwell. Cromwell, too, believed that he was an instrument of God. The comment made by Richard Baxter in 1685 concerning Cromwell holds true of Brown. "Having thus fixed his conscience to justify all his cause . . . he thinketh that the end being good and necessary, the necessary means cannot be bad."

In *The Interregnum*, historian F. I. Inderwick stated, "A complex character such as that of Cromwell is incapable of creation except in time of great civil and religious excitement, and one cannot judge of the man without at the same time considering the contending elements by which he was surrounded. It is possible to take his character to pieces and, reflecting one or other of his qualities as a cornerstone, to build around it a monument which will show him as a patriot or plotter, a Christian or a hypocrite, a demon or demi-god."

This applies with a vengeance to all assessments of the controversial John Brown. Truth must lie in the eye of the beholder if one sees him as an exalted hero and another as a cheap horse-thief and murderer. An author must tread warily in this field. Fortunately, there is a good deal of documentary evidence. Beyond that, some comment is desirable on previous treatments of Brown, to which reference will be made in this book.

The first three full-scale biographies of Brown, of the unadulterated hero-worshipping kind, were published by James Redpath in 1860, by Franklin B. Sanborn in 1885, and Richard J. Hinton in 1895. All three historians knew Brown personally, Redpath and Hinton as newspaper correspondents, Sanborn far better since he played a key role as a member of a group of men called the Secret Six,

operating from Boston, who gave Brown his necessary financial back-
ing. All three historians were early aware of the Brown conspiracy
to invade the South, though not aware of Harper's Ferry as the point
he would attack.

In an amazing hoax the public was kept uninformed until 1879 that
Brown had been the perpetrator of the murder in cold blood of five
men in May, 1856, on the banks of Pottawatomie Creek in Kansas,
who, though innocent of any crime, had been dragged from their
beds in the night and hacked to death as a bloody example or deterrent
to the proslave faction in the territory. Sanborn in his biography was
forced to accept this as fact, but continued to find Brown's soul as
unstained as that of a newborn babe, and Hinton's later book glossed
over this matter. However, backbiters in increasing numbers by now
had cropped up in the state of Kansas, including the prominent
Charles Robinson, the first free-state governor, who had been hitherto
a Brown admirer.

In 1909, the Negro educator W. E. B. Du Bois published a biography that was a rhapsodic treatment of Brown, stringing together
existing sources and putting heavy emphasis on the Negro contribution to the Brown career. In 1910, Oswald Garrison Villard, the
grandson of the great Abolitionist editor, William Lloyd Garrison,
authored a massive work which he offered as "free from bias, from
the errors in taste and fact of the mere panegyrist," but his book
was, in fact a long apologia and panegyric, and aside from the
Pottawatomie affair which he could not wholly condone, he found
Brown a verray ungentil, parfit knight.

In the decade of debunking, Robert Penn Warren in his *John
Brown; The Making of a Martyr* (1929) found considerable grounds
to "debunk" Brown. A far more severe attack, in fact a diatribe, was
gathered by James C. Malin in 1942 in his "John Brown and the
Legend of Fifty-Six," a paper printed by the American Philosophical
Society. Malin was a professor of American history at the University
of Kansas, and his research and conclusions were a culminating expression of a revulsion toward Brown in the Kansas intellectual community that seems to have begun at the time of the Harper's Ferry raid.

I shall record Brown's failings in character, judged by accepted
ethical and moral codes. But warts and all, his story impresses me as
an inspiring saga of what one human being, in the evening of his life,
saddled with a record of past failure, armed with nothing but conviction, the indomitable will to fight the devil, and consummate gall

can do to shake the national will. "One of God's side is a majority," proclaimed the famed Abolitionist Wendell Phillips in exalting Brown after his capture at Harper's Ferry and, indeed, Brown's role in bringing on the Civil War seems to me to have been underrated by history.

An aspect that has some relevance to modern times is that this was, despite Brown's own advanced years, essentially a youth activist movement, since it was youth over whom Brown wielded his great influence. Redpath, Hinton, and Sanborn at the time they fell under Brown's influence during his Kansas crusade were twenty-three, twenty-six, and twenty-five years old, respectively. Of the twenty-one men who comprised Brown's Harper's Ferry force, only two were over thirty, and the average age was twenty-five, although a good number were grizzled, three-year veterans of the war in Kansas.

They were predominantly young militants, radicals on the issue of slavery, who in a generation-gap of thinking, opposing their elders, wanted a showdown with the South, and unlike moderates of the stamp of Abraham Lincoln were unwilling to haggle with slaveholders in the interest of "Union first." They were not riffraff. Annie Brown, Brown's sixteen-year-old daughter who tended house for them in the summer of 1859 at the Kennedy farm in Maryland, which was the springboard for the Harper's Ferry operations, commented later of their caliber with a pun, "There is plenty of good bread which is not college-bred." Yet, between 1857 and 1859 Brown did attract many men to him who had fine education and talent.

Brown himself was youth-conscious, having great faith in youth, relying on them for brains as well as physical capacity. He beamed his appeal purposefully to youth on the "higher law" theme. And Brown was in person a remarkable youth-phenomenon. At the age of fifty-nine, he had the endurance of one who was twenty-five. His mind had the vibrancy, the daring, and the flexibility of youth. It was only in the crisis at Harper's Ferry, when he was engulfed by events that he could not control, that he aged years within a few hours, became befuddled and bewildered, and suddenly responded in the flesh to the appellation commonly attached to him, "Old Brown."

MAN ON FIRE

CHAPTER ONE

Man of Failure

IN EARLY 1850 when he had reached seventy-seven years of age John Brown's father, Owen, was asked by his daughter, Marian, to write a brief story of his life. In his narration Owen said, "In 1800, May 9 John was born one hundred years after his Great Grandfather, nothing [else] very uncommon."

The year 1800 was actually a "very uncommon" one. It was the dawn of a century that was to be dominated in this nation by the dispute over slavery, which would plunge it into bloody civil war. In 1909, William Dean Howells, the dean of American letters, reflected that the two great figures of the last century had been John Brown and Abraham Lincoln. "So different as they were in their lives, in their death they are not divided because they both died by the power of slavery, the one, slavery in its supremacy, the other, slavery in its extremity."

The year 1800 was important for the election of Thomas Jefferson as President, which overthrew the oligarchic rule of the Federalists by "wealth and talent" and ushered in egalitarian democracy, and the age of the common man's Brown and Lincoln. Although a slave-owning Virginian, Jefferson had written of slavery in 1782, "Indeed,

I tremble for my country when I reflect that God is just." In 1803, stretching the concept of federal power, Jefferson made the Louisiana Purchase, bringing new lands into the Union which would in future years be the source of woes in the great slavery dispute, including Bleeding Kansas in 1856.

In this year of 1800, a slave, Nat Turner, was born who was to lead a notable slave insurrection that John Brown would often discuss. In 1800, the first attempt at insurrection by slaves was led in Virginia by "General Gabriel" (Prosser), a young slave blacksmith. At a brook, six miles from Richmond, a crowd of almost a thousand Negroes gathered on September 1, a few with firearms but most with clubs and cutlasses. The attack, like Brown's in a later year, was to be concentrated on a government arsenal in Richmond. According to the *United States Gazette*, published in Philadelphia, of September 8, "They planned to issue proclamations summoning to their standard their fellow Negroes and friends of humanity throughout the continent. In a week they estimated they would have 50,000 men on their side." A heavy thunderstorm that made a swamp of the roads to Richmond caused Gabriel to call off his attack. He was captured and hanged along with thirty of his army.

In 1800, a bloody war of liberation was in progress in the French colony of St. Domingue in the eastern part of the island of Hispaniola, later named Hayti. The doctrines of the French Revolution infiltrated *affranchis*, freedmen children of white masters and Negro women, and they rose up in 1791. Then slaves on northern sugar plantations joined the rebellion with slaughter and rape of the neighborhood whites, pillage, and fire. Toussaint L'Ouverture, a slave who had learned to read and write while working as a coachman, came to the fore as a leader. British troops landed on the island and Toussaint joined forces with the French who proclaimed freedom for the slaves and made him commander-in-chief. He turned against the French and in 1800 became absolute ruler when he overcame General Rigaud who had set up an *affranchi* state in the south. Occupied with European troubles, Napoleon was unable to cope with this revolt until 1802, when he sent General LeClerc with twenty thousand men to the island. Toussaint was captured and sent to France, where he died in a dungeon while awaiting trial. Before the torch was extinguished, however, over ten thousand French were believed to have perished in the strife.

John Brown had read all the literature extant about Toussaint

L'Ouverture and often cited him as proof that Negroes were valorous, and willing and able to fight for their freedom. He shrugged aside arguments (which were valid) that conditions were different on the plantations of Hayti from those in our southern states.

Owen Brown began his narrative, "As I take up my pen to write, I say that my life has been of little worth, mostly fild with vanity." Much worth should be attached to a rugged, pioneer struggle for existence, of unremitting toil from sunrise to sunset. He worked at shoemaking and tanning, farmed, and sold butter and cheese to enable his family to survive. He married Ruth Mills of Dutch origin in 1793. John was born in Torrington in Litchfield County, Connecticut, seven years later.

The controversy about John Brown starts out with his ancestry. Sanborn intimated via a footnote that Brown must have been descended from the John Brown, listed in John Foxe's *Book of Martyrs*, who was burned at the stake in the Popish persecutions under the English Tudors in 1511. Our John Brown never made this claim. Sanborn claimed, moreover, that Brown was of distinguished New England stock, being a descendant of the Peter Brown who came over on the *Mayflower* in 1620. In his biography, Villard said that this was not so, that he was descended from an obscure Peter Brown born in Windsor, Connecticut, in 1632. The aged Sanborn angrily assailed Villard, saying that if he was not descended from Peter Brown of the *Mayflower* he must have been descended from his brother and so it was all in the family. In a recent study in 1957 in the *American Genealogist*, Donald Lines Jacobus found no proof that Brown sprang from the *Mayflower* Brown and in fact found evidence to the contrary.

This is a matter of more than academic interest. In 1857, when Brown was adopted by prominent persons of Boston society as one of their own, a factor in his social acceptance was his supposed *Mayflower* lineage. I have seen no oral statement attributed to Brown in this regard prior to 1857 and nothing in his letters, and it appears to have been an invention on his part when he cultivated Boston aristocracy.

John's grandfather, also John Brown, was a captain in the 18th Regiment of the Connecticut Colony in the Revolutionary War and died of dysentery soon after he took up arms. He left eleven children, including little Owen, who wrote: "The care and support of this family fell mostly on my mother. The laboring men were mostly in the army." John Brown's maternal grandfather, Lieutenant Gideon Mills, also served in the Revolution. His mother, Ruth, died when John Brown was eight years old. Owen married twice more and he had sixteen children in all. His only child other than John who attained distinction was Salmon, a son of Ruth. He was a lawyer, editor of the newspaper, the New Orleans *Bee*, and fought a political war with General Andrew Jackson. He died when he was thirty-three. Owen was not proud of him. "He was of some note as a gentleman but I never knew that he gave evidence of being a Christian."

In June, 1805, Owen migrated from Connecticut to the Western Reserve district of Ohio, the northeastern district of Ohio that Connecticut had refused to relinquish to the federal government but "reserved" for its own citizens. An 1805 treaty with the Indians made it safe for newcomers. After a seven-week trek by ox-cart, the family settled in Hudson, thirty miles southeast of Cleveland, named after the leading citizen, Squire David Hudson. Owen wrote, "We had some hardships to undergo but they appear to be greater in history than they were in reality," which again cushioned the truth. This was the forest primeval, peopled with Indians, a wilderness that had to be cleared; without any roads, transport was possible only by ox-carts or by rough sleds. Bears attacked the settlers' livestock and in turn were attacked by organized bear-hunts, which went on for years until they were exterminated. As an amateur surveyor, the father related he "was often calld to go into woods to make devisions of land . . . and be gone some times two week and sleep on the ground and that without injery."

In this wild country John Brown grew up from the age of five, when he was of school age. The man of letters, Henry D. Thoreau, in one of his frequent encomiums said, "He did not go to Harvard. He was not fed on the pap that is there furnished, but he went to the University of the West, where he studied the science of Liberty, and having taken his degree he finally commenced the practice of Humanity in Kansas."

Indeed, Brown had little formal education. Brown himself wrote that his was "the School of Adversity." We are fortunate to have an autobiography of his boyhood which was written under the following circumstances. On a Sunday night in January, 1857, Brown discoursed at dinner about his Kansas experiences in the home of the Boston merchant prince, George L. Stearns, who would be the most generous of the Secret Six who furnished the money for Brown's famous and fatal exploit. Stearns's twelve-year-old son Henry after dinner pressed his pocketmoney into Brown's hand begging him to use it for "some poor, little boy in Kansas," and asked the old warrior to describe what kind of boy he had been. Brown replied, "My son, I am afraid that it would be too wearisome for the ladies, but I will write it down and send it to you," which he did, from Red Rock, Iowa, on July 15 of that year.

James Russell Lowell pronounced this the finest piece of autobiography extant, which is typical hyperbole from Boston intellectuals. It is interesting and important not only as a recital of what the boy John Brown really was but for what the adult Brown wanted to appear to have been in his youth, since he was interested far less in enlightening the son than in impressing the rich father, whose support was vital for his plans.

His account was rendered in the third person:

Indeed when for a short time he was sometimes sent to School the opportunity it afforded to wrestle, & Snow ball & run & jump & knock off old seedy Wool hats; offered to him almost the only compensation for the confinement & restraints of school. I need not tell you that with such a feeling & but little chance of going to school *at all*; he did not become much of a schollar. . . . He learned nothing of Grammer; nor did he get at school so much knowledge of com[mon] Arithmetic as the Four ground rules.

Brown had no need to mention that his education in spelling had been poor.

He stayed around the Indians and learned their talk. He early learned to dress his own deer, squirrel, raccoon, or wolf skins. He grew up fast and by the time he was fifteen he was very large and strong for his age and anxious to do a man's work.

"I must not neglect to tell you of a verry *bad & foolish* habit to which John was some what addicted. I mean *telling lies*; generally to screen himself from blame; or from punishment." Perhaps if little John had been oftener encouraged to be frank, "he would not have been so often guilty in after life of this fault." Why should Brown have made this damaging admission if he had not been discovered by Mr. Stearns in some lie?

He told of an incident which "made him a most *determined Abolitionist*: & led him to declare, *or Swear Eternal war* with Slavery."

When the War of 1812 broke out, his father went into the business of furnishing beef cattle to the troops and John, though only twelve years old, was sent driving cattle a hundred miles from home. He stayed with a gentlemanly landlord who made a pet of him, but he had a slaveboy who was badly clothed and fed "& beaten before his eyes with Iron Shovels or any other thing that first came to hand."

Was this a Brown invention? Frederick Douglass, the Negro leader who was a Brown worshipper, could not help but note the similarity to the biblical tale of how the sense of justice was awakened in young Moses by seeing a Hebrew bondsman beaten by an Egyptian. Then, too, it is established that Owen Brown furnished cattle for the troop led by General William Hull, who marched from Dayton to Detroit in 1812 where he surrendered his army. Slavery was outlawed in the Northwest Territory by the Northwest Ordinance of 1787. How, one may ask, could his landlord have owned a slaveboy?

More credence can be put in other details Brown states regarding the formation of his personality. He acquired a taste for reading and became "a firm believer in the divine authenticity of the Bible," and "possessed a most unusual memory of its entire contents." There was no frivolity in his nature—he never attempted to dance and never learned one card from another. He "grew to be verry fond of the company & conversations of old & intelligent persons."

Of one facet of his personality which he discussed there can be no doubt, his imperiousness. "The habit so early formed of being obeyed rendered him in after life too much disposed to speak in an imperious or dictating way." A younger brother would call him "A King against whom there is no rising up." Sanborn corroborated this thirst for leadership with a statement made to him by Milton Lusk, the brother of Brown's first wife, that he remembered, as a classmate of Brown in early school days, Brown "doted on being the head of the heap." Brown said of himself as a boy, "He became ambitious to excel in doing anything he undertook to perform."

Now we come to a passage little short of extraordinary, Brown's advice to young Stearns: "I wish you to have *some deffinite plan*. Many seem to have none, & others never stick to any that they do form. This was not the case with John. He followed up with *tenacity* whatever he set about so long as it answered his general purpose: & hence he rarely failed in some good degree to effect the things he undertook. This was so much the case that he *habitually expected to succeed* in his undertakings."

This was at the opposite pole from the fact. Brown had failed in everything he had undertaken until he turned to the antislavery cause at the age of fifty-four, and he had wandered from one business to another aimlessly.

That he was aware of his falsehood, which Brown regarded as the tongue-in-cheek spoof that gave him much merriment, is demonstrated by an only grazing reference to his inability to study further "on account of inflammation of the eyes." When he was nineteen, along with his brother Salmon, he entered a school at Plainfield, Massachusetts, run by a Rev. Moses Halleck, to prepare himself for Amherst and a career in the ministry; but he had to abandon the course on account of inflammation of the eyes. He could not have mentioned this fizzle and yet maintained that he succeeded in all he undertook.

In his late teens, confident and self-reliant, he was foreman of his father's tanning establishment and lived away from home in bachelor quarters with a cousin. He was a cook for the men, a skill he enjoyed all his life, and had learned some surveying. When only twenty, he married nineteen-year-old Dianthe Lusk, "a *remarkably plain*; but neat industrious & economical girl; of excellent character; earnest piety"; and launched himself as "a practical *Shepherd*: it being a calling for which in early life he had a kind of *enthusiastic longing*: together with the idea that as a business it bid fair to afford him the means of carrying out his greatest or principal object," which was, of course, the attack on slavery, his "deffinite plan," which he had formed in youth.

It is a neat package. The autobiography is a vehicle for a self-serving document to justify John Brown's life to Papa Stearns, the life of a born leader who had relentlessly pursued his object to overthrow slavery through lonely years from boyhood.

This work of art he concluded with a benevolent postscript to son Stearns: "I had like to have forgotten to acknowledge your contribution in aid of the cause in which I serve. God Allmighty bless you; my son."

"I am an abolitionist. I know we are not loved by many. I have no confession for being one." Thus Owen Brown wrote in 1850 to his children, explaining how he had become one.

During the Revolution, with his father gone, he worked in the fields in Connecticut with Sam, a slave from Guinea, lent by a neighbor. "I used to go out into the fields with this slave and he used to carry me on his back and I fell in love with him." When Sam died, Owen attended his first funeral.

In 1785, a series of revival meetings in New Canaan brought the Great Awakening to Owen, the religious sense of participation in all humanity, individual responsibility to cleanse away sin, and salvation by good works. In 1790, he was deeply moved when he read a sermon by the Reverend Jonathan Edwards in which slavery was denounced as a cardinal sin against God. Then Owen related an incident that occurred in New Canaan three years before John was born. A Mr. Thomson, a Presbyterian minister from Virginia, had brought his slaves to Connecticut for safety during the Revolution and now proposed to take them back. The slave father had escaped and was in hiding, but Mr. Thomson said he was going to take back the wife and children. There was quite a ruckus in the local church when he appeared to preach. He was asked if he could separate husband and wife. "Mr. T. said he married them himself and did not enjoin obedience on the woman." Owen concluded: "I think he did not get his property as he call(ed) it. Ever since I have been an abolitionist; I am so near the end of life I think I shall die an abolitionist."

John Brown has more than once been called a pious hypocrite on his championship of the slave, but no thorough review of the evidence can leave one in the slightest doubt as to his sincerity. The abolitionism of his father made him what he himself described as a "dyed-in-the-wool Abolitionist," who regarded the Negro as his brother. One must also take into account as an environmental factor that the Western Reserve from its early years was a hotbed of rabid Abolitionist sentiment, and Brown, living there, was saturated with it.

Mary Land, writing in the *Ohio State Archeological and Historical Quarterly*, points out that this area was known far and wide as an Abolition center with more Underground Railroad stations than any other comparably sized area in the nation. Most barns had a concealed room for slave fugitives. A branch of the American Anti-Slavery Society was located in almost every little town in upper Ohio when not one was known in New England. As time went on, announcements of the activities of the Underground Railroad appeared openly in Ohio newspapers, and it was said that the southern pursuers there had to be as cautious and move with as much circumspection as the pursued. Southerners used to sneer at this area as a state, distinct and separate from the rest of Ohio. The Richmond *Republic* wrote of the residents: "A more hypocritical, canting, whining, totally depraved and utterly irredeemable set of rascals never walked the face of the earth."

Hudson was known as a rabid Abolition town. Outside Hudson there was a signpost that showed a grinning young Negro pointing the direction, "Dis Is De Road to Hudson." It was erected as a joke in 1830, but was left standing for years.

Abolitionism in higher education set off a bitter dispute in which Owen Brown took part. Squire Hudson gave a gift of land for founding Western Reserve University and two others followed suit. Owen Brown became a member of the board of trustees and the buildings started going up. Its first president, Charles B. Storrs, openly advocated immediate emancipation of the slaves and announced his plans to make it an Abolitionist school, admitting Negroes without limit.

The trustees, other than Owen, felt this was going too far, canceled their subscriptions and withdrew the enrollment of their sons. So there was a compromise policy. A new president, carefully investigated for his views beforehand, slashed the number of Negroes to be admitted and forbade debate in the school and by the faculty about abolitionism. Owen was disgusted, and resigned to shift his support to a newly formed manual arts institute at Oberlin, which got a charter as a college and became nationally famous as an Abolitionist college. Owen Brown was a trustee of Oberlin for nine years.

When Brown described himself as a "practical Shepherd" he meant that he collected animals, and tanned their skins, and in that occupation he started to build his family. He was to sire twenty children in all, and they came along fast: John Jr. in 1821, Jason in 1823, Owen in 1824, Frederick, who died, in 1827, Ruth in 1829, and another Frederick in 1830. For years his great care was to feed all these mouths.

In May, 1825, Brown made the first of many migrations. He moved to Randolph, later called New Richmond, in Crawford County in the northwestern corner of Pennsylvania not far below Lake Erie. It was at Titusville in this county that the first oil well would be drilled in 1859, but at this time it was "donation land," with which Pennsylvania had proposed to reward its Revolutionary War militia, but since no one wanted it the land was sold cheap. It was also inviting to Brown because of the abundance of oak and hemlock bark at hand for use in tanning. The hides were transported from the Western Reserve.

Brown thought "big" from the beginning of his career. Sinewy, always striding with a long, springlike step, he was a dynamo of energy. He built a tannery measuring 26 by 50 feet, of native stone, two feet thick. There were eighteen vats in the tannery and he had as many as fifteen men working for him. He erected a log house and a large barn with a secret, well-ventilated room for fugitive slaves. He established a United States post office and was the first postmaster at Randolph from 1828 to 1832. He brought the first blooded-stock into the area when he sold in Waterford in Erie County the first blooded-bull.

We have more impressions of John Brown in this period lasting until 1835, when he returned to Ohio, than we have until he became a person of note in Kansas in 1855–56. Most of them were collected by James Redpath for his "hot-off-the-griddle" book in 1860, so that we can be reasonably sure that they were not concocted out of later imagination that makes many recollections of Brown suspect.

The power of his personality made a great impression on everyone. "He was always a man of nerve from his first Start in life and Iron will, which no man could change until he was convinced . . . for courage and determination Napoleon or General Jackson was never more than his equal." Brown throughout his whole life was reserved to others unless he had something to say, but when he had an opinion he was verbose, loved debates before the roaring fire of his living room, was eager for knowledge, and had no respect for a man who had no opinions of his own. "The Bible was almost at his tongue's end." He had a tart tongue. He once got into an argument with a Methodist minister, who asked him if it was true that Brown had said that he was "no gentleman, let alone a clergyman." Brown replied that he had said more than that. "I said, sir, that it would take as many men like you to make a gentleman as it would take wrens to make a cock-turkey."

They arranged a debate, Brown to ask questions first of the preacher, and then the procedure was to be reversed. "But John Brown's questions soon exhausted and confused his opponent so that the latter retired without opening his side of the debate."

Brown always had a sense of humor, and a journeyman recalled that "He was jocose and mirthful, when the conversation did not turn on anything profane or vulgar." Even Cromwell loved horse-play.

"Upon the subject of Slavery he was always of one mind and looked upon it as a great Sin against God and menus [menace] to the morals of the country where it existed and he considered it as much his duty to help a negro to make his escape as it was to help catch a Horse Thief."

His first two questions to a prospective employee were whether he opposed slavery and whether he observed the Sabbath. He broke with his brother-in-law Milton Lusk because he disregarded his injunction not to visit on Sunday. (One is reminded of John Evelyn's definition of Puritanism at the end of the Protectorate: "Preaching and sitting still on Sundays.") He became less of a strict constructionist over the years as his religion became more a subjective matter, and it is noteworthy that part of the Pottawatomie murders and the assault on Harper's Ferry occurred on the Sabbath.

His children had memories of his interest in runaway slaves. John Brown, Jr., said that a fugitive and his wife came to the door, sent by a neighbor. "They were the first colored people I had ever seen, and when the woman took me upon her knees and kissed me, I ran away as quick as I could and rubbed my face to get the black off for I thought she would 'crock' me like mother's kettle." His father took them to the woods to hide when he heard the sound of horses' hoofs. It was a false alarm, but his father could not find the couple in the night and "finally he was guided to the spot by the sound of the man's heart throbbing with fear."

Ruth related, "Father used to hold all his children while they were little and sing his favorite songs, one of which was 'Blow, Ye Trumpet, Blow.' One evening after he had been singing to me he asked how I would like to have some poor, little black children that were slaves come and live with us, and asked me if I would be willing to divide my food and clothes with them. He made such an impression upon my sympathies that the first colored person I ever saw—it was a man I met on a street in Meadville—I felt such pity for him that I wanted to ask him if he did not want to come and live at our house."

When he returned home from the day's toil, said Ruth, he wanted psalms to be read to him while he relaxed. He seemed to know the Scriptures by heart, since he would correct any mistake in the reading. George B. Delamater recalled that his father and Brown boarded children in their homes in a school they set up—his father in the summer and Brown in the winter. At Brown's home, after breakfast, Bibles were distributed to each child and each read verses. Then Brown rose and prayed as in a trance, eyes closed, his hands swaying the back of the chair. "Everything seemed fixed as fate by the inspiring presence of him whose every movement, however spontaneous, seemed to enforce conformity to his ideas of what must or must not be done. . . ."

In Owen Brown's last letter to his son John he wrote, "I ask all of you to pray more earnestly for the salvation of my soul than for the life of my body." And the son was like the father. "The burden of Father's soul was the souls of his children, and he strove with them without ceasing." The discipline was extremely strict and absolute obedience was demanded. Years later, soon before the march on Harper's Ferry, Watson said to his father, "The trouble is, you want your boys to be as brave as tigers, and still afraid of you."

John Brown, Jr., related that as a small boy he was charged with leading a blind horse around a mill that ground bark. He would get bored and run off to play. One morning the father took the small boy to an upper room of the home and showed him an account book in which he had recorded nine lashes for unfaithfulness at work with no credits. The debt must be paid. He struck the boy three light lashes with a beech strip. Then he took off his shirt and commanded his son to whip him, ever "Harder," until the blood flowed from the wounds. Thus the debt was wiped out as he shared the guilt with his son.

The Lord was always by his side, punishing or rewarding him. In June, 1830, he wrote his father: "Our stupidity, ingratitude and disobedience we have great reason to mourn and repent of. I feel that I ought to expect God's judgment when his mercies do not awake more of my love and gratitude and zeal for his honor." Such implicit trust enabled him more easily to accept the tragedies of life. In August, 1832, his wife, Dianthe, died, along with her three-day-old son. In less than a year he had married again, to Mary Anne Day, the sixteen-year-old daughter of a blacksmith and thus only four years older than his oldest son. She was a strong girl, another "remarkably plain but neat industrious & economical" girl who would bear him thirteen children, most of whom would die in infancy. Two of her sons, Watson and Oliver, would die at Harper's Ferry; her son Salmon would have the longest life of the Brown boys.

A journeyman who worked for Brown in Pennsylvania recalled, "It became almost a proverb that Speaking of an enterprising man, 'He was as enterprising and as honest as John Brown.'" Yet, after ten years of enterprise in Crawford County, John Brown's business collapsed. His raw material, the hides, were too far away for economical transport and his market was too distant. The failure was so complete that he needed money desperately to enable him to leave Pennsylvania for Ohio to join his new partner Zenas Kent. He wrote Kent on April 24, 1835: "I was disappointed in the extreme not to obtain the money I expected; & I know of no possible way to get along without it. I had borrowed it for a few days to settle up a number of honorary debts which I could not leave unpaid and come away."

Such was the pattern of John Brown's entire career to the final fiasco. He had all the ingredients for success—enterprise, self-confidence, courage, vision, rigorous standards, command, system, willingness to toil endlessly—everything save basic judgment in his schemes.

This ten-year enterprise as a tanner was by far his longest sustained business experience. The register of the succeeding years is a lugubrious one, in which, in his own words in a letter to John Brown, Jr., he was kept running "like a toad under a harrow."

The tanning firm of Kent & Brown in Portage County, Ohio, which he had planned, never got off the ground. He became instead a contractor for part of the Ohio and Pennsylvania Canal from Franklin Mills to Akron. He became a speculator and land developer of the Franklin Mills area, which later became the town of Kent, but Brown heavily overcommitted himself and in the Panic of 1837 his property was assigned to creditors and debts were left unpaid on the books.

One of those who was left holding the bag was Marvin Kent, who later described Brown as a "man of ordinary calibre with a propensity to business failure in whatever he attempted." Brown had another explanation—overborrowing. To his oldest son he said: "Instead of being thoroughly imbued with the doctrine of pay as you go, I started out in life with the idea that nothing could be done without capital, and this pernicious doctrine has been the rock on which I as well as many others have split."

He did anything to turn a dollar, working as a surveyor, buying and selling lumber. He bred race horses for a while for racing at a track at Warren, patronized by Kentuckians like Henry Clay. John Brown, Jr., said that he argued his father out of this business on conscience grounds, the father claiming if he did not breed them someone else would and John Jr. answering "that this was the slaveholders' and gamblers' argument, and he abandoned the business." Perhaps he abandoned it because his horses did not win at the races. He went East and purchased some Saxony sheep that he conveyed by boat to Albany, and drove them from there to Ohio, becoming in fact a "Practical Shepherd."

We now encounter a transaction that raises a grave question as to Brown's honesty, despite all his pious protestations to the contrary. On June 12, 1839, he wrote his wife from New Hartford, Connecticut, that a loan he was counting on might not come through. "Should that be the will of Providence I know of no other way but we must consider ourselves verry poor for our debts must be paid." Three days later he did get what was not a "loan" but a check for $2,800 from the New England Woolen Company—for the purchase of wool by Brown for the company. Instead, he pledged the check as security for his debts and when he could not pay them his creditors cashed the check. He was fulsome with apologies and the company did not bring him into court for this diversion of funds. In 1840, he wrote the company that he was so hard up that he could not pay for postage to forward letters from its agent, but, "I most earnestly hope that the Devine Providence will yet enable me to make you full amends for all the wrong I have done," claiming that it was unintentional on his part.

He never paid off this debt but he did not forget it. On the day before his execution he made a will leaving $50 to George Kellogg, the agent of the company, to be paid to Kellogg when the money became available from settlement of his father's estate.

We are tracing the life of a man who under pressure had an uncommon genius in self-justification to himself and others. His evolving concern with the slavery question puts him in a much better light than does his mangy business life.

His interest in slavery in the early years was not intense. The first documentary proof we have is a letter to his brother Frederick on November 21, 1834, close to the end of his Pennsylvania stay. "I have for years been trying to devise some way to get a school a-going here for blacks." As a preliminary, after some discussion with his family, he was going to try to get a slaveholder to release a black boy or he would buy one, and he would "bring him up as we do our own—viz. give him a good English education, learn him what we can about the history of the world, about business, about general subjects. . . ." This might be the best way to break the "yoke effectually than in any other. If the young blacks of our country could once become enlightened, it would most assuredly opperate on slavery like firing powder confined in rock. . . ."

Brown seemed sincere in his concern about slaves, though this was an idea for profit at a time when his business was foundering. The money, he explained, could be raised under the laws of Pennsylvania by a tax on the township for the school fund. "If you will join me in this undertaking, I will make with you any arrangement of our temporal concerns that will be fair."

Wendell Phillips Garrison, the son of William Lloyd Garrison, examining the evidence, was perplexed that Brown, if deeply concerned about blacks at this time, could have been so blissfully unaware of the obstacles in educating blacks even in the northern states. The year before, Prudence Crandall, a young Quaker, became headmistress of a school in Connecticut. She admitted a young Negress, and when there was a furor she changed it to an all-Negro school, and advertised in Garrison's *Liberator*. Seventeen black students arrived. She kept the school going through stones and curses hurled at her. Garrison was amazed at her bravery, "as undaunted as if she had the whole world at her side." The state legislature passed a law that prevented students from out-of-town attending the school but she fought the law. Finally, the school was set on fire and ravaged and she had to give up. When Noyes Academy in New Hampshire admitted a few Negro students, the villagers wasted no time on legal formalities—thirty men with a hundred yoke of oxen attached ropes to the school and dragged it out of the town limits.

Of his continuing sympathy with Negroes, Brown's son John and daughter Ruth tell the same story. After he returned to Franklin Mills in Ohio in 1835, he hired a black man and his wife. They went to church one Sunday and were put in the rear, close by the stove. John Brown was indignant, and the following Sunday he made them sit in his pew while he and his family sat around the stove. John related, "This was a bomb-shell and the Holy Spirit in the hearts of Pastor Burritt and Deacon Beach at once gave place to another tenant. Next day, Father received a call from the Deacon to admonish him and 'labor with him,' but they returned with a new view of Christian duty." The incident was, according to son John, a considerable factor in alienating John Brown from churches and organized religion.

In 1840, Brown contemplated settling in the slave state of Virginia on lands belonging to Abolitionist Oberlin College. It was Brown's first contact, albeit an indirect one, with a man who was to play a large part in his life, the nation's foremost philanthropist, Gerrit Smith of Peterboro, New York, who had inherited two thousand acres of land nearby, mostly in Tyler County, Virginia, bordering on Ohio. Oberlin had asked the Abolitionist Smith for financial help, and he gave them these lands in April, 1839, saying, "The land is so far from me that I cannot make judicious and profitable use of it." Since titles were in dispute he added a cash gift of $2,000. In thanking him for the gift, Oberlin replied that although in a slave state the lands would become available "to Christian tenants and free laborers." (No slaveholder in Abolitionist eyes could be a Christian.)

John Brown learned of these lands through his father, Owen, who was a trustee. He wrote in April, 1840, to the Prudential Committee of the college saying that he would like to see the lands with a view to settlement. He believed the "institution can well afford to be quite liberal towards a family like my own." His three eldest sons were "all resolute, energetic, intelligent boys & as I trust of very decided religious character such as I think will if they are continued prove to be valuable members of any community or faithful and competent agents should they be kneeded. The business we now follow is mainly wool growing in which I have been hitherto prosperous [sic]."

He offered to survey the lands on an inspection tour and the college voted him $50 as a fee and for expenses. The treasurer was enthusiastic, and wrote father Owen that "by proper efforts," after clearing titles, they would "with the blessing of God soon see that wilderness bud and blossom as the rose."

Brown left on April 14 from Franklin Mills and returned on May 16. On April 27, he wrote his wife from Ripley, Virginia, "I like the country as well as I expected, and its inhabitants rather better; and I have seen the spot where if it be the will of Providence, I hope one day to live with my family." The southerners were inferior to the northerners: "Were the inhabitants as resolute and industrious as the Northern people and did they understand how to manage as well, they would become rich." Brown was never daunted by his failures into believing that he could not teach the rules of success. "They have so little idea of moveing off anything they have to sell or of going away for anything they kneed to buy that their merchants extort uppon them prodigiously. By comparing them with the people of other parts of the country & world I can see new and abundant proof that Knowledge is power. I think we might be very useful to them on many accounts, were we so disposed."

On his return, on July 14, he made a proposition that one thousand acres should be given him in a deal as a return for acting as agent in selling twenty thousand acres, a formidable responsibility since squatters had cabins all over and in fact litigation was to go on for years as to titles. The trustees agreed. But Brown kept delaying. Finally, on January 2, 1840, he wrote that, "I have sometimes allmost given up the idea of going to the south," but now, "I shall expect to receive a thousand acres of land in a body that will include a living spring of water dischargeing it at a heighth sufficient to accomodate a tanery as I shall expect to pursue that business." Oberlin changed its mind and, on January 20, its secretary, Levi Burnell, notified Brown that the offer was withdrawn and refused, despite Brown's further letter, to give any reason.

There are three observations as to this abortive project.

This was the only time that John Brown ever saw the Appalachian Mountain range in the South before he formulated his Harper's Ferry plan. No doubt their height and forests made a lasting impression on his mind, which might have inspired the plan. In later years when he was putting together his conspiracy and gave assurances to friends that he had inspected the southern Appalachians personally, he neglected to mention that he had viewed the foothills not on the eastern side where Harper's Ferry lay but two hundred miles away on the western side where the terrain was more rugged.

There is absolutely no proof, as his savage critics, Hill Peebles Wilson and G. W. Brown, have claimed, that he planned to stock his Virginia farm with slaves after settling there. On the other hand, there is absolutely no proof that the acquisition of these lands had anything to do with plans for Negro emancipation, as Sanborn and Du Bois have claimed. Wendell Phillips Garrison commented that if Brown had had anything ulterior in his mind along this line such a purpose would have been set down in the notebooks he kept; but, on examining them, Garrison could find only notations relating to farming possibilities, such as this: "28th April found on big Battle below the forks good bottom land good Stone & on the left hand fork a fine bottom with one of the best Sugar orchards I ever met with."

In the hearings in 1860 of the Mason Committee of the United States Senate investigating the Harper's Ferry raid, a most reputable man, William F. M. Arny, testified that he met Brown while he was in Virginia at this time and they talked at length. In late 1858 he met Brown again in Kansas and said to him, "Brown, when I knew you twenty years ago in Virginia you professed to be an Abolitionist and

an Abolitionist of that class that are termed non-resistant and you refused to use arms in any shape and form and you were considered
ultra on that subject at that time." He asked Brown why and how he
had changed his views and Brown replied that it was on account of
the persecutions to which he and his family had been subjected in
Kansas.

One can readily guess why Oberlin backed out of the project.
Brown was sunk in such a morass of financial woes that it is doubtful
that he could have disengaged himself sufficiently to move out of
Ohio and in any case he seemed to be a misfit in business and a bad
risk. He was up to his neck in lawsuits on promissory notes he had
signed and on which he had defaulted. Portage County court records show that he was sued no less than twenty-one times between
1820 and 1845. The Bank of Wooster sued him on a bill of exchange
drawn on the Leather Manufacturers Bank of New York where he
had no funds.

One transaction smacks of flagrant dishonesty. In 1836, Brown
raised $6,000 from the Western Reserve Bank on a note on which
Heman Oviatt and others were security. When Brown defaulted,
Oviatt, who had befriended Brown in the past and had given him
work, assumed the whole liability and sued Brown. Brown acquired
a property, Westlands, under a penal bond of conveyance and endorsed it to Oviatt. However, when Brown later got a deed, free
and clear, he recorded it in his own name without letting Oviatt
know, and then mortgaged it. Another creditor of Brown's on the
mortgage brought suit, and in a sheriff's sale Westlands was sold to
one Amos Chamberlain. Oviatt was left out in the cold when the
Supreme Court of Ohio held Chamberlain's title good.

Villard attributed this to "the great confusion of Brown's affairs
and his own poor business head." Realistically, it could be nothing
but a conscious fraud.

Brown claimed that he had a secret understanding with Chamberlain to turn the land back to him and anyhow he claimed pasture
rights. He built a shanty on the land in April, 1841, and with his
sons Jason and Owen, who were armed with muskets, prepared to
hold it. As early as this date he relied on *vi et armis* to attain his objectives. With this display of force he combined a letter full of flattery, a plea for sympathy and whining cant. He reminded Chamberlain of the "days of cheerful labour we have performed together";
he had made Chamberlain's "happiness and prosperity my own in-

stead of feeling envious at your success." He pleaded for sympathy
for the Brown family and then had the gall to ask for clemency for
his poor creditors. "I ask you why will you trample on the rights
of your friend and of his numerous family? Is it because he is poor?
Why will you kneedlessly make yourself the means of depriveing all
my honest creditors of their Just due? Ought not my property if it
must be sacrifised to fall into the hands of honest and some of them
poor and suffering Creditors?" Did he forget defrauded Mr. Heman
Oviatt?

Mr. Chamberlain was unmoved. The sheriff of Portage County
arrested Brown and his two sons and they were lodged for a while
in Akron jail. This seemed the bottom but worse disgrace was to
follow. In September, 1842, he was declared a bankrupt and was
allowed to keep only a little property among which were two mares,
two cows, two hogs, three lambs, nineteen hens, seven sheep, eleven
Bibles and testaments, and three pocket knives valued at 37½ cents
each.

Bankrupt at the age of forty-two after years of running "like a
toad under the harrow!" This was tasting the dregs for a proud,
ambitious man, whose reading, aside from the Bible, was, *The Life of
Oliver Cromwell*, *The Life of Napoleon*, *Plutarch's Lives*, and the
histories by Josephus, in which Brown, no doubt, pictured himself
as the Hebrew commander in the wars against the Romans.

And the year after his bankruptcy, tragedy struck hard when he
lost by sickness four of his children ranging in various ages up to
nine. Despite the stony appearance he gave, he was in his home a most
affectionate and sentimental husband and father. There are many
stories bearing this out, such as that when his wife was ill, he would
stay up all night by the fireplace for fear that the fire might go out
and she might get a chill.

Some of his letters to his family are quite moving. Writing from
New York City in December, 1838, he said: "My increasing and
anxious care for the present and everlasting welfare of every one of
my family seems to be threefold as I get separated further and
further from them. Forgive the many faults and foibles you have seen
in me and try to profitt by anything good in either my example or
my Council." From Springfield, Massachusetts, in May, 1844, he
wrote: "There is a peculiar music in the word, HOME," after a long
absence. In the same letter he told Mary that when he reflected "on

the considerable difference in age as well as the follies and faults with which I am justly chargeable, I really admire at your constancy and I really feel notwithstanding I sometimes chide you severely that you are *really* my better half."

Further heavy grief came in 1846 when one-year-old Amelia was accidentally scalded to death by hot water poured by eighteen-year-old Ruth. He comforted his wife:

One more dear little feeble child I am to meet no more till the dead small & great shall stand before God. . . . Notwithstanding God has chastised us often & sore, yet he has not Himself entirely withdrawn from us nor forsaken us utterly. . . . I have sailed over a somewhat stormy sea for nearly half a century & have experienced enough to teach me thoroughly that I must reasonable buckl up & be prepared for the tempest. Mary, let us try to maintain a cheerful self command while we are tossing up & down & let our motto still be Action Action as we have but one life to live.

He recalled with grief these lost children for years thereafter. Nine of his twenty children died in infancy. In January, 1847, he wrote Ruth from Springfield: "Sometimes my imagination follows those of my family who have passed behind the scenes & I would almost rejoice to receive permission to make them a personal visit. I have outlived nearly half my numerous family & I ought to realize that in any event a large proportion of my journey is travelled over."

How did he live after his bankruptcy? There is a document dated January 24, 1843, in which Everett Farnum leased to John Brown of Richfield, Summit County, "A certain farm being about 150 acres contained in what is called the Marcus Newton farm and 20 acres lying directly west and adjoining the same." There is a record of prizes won by him for sheep at the Summit County fairs. He was over the hump financially, so to speak, since his sons John Jr., Jason, and Owen were old enough to obtain work, support themselves, and add to the family exchequer. In 1841, John Jr. started to teach at a little country school. We have a letter from father to son dated January 18, 1841, in which the elder Brown reproves his son for his complaint that he could not maintain discipline. If he cannot manage at the school, the father wonders, "How are you to stimulate Asses to attempt a passage of the Alps?"

The years were slipping by, and the man soon to be a grandfather wrote his wife in early 1844 about his fears of a wasted life. "I feel considerable regrets by turns that I have lived so many years and have, in reality, done so verry little to increase the amount of human happiness." He had so few friends since his abrasive personality alienated so many. "I often regret that my manner is no more kind and affectionate to those I really love & esteem but I trust my friends will overlook my harsh rough ways when I cease to be in their way."

Then he had a stroke of good fortune when very wealthy Simon Perkins of Akron took him into partnership in the sheep business, a fifty-fifty profit-sharing arrangement under which Perkins furnished capital, feed, and shelter and Brown did the work. Moreover, Perkins permitted the Brown family to live in a fine home he owned outside Akron. Brown wrote exultantly to John Jr. that "This is the most comfortable and favorable arrangement of my worldly concerns that I ever had," and Perkins had taken him in with him although he knew all the disgrace, including the episode on Westlands when he and his sons had been "Belted Knights."

Brown found it hard to believe that a fellowman could have such sublime trust. "It is certainly indorsing the poor bankrupt and his family, three of whom were but recently in Akron jail."

Mr. Perkins was to rue the day that he ever went into business with John Brown. In 1878 when questioned by Sanborn about Brown as a business partner, he replied brusquely, "The less you say about this the better." As far as the machinery of making money was concerned, the gears of Brown's mind were in reverse. DuBois put it aptly, "To him business was a philanthropy. We have not yet even today reached this idea but urged on by the Socialists we are faintly perceiving it . . . the prospect of great wealth did not tempt him but rather repelled him."

At first things went famously for Brown in his alliance with Perkins. He made trips east to sell their wool to manufacturers and they made money. The demand for wool was high. Tariffs had been raised to keep out foreign wool. Our Industrial Revolution may be said to have begun with textile factories in New England. By 1850, there were hundreds of mills—in Lowell and Lawrence, Massachusetts, in Pawtucket and Woonsocket, Rhode Island—producing flannel, blankets, and coarse worsteds. When the United States moved toward war with Mexico in 1845, the price of wool started to soar.

His confidence in himself restored, Brown was obviously in high fettle when he reported in the *Ohio Cultivator*, in November, 1845, that he had attended a fair in his birthplace, Litchfield, Connecticut, with William A. Ladd and that he had exposed a damn-Yankee trick of greasing sheep with sperm oil "in order that they may collect more dirt and appear a darker hue."

Brown and his partner conceived the idea of establishing a commission house in Springfield, Massachusetts, to act as agent for the western sheepfarmers in selling their wool to eastern manufacturers. There is a printed circular, dated March 16, 1847, in which Perkins & Brown announce to farmers that they will undertake to grade wool for a commission of one cent a pound and sell it to manufacturers for another cent a pound. Thinking "big," Brown got the idea that the firm would put all the sheepraisers under its fatherly wing. He delivered lectures on proper methods of shearing sheep, and Perkins & Brown offered gold medals to farmers who produced the best fleeces. There is a record of the personal presentation by Brown of a medal to one John Gilmor of Ohio County in West Virginia.

In July, 1847, Brown wrote with delight to Perkins in Akron that he was receiving from fifty to eighty bales a day, and though selling only "a little" was getting a lot of inquiries from mills. In the first year they did not sell much, and only a large export sale of their own wool to an English buyer enabled the firm to show a profit.

The business could not get off the ground, and the sheepfarmers who were their clients ground their teeth. Brown organized a meeting of the farmers in Steubenville, Ohio, and explained to them that it was a conspiracy on the part of the manufacturers. "We have at last found out that some of the principal manufacturers are leagued together to break us down." He mollified many by giving them advances on shipments on which he was oversanguine, and cost the firm heavily. A neighbor-businessman in later years explained that part of the trouble was that "Brown was not a trader. He waited until his wools were graded and then fixed a price. If this suited the manufacturers, they took the fleeces. If not, they bought elsewhere." By the time he offered his wool, they were already well stocked-up.

The letter-book of Perkins & Brown is preserved in the Ohio Historical Society with copies of most letters in Brown's handwriting. Thumbing through it, one finds abundant evidence of a man in an enterprise in which he was over his head and constantly embroiled. On December 2, 1847, there is a letter of apology to John Gilmor. "We would further say that we have certainly intended to reply to all our numerous correspondents with as much promptitude as possible. The only excuse we have to offer is a great deal of sickness in our Mr. Brown's family which occasioned the oversight." The very next day, there is an outburst in a letter to L. Tucker enclosing $300 for the amount of his claim. "What sufficient reason you have for the one-sided ungentlemanly course you have ever taken since we became your subscriber, we know not, or what satisfaction or reward you look for in stating downright falsehoods, we know not. We leave the matter with yourself and you will save one number of the Cultivators by stopping it at once and we will save the trouble of taking it from the Post Office." There are excuses constantly to his clients. Thus on November 6, 1848, he wrote to I. and N. Peterson, "We are always ready to sell but manufacturers are not always ready to buy and you know it takes Two to make a bargain."

On April 7, 1849, Brown wrote to Perkins in Akron that he had twenty letters "crowding me for money ahead of what I am able to reply to. I am keeping them along as well as I can but find I need my face hardened over every morning."

Another businessman in the trade, Aaron Erickson, gave this version. Brown had an obsession (which Erickson thought cockeyed) that wool had never before been properly graded, "or if so at all so imperfectly as to be useless." He claimed that he alone could grade wool with accuracy. Once when Brown's back was turned, said Erickson, "I had the cruelty to switch" two grades Brown was discussing, and when Brown resumed the discussion and handled the wool, the self-proclaimed expert did not realize that they had been switched.

Brown fixed his own prices on the lower grades 50 percent below market value and on the higher ones 50 percent above. Erickson said to him, "Those lower grades are priced so low that they will be snapped up by the first speculators who see them." Brown replied, "They are graded right. I shall make it up on the fine wools which I am determined shall be appreciated." Sure enough, the lower grades were snapped up the next day and then Brown faced a suit for damages by his wool-grower clients on the ground that he had sold their wool at throwaway prices.

And what of the higher grades? Several months later Erickson found Brown "more than ever confirmed in his theory but greatly depressed in spirits." He had sold none of his fine wools because the manufacturers had made a combination against him. He was going to ship them to England. Erickson was aghast. Didn't he know that wools were selling so cheap in England that they were being shipped to the United States despite shipping costs and the high tariff that shippers had to pay? "I tried in kindness to explain the inevitable consequences of his delirium but Brown interrupted, 'Your wool was not graded like mine.' "

The result—a Mr. Musgrave of the Northampton Woolen Mills offered him sixty cents a pound for his fine Saxony fleeces, which Brown declined. A few months later Musgrave invited Brown to accompany him to the Hartford Railroad depot to see some wool he had purchased, and Brown did so. Musgrave said that this was Brown's wool which he had bought in England; even with the tariff charge it had cost him in all only fifty-two cents a pound. E. C. Leonard, who, as a boy, went along with Brown to the depot, recalled "Uncle John wheeled and I can see him now as he 'put back' to the lofts, his brown coat-tails floating behind him and his nervous strides fairly devouring the way."

Brown remained unconvinced and in August, 1849, he sailed for Europe to oversee the sale of his fleeces. No success. He wrote John Jr. on September 21 that he had sold only a hundred and fifty bales. "I have a great deal of stupid, obstinate prejudice to contend with as well as conflicting interests; both in this country and from the United States." He sold a bit more and returned in six weeks with a colossal loss from the venture.

While abroad he spent two weeks on the Continent and visited battlefields of Napoleon—Waterloo, Jena, and perhaps Leipzig. He would often cite this inspection trip in later years as one that had given him military expertise.

When did John Brown turn from a passive Abolitionist to a fire-eating Abolitionist? That seems to be an unanswerable question. That Brown had made antislavery "his greatest or principal object" through life, as Brown stated, and as Sanborn and Villard repeated, is completely unacceptable. His "greatest or principal object" up to 1855 was to feed and clothe himself and his numerous family, and his intense interest in slavery dates only from 1847. Brown himself on a prairie in Kansas in 1858 indicated to Richard J. Hinton that his commitment to the cause had been of shorter duration than a lifetime. He said, "For twenty years I have never made any business arrangement which would prevent me at any time answering the call of the Lord.

I have kept my affairs in such a condition that in two weeks I could wind them up and obey that call, permitting nothing to stand in the way of that call, neither wife, children or worldly goods." That would set the date from 1838. DuBois was driven to this conclusion: "Human purposes grow slowly and in curious ways; thought by thought, they build themselves until in their full, panoplied vigor and definite outline not even the thinker can tell the exact process of growing or say that here was the beginning or the ending." In other words, he could not trace the growth process.

In Brown's notebooks from 1838 to 1845 there are a hodgepodge of entries relating to business transactions, since Brown was a systematic man. Beyond that, there are humdrum thoughts:

Deacon Abel Hinsdale left off entirely the use of Tobacco at the age of 66 now 73 and has used none since that time. No ba(d) consequences have followed Qery when will a man become too old to leave off any bad habit.

That kind of news which we most like to hear of others, affords the best possible index to the true character of our own hearts. John Brown.

Wendell Phillips Garrison concluded: "In the foregoing ethical commonplaces we have all that John Brown confided to his pocket-companion from which no one would guess that slavery was his remotest thought. The Darwinian defense, the 'imperfection of the geologic record,' is of course valid here; yet one cannot resist the general impression that the struggle for existence and (so far as this permitted) religious concern of the common orthodox type were the Practical Shepherd's main preoccupations during the seven years 1838–1845."

His letters to his family show that he was wrapped up in business. In June, 1844, he wrote, "The general aspect of our worldly affairs is favorable. Hope we do not entirely forget God. I am extremely ignorant at present of miscellaneous subjects," which would include abolitionism. In a later letter he said, "I trust that getting or losing money does not entirely engross our attention, but I am sensible that it occupies too large a share of it."

The evolution of Brown into the crusader must be viewed in the context of the evolution of the slavery controversy. In the long years while Brown was quiescent, the slavery issue was dormant save for the Abolitionists who were regarded on the whole as "obnoxious pests." The antislavery candidate for President in 1840, James G.

Birney, who ran on the Liberty party ticket received a grand total of 7,000 votes. For a generation after the Missouri Compromise of 1820, which admitted Missouri as a slave state but prohibited slavery in the remaining territories north of the parallel of 36° 30', there was a delusive tranquillity. Sage minds sensed that the peril had only temporarily been shelved. Thomas Jefferson wrote in 1820: "This momentous question, like a firebell in the night, awakened and filled me with terror." In his diary, John Quincy Adams confided, "I take it for granted that the present question is a mere preamble—a title-page to a great, tragic volume."

The slavery issue flared up in 1846 when the United States went to war with Mexico. Many in the North saw it all as plot to bring in new slave states and augment the political power of the existing slave states. Opposition to the war was particularly virulent in Massachusetts where Brown was now living. The state legislature officially labeled it as a war to strengthen the "slave power." Henry D. Thoreau as a protest against the war refused to pay the state poll tax, went to jail, and then in self-justification published his "Essay on Civil Disobedience."

Now tangible evidences of Brown's concern with slavery begin to surface. Frederick L. Douglass, who was considered the unofficial president of the Negroes before and after the Civil War, had a talk with him one evening on Brown's invitation in late 1847. The son of a white slaveholder and a black mother, Douglass had escaped to freedom when twenty-one and became a shipyard laborer at New Bedford. He made a great impression by his eloquence at an antislavery meeting and became a lecturer on abolitionism and the publisher of the paper *Northern Star* in Rochester. (Runaway slaves followed the North Star to Canada and freedom.) It was while on a lecture tour in Springfield that he met Brown who invited him to his home for dinner.

The house was much simpler than Douglass would have expected of the businessman, in a back street where laborers and mechanics lived. The plainness and lack of furniture "almost suggested destitution," and "the meal was such as a man might relish after following the plow all day." After dinner they talked at length.

Douglass later recalled, "I have talked with many men, but I remember none who seemed so deeply excited upon the subject of slavery as he. He would walk the room in agitation at the mention of the word." In editorial correspondence in the *Northern Star* he reported a private interview with a man who "though a white gentleman is in sympathy a black man and as deeply interested in our cause as though his own soul had been pierced with the iron of slavery."

Brown not only condemned the institution but added that slaveholders "had forfeited their right to live, that slaves had the right to gain their liberty in any way they could." Douglass wrote that his own utterances became tinged by the color of Brown's radical sentiments, and a year later he was repeating editorially Brown's words, that slaveholders had "no rights more than any other thief or pirate. They have forfeited even the right to live."

Douglass also recalled that Brown outlined a plan for establishing himself and a force in the Appalachians to run off slaves. Sanborn is apparently on firm ground in stating that several decades later when he wrote his autobiography Douglass was confused as to the time and this disclosure actually came eleven years later. At this stage Brown's ideas for achieving emancipation were naive. Thomas Thomas, a slave from the eastern shore of Maryland, was hired by Brown as a porter in Springfield in 1846. The work was to begin at 7 A.M., but Brown told him to report earlier, at 6 A.M. when he would expound to him his plan for freeing the slaves. According to Thomas' story to Sanborn, the Brown plan was this: "to occupy land in the South as a slaveholder and, using trusty colored men as his nominal slaves, through them indoctrinating the real slaves with the hope of freedom."

The Springfield experience of Perkins & Brown was coming to a disastrous close. Perkins summarized it: "In the wool business at Springfield, I furnished the capital. Brown managed according to his own impulses; he would not listen to anybody but did what he took into his head. He had little judgment, always followed his own will and lost much money."

Brown's financial harassments remind one of the sculptured figure of Laocoon writhing in the snake coils. On April 12, 1850, from Burgettstown, Pennsylvania, he wrote his family that he had had an interview with Perkins and, "He met a full history of our difficulties and probable losses without a frown on his countnance, or one syllable of reflection, but on the contrary with words of comfort and of encouragement. . . . Mr. Perkins has in this whole business from first to last set an example worthy of a Philosopher, or of a *Christian*. [I] feel nerved to face any difficulties while God continues me such a partner."

By the Autumn months, matters had taken a turn for the worse and he felt alarm. On November 4, he wrote to John Jr. in Ohio: "We have trouble with Pickergills, McDonald, Jones, Warren, Burlington & Patterson and Ewing. These different claims amount to $40 M; ($40,000) & if lost will leave me nice and flat. (This is in confidence.) Mr. Perkins bears the trouble a great deal better than I had feared." In those times $40,000 was a colossal amount of money.

In a letter of December 4 he wrote his sons in Akron indicating that Perkins had given the signal to close shop and that Brown's major concern was simply to get himself disentangled from the ghastly wreck. "What burdens me most of all is the apprehension that Mr. Perkins expects of me in the way of bringing matters to a close what no living man can possibly bring about in a short time and that he is getting out of patience and becoming distrustful. . . ." He made a poignant request. Would they send him a "fine-looking, Black Shepherd Puppy whose ears stand erect"? He planned to give it to the New York lawyers who were representing them in the Pickergills suit, believing this would obtain from Messrs. Cleaveland & Titus better legal services than $100 in legal fees. Two days later he wrote John Jr. saying that he saw a chance of survival if John, Jason, and Frederick kept in Perkins' good graces in Akron and kept their father informed. "I have often made mistakes by being too hasty, and mean 'to ponder well the path of my feet' in the future."

He was trying to figure out means of supporting himself. He wrote to Jason in Ohio, who grew grape vines on a farm in Ohio, to get two junk bottles, fill them with cherry wine, and send them to him express. "We can effect something to purpose by producing unadulterated domestic wines. They will command good prices." (Brown was himself a total abstainer since 1829 and had never smoked.)

Never, never, he told John Jr. think of entering the wool business. Don't barter away your conscience for a niggardly commission. "Wool buyers generally accuse each other of being unscrupulous liars, and in that one thing perhaps they are not so."

The clearing away of the wreck went on for years. Burlington Mills of Vermont brought a suit for $60,000 for breach of contract in failing to supply wool at the contracted price, which was settled out of court in 1853. Brown claimed that one Warren defrauded the firm of thousands of dollars and brought suit in Troy, New York, winning in the trial court, but losing on appeal. Even years later, in 1858, two years after his great exploits in Kansas, he had to warn his family to conceal his title to newly acquired land for fear that these ravenous creditors might attach it. As they well knew, he wrote them, he had given up everything he had to Perkins and besides he was acquitted of all further claims "for my service in Kansas."

He had moved his family from Springfield in 1848, but he had to spend considerable time alone in Springfield tending to the liquidation details. Homesick, he wrote his wife in 1850: "I can look back to our log cabin in the centre of Richfield with a supper of porridge and Johnny Cake as a place of far more interest to me than the Massasoit Inn of Springfield."

Gerrit Smith, the nation's foremost philanthropist, with whom Brown's life was destined to be intertwined, again enters the picture. Smith was by now a confirmed Abolitionist, one whom Horace Greeley described as an "Honest, brave, kind-hearted Christian philanthropist, whose religion is not put aside with his Sunday cloak but lasts him clear through the week." On August 1, 1846, to celebrate the 12th anniversary of British emancipation of the slaves in the West Indies, he donated 120,000 acres of land in Franklin and Essex counties in the Adirondacks in New York State to worthy black folk in thirty- or forty-acre parcels. His purpose was not only to give the freedmen the chance to be independent and self-respecting husbandrymen, but to qualify under the $250 New York property requirement for voting, which Smith called a "mean and wicked exclusion."

Brown saw an opportunity to combine idealism with sound business practice. In April, 1848, he wrote to Smith, "I am something of a pioneer. I grew up among the woods and wild Indians of Ohio and am used to that climate and way of life. I will take one of your farms myself, clear it up and plant it and show my colored neighbors how such work should be done, will give them work as I have occasion, look after them in all needful ways and be kind of a father to them." To his father, Owen, he said that he had found the lands inviting, even though they were in a high northern latitude. He had visited with a number of black families in the area. "I can think of no place that I think I would sooner go all things considered than to live with these poor despised Africans to try & encourage them & show them a little as far as I am capable how to manage."

Smith did not agree to the proposition. Outsiders who try to take a free ride on a philanthropy are a too-familiar type to the almoner. Nevertheless, Brown on his own moved his family in 1848 from Springfield into this community. It was here they were living when he died; it is here that he lies buried today.

The Adirondacks farm community was reached by going to Rutland, Vermont, then to Vergennes, crossing Lake Champlain by boat, then from Westport to Keene, New York, across the Keene mountain road, a steep and wooded passage, and then into North Elba. The first clearing was the Scott farm and then the Flanders farm which Brown leased on arrival. Ruth told of their first journey there with their father who was buoyant while everybody else was filled with uncertainty. "The day we crossed the mountains from Keene was rainy and dreary and father wanted us to notice how fragrant the air was with the perfume of the pines, hemlocks and balsams." The house on the Flanders farm was only one story high, and Ruth wondered how nine people would ever manage to live in it.

They moved from one leased farm to another, before he purchased a farm. There is a deed dated November 9, 1849, in which Gerrit Smith and his wife, Ann, sold a tract of land of 244 acres to John Brown for $244, a dollar an acre. Brown did not finish paying for it until 1853.

North Elba. The very name has the chill of cold, bleak exile. The farm was a mile below Lake Placid, which in a later day would become a favorite spot for winter sports. The winter was six months in duration and the summer was quite short; in fact, there was only one month in which there was no frost at night. Ruth related that one day, walking to the farm from Keene, Brown was almost buried by snowdrifts. The first task on his new farm was to uproot trees and dislodge rocks to make farmland. "The main thing is for all of us to keep good-natured," Brown exhorted his family from Springfield.

In the *American Agriculturist*, in 1959, Edward Eastman said, "As I looked at the small, barren fields of this mountain-top farm, I wondered how Brown and his large family ever managed to subsist there." It was a struggle to make ends meet. In the forests there were berries aplenty and some money could be made in the spring from maple-sugar. In the streams there was as much trout as could be carried off. Oats were hauled in winter to the Adirondack Iron Works for food for the men. There was a starch factory to which potatoes were sold for fifteen cents a bushel. Vegetables and winter corn were grown. Sheep could graze and the boys drove Devon cattle up from Connecticut. A local paper reporting the Essex County fair in 1850 said, "The appearance upon the grounds of a number of very choice and healthy Devons from the herd of a Mr. John Brown residing in one of our most remote and secluded towns attracted great interest."

The farm had to be extensively provisioned from without, which Brown did continuously. We have a letter of his from Troy, New York, to his wife, saying that he was sending the following: 130 some lbs. codfish, 40 odd yards calico, 2 lbs. tea, 1 lb. allspice, 1 oz. nutmeg, 10 spools thread, a few dollars worth of clover seed, one barrel clear pork, 2 barrels flour, 1 side sole leather, 1 calf-skin, 2 bunches of yarn.

Why did Brown move his family to this remote and unprofitable mountain eyrie? There can be no doubt as to his motivation, which was a warm-hearted philanthropic one—he wanted to do some good for the black people living in the environs. Most of the money he brought with him to North Elba to buy furniture he gave to the neighborhood blacks to buy some warm clothing. He fraternized with them, he gave them advice, he surveyed their lands for them, since boundaries were a big problem, he lent them his oxen and his tools. But again, the basic plan and goal were unsound. Son Salmon Brown recalled, "It was the wildest scheme he ever got in his head." The colored people could not adjust to the cold climate; they were not skilled in agriculture, the freedmen having worked in cities as barbers, coachmen, and the like. The neighboring white farmers would not give them work in off seasons and the merchants skinned them mercilessly for provisions.

Richard Henry Dana, Jr., the author of *Two Years Before the Mast*, recalled in 1871 that he and two companions got lost in the woods up there in the summer of 1849. Three worn, weary and black-fly–bitten travelers found succor at Brown's home. In his diary, Dana recorded, "The place belonged to a man named Brown, originally from Berkshire in Massachusetts, a thin, sinewy, hard-favored, honest-minded man, who had spent all his days as a frontier farmer. On conversing with him, we found him well informed on most subjects, especially on the natural sciences. He had books and evidently had made a diligent use of them."

Dana was especially struck by Brown's kindliness to the black folk whom he had sitting with him at dinner. He introduced Negroes

as "Mr." and "Mrs." and it was plain, Dana said, that they had never
been treated so before, perhaps never until that day, since they had
the awkwardness of laborers on a plantation and it seemed that what
to do on this formal introduction was quite beyond their experience.

With his family located elsewhere, Brown bustled around a great
deal in Springfield. One night he attended a demonstration where a
woman was hypnotized. He got up and denounced it as a fraud and
asked to test the entranced lady. The lecturer on Panthetism consented but only if Brown would submit himself to the same tests. The
next night, Brown came with a vial of concentrated ammonia and
dolichos pruriens, or "cow itch." The entranced lady survived the
tests but Brown suffered terribly when the ammonia was applied to
his nose, and as for the "cow itch," he was not able to sleep for three
nights afterward.

He dabbled in phrenology, which was popular at the time (reading character from the shape and bumps of the head). We have a
phrenological report on Brown of February 27, 1847, by O. S.
Fowler, the nation's leading wheeler-dealer in phrenology. John
Brown, Jr., went to work for Fowler the next year as a lecturer, and
so this report may by indirect means reflect the son's advice to the
father.

You are positive in your likes and dislikes, "go the whole figure or nothing" and want others to do the same. . . . You are more practical than
theoretical. . . . You have a pretty good opinion of yourself and would
rather lead than be led . . . have great sense of honor. . . . In making up
your mind you are careful and judicious but as firm as the hills once
decided. . . . You like to do business on a large scale and can make money
better than save it. Your ability to read the character of others is excellent
but have little tact in adapting yourself to them. You are too blunt and
free spoken.

What is more important for the future, he attended many antislavery meetings and fraternized with black people. In 1848, he contributed a piece to an obscure antislavery paper run by blacks in
New York called *The Ram's Horn*, of which we would not know if
the clipping had not been found with the personal effects he carried
with him to Harper's Ferry.

It was entitled "Sambo's Mistakes," and Brown wrote as if he were
a Negro reciting his own errors, which were in large part his failure

to obey the maxims of Ben Franklin's *Poor Richard*. One passage is notable because it exhorts the Negro to stand up and fight for his rights.

Another trifling error of my life has been that I always expected to secure the favour of the white by tamely submitting to every species of indignity contempt & wrong, instead of nobly resisting their brutal aggressions from principle & taking my place as a man & assuming the responsibilities of a man, a citizen, a husband, a father, a brother, a neighbour, a friend as God required of every one, but I find that I get for all my submission about the same reward that the Southern Slaveocrats render to the Dough-faced Statesmen of the North for being bribed & browbeat & fooled & cheated, as the Whigs & Democrats love to be, and think themselves highly honored if they may be allowed to lick up the spittle of a Southerner.

Events on the national scene would shape his life. From August, 1846, less than three months after the start of the Mexican War, the nation had been agitated by the Wilmot Proviso, an amendment to an appropriation bill introduced by Congressman David Wilmot of Pennsylvania, banning slavery in the territories acquired from Mexico. This proviso was endorsed by all but one of the state legislatures of the North. Bitter debate held up the organization of the newly won territories for a full four years. Finally, the Compromise of 1850, pushed through by the pleas of Henry Clay and Daniel Webster in the waning days of their lives, purchased peace in the Union for another eleven years. California was to be admitted as a free state, Utah and New Mexico were to be organized as territories with no reference to slavery, the issue to be decided when they became states, and most controversial of all, the South won a stringent new provision for recovering its fugitive slaves, using federal power and denying the fugitive slave a jury trial before extradition.

The North howled. Ralph Waldo Emerson, who had hitherto been a moderate on the slavery issue, confided to his journal, "This filthy enactment was made in the nineteenth century by people who can read and write. I will not obey it, by God." It was to prove a notable miscalculation in the long series that would bring on the Civil War. Statesmen whose minds were ruled by cold logic could not appreciate the effect of emotion in men's hearts on the slavery issue. Webster talked of the "strange enthusiasm" of the Abolitionists, and Clay, asking for a calm weighing of the issues, said, "On the one scale, we behold sentiment, sentiment alone. On the other, property, the social fabric, life, all that makes life desirable and happy." Could "sentiment" mean much compared to that?

It was a mistake for the South to ram this bitter pill down the throat of the North. Fugitive slaves were in fact a safety valve for slavery by allowing the peculiar institution (viz. slavery) to be purged of its most rebellious spirits. Du Bois wrote, "These men [fugitives] saved slavery and killed it. They saved it by leaving it to a false, seductive dream of peace. . . . They destroyed it by presenting themselves before the eyes of the North and the world as living specimens of the real meaning of slavery."

Brown sensed the major change in sentiment that was taking place. To John Jr. he wrote on April 21, 1848, that the slave cause "seems likely to set the pot a-boiling again in Congress." Two months after the enactment of the 1850 law, writing to his son in North Elba giving farming instructions, he added, "It now seems that the fugitive slave laws was to be to be the means of making more Abolitionists than all the lectures we have had for years. It really looks as if God had his hand in this wickedness, too."

Soon after he wrote his wife about his increased activity in his nonbusiness hours in circulating among the blacks and giving them advice and encouragement. "They very much need encouragement and advice. I can only say that I think I have been enabled to do something to revive their broken spirits."

On January 15, 1851, Brown organized the first and what was to be the only branch of an organization of Negroes in and around Springfield to resist the fugitive slave dragnet, and it had apparently only one meeting. He called it The United States League of Gileadites, from Judges, Chapter 7, "Whosoever is fearful or afraid, let him return and depart early from Mount Gilead." He gave it the motto, "Union is Strength," and wrote his "Words of Advice," excerpts from which follow:

Nothing so charms the American people as personal bravery. . . .
No jury can be found in the Northern States that would convict a man for defending his rights to the last extremity. This is well understood by Southern Congressmen who insisted that the right of trial by jury should not be granted to the fugitive. Colored people have more fast friends amongst the whites than they suppose. . . . Should one of your number be arrested, you must collect together as quickly as possible so as to outnumber your adversaries. . . . Let no able-bodied man appear on the ground unequipped. . . . Your plans must be known only to

yourself and with the understanding that all traitors must die. . . . Do not delay one moment after you are ready; you will lose all your resolution if you do. Let the first blow be the signal for all to engage; and when engaged do not do your work by halves; but make clean work with your enemies. . . . Your enemies will be slow to attack after you have once done up the work nicely.

Brown added that a lasso could be "applied to a slave-catcher for once with good effect. . . . Stand by one another while a drop of blood remains; and be hanged if you must, but tell no tales out of school."

The credo of John Brown, the warrior, had emerged—fight slavery as a sin, spring when ready without delay, fight to strike terror, and fight total, "make clean work with your enemies."

Under what influence had Brown become an extremist? Undoubtedly the more heated antislavery political atmosphere in the North, and particularly in Massachusetts, had had a great deal to do with it. One wonders, too, if Brown's frustration and bitterness from his failures in business had built up a store of venom which was unleashed on a convenient devil, the Slave Power.

Brown after turning fifty, as his hatred for slavery mounted in intensity, became increasingly a Bible fanatic. That his children did not accept the Bible literally as their guide to life gave him profound grief and a feeling of personal loss. He wrote to his children in January, 1852, "When I look forward as regards the religious prospects of my numerous family (the most of them) I am forced to say and feel too; that I have little, very little to cheer. That this should be so is I perfectly well understand the legitimate fruit of my own planting; and that only increases my punishment." In August of that year he wrote John Jr., "One word in regard to the religious belief of yourself and the ideas of several of my children. My affections are too deep rooted to be alienated from them, but 'my Grey Hairs must go down to the grave in sorrow,' unless the 'true God' forgive their denial, & rejection of Him, & open their eyes." In August, 1853, he wrote John Jr. a letter of many pages, an extraordinary document, almost a pamphlet in size, all made up of scriptural texts, arranged so as to bring forcibly to him the moral Calvinist theology, point by point, its terrors as well as its promises.

The Calvinist ideas of predestination and salvation by the works of the elect were strong in his mind. For long he had told his wife and half-brother Jeremiah that he was "an instrument of God." Now he searched the Bible even more closely to discern God's will. His belief in the scriptures and that his destiny was decreed by God would never falter in the following years and sustained him when he was about to ascend the gallows. In his last letter to his family he wrote, "I beseech you every one to make the bible your dayly & nightly study; with a child-like, honest, candid, teachable spirit."

The Lord continued to vex him severely in his business life. The long-suffering Perkins, possibly because he felt that he was saddled with Brown, made an arrangement with him, like the one a decade earlier, under which Brown tended sheep in Ohio, boarded hands, and toiled while Perkins furnished the capital, the partners splitting the profits. So Brown moved his family back to Akron in 1851, temporarily abandoning inhospitable North Elba. Sons John Jr. and Jason worked small farms in other counties of Ohio.

For a while things worked out well. The operation must have been a large one since he wrote John Jr. in May, 1853, that he had raised five hundred and fifty lambs that spring, and there was besides sheepfarming, planting of crops such as oats and potatoes. "Yesterday I began my 54th year & I am surprised that one guilty of such an incredible amount of sin and folly should be spared so long."

Concerning Perkins, he said, "He seems so pleasant and anxious to have me continue that I cannot tear away from him." But the following year, Perkins felt differently. Brown wrote his eldest son announcing the end at last of the relationship between the two men. He explained: "The world is not yet freed from real malice and envy."

Brown, at the age of fifty-four, was almost stone-broke, having been able to salvage only a few farm animals. He had moved his spouse and young children (his twentieth and last, Ellen, was born in 1854) back to North Elba.

The Compromise of 1850 was a nasty-enough experience. With that unpleasantness hurdled, North and South hoped for a surcease from trouble. Forty-four members of Congress, including leaders from North and South, pledged themselves to oppose any national candidate for federal office from President down who favored "a renewal of sectional controversy upon the subject of slavery." But soon after in 1854 came a bombshell, the Kansas–Nebraska bill.

This bill was bulled through Congress by Senator Stephen A. Douglas of Illinois, five feet tall, the "Little Giant," and the forceful

Douglas perhaps more than any other one man was responsible for the Civil War by setting in motion a chain of events. In his diary, John Quincy Adams wrote a description of Douglas in forensic action: "His face was convulsed, his gesticulation frantic, he lashed himself into such a heat that if his body had been made of combustible material it would have burnt out. In the midst of his roaring, to save himself from choking he stripped off and cast away his cravat, unbuttoned his waistcoat and had the air and aspect of a half-naked pugilist."

The problem was the organization of the territory of Nebraska, which stretched west to include what are today the Dakotas, Montana, and parts of Wyoming and Colorado. It all lay north of the 38° parallel, and therefore under the Missouri Compromise of 1820 it was all barred to slavery. So the South objected and a deadlock threatened. Douglas, as chairman of the Committee on Territories, proposed a repeal of the Missouri Compromise, specifically declaring it in the bill as "inoperative and void." Declared Douglas, "It is due to the South, it is due to the Constitution, it is due to that character of consistency which I have heretofore labored to maintain. . . . I am prepared to make the sacrifice." Senator Archibald Dixon of Kentucky expressed the pleasure of the South: "Sir, I once recognized you as a demagogue, a mere manager, selfish and intriguing, I now find you a warm-hearted and sterling patriot."

The bill was passed by the Senate on May 25, 1854, and was signed by President Franklin Pierce. Northern Democrats had been persuaded to go along by Douglas' slogan of "popular sovereignty," that the people living there should be able "to regulate their domestic institutions in their own way." He himself later proclaimed that he did not care whether "slavery is voted up or down." A political pragmatist, Douglas had no conception of the strength of human moral and ethical values as a political force. He was frankly astonished when he said after the bill became law, "I could travel from Boston to Chicago by the light of my own burning effigies."

There was an outcry and wailing in the North against this alleged sellout to the South. Horace Greeley, in the New York *Tribune*, said, "The revolution is complete and Slavery is King." Senator Ben Wade of Ohio said, "The humiliation of the North is complete and overwhelming." Many newspapers printed the names of those who had voted for the bill, bordered with black. (Almost all in the House and Senate who voted for it would be gone by 1858). The clergy entered politics as they had never done before, and Congressman William Marcy Tweed of New York lamented, "Alas, alas, such a profanation of the American pulpit was never before known. The head of the devout follower drops."

This was the great watershed of the slavery controversy, as it moved from words to deeds. The Whig party died and the movement to form a new Republican party, proposed in a little schoolhouse at Ripon, Wisconsin, on February 28, gained momentum.

By this time John Brown was totally involved in the cause. He was now apparently a deep reader of Garrison's *Liberator* paper since a letter of his on January 9, 1854, to Frederick A. Douglass is filled with Garrison-type choice invective and a general curse against all and sundry on the other side, whom Brown labeled

malignant spirits, such fiends clothed in human form. . . . Among the first who neglecting himself and useful labor to seek office and electioneer have come to be a majority in our national legislature and most of our state legislatures and who there pass unjust and wicked enactments and call them laws. The chief magistrate, judges, commissioners, marshals, sheriffs, constables and policemen and "last but not least" come the devil's drummers and fifers—such fellows as in the black cloth get in the "sacred desk" there to publish the Gospel (no doubt) for numbers of them are Doctors of Divinity. But what Gospel do they preach? Is it the Gospel of God or the Son of God? God commands "That which is altogether just shalt thou follow" and every man's conscience says Amen. God commanded, "That thou shalt not deliver unto his master the servant which is escaped from his master unto thee!" . . . There is another set of the same throngers of the broad way which I have not mentioned (Would to God I had already done!) I mean editors and writers in the pro-slavery newspapers and periodicals. These seem to vie with each other in urging men on to greater and still greater lengths, stifling conscience and insulting God.

At the time of the passage of the Kansas–Nebraska bill, Brown was in New York near Troy in connection with one of his lawsuits flowing from the defunct wool business. The day after the bill was enacted a dramatic event took place in Boston when a mob tried unsuccessfully to free fugitive slave Anthony Burns, and he had to be escorted to the wharf by two thousand federal troops while fifty thousand jeering and hissing spectators along the third of a mile route from the courthouse were held back by twenty-two companies of state militia. "A few more such victories and the South is undone," commented the Richmond *Enquirer*. A southern visitor to Boston predicted correctly that with the passage of the Kansas–Nebraska bill this would be the last fugitive slave ever recovered from the state of Massachusetts. "As easily could a law prohibiting the eating of codfish and pumpkin pies be enforced."

When Brown read the account in the Troy paper, according to his lawyer, he became greatly agitated. He walked rapidly across the room several times, then turned and said, "I am going to Boston." His counsel restrained him by pointing out that it was too late for him to do anything for Burns, and besides his case was coming up in court the next day.

Douglas had consented to the division of the Nebraska territory into two territories, Kansas and Nebraska, the tacit understanding being that Nebraska would be free and Kansas, lying adjoining the slave state of Missouri, would be slave. The North was determined that Kansas would not be slave, and the contest was announced by Senator William H. Seward of New York immediately on passage of the bill: "Come on, then, gentlemen of the slave states. Since there is no escaping the challenge, I accept it on behalf of Freedom. We will engage in competition for the virgin soil of Kansas. God give the victory to the party which is strongest in numbers as in right."

The newspapers of the North filled with appeals to lovers of freedom to migrate to Kansas. There were glowing accounts of the extraordinary fertility, healthfulness, and beauty of the new land—the soil was rich, timber was plentiful, the streams were full of fish, and the woods full of game. Ohio had a bad drought in 1854, and the Brown boys told their father that summer that they contemplated moving to Kansas. On August 21 he wished them godspeed. If they were bent on going "with a view to help defeat Satan and the legions in that direction I have not a word to say, but I feel committed to operate in another part of the field." He did not say where or how.

In October, Owen, Frederick, and Salmon started out, taking eleven head of cattle and three horses by boat over the Great Lakes to Chicago, drove them to Meridosia, Illinois, where they wintered. Resuming this journey in warmer weather next year they walked three hundred miles across Missouri and arrived in Kansas on April 20, 1855. John Jr. and Jason with their wives and children started their journey that spring at the opening of navigation, going by the Ohio and Mississippi rivers to St. Louis. Jason took along boxes of fruit trees and grapevines, John a plow and agricultural tools. There was no railroad west of St. Louis and so they went by the steamer *New Lucy* on the Missouri River in preference to the arduous trip west by stagecoach. On board they saw southerners without any farm supplies but profusely armed with revolvers and bowie knives. The thought struck the Browns—must the fertile Kansas prairies be first secured by a struggle by arms? If so, how poorly they were prepared for such work, since the five boys had altogether two small squirrel guns and a revolver.

Cholera broke out, and Austin, the four-year-old son of Jason, died. At Waverly, Missouri, while a broken rudder of the boat was being repaired, they buried him in pitch-dark, illuminated only by the lightning of a furious thunderstorm. The southern captain cast off his lines and left the Browns stranded, and so they had to get to Kansas City by stage. On the way they could get no food at farmhouses since their speech branded them as northerners and all the farmers turned them away, saying, "We have nothing for you." They were half-starved when they were finally fed at a stage house in Independence, Missouri.

In Kansas, they joined up with the other three boys on a claim twelve miles west of Osawatomie, in the southeastern corner of Kansas. Between them and the settlement lived their father's half-sister Florilla and her husband Rev. Samuel Adair, both graduates of Oberlin. There was no time to build homes, if they were to eat. They pitched the tents they had transported there and set to work plowing the fields, planting corn and other crops, fruit trees and vines, securing hay from the waving grass for their stock.

John Brown, left in the East, was champing at the bit. On September 30, 1854, he wrote from Akron to his daughter Ruth Thompson at North Elba (she had married a neighborhood boy, Henry Thompson) asking her advice about going to Kansas. Would it be more likely to benefit the black people than going back to North Elba? As he had volunteered in their cause "they have a right to vote as to the course I take." We do not have her reply, and no doubt she knew that her father would make up his own mind.

The trumpet sounding in Kansas was heard in the East in the spring of 1855. Border-ruffians swarming from Missouri were strong-arming Kansas and had on March 30 entered Kansas in force and elected a proslave legislature for the Territory. John Brown, Jr., wrote his father on May 20 a letter that made the old man's hackles rise: "I tell you the truth, when I say that while the interest of despotism has secured to its cause hundreds and thousands of the meanest and most desperate of men, armed to the teeth with Revolvers, Bowie Knives, Rifles & Cannon—while they are not only thoroughly organized, but under pay from Slaveholders—the friends of freedom are not *one-fourth* of them *half-armed*. . . . The result of this that the people here exhibit the most abject and cowardly spirit, whenever their dearest rights are invaded and trampled down by the lawless bands of Miscreants which Missouri has ready at a moment's call to pour in upon them." Unless the free-state settlers got arms, it was not a question of Negro enslavement any longer but their own enslavement. "Now we want you to get for us these arms. We need them more than we do bread."

Hearing this Macedonian cry, John Brown determined to go to Kansas to join his five sons. He wound up his business affairs as best he could, selling his cattle at sacrifice prices, and made some provision for his family at North Elba. Most important, he set out to accumulate a cache of arms. He collected a boxful of firearms in Springfield. On June 28, he attended a convention of Radical Political Abolitionists in Syracuse, New York, called by philanthropist Gerrit Smith. Brown made an emotional speech saying he wanted to go to Kansas to bring arms to his embattled sons there but his poverty prevented it. Gerrit Smith read his son John's letter "with such effect as to draw tears" to everybody's eyes. "I have reason to bless God that I came; for I have met with a most warm reception from all," he wrote his wife. But he raised only a small sum, $60 in all. Gerrit Smith, who at this time was unexcited about Kansas, donated only $20.

In the Western Reserve area of Ohio, Brown's own stamping grounds, he met in August with more success. After an appeal in a meeting in a public hall of Akron he collected ammunition and clothing. A case of guns belonging to a disbanded militia company of Ohio and located in a dusty attic was "spirited away." Then he acquired about ten broadswords, which were to be employed the following year in a celebrated carnage. Resembling the deadly Roman double-edged shortswords or the claymores used by Scotch Highlanders, they had on their hilt the device of an eagle. They were given to Brown by "General" Lucius V. Bierce, head of a defunct filibustering company, a secret society in northern Ohio called the "Grand Eagles," organized to help Canadians in the 1840s to secure their independence from Great Britain.

On August 18 he left Cleveland with his son-in-law Henry

Thompson, a strapping farm boy of twenty-three, and they picked up Brown's youngest son in Detroit, sixteen-year-old Oliver Brown, tall and muscular for his age. On August 23 the three left Chicago for Kansas in a wagon heavily laden with arms, and drawn by "a nice young horse for which we paid here $120 but have so much load that we shall have to walk a good deal." They would not arrive in Kansas until October 7.

John Brown went to Kansas only to fight. "I did not go there to settle but on account of the difficulties," he said to his interrogators soon after his capture at Harper's Ferry. He would never own a home or land in Kansas. In March, 1859, he wrote to John Teesdale, editor of the Des Moines *Register*, that, "It has been my deliberate judgment since 1855 that the most ready and effectual way to retrieve Kansas would be to meddle directly with the peculiar institution."

Thirty-five years of wandering in the wilderness in his adult life had come to a close. In his fifty-sixth year, at a time when most men are thinking about closing their careers, life began for John Brown. The previous stream of disasters had not diminished his confidence in himself a jot, had only added toughness to his hide. Stephen Vincent Benét described him now:

> He was a stone,
> A stone eroded to a cutting edge
> By obstinacy, failure and cold prayers. . . .

He had commenced this new career in the role of a professional fund-raiser and he was to spend a good deal of time in the future, as he described himself, in being a professional mendicant. Money had been a constant care of his life till now and it was to be a constant care through four more crowded years, but the purpose now was to enable him to carry on his personal confrontation with the evil for which he had a consuming hatred—slavery.

CHAPTER TWO

Firebrand in Kansas–To the Pottawatomie Murders

꧁꧂

"No other territory has ever had such a history," said Abraham Lincoln in his first speech in Kansas on November 30, 1859. He was a thousand times right about that.

The turbulent struggle for control of Kansas between North and South was initiated on July 1, 1854, when the Territory was opened for settlement. In 1909, looking back a half century, William Dean Howells wrote, "We can hardly imagine the intensity of sympathy in the non-combatant witnesses on both sides or the frenzy of anxiety and resentment with which they followed the small events in the mighty struggle as it raged in that naked country." By the time John Brown arrived on the scene in Kansas in October, 1855, a good deal had happened, though the issue of slave or free was still in the balance.

The South believed that a proslave Kansas was vital to its survival. The Charleston, South Carolina, *Mercury*, a leading southern paper, said, "By consent of the parties the present contest is made the turning point in the destinies of slavery and abolition. . . . If she [the south] is defeated, abolition will grow more insolent and aggressive until the utter ruin of the South is consummated."

There were fifty thousand slaves in Missouri. Former Senator David R. Atchison, of Missouri, who would be the leading spirit for the South in Kansas, said, "If Abolitionism is established in Kansas there will be constant strife and bloodshed between Kansas and Missouri. Negro stealing will be a principle and a vocation. It will be the policy of philanthropic knaves until they force the slave-holder to abandon Missouri." Once Missouri was lost, said Senator Alfred Iverson of Georgia, then West Texas would go, the South's "institutions will be confined to the narrow limits they now occupy and their overthrow will be only a question of time." The South claimed that honor was at stake since the North was reneging on a gentlemen's understanding in Congress that Kansas would be a slave state while Nebraska would be free.

In the early months there seemed little question that the South would prevail. Missouri men streamed into Kansas and founded the towns of Atchison, Leavenworth, and Kickapoo on the Missouri River. Their weapons, bowie knives and revolvers, part of their dress, were freely brandished. Under the system of land sale, "squatters" settled on the land. They could have it free until the land offices were set up in two or three years and then could buy it at the "upset" price of $1.25 an acre or $200 for a 160-acre tract of land. Some men from Missouri settled on the land, a few bringing their slaves while others proclaimed title by making a quadrangle of four logs and putting a placard with their names on an upright stake in the center.

A countermovement started in the North. Eli Thayer, a member of the Massachusetts General Court, the lower house of the legislature, organized the Massachusetts Emigrant Aid Company, a joint stock company with a capital in its charter of $5 million. His original idea that it would make money for investors was dropped and it became a philanthropic venture under the name of the New England Aid Company, with the wealthy textile manufacturer Amos Lawrence as treasurer and leading contributor.

The first colony of twenty-nine men left Boston on July 17, 1854, amid cheering from an immense crowd that filled the station and lined the railroad track for several blocks. The chief agent in Kansas designated for the company was Dr. Charles Robinson, a physician of Fitchburg, Massachusetts, who had traversed Kansas on his way to California in the gold rush in 1849, and while in California had undergone some rough experiences, including four months' political imprisonment on a prison ship. Of the first contingent of twenty-nine,

Robinson wrote, "These men were regarded with as much interest as would be a like number of gladiators about to enter the arena into deadly conflict with wild beasts or with each other."

Other companies followed, all men, and as they moved toward the West they snowballed in number with the addition of new recruits. John Greenleaf Whittier, the poet laureate of the antislavery movement, wrote the "Emigrants' Song."

> We cross the prairies as of old
> Our fathers crossed the sea,
> To make the West as they the East,
> The homestead of the free.

On August 1, with the arrival of the twenty-nine, the town of Lawrence was established forty miles west of the boundary formed by the Missouri River. It was called Wakarusa and New Boston before acquiring its name from Amos Lawrence. As other contingents arrived in Kansas, the southern faction was getting nervous. Senator Atchison was on a wharf at Kansas City with a dozen Missourians. "What is that on the deck of that steamer?" he asked one of them. "Senator, that is a steam-engine and steam-boiler." He asked another and got a similar reply. "You are all a bunch of damned fools," he said. "That is a Yankee city going to Kansas and in six months they will cast a hundred Abolition votes."

If invective and blood-curdling threats in the press could have won Kansas for the South, the papers such as the Leavenworth *Herald* and the *Squatter Sovereign* of Atchison would have done it. The new arrivals were called "hellish immigrants and paupers whose bellies are filled with beggar's food," or "psalm-singing buttonmakers and tin-peddlars of New England, whining and intermeddling with everybody's business . . . thieving paupers and tract-distributors of Lawrence." As for threats, the editor of the *Squatter Sovereign* was a new Herod as he swore that he was "prepared to kill a baby if he knew it would grow up to be an Abolitionist."

The North responded in kind. Senator Charles Sumner of Massachusetts branded the Missouri invaders as "hirelings, picked from the drunken spew and vomit of an uneasy civilization." The term "border-ruffians" was commonly used, and Thomas H. Gladstone, correspondent of the London *Times*, saw these young toughs gathered in hotels, gambling houses, and barrooms. "At night they throw themselves on the floor if beds be scarce, their revolvers by their side

and thus a dozen in a row prepare themselves for next day's action."
They gloried in the name. "I am a border-ruffian, sir. I am none of
your city-raised, down-eastern. I can draw my bead at forty rod and
bound to shoot center, anyhow. I can scream louder, jump higher,
shoot closer, get drunker at night and wake up soberer in the morning than any man this side of the Rocky Mountains."

By the spring of 1855 it was clear to many in the North that
fighting was inevitable. C. B. Lines, a deacon of a church at New
Haven, Connecticut, enlisted a contingent of seventy-five Kansas
pioneers. The send-off meeting heard an earnest address from the
famed Rev. Henry Ward Beecher. Lines announced that the group
lacked the new Sharp's rifles made in Hartford, which were breech-
loading, could fire ten times a minute, and hit a target a mile away. A
subscription for fifty rifles began in the audience, and the Reverend
Mr. Beecher declared that if twenty-five were pledged, his Plymouth
Congregation Church of Brooklyn would furnish the remainder,
since for the slaveholders of Kansas the Sharp's rifle was a greater
moral agency than the Bible. Henceforth these rifles were known as
Beecher's Bibles and were often shipped to Kansas in boxes marked
"Bibles."

The prevailing opinion of the southern faction was that the free-
staters would not and could not fight. The St. Louis *Intelligencer*
warned the South that, "Never was a greater mistake . . . fight they
will if need be. Remember, the sons of New England shed the first
blood in the American Revolution and they were last to furl their
flags in that terrible struggle."

A territorial delegate to Congress, a proslavery man, General J. W.
Whitfield, was easily elected in November, 1854. Horace Greeley
mourned, "We believe that there are four chances to one that Kansas
will be a slave state to one that she will be free." The first territorial
governor, appointed by the President, Andrew H. Reeder, a Democrat from Pennsylvania, called for a free election for a territorial
legislature on March 30, 1855. The Missourians were determined to
win. General J. H. Stringfellow, an ally of Senator Atchison, gave
orders at a meeting in St. Joseph, Missouri: "I tell you to mark any
scoundrel among you who is the least tainted with Abolitionism, in
Free-Soilism, and exterminate him. . . . I address you one and all, to
enter every election district in Kansas and vote at the point of a
bowie knife or revolver."

The Missourians were organized into Blue Lodges, with the password "sound on the goose," and the test for eligibility was "sound-ness on the goose." They overran the Territory in military companies on election day. Election officials were easily intimidated, but where one raised a question of residence, a border-ruffian took out a watch and gave him five minutes to decamp—which he did. Although according to the census of 1855 there were only 2,905 white males of voting age in the Territory, there were 6,307 votes cast of which only 791 were against slavery. Of thirty-nine representatives elected, thirty-eight were proslave, and the lone free-stater resigned. The Independence (Missouri) *Messenger* crowed, "Abolitionism has been driven to the bush. The fanatical propagandists of the North have only received a lesson in the Southern political alphabet and it may be well for them if they do not push their inquiries any further."

The legislature met on July 2 at Pawnee, an embryonic town in which the capitol was an unfinished stone warehouse, and the members had to camp out, sleep, and cook on the surrounding fields. Governor Reeder, while recognizing the legality of the legislature, showed some courage by ousting seven members for technical reasons in their election. Infuriated, the legislature after six days voted to remove itself to the Shawnee Methodist Mission, accusing Reeder of engaging in land speculation at Pawnee. It petitioned President Pierce to remove him, which Pierce did.

At Shawnee the legislature passed a series of draconic laws called the Black Code. The mere statement by any resident that slavery was illegal was punishable by five-year imprisonment, and death was the penalty for inciting slaves to rebellion even by the printed word. Only persons who favored slavery in the Territory could hold office or even serve as jurors.

Intelligent southerners realized that this only played into the hands of their opponents. The New Orleans *Bulletin* called it "outrageously proscriptive, violent and disgraceful," and the Missouri *Democrat* called it "ill-tempered, senseless, school-boy legislation." The New York *Times* headed an editorial about it with simply "Hellish."

James H. Lane, an extraordinary character who was to dominate Kansas politics until his suicide in 1866, entered the fray. A politician from Indiana who had distinguished himself in the Mexican War, he had been a Democratic congressman who had voted for the Kansas–Nebraska bill but decided in 1855 to take the gamble of becoming a free-stater. He was a great orator and it was said that no man of his time in all the country had such a magnetic control over a crowd as he. In a speech he said, "The proslavery people delight in the term 'nigger-worshipper' for free-state men. I will show you that the pro-slavery men are of all 'nigger-worshippers' the most abject. Accord-ing to the Kansas code [and he read from it] if a person kidnaps a white child, the utmost penalty is six months in jail. If a nigger baby, the penalty is death. Who worships niggers and slave-niggers at that?"

The free-staters denounced the "bogus laws" passed by a "bogus legislature" and decided to set up a government of their own. A series of conventions took place at Lawrence, Big Springs, and Topeka. From now on there would be dual government in Kansas Territory. This culminated in the election of former Governor Reeder as the free-state territorial delegate to Congress while the proslave element chose Whitfield again, and a free-state constitution was drawn up in Topeka. The proslave forces had their elections which the free-staters boycotted while the free-staters had their own elections which the proslave men boycotted.

The free-staters split among themselves into Abolitionist and anti-Abolitionist factions with the latter in the majority. New England Abolitionists had taken no part in the settlement of Kansas, saying they did not care about "a squabble about the ballot box," and that Thayer's project was doomed to failure. In turn, Thayer's pet hatred was the Garrisonites, whom he branded as only "resolution-passers"; the *Liberator* to him was "the birthplace and sepulchre of all their hopes, purposes and aspirations."

The Topeka constitution, which was accepted in an election by the free-staters, banned slavery, but also excluded all Negroes from the Territory, bond or free. The reasoning put forth was that there were many poor whites from the South in Kansas who had never owned slaves, but their prejudice against Negroes was such that if there were free Negroes in Kansas they were proslave men, and if there were none, they might be free-state men. Eli Thayer in a speech said, "I would prefer to see Kansas a free state for the worst reasons than a slave state for the best reasons."

This provision was unacceptable to Abolitionists of the John Brown type and would always stick in their craw. Horace Greeley could not approve it but yet accepted it as a stopgap. "An error of this character may be corrected, but let slavery obtain a foothold there and it is not so easily removed."

Kansas did not start to "bleed" until late 1855, though there were many cases of physical violence foreshadowing the future bloodshed. William Phillips, a free-state lawyer at Leavenworth, disregarded orders to leave the Territory. He was kidnapped to Missouri, one side of his head was shaven, his clothes were stripped off, he was tarred, ridden on a rail for two miles and then sold at auction for $1. The Leavenworth *Herald* commented that, "The joy, exultation and glorification produced by it in our community are unparalleled." General Stringfellow's brother, B. F. Stringfellow, said in the *Squatter Sovereign* of August 28, 1855, that it did not matter how many millions or billions the Emigrant Aid Societies spent or how many men they sent to Kansas, "We will continue to tar and feather, drown, lynch, and hang every white-livered Abolitionist who dares to pollute our soil."

John Brown was on his way to the battleground in the wagon drawn by a single horse with his son Oliver and son-in-law Henry Thompson, often making only eight or ten miles a day, walking almost all the time to ease the burden on the horse.

In a tent during a storm on September 15 in Adair County, he wrote home. They fortunately were all well, had had some "Bowel complaints" which had been checked. The inhabitants were unfriendly and would not give them even a pail of water for the horse. He had caustic comments on the "effect of the peculiar institution generally" on Missouri. The soil was good, timber plentiful, but the land was unoccupied and cheaper than in Kansas. Although they had no money, "We are not however disheartened and shall somehow shift to get along."

He wrote a brief account of this journey in 1858 for a book he began about himself, but dropped. While he traveled through Missouri, approaching Kansas, "Companies of armed men, and individuals were constantly passing and repassing Kansas-wise, continually boasting of what deeds of patriotism & chivalry they had performed in Kansas; and of the still more mighty deeds they were yet to do. No man of them would blush when telling of their cruel treading down & terrifying of defenceless Free State men . . . coarse, vulgar, profane jests & the bloodthirsty brutal feelings to which they were giving vent would have been a most exquisite treat to Ears."

On October 7, John Brown arrived at the Osawatomie settlement of his five sons with his total wealth in his pocket, sixty cents, but with an armory of weapons in his wagon with which he would establish a small fort there he called Brown's Station. The new arrivals were sick with chills and ague—even their horse was sick. The Browns resident there were down, too, with sickness, all with the exception of Mrs. John Brown, Jr. They had been living in tents while they concentrated on growing crops.

The forerunner of an extremely cold winter was upon them. Brown wrote to his wife in cold North Elba assuring her that those in Kansas "are not altogether in Paradise." There were rains driven by winds that fell as ice and, even without rains, the ground turned into ice at night. "Still God has not forsaken us; and we get 'day by day our dayly bread.' " He thought much of his "widowed wife," he said, and sometimes allowed himself to dream a little of again enjoying the comforts of home but did not dare to dream too much.

Father Brown cheered up his small clan of Browns and exhorted them to start building more permanent homes. And so they built a shelter for the winter, a shed open in front, its roof of poles covered by long shingles and its three sides formed of long prairie grass pressed close between upright stakes. On the unexposed side there was a large fire kept burning continuously with logs. They were visited by Indians, Sac and Foxes, and John Jr. once asked the old chief why they did not build permanent residences and get civilized. The chief made a pointed observation about the white men when he replied, "We want no houses and barns. We want no schools and churches. We want no preachers and teachers. We bad enough now."

Two days after he arrived, Brown and sons left their claim to cast their votes for the free-state territorial delegate, Reeder. They were, he wrote his wife, "most thoroughly armed (except Jason who was too feeble) but no enemy appeared."

On November 22, Charles Dow, a free-stater who had just arrived from Ohio, went to a blacksmith shop in Hickory Point in Douglas County north of Osawatomie and had a wordy quarrel with pro-slavery Franklin N. Coleman from Virginia. On his way home, Dow was shot in the back and was left to die on the road. An old man at whose home Dow lived, Jacob Branson, who was usually a quiet man, uttered loud threats against Coleman, and a friend of Coleman's got a warrant for Branson's arrest on a charge of breach of the peace for uttering these threats. Branson was pulled out of bed at night by county sheriff Samuel J. Jones, who haled from Westport, Missouri, and was strongly pro-southern.

A posse of fifteen men guarding Branson set out for Lecompton by way of Lawrence. On the way it met a posse of free-staters leveling guns, and there was an exchange of words. "If you want to be among your friends, Branson, come over here." "If you move, Branson, we will shoot you." "Gentlemen, shoot and not a man of you shall leave alive." Branson got off the mule belonging to the Jones's posse, kicked it away and said, "I will do as you say." He was taken by his rescuers to Lawrence.

The new territorial governor was Wilson Shannon, formerly governor of Ohio, a staunch Democrat. He was imposing-looking, six feet five, "as straight as a liberty pole." But beneath the surface he was weak and wobbly. As soon as he arrived in Kansas he had attended a convention in which the proslaveryites formed themselves into what they swaggeringly called the Law and Order Party. Shannon addressing them said, "The President is behind you, the President is behind you."

Sheriff Jones yelled to Shannon for help, saying that the free-staters had organized an "open rebellion." It did not occur to Shannon to acquaint himself with the facts or send a message to Lawrence, but he ordered Major General William P. Richardson of the state militia to Lawrence. Then, getting into a panic, he appealed to President Pierce for aid and asked Colonel Edwin V. Sumner, commanding United States troops at Fort Leavenworth, to march to Lawrence. Sumner, without orders, refused. Missourians with artillery started out from Lexington, Missouri, in a boisterous mood heightened by plentiful supplies of drink. A force of two thousand men gathered close to Lawrence on the Wakarusa, a branch of the Kansas River south of Lawrence.

Free-staters rushed to the defense of Lawrence. Men drilled with their Sharp's rifles, and embankments and circular earthworks were hastily thrown up.

On December 6, John Brown, whose ears were pricked to the wind, heard the war cry. John Jr. who had been on the way to Lawrence on horseback brought back the news and immediately, dropping everything, Brown mustered his brood and together with John Jr., Owen, Frederick, and Salmon drove through the night, arriving at Lawrence in the forenoon of the next day.

Their appearance at Lawrence was striking. They were standing in a small lumber wagon as they drove up before the Free State Hotel. Poles were standing upright around the wagon with fixed bayonets attached and from one pole floated an American flag. To each man was strapped a broadsword and inside the strap were revolvers. They looked formidable, particularly their grim-visaged chief.

The first appearance in print of John Brown in connection with the slavery struggle was published in the Lawrence *Herald of Freedom* the next day.

About noon a Mr. John Brown, an aged gentleman from Essex County, New York, who has been a resident of the Territory for several months, arrived with four of his sons, leaving several at home sick, bringing a quantity of arms with him, which were placed in his hands by Eastern friends for the defense of the cause of freedom. Having more than he could use for advantage, a portion of them were placed in the hands of those more destitute. A company was organized and the command given to Mr. Brown for the zeal he had exhibited in the cause of freedom both before and since he had arrived in the Territory.

John Brown was made a captain of a twenty-man company in the Fifth Regiment, First Brigade of Kansas Volunteers, the company being named the Liberty Guards. Although the active service of this company was of two days' duration, that Friday and Saturday, he was henceforth to be known as Captain John Brown.

Governor Shannon, foaming at the mouth, was in camp with the Missourians. Emissaries asking peace were sent to him from Lawrence, saying that to hold the town responsible for the Branson rescue was like holding it responsible "for the procession of the equinoxes." Shannon said, "I shall go to Lawrence and insist upon the people agreeing to obey the laws."

At the Free State Hotel in Lawrence, Governor Shannon conferred with Charles Robinson and James H. Lane about some formula to resolve the dispute. Shannon was a heavy drinker, and it seems that, knowing his weakness, the Lawrence people furnished him with much liquor. He was visibly shaken when, coming down the stairs for dinner, he saw the dead body of free-stater Thomas W. Barber being brought in. His widow had been summoned, and Salmon Brown related, "The scene that followed was heartrending to the extreme. I never heard such screams of anguish come from any human being." Thomas Barber had been riding outside Lawrence with his brother, Robert; they were stopped by an Indian agent, Major George E. Clarke, who said he was acting under orders of the governor and ordered them to turn around and ride back to

Lawrence with him. They refused, and Clarke and Robert Barber exchanged shots. A bullet killed Thomas Barber.

Shannon did not want more bloodshed. There was an agreement on a treaty of peace which was acceptable to the free-staters. It commenced: "Whereas, there is a misunderstanding between the people of Kansas or a portion of them and the government thereof; WE, the said citizens of the Territory, protest that the said rescue was made without our knowledge or consent, but if any of our citizens were engaged, we pledge ourselves to aid in the execution of any legal process against them."

At the very end, all this was hedged by an underlined statement, "We wish it understood that we do not express any opinion as to the validity of the enactments of the Territorial Legislature."

Senator Atchison was ready to accept the treaty as a concession and, addressing the Missourians, he said, "If you attack Lawrence now, you attack it as a mob and you would cause the election of an Abolition President and the ruin of the Democratic party." The pro-slave army had been greatly intimidated by the Sharp's rifles facing them, and the Kansas historian, A. T. Andreas, states that in fact a corporal's guard could not have been gotten up to attack Lawrence. On the other hand William A. Phillips, correspondent of the New York *Tribune*, said that they would have attacked but they were dispersed by a windstorm that night. "It came down with icy keenness and driving a snowy sleet. Around the camp-fires the wild gale swept the flames and sparks through the gnarled lumber of old oaks and walnuts."

There was an open-air meeting on Saturday afternoon in front of the Free State Hotel in which Robinson explained and justified the peace pact. Then John Brown elbowed himself to the front of the steps and started ranting against the treaty, saying that it was a surrender and that "I spit on it." He said that with a little support he would lead a night party against the border-ruffians outside Lawrence on the Wakarusa and would rout them.

The editor of the Lawrence *Herald of Freedom*, George Washington Brown, who became one of the most vitriolic John Brown critics, writing of this in 1902, said he thought at the time this project was mad:

[We were] beleaguered by Missouri ruffians, 2,000 strong, with munitions and filled with whiskey, back of them the Missouri administration with abundant resources, the governor of the Territory, the United States military at Forts Leavenworth and Riley. And in Kansas a few, scattered settlers, poorly housed, roughly clad, without arms or ammunition, the Missouri River closed for the winter, no railroad or telegraphic communication nearer than St. Louis. And yet John Brown, pointedly showing an insane mind, when all danger of violence was passed, desired to precipitate a bloody combat. He would endanger the lives of all of us, see our homes going up in smoke, women and children homeless and foodless, exposed to excessive cold, fleeing from their pursuers, with no refuge within 500 miles, whilst their defenders would be sleeping in death.

Brown was silenced by being pulled down and then he calmed. He spent some time in the evening with one James F. Legate, who had lived in the South, asking him particulars about whether the slaves would fight for their freedom. He then asked Legate to join him in a prayer for freedom of mankind through the world and power to vanquish the southern slaveholders.

Brown was not content with the settlement of the dispute, but things would have to rest that way for the winter. To his brother-in-law Orson Day, in Whitehall, New York, he wrote on December 14 that peace had been secured, "by means of some bravery and tact with a good deal of trickery on One side & of cowardice, folly & drunkenness on the other. Yet so it is & I believe that the Missourians will give up further hope of making Kansas a Slave state." Hot-blooded, young Oliver, reflecting his father's thoughts, wrote home that this bloodless confrontation was unsatisfactory. "The facts are that Colonel Lane and General Robinson got poor old Shannon drunk and fooled him instead of meeting him like men and cursing him out and the character of the writings drawn by them was such as to decieve the Missourians rather than to back them out."

To his wife, Brown put the best complexion on it. "So ended this last Kansas invasion, the Missourians returning with *Flying Colors* after incurring heavy expences; suffering great exposure, hardships & privations, not having fought any Battles, Burned or destroyed any infant towns or Abolition presses; leaving the Free-State men organized & armed in *full possession* of the Territory; not having fulfilled any of all their dreadful threatenings, except to murder One *unarmed* man."

The winter of 1855–56 in Kansas was most frigid, Siberia-like, and the main concern of the Browns, as it was for others, was survival in their makeshift shelters. For weeks the temperature hovered from 10 to 30 degrees below freezing. Mrs. Sara Robinson, the wife of Charles Robinson, related that at breakfast the water would freeze in the tumblers on the table, and the bread could be cut only as it was thawed before the fire. "To face a Missouri mob was nothing to facing the winds which swept over the prairie." Another settler, Captain Samuel Walker, recalled that families went to bed often at midday as the best refuge and, with doors and windows made of cotton cloth, they often awoke with six feet of snow around them. A few southerners wondered if they were not engaged in a doomed cause since many of the hundred and seventy-five slaves in Kansas died or were maimed by the cold.

When the weather let up sufficiently, Brown drove his wagon to Missouri to buy provisions but he had to part with his transport to Kansas. On February 1 he wrote his wife, "By means of the sale of our Horse and Waggon; our present wants are tolerably well met . . . we have middling tough times (as some would call them) but have enough to eat." Despite the forbidding climate they would carry on. "It is now nearly Six Weeks that the Snow has been almost constantly driven (like dry sand) by the fierce winds of Kansas."

The weather may have had a political influence in deferring hostilities. He told his wife on January 1 that "there seems to be little feeling on the slave question." On February 1, however, he said that trouble might erupt, though he doubted that would happen until the weather got warmer. "*Should* that take place we may soon again be called on to 'buckle on our armor'; which by the help of God we will do."

A most brutal murder had aroused the free-staters, this one on January 15 at the time of the elections for members of the territorial legislature and state officers under the Topeka constitution, elections boycotted by the southern faction. The proslave papers, organs of the Law and Order party, openly preached violence, the Kickapoo *Pioneer* saying, "RALLY RALLY! Sound the bugles of war! Leave not an Abolitionist in the Territory to relate their treacherous and contaminating deeds. Strike your piercing rifle balls and your glittering steel to their black and poisonous hearts." On the day this was published, some Kickapoo Rangers acted on the advice. They captured Captain Reese P. Brown, a leader on the free-state side, and chopped him to pieces with hatchets. On one of the coldest days of that winter they threw the dying man, iced with gore, on the floor of a farm wagon. After jolting him around for miles, they knocked on the door of his cabin, and, when his wife opened it, they shouted, "Here's Brown," throwing the corpse at her feet.

On January 24, President Pierce, after conferring with Governor Shannon in Washington, in a special message to Congress put his stamp of approval on the Shawnee legislature and said that those who stood behind the free-state Topeka constitution threatened "treasonable insurrection." Brown on February 20 wrote to Congressman Joshua R. Giddings of the Ohio Western Reserve that he feared that United States soldiers were about to move in to enforce those "*Hellish enactments*" of the bogus legislature. Giddings replied to Brown, "You need have no fear of the troops. The President will never *dare* to employ the troops of the United States to shoot the citizens of Kansas. The death of the first man by the troops will involve every free state in your own fate."

By and large the winter was a peaceful prelude to the havoc that would break loose. Brown was building a house for brother-in-law Orson Day, and on February 21 he wrote him that he had little to fear on arrival. "I think that Free State people who go quietly along their way will not now meet with any difficulty."

Brown, however, had some plan in mind that spring, some mischief aimed at meddling with the peculiar institution. He was not going to sit by idly at Brown's Station. On April 7 he wrote his wife, "We do not want you to borrow trouble about us but trust us to the care of 'Him who feeds the young ravens when they cry.' We are doing off a house for Orson Day which we hope to get through soon, after which we shall probably soon leave the neighborhood." He did not say where he was going. That Brown sought trouble and not peace is clearly indicated by his adding, "For one, I have no desire (all things considered) to have the Slave Power to cease from its acts of aggression. Their feet shall slide down in time!"

Another indication of a hatching plan is in a letter that Henry Thompson wrote his wife, Brown's daughter, Ruth, that on Brown's plans would depend his own "until School is out." (In 1858 when Brown wrote to North Elba asking Thompson to join him in his southern expedition, he used that very same code word, asking Thompson to be his "Scholar.")

John Brown, Jr., wrote to a "Friend Louisa" back in Ashtabula County in Ohio that real trouble would soon explode. "To those who contemplate coming, I would say to them by all means come thoroughly armed with the most efficient weapons they can obtain and bring plenty of ammunition. The question here is—shall we be free men or Slaves? The South is arming and sending in her men. The North is doing the same thing. It is now decreed and certain that the Slave Power must desist from its aggressions in Kansas or if they do not, the war-cry heard upon the plains will reverberate not only through the hemp and tobacco fields of Missouri but through the Rice Swamps, the Cotton and Sugar plantations of the Sunny South. From the present appearance the first act of the Drama of insane Despotism is to be performed here."

Whatever initiative was planned by the Browns was canceled by events to which they were to respond, unplanned.

Defying President Pierce, the free-state legislature met at Topeka on March 4 and heard an inaugural address by its first governor, Charles Robinson. John Brown, Jr. was one of the members signing a memorial to Congress asking for the admission of Kansas as a free state and, in the remote event Congress complied, it elected James H. Lane and former territorial governor Reeder as its first United States senators. The session lasted only eleven days—the members realized that in effect it was only a mass-meeting in a costume of legality to win sympathy in the North, to demonstrate to Washington that the free-state element was alive in Kansas and did not propose to abide by the rule of the bogus legislature.

On April 16, there was a meeting of settlers at Osawatomie to review the whole bedeviled situation. Rev. Martin White presented the case from the point of view of the southern faction. John Brown followed and what he had to say was this: He was a dyed-in-the-wool Abolitionist who regarded the Negro as his brother. Rather than recognize the bogus legislature by paying taxes to the amount of one-hundredth part of a mill, he would rather see the Union dissolved and the country drenched with blood. The meeting adopted a resolution repudiating the Shawnee legislature as emanating not from the people of Kansas but "forced upon us by a foreign vote." Soon after, the Reverend White's home was raided in the night, his horses stolen, and he fled to Missouri.

John Brown and his tribe were gaining a reputation as troublemakers and leading spirits of the Abolitionist faction. A territorial judge, Sterling G. Cato, came to Dutch Henry's Crossing on Pottawatomie Creek, ten miles from Brown's Station, to hold court, and the word circulated that he had issued warrants for the arrest of the Browns for defying President Pierce's proclamation that the Shawnee legislature was the only legal lawmaking body in Kansas. Brown sent Salmon Brown and Henry Thompson to the court and they spent half a day there, inviting arrest, but there was none. Salmon in his reminiscences wrote that he had not approved of the idea as it was too hazardous. "I think Father trusted a little too much to Providence."

As Judge Cato was holding court next day, John Brown, Jr., left the courtroom with some men, and in the adjoining yard shouted in a voice that could be heard clearly by Cato, "The Pottawatomie Rifles will meet at the parade grounds." When darkness came, Judge Cato abandoned those precincts, and when he reached Lecompton he said that he had had no choice but to flee for his life.

Sheriff Samuel J. Jones had an indomitable pride that had been badly bruised. Since early December he had brooded on the insult he had suffered when Old Branson had been released from his grip and taken to refuge in Lawrence. But his authority could be vindicated. Had not the town of Lawrence agreed in the December treaty that they would not resist any legal process to punish the law-breakers?

He appeared on the streets of Lawrence to place under arrest S. N. Wood who had commanded the party of rescuers. He took him into custody but lost him in a confusion when a crowd gathered around him. Jones returned the following day and called on the citizens of Lawrence to assist him in serving four warrants. He was jeered. He seized one man who struck him in the face and then he retreated. He returned three days later with twelve of the United States Cavalry and arrested six citizens on the charge of contempt of court—for failure to help him in serving warrants.

He and his prisoners spent the night in a tent pitched outside of town. Jones left the tent to get a drink from a pail of water. A shot rang out. "That was meant for me," he said to U.S. Lieutenant James McIntosh. "It was just a threat," was the soldier's casual reply. Jones showed him a hole the bullet had made in his pants leg. He went back into the tent and, as his form was outlined by the light within, another shot rang out—and this one landed.

The *Squatter Sovereign* screamed, "We are not prepared to hear of such lamentable news, the death of the patriot Jones. HE MUST

BE AVENGED. HIS MURDER MUST BE AVENGED, if at the sacrifice of every Abolitionist in the Territory. . . . We are now in favor of levelling Lawrence and chastising the Traitors there congregated, should it result in the total destruction of the Union."

Jones was not dead. The truth was tardily revealed that he had suffered a superficial wound. Poor dead Jones was the excuse for more violence. A twenty-year-old youth, John Jones, who allegedly talked abolitionism, was shot to death at Blanton's Bridge near Lawrence. Then another killing. Three young men rode out to the site of this murder to find out about it and on the way accosted a group of mounted Missourians who shot one of the three, John Stewart, to death. Men were dropping more rapidly now in Kansas.

The pro-southerners shut their eyes to these murders of free-staters. Governor Shannon reported to President Pierce the terrible threat the Territory faced from the lawless Abolitionists, a "plan of resistance" by a "dangerous, secret, oath-bound organization, unscrupulous as to the use of means to accomplish their objects." The pro-southern papers rang with the demand that Lawrence, a foul blot on civilization, must be taught a lesson. Of the word "caution" the Leavenworth *Herald* said, "Hush that damnable sound for it has already hissed too long in our ears. It must come and the sooner the better. *The blow must be struck.*"

The proslavery legal machinery of the Territory swung into action to crush the free-staters. A grand jury sitting at Lecompton was charged by Chief Judge S. D. Lecompte on May 14 that, since the Shawnee legislature was backed by the United States government, all those who resisted its laws were guilty of "high treason," a unique definition, since according to the United States Constitution, treason consists of levying war or giving aid and comfort to the enemy. Even if there was no resistance but combinations had been formed with the intent of resistance, all who aided and abetted such combinations were guilty of "constructive treason." Governor Robinson, former Governor Reeder, James H. Lane, and five others were indicted by the grand jury for treason without any witnesses having been heard.

Governor Robinson, on his way east to raise friends for the cause which was now in gravest peril, was arrested on a steamer at Lexington, Missouri, on a charge of being a fugitive from an indictment, although the indictment was not returned until several days later. He was conducted to Leavenworth for imprisonment where he was not released on bail until September 10. Former Governor Reeder who was in Kansas City disguised himself as a woodchopper and was rowed down the Missouri River in a canoe. Lane escaped capture since he was visiting Indiana and remained there.

The grand jury took further remarkable action. It branded the two free-state newspapers of Lawrence, the *Herald of Freedom* and the *Kansas Free State*, as nuisances which should be abated, and likewise declared the Free State Hotel a public threat which should be erased, since it was a military fortress, "regularly parapeted and portholed for the use of cannon and small arms." This grand jury action, said the *Squatter Sovereign*, was the answer of the legally constituted authority of the Territory to the "seditious fanatics of the crack-brained town of Lawrence."

A posse was assembled to enforce the writs on Lawrence, consisting of mostly border-ruffian Missourians, Platte County Riflemen, and Kickapoo Rangers. The ranks were swelled by members of a group of three hundred men who had been mustered as settlers in Montgomery, Alabama, under Major Jefferson Buford. There was no call on the United States forces at Fort Leavenworth commanded by Colonel Sumner. Too late, President Pierce sent a message to Shannon: "My knowledge of the facts is imperfect, but with the force of Colonel Sumner at hand, I perceive no occasion for the posse, armed or unarmed."

A force of eight hundred men assembled on Mount Oread, overlooking Lawrence. Lawrence sent word that with its leaders gone it would not fight, and its committee of public safety submissively said, "We only wait an opportunity to test our fidelity to the laws of the country, the Constitution and the Union." The town sent a desperate appeal to Governor Shannon, who replied curtly that as long as Lawrence kept up a military organization to resist the territorial laws, "I shall not interpose to save them from the legitimate consequences of their illegal acts."

There was no resistance when Deputy Marshal Fain made two arrests in Lawrence on the evening of May 20. Citizens of Lawrence assisted Fain the following morning when he arrested three men who had been indicted for treason at Lecompton. The manager of the Free State Hotel treated Fain and his men to a sumptuous lunch. All Lawrence citizens were meek and mild, trying to give not the least offense.

The marshal and his men returned to the posse on Mount Oread, who were by now plentifully fueled with drink. Atchison addressed them: "Boys, this day I am a Kickapoo Ranger, by God! We have entered the damned town and taught the damned Abolitionists a Southern lesson they will remember until the day they die. And now, boys, we will go in again with our highly honorable Jones and test the strength of the damned Free State Hotel and teach the Emigrant Aid Company that Kansas will be ours. If man or woman dare stand before you, blow them to hell with a chunk of cold lead."

They descended the heights and marched down the main street, Massachusetts Street, dragging five pieces of artillery. They had no banner of the Union but one banner had a single white star and the inscriptions, "Southern Rights" and "South Carolina." Another banner, with blue letters on a white background, read, "Let Yankees tremble, Abolitionists fall/ Our motto is, Give Southern rights to all." The two newspaper offices were destroyed and the presses and type thrown into the river. In front of the Free State Hotel, S. C. Pomeroy, agent of the Emigrant Aid Company, refused to tell where their Sharp's rifles were hidden, since they were private property, but gave up two cannon. Thirty artillery shots were fired into the hotel but the walls, two-feet thick, held up and explosions from kegs of gunpowder did not demolish it. It was put to the torch, and finally the hotel all caved in.

Sheriff Jones burst out with joy, "I have done it! By God, I have done it! This is the happiest moment of my life! I determined to make the fanatics bow before me in the dirt."

Governor Robinson's home on a hill was burned. The border-ruffians tanked up further on the liquor stores in the cellar of the hotel. Homes were pillaged and cupboards and drawers emptied. Jubilant and cavorting they left the town, toasting the great "victory." London *Times* correspondent Thomas H. Gladstone saw them celebrating in Kansas City in "grotesque intermixture in dress," wearing narrow dresscoats over their red shirts or having girded themselves with cords and tassels which had ornamented the curtains of the Free State Hotel.

The *Squatter Sovereign* said of the sack of Lawrence: "We simply executed to the letter what the law decreed and left as though we had been to church. By the way, there is no church in Lawrence, but several *free love associations*." This was an American town, sacked by a force acting under the instruction of a United States court in a time of peace.

John Brown, Jr., was at work in the corn fields on Thursday, May 22, the day after the attack on Lawrence, when a messenger

brought him the startling news. "Without delay I rode to Osawatomie with the word and then rallied the men of my company whose
homes were mostly on Pottawatomie and Middle Creeks." Thirty-
four armed men of the Pottawatomie Rifles commanded by John
Jr. at 6 P.M. pushed on northwest toward Lawrence. The company
included his father and his brothers. The first message conveyed
the impression that fighting was in progress. Two miles from the
river called Marais Des Cygnes (French explorers saw or thought
they saw swans on it) they met a messenger from Lawrence who reported that the town had been taken without resistance and the
border-ruffians were razing it to the ground. The shocking news
was received in silence and then the word was passed along the line,
"Onward." They camped that night at Prairie City. The next day,
they joined up with the Pomeroy Guards and some more men under
the command of Captain Samuel T. Shore. They went up Ottawa
Creek to a spot near Palmyra, later the town of Baldwin, twelve
miles from Lawrence. They had marched twenty-five miles from
home.

That day, at noon, John Brown formed a vigilante squad of his
own for special duty. It included his sons Owen, Frederick, Salmon,
and Oliver. His two sons John Brown, Jr., and Jason stayed behind.
In addition, his company had his son-in-law, Henry Thompson, an
Austrian-Jewish immigrant, Theodore Weiner, who ran a small
store in the neighborhood, and James Townsley, a forty-one-year-
old member of the Pottawatomie Rifles. Townsley drove them off
in his wagon and team while Weiner rode beside the wagon on his
pony.

It seems fairly well agreed that in the intervening time between
noon and 2 o'clock, when the wagon left, the broadswords they had
were sharpened on a grindstone. From the various accounts it appears that when the party left in the wagon there were cheers. Beyond that, there is disagreement as to what talk went on in the
company before they left.

It was not until Townsley made a full confession in the Lawrence
Daily Journal of December 10, 1879, that the whole affair and John
Brown's responsibility for it came to light. After that time, Brown's
sons made fragmentary admissions. In 1913, Salmon Brown, then
seventy-seven years old, and again in 1917, gave what purported to
be a full story. Salmon's account seems untrustworthy in many ways.
He told of the men viewing Lawrence afire from the top of a hill

south of the Wakarusa on the morning of May 23. This is contradicted by others, who stated they were miles away. Then he told how a messenger that morning brought news of the brutal caning in the United States Senate in Washington, D.C., the day before of Senator Charles Sumner of Massachusetts by Congressman Preston Brooks of South Carolina. "I do not think there was a tired or hungry man in that crowd as they were too excited to think of creature comforts. . . ." This must have been Salmon's imagination, since the telegraph did not extend further west than St. Louis at the time and the news could not have come until several days later.

Salmon and John Brown, Jr., insisted that everybody knew what was contemplated and the father acted in response to the general vote. Salmon said, "The general purport of our intentions—some radical retaliatory measure—some killing was well understood by the whole camp." Henry H. Williams, John Jr.'s chief lieutenant, Salmon said, was the most active in urging it, and in fact fifteen minutes before they left he had made a list of those to be killed and handed it to his father. John Brown, Jr., in statements to newspapers backed him up. "It was now and here resolved that they, their aiders and abettors, who sought to kill our suffering people should themselves be killed. . . . No man of our entire company could fail to misunderstand that a retaliatory blow would fall."

Jason Brown was allergic to bloodletting of any kind. (Salmon Brown told how in the previous winter they had no meat for two months and managed to catch some quail which the father dressed and cooked, but Jason having seen the fluttering of the trapped birds in their death-throes refused to eat their meat.) Jason later insisted that he did *not* know the purpose of the expedition, though he heard his father say to Weiner while he was cooking breakfast for the company, "Now, something *must* be done. We have got to defend our families and neighbors as best we can. We must show by actual work that there are two sides to this thing."

Since Townsley was the one who made the whole business public, his testimony is entitled to great weight. He was emphatic that he did not know what service he was being tapped for. John Brown came to him while in camp and said that trouble was expected in the settlements along Pottawatomie Creek. He asked Townsley if he would take him and his boys back there in his team and wagon, to which Townsley assented. Townsley said that when they left the camp, he heard John Brown, Jr. call out, "Father, be careful, be careful," showing his apprehension as to what Old Brown might do.

It is fair to say that all knew that Brown was poised for drastic action of some type or another. James Hanway related that he saw a member of the camp approach Brown when he was packing camp fixtures and urge "caution" on him, to which Brown responded angrily, "Caution, caution, sir. I am eternally tired of that word. It is nothing but the word of cowardice."

There is one quite persuasive piece of evidence that no one knew what John Brown had in mind. Salmon admitted that when they returned to the camp and the news had broken of the massacre, "Jason had the awfullest look on his face that I have ever seen." If the word had been passed around before Brown left, why should Jason have been so shocked?

James Blood, riding a horse from Osawatomie on his way to Lawrence, met the party on a plain as the sun was setting. "I could see the gleam of the sun's rays reflected from the moving gun-barrels of the party in the wagon." The cry "Halt" rang out when he was a hundred yards away and then he was ordered to ride up. They seemed to him strangely nervous, halting a solitary traveler, who was apparently unarmed, upon the open prairie.

When he drew up to the wagon, with Weiner on his pony beside it, he saw the six men armed to the teeth, with swords hanging from their sides and with revolvers in their belts. John Brown, whom he had found in the past reserved in speech, was now voluble after greeting him, denouncing the men of Lawrence as cowards and worse for giving up the town without a fight, or even a single shot. "His manner was wild and frenzied, and the whole party watched with excited eagerness every word or motion of the old man. Finally, as I left them, he requested me not to mention the fact that I had met them, as they were on a secret expedition and did not want anyone to know they were in the neighborhood."

Blood (is not the name an eerie coincidence?) rode off, the wagon rolled along in the opposite direction, and soon it was night.

In contrast to the plains lying farther west, the country around Osawatomie was wooded, with swelling hills, ravines, and crossed by rivers and winding streams. Pottawatomie Creek was misnamed since it is not a creek but a broad river, and to its north flows the river Marais des Cygnes, both meeting to form the Osage River. (Osawatomie was named by taking syllables of Osage and Pottawatomie.)

Along the Pottawatomie, there were located many cabins of settlers. Dutch Henry's Crossing was a tiny settlement where a German immigrant, "Dutch Henry" Sherman, operated some kind of a ford across the river.

There were grisly sights on the banks of the Pottawatomie on the morning of Sunday, May 25. On a road about two hundred yards from the cabin of the Doyles, poor-white settlers from Tennessee, there were two corpses. Mr. Doyle, the father, had been stabbed in the breast and shot in the forehead. His son, William Doyle, age twenty-two, lying beside him, had holes in his side and jaw and his head was cut open. Another son, Drury Doyle, age twenty, was lying in the grass about a hundred and fifty yards from the cabin. He had a hole in his breast and his arms and fingers had been cut off.

A hundred yards from the cabin of Allen Wilkinson, a member of the Shawnee legislature, the lawmaker lay dead with gashes in his head, throat, and side. In a creek near the cabin of James Harris was the corpse of William Sherman, the brother of "Dutch Henry" Sherman. His skull had been split open in two places and some of his brains had been washed out into the creek. His left hand was cut off and there was a large hole in his breast.

The midnight mass murder sent a chill of horror through Kansas. Since the victims were all of the proslavery side, it was immediately recognized for what it was, political reprisal. There had been murders of free-staters before this event, but they were the outcome of angry encounters in broad daylight, often the result of brawls, between men armed or in the company of armed companions. The painstaking chronicler of Kansas minutiae, A. T. Andreas states, "Thus these [previous] unavenged murders, numerous and atrocious as they were, lacked the ghastly horror of this silent, stealthy, midnight massacre of defenseless men."

The Westport, Missouri, *Border Times*, on May 27, was first to announce the atrocity, while increasing the victims by three.

WAR! WAR!

Eight Pro-Slavery men murdered by the Abolitionists in Franklin County, K.T.

LET SLIP THE DOGS OF WAR!

We learn from a dispatch just received by Col. A. G. Boone, dated at Paola, K.T., May 26, 1856, and signed by Gens. Heiskell and Barbee, that the reported murder of eight pro-slavery men in Franklin County, K.T., is but too true.

The dispatch explained the murders this way: "The Abolitionists (the court being in session) were afraid that these men would be called upon to give evidence against them, as many of them were charged with treason."

The St. Louis *Morning Herald* declared that "midnight assassination which revives in all their atrocity the most fiendish barbarities of the darkest ages and which, we repeat, is without parallel in Christendom since the Revolution in France, is *deliberately* planned to strike terror into the hearts of political opponents! Whether such will be the effect of the lesson remains to be seen." The fire-eating *Squatter Sovereign* said that the exemplary patience of the proslave government had its limits in the face of these midnight murders and assassinations. "Whilst these rebellious subjects confined themselves to the resistance of the law . . . the pro-slavery party in the territory was determined to stand by the law. And that we have no doubt is still the determination of every pro-slavery man, but there is a time for all things."

The Leavenworth, Kansas, *Weekly Herald* poured scorn on the free-staters "who have been outraged by the Law and Order party, but have like martyrs, passed through the fire, without the stain of blood upon their skirts." Then, reinterring Sheriff Jones, it sneered, "This is the party so pure and untarnished with dishonor that their very natures revolt and recoil from the countenancing of even a minor disgrace, much less the *foul assassination* of Sheriff Jones." On June 14 on its front page the Leavenworth *Herald* pleaded for the sympathy of the world for the oppressed southern men of Kansas. "We have proclaimed to the world that although we preferred Kansas being made a Negro Slave state, yet we never dreamed of making it so by the aid of bowie knives, revolvers and Sharp's rifles until we were threatened to be driven out by a band of hired Abolitionists, bought up and sent here to control our elections and steal our slaves and those of our friends in adjoining states."

Remarkably, the heinous crime failed to attract much attention outside of Kansas and John Brown's name was never even connected with it in reports. In Congress, only Senator Robert Toombs of Georgia and Congressman Mordecai Oliver of Missouri made passing references to it. The press in the southern states passed it up. In the North it could not be credited as the horrible deed it was, as historian James Ford Rhodes explained, because it did not fit the picture of the previous good character of the free-staters. "The testimony of impartial observers was that the proslavery men were lawless and aggressive, and the free-state settlers submissive, industrious, and anxious for liberty and order."

The New York *Times* carried a full story of the sack of Lawrence on its front page. On an inside page there were a few lines about the massacre, and the comment that it had appeared in the St. Louis *Republican* and therefore was "a story quite as improbable as many others that have appeared in that journal."

Where details were reported, they were badly garbled so that it became fiction. The New York *Tribune* ran a story that a party of border-ruffians went to the home of a free-state man residing near the Pottawatomie, dragged him out of bed, and took him to a grove nearby where they prepared to hang him. A rope was put around his neck and he was given time to say his prayers. Five of his neighbors armed themselves and went to his rescue, reaching the grove just as he was being swung up. They poured a volley into the gang killing five instantly while the other five fled. On June 10 it supplied more details of the affair from an eyewitness. A free-state man went to a store to buy lead. He was told that it was eighteen cents a pound but twenty-five cents a pound to a free-stater. When asked why he wanted it, he replied, "Wolves, if they come my way or even a man if attacked." He was then hustled to the timber to be strung up.

In the disorder which prevailed at the time of the murders and that continued after them, it is quite probable that the facts got mangled even in Kansas. London *Times* correspondent Thomas H. Gladstone published a book in 1857 about the border warfare and he most assuredly had no motive for concealing the truth. He was at Leavenworth at the time, and "as far as I could ascertain, a fight had occurred between half a dozen pro-slavery men and as many or more of the opposite party. Every pro-slavery man was left dead as well as three of the free-staters."

William A. Phillips published a book in 1856, *The Conquest of Kansas by Missouri Ruffians*, in which he reported the murders a result of an attack by free-state men on proslave men to forestall an attack on themselves. He reported executions of proslave men after a trial. He said, "Lynch-law is terrible always, but Kansas was the seat of guerrilla warfare and this was its sternest phase." Phillips had, of course, a strong free-state bias, but he may have been genuinely misinformed. He reported the death of a "Mr. Sherman who was killed at the time by the Comanches, he having gone out on the plains to hunt buffalo. The Indians not only killed him but mutilated his body, and his friends, when they found the body, brought it back to Pottawatomie. The pro-slavery men in the neighborhood took advantage of this circumstance to confound this affair with the other and to charge it to the Abolitionists."

The identity of the leader of the nighttime murder party, calling itself part of the Northern Army, which invaded the cabins on the Pottawatomie and selected the men for slaughter, was instantly known. Mrs. Mahala Doyle, who lost her husband and two sons, gave a full description of the old man, and the broad-rimmed old straw hat pulled down on his head would have been almost enough to identify Brown. Then James Harris said he had recognized two, "namely a Mr. Brown, whose given name I do not remember, commonly known as Old Man Brown, and his son Owen Brown."

Henry Clay Pate, correspondent for the St. Louis *Republican* in a dispatch of May 30 named Brown:

The leader of the party showed the bloody dagger and boasted that it did the evil deed. His name is Brown. . . . Brown told me he would take the life of a man as quick as he would that of a dog if he thought it was necessary. He said if a man stood between him and what he considered right, he would take his life as coolly as he would eat his breakfast. His actions show what he is. Always restless, he seems never to sleep. With an eye like a snake, he looks like a demon. Apparently a miserable outlaw, he prefers war to peace, that pillage and plunder may the more safely be carried on.

On May 24, the company led by John Brown, Jr., had gone to Lawrence to inspect the ruins of the town and then returned. The next afternoon a rider came tearing into their camp near Ottawa Creek, shouting, "Five men have been killed in Pottawatomie Creek, butchered and most brutally mangled, and old John Brown has done it!" John Brown, Jr., resigned his captaincy in favor of Henry H. Williams. At midnight, John Brown and his squad rejoined the company.

Jason Brown asked his father tremblingly, "Did you have anything to do with the killing of those men on the Pottawatomie?" John Brown said, "I did not do it but I approved of it." Jason said, "I think it was an uncalled for, wicked act." Jason recounted his father's answer, "God is my judge. It was absolutely necessary as a measure of self-defense, and for the defense of others." Jason said he could not give his exact language, but this was the purport of it. "It seemed to hurt his feelings that I felt so about it." Jason then asked Frederick who the murderers were and his brother said that he could not tell. "Did you kill any of them with your own hands?" With tears rolling down his face, Frederick said, "No. When I came to see what manner of work it was, I *could not* do it."

John Jr. and Jason went off by themselves back to Osawatomie. Already there were men patrolling the roads looking for them, they were warned, and so they headed through the brush for the cabin of the Reverend Samuel Adair and their aunt Florilla, who told them it was too dangerous to give them shelter. "Our lives are threatened and every moment we fear that our house will be burned over our heads." They pleaded that they had eaten nothing since morning and had had nothing to do with the murders. "Let us lie on your floor until morning—in your out-house if nowhere else." The Adairs let them sleep on a mattress on the floor. Owen Brown rapped on the door at two o'clock in the morning. The Reverend Mr. Adair closed the door in his face. "Get away as quick as you can! You are a vile murderer, a marked man and you endanger our lives." John Jr. could not sleep all that night. "I feel that I am going insane," he said over and over again, and in the morning he acted like a thoroughly deranged man.

Brown, with his four sons, Owen, Oliver, Salmon, and Frederick, went into hiding on Tanway Creek. It was not until two weeks after the massacre that John Brown wrote to his wife a letter headed, "Near Brown's Station, K.T. June 1856." He said, "We were called to go to the relief of Lawrence, May 22. . . . On our way to Lawrence we learned that it had been already destroyed, and we encamped with John's company over night." His account of the ghastly Pottawatomie affair was crisply stated: He had formed a little company of his own. "Next day our little company left, and during the day we stopped and searched three men. . . . On the second day and evening after we left John's men we encountered quite a number of proslavery men, and took quite a number of prisoners. Our prisoners we let go; but we kept some four or five horses. We were immediately after this accused of murdering five men at Pottawatomie, and great efforts have since been made by the Missourians and their ruffian allies to capture us."

John Brown had crossed his Rubicon in Kansas. From then on he was an outlaw, as he stated in picturesque language in his letter's last paragraph. "Since then we have, like David of old, had our dwellings with the serpents of the rocks and wild beasts of the wilderness, being obliged to hide away from our enemies." Though there was nothing incriminating in the letter, in the last sentence he acquitted himself of all moral guilt. "We feel assured that He who sees not as men see, does not lay the guilt of innocent blood to our charge."

John Brown might judge the crime by his own lights, as "*He* sees." We must look at it "as *men* see."

On the night of May 23, related James Townsley, the John Brown party in his wagon came to within two or three miles of Pottawatomie Creek. Then at Brown's direction they turned off the main road, drove down to the edge of the timber between two deep ravines and set up camp a mile above Dutch Henry's Crossing. There Brown informed him of the purpose of the expedition, wholesale murder of proslavery men. Townsley said he was shocked and wanted to take his wagon and team back to his home, which Brown refused to let him do.

They talked back and forth. Brown said that it had to be done for the protection of the free-state settlers, that it was better that a score of men should die than that one man who came to make Kansas a free state should be driven out. "I have no choice. It has been decreed by Almighty God, ordained from Eternity, that I should make an example of these men." Townsley interrupted, "If God is such a powerful man as you say, why doesn't he attend to this business himself?"

Accepting Townsley's statement as true, that he then learned Brown's purpose for the first time, the question arises—when did the others learn of it? The probability is that the others learned about it at the same time, the night of May 23, and that their habit of obedience to the stern patriarch of the family was such that they accepted it without demurrer. Weiner was a "big, savage, bloodthirsty Austrian" who did not need any spur of persuasion.

The party stayed in the ravine a full day and did not start out until the following night. Townsley insisted that the twenty-four-hour delay was necessitated by his protests until he finally capitulated to the iron-willed Brown. Possibly the party needed a rest after the day's hard drive. Salmon Brown said his father set the time not only as the hour when their quarry would be in hand but also, "Father took into consideration the terrifying effect" of a slaughter in the night.

At ten o'clock on Saturday night, May 24, the party set out. Townsley was now an active participant, armed with a broadsword, and he acted as guide. They crossed Mosquito Creek and at eleven o'clock approached the cabin of the Doyles. They knocked on the door. The Doyles told them to go away. They made torches from bundles of prairie grass, and threatened to burn the cabin down and so they were admitted inside. They announced that they were members of the Northern Army and that Doyle and his three sons were prisoners and must come with them. Mrs. Doyle on her knees begged them to spare the youngest son who was a mere boy and the old man assented. They departed and soon after there was a pistol shot. Terrified, she did not leave the cabin until dawn, when she found the bodies of her menfolk.

Townsley said that John Brown drew his revolver and shot old man Doyle in the forehead to nerve the others to the work, and then the two youngest Browns, nineteen-year-old Salmon and sixteen-year-old Oliver, fell on the Doyles with their short, two-edged swords. A Doyle boy tried to run away and Oliver overtook him. Salmon claimed that his father shot father Doyle when he was already dead. His explanation seems implausible, that Brown fired a bullet into the corpse to let Townsley and Thompson, who had wandered off, know where he was. But if Doyle was already dead, then John Brown was technically correct when he said that he killed no one that night.

The next destination was the home of Allen Wilkinson. The sound of a barking dog about an hour after midnight awakened Mrs. Wilkinson, who was sick with measles. Men knocked on the door and asked the way to "Dutch Henry's." They wanted Wilkinson, who was in bed, to come out and show them the way but the wife dissuaded her husband from doing so. After a whispered conference they loudly announced, "You are our prisoner. Do you surrender?" Wilkinson said, "Gentlemen, I do." They made him open the door, four men entered, and told Wilkinson to put on his clothes.

Mrs. Wilkinson begged them to let her husband stay with her, since she was sick and helpless. The old man, who seemed to be in command, said, "You have neighbors." She said, "So I have but they are not here, and I cannot go for them." The old man replied curtly, "It matters not."

Wilkinson had to dress in a hurry. He wanted to put on his boots as a protection from the damp, but they would not let him. They left, and soon afterward one of the strangers returned to take possession of two horse saddles. He told the frantic Mrs. Wilkinson that her husband was being taken "a prisoner to the camp."

James Harris, in a cabin across the river, was in bed with his wife and child when they were aroused at two o'clock in the morning by a group of men who styled themselves the Northern Army. With drawn swords and revolvers they took possession of the cabin. The occupants of the cabin included three men who were sleeping over-night and were to leave the next morning. One of the three was William Sherman, known as "Dutch Bill." They asked where his brother "Dutch Henry" was and were advised that he was out on the plains in search of cattle which he had lost. They took James Harris outside and quizzed him—had he taken any hand in harming free-state men or aiding the proslavery cause; had he taken any part in the troubles at Lawrence a few days before? He said firmly no, and they brought him back to the house. They searched the house for arms and ammunition, took a saddle, and made Harris saddle "Dutch Henry's" horse which was there.

The old man then led William Sherman away while two of the Northern Army remained in the cabin. Fifteen minutes later without explanation the two men disappeared into the night.

According to Townsley, there was no intentional mutilation of the bodies after death. "They were slain as quickly as possible and left, and whatever gashes they received were inflicted in the process of cutting them down with swords. I understand that the killing was done with these swords so as to avoid alarming the neighborhood by the discharge of firearms."

These fiendish murders, without doubt, were the result of an emotional decision by John Brown. His frenzied appearance and impetuous speech as described by James Blood on meeting him the day before were the marks of an overwrought mind which had fastened on the idea that the crisis for the free-staters called for a ringing protest against nonresistance and an unforgettable lesson to their enemies.

The decision could hardly have been reached after cold calculation since Brown and his sons were lucky, indeed, to have escaped with their lives. The law was in the hands of the proslave party and that area was overrun with border-ruffians. It is an irony that in this case where the violence was done after an emotional, snap decision and the odds were heavily against him, John Brown managed to stay clear of the law and private revenge—the Harper's Ferry attack, on the other hand, was long planned and the chances of extricating himself were good, but the result there was fatal to him.

In his own mind, heeding the command of the Lord he had unleashed the sword of Gideon, he had exterminated the Lord's enemies as Joshua put Canaan's guilty cities to the sword. In their book on Lincoln, John C. Nicolay and John Hay said that in Brown's fanatical belief, "in the sacrificial sternness of his prototypes in Jewish history, he could lay his own child on the altar without a pang." The Kansas historian, Professor Leverett W. Spring, writing in 1885, said:

In behalf of the cause which fascinated and ruled him he was prepared to sacrifice his enemies and if the offering proved inadequate to sacrifice himself. He belonged to the Hebraic, Old Testament, iron-type of humanity, in which the sentiment of justice—narrowed to warfare upon a single evil, pursuing it with concentrated and infinite hostility as if it epitomized all the sinning of the Universe—assumed an exaggerated importance. It was a type of humanity in which the lives of individual men, weighed in the interests of the inexorable cause, seemed as light and trivial as the dust on a butterfly's wings.

In the same spirit, Oliver Cromwell after massacring the inhabitants of the fortified town of Drogheda in Ireland in 1649 because they had refused to surrender said, "This was a righteous judgment of God upon these barbarous wretches who have imbrued their hands in so much innocent blood and will tend to prevent effusion of blood for the future—which are satisfactory grounds for such actions, which otherwise cannot but work remorse and regret."

Sanborn related that at the morning meal after the massacre, Brown raised his hands in prayer and the hands were dyed with blood. The motive of his conduct was "an impression that God had called him to a high and painful work and he must accomplish this even with bloodshed."

The historian Rhodes stated that Brown counted up the number of free-state victims starting with the murder of Charles Dow. "This blood must be expiated by an equal number of victims." There are flaws in this reasoning. Brown could not have been a careful arithmetician, since he killed five while the number killed on his side had mounted by this time to six. Then, too, if Townsley is to be believed, Brown had further killings in mind that night but was dissuaded. "Brown wanted me to pilot the party into the neighborhood where I lived and point out all the pro-slavery men in it, whom he proposed to put to death. I positively refused to do it."

Theodore Roosevelt wrote a sympathetic article about Brown in *Outlook* magazine in 1910. Roosevelt, who cannot be described exactly as an apostle of nonviolence, said in an obvious reference to Pottawatomie, "It was a heroic struggle and as is inevitable in all such struggles it had also a dark and terrible side. Very much was done of good and much also of evil, and as was inevitable in such a period of revolution often the same man did both good and evil."

All too true. In this world good and evil live side by side and often in the same man. However, a state of war had not broken out in Kansas, no free-stater had died in the sack of Lawrence, the murders of free-staters had taken place further north in Douglas and Doniphan counties, and the area around Osawatomie was undisturbed.

Then—the murdered men, although proslavery in their sympathies, could hardly be classed as combatants. Not one owned a slave. Allen Wilkinson, although a member of the Shawnee legislature, was nonvocal and inoffensive. His wife testified, "My husband was a quiet man, and was not engaged in arresting or disturbing anybody. He took no active part in the pro-slavery cause, so as to aggravate the Abolitionists." "Dutch Bill" Sherman with his brother, "Dutch Henry," operated a saloon, a rendezvous for border-ruffians, which seemed to be the sum total of their activities in behalf of slavery, excluding their mouthings of hostility to free-staters. The Doyles, "poor whites" from Tennessee, almost illiterate, had come to Kansas because, according to Mrs. Doyle, slavery was "ruinous to white labor." Yet, because they were southerners by origin they voted with the southern party of the state. It seems that the father Doyle was the only one of the five victims whom John Brown had met previously. They had had a bitter political argument, according to one witness. It was Brown's attitude that southerners who owned no slaves but were politically proslave were "worse than slaveholders," since lacking any pecuniary interest they could be motivated only by moral depravity in approving the curse of slavery.

There were many statements made afterward that all the men killed were worthless, no-good types whom the world was well rid of. If such be the criterion, then a good part of the human race would be sluiced away at once—and who shall be the judges? Even the legislator, Wilkinson, who had a fair education, was relegated to this degraded category. Thus, "Wilkinson was a most evil-looking man who fearfully abused a nice wife, well liked by the neighbors."

That such rumors were irresponsible claptrap is evidenced by an assessment of the victims given by Montgomery Shore to historian William E. Connelley in 1892. This Shore was a brother of Captain Samuel T. Shore, who later fought with Brown. He said the Doyles were the lowest people imaginable. They brought five bloodhounds with them to Kansas and settled near Dutch Henry's Crossing to capture slaves that escaped from Missouri, and they lived on wages from plantation guards. Wilkinson was a "worthless, drunken and dangerous man." There was neighborhood talk that the Shermans were criminally intimate with Mrs. Doyle, that one of her sons was "the fruit of some incest or other scandalous criminal intercourse in the South. They were all thieves and stole cattle and hogs. The old woman was as great a drunkard as were the husband and boys. She chewed tobacco, smoked and ate snuff." As for "Dutch Henry," he was supposed to have killed several people and had raped a number of women. "He always kept two or three Indian women at his home for criminal purposes." "Dutch Bill" was as bad as his brother and obviously did not deserve to live.

Turning to the next excuse for Brown—it was said that he grabbed time by the forelock and acted to prevent the Osawatomie settlers from being driven from their homes by the border-ruffians. In Weiner's store, a mile and a half from the Doyles, a notice was allegedly posted that all free-state settlers must leave within thirty days or have their throats cut.

There are two observations that are pertinent to the various allegations that the free-state settlements were in imminent danger. First, bloody threats were a chief stock in trade of the border-ruffians and the pro-southern press. If words had been bullets, bodies of all the free-state settlers would have littered the fields of Kansas from an early date. Second, if such a deadly menace had existed, it is unlikely that John Brown and his sons would have taken off for Lawrence, leaving unprotected among others the wives of John Brown, Jr., and Jason Brown.

This yarn had been embellished with a messenger who rode into the camp on Friday morning with news of an impending outrage, and that this galvanized John Brown into action, impelling him to return and take preventive action. There was a search made for the identity of this messenger but one after another person was marked off as unavailable, and so he remains unknown. There are a pile of difficulties that roadblock the existence of any such messenger and he must be put down as fictional. Such a messenger could hardly have traveled faster than the expedition itself, and John Brown stayed only a few hours in camp before he returned home in the Townsley wagon. If in the interim there had been an outcropping of such trouble, why had he not inquired about it from James Blood whom he met on the way back since Blood had just departed from Osawatomie? Then, again, if such peril had existed why did the party idle away a whole twenty-four-hour period in the ravine above Dutch Henry's Crossing, while presumably their kin were in such jeopardy?

Yet a fable will be believed if people want to believe it. Du Bois wrote, "Although the exact facts have never been told, it seems clear that a meeting of the intended victims was secured at which John Brown himself presided. Probably it was then decided that the seven ringleaders of the projected deviltry must be killed and John Brown was appointed to see that the deed was done." Sanborn went further than that. He said that the victims were tried, found guilty and given time to pray—this in the face of the categorical denials of the Brown sons and Henry Thompson that there had ever been such a trial.

The victims were well chosen by Brown not because they were guilty *but because they were innocent.* He instinctively grasped the essence of maximum terror. It is its unreasonableness and consequently its unpredictability which makes terror the most fearsome. Dr. Hannah Arendt in her book, *The Origins of Totalitarianism,* has a brilliant discussion of the use of terror as an instrument of power, saying that Stalin and Hitler realized that terror has its greatest effect when directed against those who are not the true enemies. Thus Stalin in the purge trials of the mid-thirties picked on the assassination of Kirov as a convenient excuse to put the innocent to death *pour encourager les autres.* It was this same principle of terror that was used by Charles A. Hamelton in his 1858 Kansas massacre, as we shall see, when he selected his victims at random.

The supreme absolutist Brown made his resolve after the sack of Lawrence according to his own personal concept of the need for most effective retribution, according to his own reading of the will of the vengeful Deity.

One evening three months later, Brown was at the home of E. A. Coleman in Kansas, who asked Brown if he had killed those men on the Pottawatomie. Brown answered, "I did not but I do not pretend to say they were not killed by my order. In doing so, I believe I was doing God's service." Mrs. Coleman said, "Then, Captain Brown, you think that God uses you as an instrument in his hands to kill men?" He replied, "I think he has used me as an instrument to kill men, and if I live I think he will use me as an instrument to kill a good many men."

Such an edict directed to the individual from the "higher law," exculpating him from man-made law, was familiar in Cromwellian doctrine. It was justified by John Milton in his "Samson Agonistes":

> And hath full right to exempt
> Whom it so pleases Him by choice
> From natural obstruction, without taint
> Of sin or legal debt;
> For with His own laws He can best dispense.

Yet, if everyone took it into mind to act according to his own concept of the "higher law," what would become of society's laws, which are founded also on the belief that they carry out the will of God? The biblical *lex talionis*, for example, has been the Judeo-Christian rationale for capital punishment. Villard, who found excuse and palliation for all else that John Brown did in his life, could not bring himself to condone this, which he said was a "dark blot on his memory. . . . If he deserves to live in history, it is not because of his cruel, gruesome, reprehensible acts on the Pottawatomie, but despite them." William Dean Howells condemned Brown not only for what he did but, worse yet, made others do for him. One of Brown's favorite biblical quotations was that "without the shedding of blood, there is no remission of sins." Howells commented that even if this were true, "it is the blood shed by the martyr, and not by the murderer, which shall serve us."

We have discussed the smokescreen of excuses that have been tendered for Brown's crime, which quickly dissolves on a candid examination. What is far more astonishing is that Brown, after the short initial excitement, escaped being stigmatized with the crime during his lifetime and not until 1880 was he recognized by history as its perpetrator, although he was one of the prominent figures of the age. If history can thus be perverted, we may well ask with Pontius Pilate, "What is truth?"

From 1856 on, he had little or nothing to say about it. If he was proud of having been chosen as an instrument of the Lord, he might have felt that the Lord had slipped in this instance. Perhaps he remembered that night with a cold shudder. Riding alongside him in August, 1856, Captain Samuel Walker said that he would not have the Pottawatomie massacres on his conscience for all the world. Brown replied that although he was in command of the party he had not raised his hand against any one of them. This is the one and only time that Brown ever admitted to anyone that he was actually at the scene; in his remark to E. A. Coleman, which we have mentioned, he did not admit he was there. James Hanway was a member of the company from which Brown took his departure with his squad on May 23, 1856. He remained a lifelong admirer of Brown whom he termed "The Cromwell of America—though more humane." He told of a conversation in Kansas in 1858. "The old man remarked that the first shock frightened the free-state men almost as bad as the ruffians but he knew then that when the facts were understood that a reaction would take place. He then remarked, 'If the killing of these men was murder, then I was an accessory.'" On one occasion in Boston in 1859, Brown was asked about the Pottawatomie murders and said that he had had no part in them although he endorsed them.

Brown was never backward in boasting of his accomplishments in Kansas but one can search and find nothing more, even by oblique reference. It seems that by an effort of will he had brainwashed himself of this gruesome memory. He seemed to believe he was making an honest statement when, in the interrogation a few hours after his capture at Harper's Ferry, he said, "I killed no man except in fair fight. I fought at Black Jack and Osawatomie and if I killed anybody it was at one of those places."

There was some discussion of the Pottawatomie atrocity at the time of Brown's Harper's Ferry raid, trial, and execution in 1859. The New York *Herald* printed the damning affidavits on its front pages but it was a Democratic and violently anti-John Brown paper and so all this was termed a southern lie. In Lawrence, Kansas, G. W. Brown in his *Herald of Freedom* was castigating Brown as the Pottawatomie murderer but this was discredited as a personal vendetta. The attention, the focus of public interest, at the time, was all on Harper's Ferry, not on Kansas of 1856.

The Pottawatomie murders were discussed in the United States Senate on December 12, 1859, soon after Brown's execution, by Senator Andrew Johnson of Tennessee (later President on Lincoln's death): "The Senator [Doolittle] talks about the school in Kansas in which John Brown was taught. He did not go there to be taught but he went there as a teacher. These were his teachings. Imagine the cries and lamentations on the one hand and the shrieks of the dying and mutilated on the other. I think sometimes that I hear the shrieks so loud, so wild, so clear, that even listening angels stoop from heaven to hear. This is the man for whom an apology is offered."

Brown murdered Doyle and his two sons, Johnson went on. He lost two sons at Harper's Ferry. "Justice seemed a little tardy but it kept constantly in pursuit of its victim. I do not say that was a stroke of Providence, but it was a singular coincidence. He whose hands were red, crimson with the blood of a father and two sons, fell a victim at Harper's Ferry with his own two sons."

After his execution, there was almost a concerted conspiracy to save Brown's reputation on this score. His sons naturally joined in. Salmon Brown wrote Sanborn in December, 1859, "I was one of the company at the time of the homicide. . . . I say positively that he was not a participator in the deed—although I should think none the less of him if he had been there, for it was the grandest thing ever done in Kansas." The correspondent Richard J. Hinton wrote in the Boston *Evening Traveller*: "John Brown told me he was not a participator in the Pottawatomie homicide. John Brown was incapable of uttering a falsehood."

In an 1859 article, Thomas Wentworth Higginson, one of the Boston Brahmins who financed Brown, commented on a letter from Mrs. Mahala Doyle rejoicing over Brown's execution, ". . . which common charity bids us suppose a forgery, uttering fiendish revenge in regard to a man against whom, by her own showing, there is not one particle of evidence to identify him with her wrongs." This seems disingenuous on his part since this same Higginson was in Kansas in 1856 and in his 1898 book, *Cheerful Yesterdays*, admitted that he knew of the act and Brown's connection with it. "I heard no one who did not approve of the act and its beneficial effects were universally asserted."

The James Redpath book of 1860 established the John Brown legend for a generation. Redpath had little regard for accuracy. Once when reproached for inaccuracy he replied that, "It sounded better as I reported it, and will have a more telling effect in the East." He dealt with Pottawatomie in this fashion. "John Brown did not know these men were killed until the following day; for, with one of his sons, he was twenty-five miles distant at the time—he was at Middle Creek." He quoted Brown, "But remember, I do not say this to exculpate myself; for although I took no hand in it, I would have advised it had I known the circumstances." Redpath had been a correspondent in Kansas for the New York *Tribune* in 1856 and knew the truth.

John Brown was so great a hero after the Civil War that there would have been no audience for the truth even if it had been published. It was years later, in Kansas, that the anti-John Brown school of thought sprang up. An account written by James Hanway and revised in 1879 was given credence in which he made it clear that John Brown headed the murder party which left the main company on May 23. In December, 1879, came the Townsley confession. The truth could no longer be suppressed. Sanborn wrote to Redpath: "You and I must give in that the Old Hero was at Pottawatomie and gave the orders."

In his 1885 book, Sanborn had three choices: to brand Brown as a murderer, as insane, or as acting under Divine guidance. He chose the last: "The story of John Brown will mean little to those who do not believe that God governs the world and that he makes His will known in advance to certain chosen men and women who perform it consciously or unconsciously. Of such prophetic, Heaven-appointed men, John Brown was the most conspicuous in our time and his life must be construed in the light of that fact. . . . Such a deed must not be judged by the everyday rules of conduct. . . ."

Furthermore, he said, "Upon the swift and secret vengeance of John Brown in that midnight raid hinged the future of Kansas, as we can now see it, and on that future again hinged the destinies of the whole country." Most Americans agreed with him, and said "Amen," although they knew little about Kansas in 1856.

CHAPTER THREE

Firebrand in Kansas—
The Outlaw

A DETACHMENT of Alabamans and Georgians of Major Buford's company rode in from Missouri on May 27, two days after the massacre, scouring the countryside for the criminals, the Browns. They burned to the ground all the buildings at Brown's Station, and drove off all the cattle. John Brown, Jr., lost all his personal possessions, one of the most precious being his library of four hundred volumes, which he had started to collect when he was a boy of twelve.

Jason left the Adair cabin to surrender to United States troops. Instead, he walked straight into a group of border-ruffians led by the Reverend Martin White who had returned from Missouri. "You are one of the very men we are looking for," said White. "Your name is Brown. I knew your father." "My name is Jason Brown. I have never knowingly injured a human being. Now, if you want my blood, there is a mark for you," and he pulled open his shirt, expecting to be shot to pieces. White answered, "We won't kill you now. But you are our prisoner and we hold every man a scoundrel till he is proved honest."

Jason was weak with excitement and fatigue, and trembling with the chills. They made him walk four miles at a fast walk and then put him on a horse, tying his arms behind him and his feet beneath the horse. With a guard of twenty men he was taken to Paola, eight miles from Osawatomie where he found three hundred proslavery men massed. "Swing him up! Swing him up!" was the shout he heard. He was hustled over to a tree, a hemp rope was flung over a limb, and all seemed ready, but his life was spared.

While he was there, John Brown, Jr., was brought in as a prisoner. He had been found wandering in the woods. After a brief confinement, both were taken to Osawatomie. Jason was transported in a wagon but John Jr. was given special treatment. His wrists were bound tight by a hard hemp rope and also his upper arms; he was driven afoot at full trot pace to Osawatomie, led by a forty-feet-long rope attached to a horse. By the time he reached there, he was a terrible sight. His clothes were torn, the flesh of his upper arms was all cut and swollen; having been dragged through the water of creeks, the flints at the bottom had cut through his boots and badly lacerated his feet. Then he was chained by each ankle with an ox-cart chain to the center pole of the guard tent. He was out of his mind, shrieking and jumping up and down. He was told to shut up, but kept on yelling. A trooper knocked him down with a terrible blow on the jaw, a second knelt on him and pounded him with his fist, and a third kicked him with all his force on his neck. Jason cried, "Don't kill a crazy man!" and a ruffian replied, "We'll fetch the craziness out of him." After this beating, John lay unconscious for three hours.

Henry Clay Pate reported this way in the Missouri *Republican* the ordeal of John Brown, Jr.: "The one who feigns to be crazy has just left in charge of the dragoons. He is made to accompany them on foot, at a pretty rapid gait, of course, as the troops are mounted. His day's march will help the craziness and perhaps cool down the fanaticism which has laid five innocent men in their graves."

Mrs. T. B. Alexander, John Brown, Jr.'s daughter, said that when her father's body was laid out for burial in May, 1895, the marks on his arms where the ropes sank into his flesh were still clearly visible.

John Brown eluded capture. He was hidden in the thickets of Tanway Creek with ten men. Besides his four sons, there were Weiner, Henry Thompson, another Austrian-Jewish immigrant, Augustus Bondi, Townsley, Ben Cochran, and Charles Keiser. Brown, acting as cook for the men, baked in a skillet a twice-a-day ration of pone of bran bread. On the last two days all they had to eat was some molasses donated by a free-state housewife who said it was too sour for her to use. The men were desperately hungry. Weiner, who weighed two hundred and fifty pounds, groaned, "A little more of this and I'm going to be as thin as a rail."

James Redpath, who was a correspondent for the New York *Tribune* and other newspapers, found his way to the Brown camp on May 30. The British-born journalist, not yet twenty-three, already had a considerable reputation from his dispatches in the New York *Tribune* covering the bogus legislature proceedings. He was the man who would found the John Brown legend with his 1860 book.

He first ran into a big, blond youth who looked wild and strange, unshaven for days, his hair matted and tangled. This was Frederick Brown, who was quite a problem to his father on account of attacks of insanity. There is repeated reference to this in his letters. A memorandum found in John Brown's papers at North Elba read, "Frederick, though a very stout man, was subject to periodical sickness for many years ATTENDED WITH INSANITY. Before going to Kansas he had subjected himself to a most dreadful surgical operation." We do not know what that was.

On this meeting, Frederick was swinging a pail back and forth, talking gibberish to Redpath about how his father was accused of the Pottawatomie murders but was innocent. His excitement seemed to increase as he led Redpath back and forth across a creek. Finally Redpath lost patience and told Frederick he would hear no more, and his demented guide led him by a devious route to the camp.

Redpath introduced himself to Brown as a devoted friend of the free-state cause. He said that the situation was in a crisis stage and he must hold out until the tide turned. He asked him if he had anything to say about the Pottawatomie murders. Brown would say only that it was a "summary execution," but would not discuss his personal responsibility.

At ten o'clock on the night of May 31, Brown was visited by Captain Samuel T. Shore and Orellius Carpenter. They held a council under a big oak tree in the center of the camp. Their visitors told of outrages that were being committed by border-ruffians in reprisal for the murders. They decided to hold a meeting the next day in a church at Prairie City after the Sunday service and to send out runners to notify the free-state families. Salmon related that at 5 A.M. the next morning Carpenter came to guide them out. "We saddled our horses and started, a funny-looking cavalcade, our clothes nothing but rags, stitched together with locust thorns." Salmon was joyful, saying to Bondi, "Hurrah! At last we're going to eat."

At Prairie City there was no breakfast. A Methodist minister gave a long sermon and then there was a recital amid weeping of the depredations of the Missourians. "I began to get pretty disgusted," said Salmon. "I thought they might better have been employed molding bullets than weeping and groaning so long." However, at two o'clock in the afternoon the lament was over and, hallelujah!, the women baked biscuits.

While they were eating their biscuits, three strangers rode by at a distance. "They must be Missourians," said Brown and he dispatched his boys to overtake them. They were brought in, and gave the information that they were from the camp of Captain Pate, who had a force of Missouri militia whose mission was to apprehend John Brown, the murderer, and his sons. They had pitched their tents a few miles away at a spring on the Santa Fe Trail called Black Jack because of the many black jack oak trees there.

Brown announced that he was not going to wait to be attacked; he would attack Pate the next morning. Five men said they would join his company, giving him a total of fifteen. Captain Shore would join him in the attack on Pate, and he had twenty-five men. Opposing them, Pate had eighty men in camp. The battle of Black Jack took place, the next day, June 2. It was the first pitched battle between the opposing sides in Kansas and this mini-battle may appropriately be termed the curtain raiser to the gigantic Civil War. The victory was rightly claimed as one belonging to John Brown and his sons.

"I went to take Brown—and he took me." That was Captain Henry Clay Pate's own summary of the battle. Pate, wrote Redpath, was "a man-butterfly, whom no one would have thought of disturbing. With the vanity of the fabled frog, he aspired to equal John Brown and flew against his soul of fire—but only to be scorched for his pains and pinned to a page of history by the stern, old Puritan and then placed in the cabinet of human imbecilities forever."

Pate, then only twenty-four years old, was, as we have noted, a correspondent of the Missouri *Republican*. He had attended the University of Virginia in his native state. He had aspired to a literary career in Cincinnati and later in Missouri and distributed cards with an engraved portrait of himself over "H. C. Pate, Author." He was leading this company not only as a captain of the Missouri militia but also as a deputy United States marshal.

At daybreak, Brown and Shore dismounted a mile from Pate's camp. "Advance!" Brown shouted the command, and his men ran down a hill. "Halt!" he shouted when they reached the bottom. Shore's men jumped into a ravine on the left and started to fire. Pate's men had been surprised while eating breakfast, and they returned the fire but they were in a panic and their shots went wild. Brown's force ran down into a ravine on the right and started shooting from behind a two-foot-high embankment. Pate's men became demoralized under the crossfire, and they started to desert.

Shore sent Brown word that he was leaving with his men. They were too hungry to fight any more. Later he explained to the New York *Tribune* that he had gone for more help. At any rate, Brown was left to fight alone. Pate's men were shielded by wagons and Brown told his men to shoot all the horses and mules in sight. This they did, and the air was thick with buzzards over the dead animals. Two of his force were wounded, and three helped them away from the field of battle. Then Townsley deserted and so there were only Brown and nine free-staters left fighting, of whom six were Browns, including Henry Thompson who kept firing till the end although he had been shot through the lungs.

The decisive event was the action of Frederick, who had been left in the rear to guard the horses. He could not be trusted with a gun since he might fire on his own family. In the thick of the battle he mounted a horse and rode around Pate's rear, shouting wildly, "Father, Father, we have them surrounded!" Pate must have thought he was surrounded. He knew that Shore's men had gone up the ravine, and not aware that they had departed for good, Pate undoubtedly thought they must have taken positions in his rear and that he and his men might be shot in the back at any instant. Two men walked out from his line, under a flag of truce, one a free-state prisoner, the other, Pate's young aide, Henry James.

Brown met them in the open field. He told them that if their commander had anything to say to him he should come out himself, and so Pate strode out to parley with Brown.

Pate told Brown that he was a deputy United States marshal, and he assumed that Brown would not resist an officer of the national government.

Brown: "Captain. I understand exactly what you are and do not want to hear more about it. Have you a proposition to make to me?"

Pate: "Well, no, that is——"

Brown: "Very well, Captain, I have one to make to you, your unconditional surrender."

Pate: "Give me fifteen minutes to talk it over with my men."

Brown: "Not fifteen seconds."

Pate looked at the muzzles of Sharp's rifles sixty rods away and agreed to surrender.

Pate denounced Brown later, saying he had been taken prisoner under a flag of truce, "a barbarity unlooked for in this country and unheard of in the annals of honorable warfare." Pate and Brown conducted a debate about this battle in the columns of the New York *Tribune*, and in his first statement Pate made an admission as to his use of the flag of truce: "My object was to gain time, and if possible, have hostilities suspended for a while." Brown in his *Tribune* reply emphasized this admission: "So much in his own language for good faith of which he found me so destitute."

Brown alone with Pate, James, and the free-state prisoner walked back to Pate's line. We must bow to Brown's bravery as he described it in his *Tribune* account: "I, an old man of nearly sixty years [he was fifty-six], and fully exposed to the weapons of two young men at my side, as well as the fire of their men in their camp, so far and no further, took them prisoners under their flag of truce." Brown told Pate to order his men to put down their guns. Pate's lieutenant, W. B. Brockett, said, "We won't do it unless Captain Pate tells us to." Brown shoved his revolver under Pate's breast and, according to Brown, Pate gave the order, saying, "Boys, why don't you throw away your guns while we talk this thing over?"

Brown took twenty-nine prisoners and much provisions and equipment. Immediately after the surrender, Captain J. B. Abbott arrived on the scene with a hundred mounted men. Brown objected to the fact that they helped themselves to Pate's booty which should have been all his as the victor entitled to the spoils.

Pate, a proud southerner, was thereafter much concerned about the imputation on his honor, about having shown the "white feather" at Black Jack. Pate visited Brown on November 22, 1859, at Charlestown, Virginia, while Brown was awaiting execution, and Pate quickly published a pamphlet at his own expense upholding his honor. It is an interesting document. He said that Brown's party at Black Jack numbered all of a hundred men. He said that he did not give the order to his men to throw down their arms; they did so voluntarily to save him. "Brown might have shot me, his men might have riddled me, but I would not have given the order for a world, much less my poor life." He supplied an affidavit in his pamphlet, signed by Brown's jailer, that Brown admitted this to him: "During this interview, Capt. Brown said that he had never imputed cowardice to Capt. Pate, but declared then, as he had done on all occasions, public and private, that the latter gave him the hardest fight he had in Kansas, that he and his company bore themselves bravely during the fight and gentlemanly during their imprisonment . . . that Black Jack was the only good fighting by pro-slavery men that he ever saw in Kansas."

From the account given by Pate one would have supposed that the interview in Charlestown was a hearts-and-flowers reunion. The New York *Herald*, of November 26, 1859, gave an entirely different version from its Charlestown correspondent. It said that the meeting of Brown and Pate "was not of the most cordial character on the part of the former. Brown declared he had met a great many men in his life of more courage than Captain Pate, to which the Captain responded by charging Brown with all kinds of villainy."

Brown took Pate and his men as prisoners to a camp he established in Middle Ottawa Creek. Recognition was coming to Brown as a natural leader, and free-state men joined his standard, so that he now had a hundred and fifty men under his command. Colonel Edwin V. Sumner, of the First United States Cavalry, heard of the whereabouts of Brown and advanced against him with fifty men. He had two purposes. First, President Pierce, alarmed about the disorders, had sent a message that all illegally formed companies must disperse and Governor Shannon had issued a proclamation to that effect, and second, a deputy United States marshal, William J. Preston, accompanied him to arrest Brown for murder. On the outskirts of the camp, Brown met Sumner and proposed a parley. He had in mind a swap of his prisoners for the liberty of his sons John Jr. and Jason. Sumner said, "I make no terms with lawless men." So Brown led him to the camp on an island which Sumner said later was so heavily fortified that it would have required a thousand men to storm it. Colonel Sumner, with a young Virginia lieutenant, J. E. B. Stuart, by his side, ordered the Brown company to disperse and release Pate, his men, and his horses.

Then Sumner told Preston to make his arrest. Preston must have lose his nerve. "Well, I'm afraid I lost the warrants." Sumner exploded, "You are a damn liar and a coward! I saw the warrants in your hand last night." Pate got up on a log and started to denounce the troops for letting the murderer, Brown, get away a free man. Sumner ordered him to get down. "I don't want to hear a word from you, sir, not a word."

Even if Preston had no warrant, it would have been an easy matter for Sumner to have held Brown overnight until one was obtained. Brown said that Colonel Sumner had expressed a private sympathy for him, although he was ready to follow official orders. A fascinating "If" of history is: Suppose Brown had been held that day for arrest on a charge of mass murder of which there were many witnesses?

Two fighting Virginians met that day—Pate and "Jeb" Stuart. They would each see John Brown once again, in connection with his attack on Harper's Ferry. Colonel Henry Clay Pate, of the Fifth Virginia Cavalry, would die on the same day when General J. E. B. Stuart was mortally wounded, on May 5, 1864, and within a hundred yards of him, near Yellow Tavern, Virginia.

There can be no doubt but that the Pottawatomie massacre was a turning point in Kansas history. It galvanized the struggle, and from that time on the two parties were at each other's throat with guns instead of words. Kansas historian Leverett W. Spring said: "To Dutch Henry's Crossing must be charged much of the havoc in which the Kansas of 1856 weltered. That affair was a festering, rankling, envenomed memory among pro-slavery men. . . . So far from befriending anti-slavery interests, the Pottawatomie massacre at once fomented and embittered the struggle. A period of lawlessness and marauding now set out that left stains on both parties as inevitably as the snail slurries its track."

Initially, the murders filled the proslavery people in the border areas with terror. The Reverend Mr. Adair, in a letter he wrote a few days after the massacre, told of the consternation it created: "The excitement produced has been most tremendous. Money, arms, horses, etc., were taken. Some pro-slavery men took the alarm and fled. . . . Runners were sent to Missourie for help, and pro-slavery men in different localities gathered together or stood in fear of their lives. Missourie troops have not come and it is thought they will not come in large numbers. . . ."

But they did come over in great numbers. Richard Hinton's explanation of the salutary effect of the massacre is unintentionally humorous: "The execution of these men was the dawn of peace in

Kansas. There was no more murdering except by ruffians attached to forces coming over in large numbers."

What is important is that the audacious and defiant deed raised the morale of the free-state side, invigorated them with the spirit of fight. Many have certified to that. Senator John J. Ingalls years later said, "It vertebrated the free-state party." Luke F. Parsons, a youth who joined up with Brown, in a subsequent account, gave a vivid impression of the turmoil following Pottawatomie: "Men who were astride the fence now had to get down on one side or the other. The whole country became aroused. All over the Territory sprang up captains who had never been heard of before. There were Captain Samuel Walker's Bloomington Rifles, Captain Joseph Cracklin's Lawrence Stubbs, Captain J. B. Abbott's Blue Mound Infantry, Captain McWhinney's Wakarusa Boys, and Captain Samuel T. Shore's Prairie City Rifles." Free-state men in large numbers left the plow now to fight.

John Brown came to Kansas, as he said, not to settle but to fight. His dearest wish was to promote a collision of the two sides, and that is precisely what he accomplished. It is highly possible that had it not been for Pottawatomie, the proslave faction flushed by its "victory" at Lawrence might have steamrollered all opposition.

In the 1870s, Governor Charles Robinson applauded Brown with the highest encomiums. He wrote to James Hanway: "I never had much doubt that Captain John Brown was the author of the blow at the Pottawatomie for the reason that he was the only man who comprehended the situation and saw the absolute necessity of some such blow and had the nerve to strike it." Dedicating a monument to Brown in 1875, Robinson said: "To the superficial observer John Brown was a failure. So was Jesus of Nazareth. Both suffered ignominious deaths as traitors to the government. Yet one is hailed as the savior of the world from sin and the other of a race from bondage."

The same Robinson led a hate-campaign against John Brown in Kansas in the 1880s. His somersault is one of the most striking features of the reversal of opinion in Kansas. Thomas Wentworth Higginson was in Kansas in 1856 and said that Robinson personally endorsed the deed to him. His change of attitude, wrote Higginson, "appears to me to have been either simply disgraceful or else the product of a disordered mind."

As the free-staters put up increasing, organized resistance, the realization grew in the South that the tide in Kansas was turning against it. The Charleston, South Carolina, *News* said, "There never was a completer or more disastrous miscarriage than the Kansas–Nebraska bill. It has not only blasted every expectation that was originally formed of it but proved to its authors a positive and unmitigated curse." The South could not compete with the North in colonizing Kansas. Major Buford's force of three hundred would-be settlers, filtering back to the South, demonstrated that.

Missouri tightened the screws on Kansas. An absolute blockade was imposed on Missouri River traffic. Boats were boarded, passengers were catechized about their destination, and, if free-state settlers, they were plundered or thrown off. The *Squatter Sovereign* said that if the citizens of Leavenworth "would hang one or two boatloads of Abolitionists it would do more for the peace of Kansas than all the speeches that have been delivered in Congress." This was well publicized in northern journals.

When Brown was ordered to disperse his company, he complained to Colonel Sumner about an army under General J. W. Whitfield of two hundred and fifty men that had invaded Kansas from Missouri. Sumner said that he had read aloud Governor Shannon's proclamation to Whitfield, who had agreed to disperse. Instead of withdrawing promptly, Whitfield plundered the settlement of Osawatomie, pillaging houses, stealing horses and even stripping the women of earrings. The army then crossed over to Westport in Missouri and disbanded.

Whitfield's men did no bodily injury in Osawatomie, but murders were occurring in the area of the Missouri border with proslavery parties on the prowl. There is no exact tally. William A. Phillips, in *The Conquest of Kansas by Missouri Ruffians*, his 1856 book on the Kansas warfare, said that in the month after the Pottawatomie affair, "Murders were frequent, many of them passing secret and unrecorded, some of them only revealed by some moldering remains of mortality." A figure of two hundred deaths through December, 1856, has been given, but no one really knows.

While the Pottawatomie murders got somehow shunted off, it was the misfortune of the proslave faction that the murders of free-staters like Dow, Barber, and R. P. Brown had dramatic qualities that could be used to whip up emotion in the free states. Another murder of this type was attributed to Whitfield's men. They allegedly tried a Missourian named Cantrall in a mock court-martial on the charge of "treason to Missouri" because of an expression of sympathy for the free-state cause. The New York *Tribune* reported it as a thriller.

The story said he was taken to a ravine, "there was a shot, followed by the cry, 'O God! I am shot! I am murdered!' Then all was silent."

There was the incredibly wanton killing (if the circumstances are to be believed) of William Hoppe in a buggy two miles from Leavenworth. He was shot and scalped by a border-ruffian named Fugit, who had made a bet in Leavenworth of $6 against a pair of boots that he could bring back the scalp of an Abolitionist within two hours. Waving Hoppe's scalp, Fugit rode back to Leavenworth and collected the pair of boots.

From the time of Sumner's dispersal order until July 1, Brown and a band lay hidden in the thickets of Middle Ottawa Creek in the vicinity of Palmyra. James Redpath visited him again. In a clearing there were five or six armed men lying down or standing and a woman picking blackberries from the bushes. In the center there was a great, blazing fire with a pot on it. "Old Brown himself stood near the fire with his shirt-sleeves rolled up, and a large piece of pork in his hand. He was cooking a pig. He was poorly clad, and his toes protruded from his boots."

His camp, Brown explained, was conducted on the highest principles. No immoral men could join, there could be no profane language, there were morning and evening prayers, grace before and after meals. "I would rather have the smallpox, yellow fever, and cholera all together in my camp than a man without principles."

The principles to which Brown referred were, of course, his own "higher law" principles, and therefore it was perfectly consistent for his band to live by depredations on the property of those who were suspected of being proslave. A store owned by J. M. Bernard at Centropolis was raided. An employee said, "A party of thirteen came on horseback. Some of them came into the store and the rest remained outside. They called for such goods as they wanted and made Mr. Davis and myself hand them out and said if we didn't hurry they would shoot us. After they had got the goods—they wanted principally blankets and clothing—they packed them upon the horses and went away. Then the next day they came back with a wagon and took the remainder of the goods in the store, including flour, sugar, coffee, bacon, and all kinds of provisions, as well as two fine horses, three saddles, two bridles and all the money that was in the store." Bondi said that this store was raided by John Brown's orders, but, as far as he could recall, the booty was clothing, "to improve our exterior, the Brown outfit being altogether in rags."

Brown had a visit from W. A. Phillips of the New York *Tri-bune*. In his 1856 book, *The Conquest of Kansas by Missouri Ruffians*, he has a discussion of the battle of Black Jack, and in that connection introduced John Brown in a description which is the first in time that we have:

Captain Brown moved to the Territory from the state of New York early in 1855, but he is by birth a Vermonter. He is an old soldier and was through the war of 1812. Tall and stern-looking, hard-featured and resolute, there is something in Captain Brown's air that speaks the soldier, every inch of him. He is not a man to be trifled with and there is no one for whom the border-ruffians entertain a more wholesome dread than Captain Brown. They hate him as they would a snake, but their hatred is composed nine tenths of fear. Although the captain is a practical man, he is one of those abstruse thinkers who have read much and *thought* more. In his opinions he is inexorably inflexible and the world generally would pronounce him a "fanatic." He is one of those Christians who have not quite vanished from the face of the earth—that is, he asks the blessings of God when he breaks his bread, and does not, even in camp, forget his devotions in his zeal against the border ruffians.

There is not a more stern disciplinarian in Kansas; he is a regular martinet, and so carefully can he conceal his quarters, that when you wish to find him when he does not wish it, you might as well hunt for a needle in a haystack as for Captain Brown. He is a strange, resolute, repulsive, iron-willed, inexorable old man. He stands like a solitary rock in a more mobile society, a fiery nature, and a cold temper, and a cool head—a volcano beneath a covering of snow.

Then Phillips added: "Whether with reason or not, I cannot say, but he was regarded as a participator, if not leader, in the Pottawatomie affair. . . ." Phillips could not *swear* to it, since he was not on the scene.

In mid-June Brown got word that his two sons, John Jr. and Jason, along with other prisoners were being moved from Osawatomie to Lecompton by way of Lawrence, a distance of sixty-five miles. Their march under a burning sun was described by a New York *Times* correspondent: "A scene then followed which has no parallel in a republican government. They were chained two and two by taking a common trace chain and using a padlock at each end which was so fixed as to make a close clasp around the ankle. Like a gang of slaves, they were thus driven on foot the whole distance at the rate of twenty-five miles per day, dragging their chains after them. . . . What a humiliating, disgusting sight in a free government!"

This barbarous treatment of his sons understandably embittered John Brown even more against the savages supporting the southern cause and the next year in the East he would exhibit the supposed chains around John Brown, Jr., to rouse sympathy and funds for his continuing campaign against slavery.

All during this march, John Brown and a band he had collected marched in concealment on a parallel course, hoping to effect a rescue of his sons, somehow. Jason related that his father would show himself from time to time, so that the guards were ordered to chase after him. They would push through river bottoms and dense, prickly tangles, coming back at night exhausted and furious, their horses all done in. He heard one exclaim on his return, "Damned if I'm going out after Old Brown any more!"

At Lecompton Jason was released shortly, having convinced a magistrate that he had no part in the murders, but John Jr. was held for three months until his release in September.

G. W. Brown, of the Lawrence *Herald of Freedom*, who had been indicted for treason, was a fellow prisoner. His veracity in view of his anti-Brown bias is highly suspect, but he gave this account of John Jr. during the term of imprisonment:

Yea, for months, whenever conversation turned, as it sometimes did, upon the Pottawatomie murders, and we attempted to excuse his father for that act, giving the mitigating circumstances current among Free State men at the time, his eyes would sparkle with unwonted brilliancy, his manner would assume the wildest excitement, and in a loud and boisterous voice, which was uncommon to him on other occasions, he would exclaim: "Do not attempt to offer anything in palliation of such a crime! Nothing can excuse it! It was unequalled in atrocity, and displayed only cowardice. . . ."

On July 2, Brown appeared in Lawrence and asked the New York *Tribune* correspondent William A. Phillips to accompany him and his men to Topeka where the free-state legislature was scheduled to convene on July 4 amid rumors of possible trouble, since President Pierce was said to believe that in the interest of peace in Kansas it should not meet. Brown's company bivouacked that night for a few hours under the stars before they resumed the march at two o'clock in the morning. Brown lay sleepless next to Phillips and discoursed to him. "How admirable is the symmetry of the heavens. How grand and beautiful! Everything moves in sublime harmony in the government of God. Not so with us poor creatures." Phillips recounted: "He criticized both parties in Kansas. Of the pro-slavery men he said that slavery besotted everything, and made men more brutal and coarse. Nor did the free-state men escape his sharp censure. He said we had many noble and true men, but too many broken-down politicians from the older states, who would rather pass resolutions than act, and who criticized all who did real work," meaning, of course, Brown.

Brown did not choose to enter Topeka but stayed on Willets farm on Shunganung Creek outside the town. It would have been most indiscreet for him to have been there since it was jammed with United States troops. Colonel Sumner was there to command the free-state legislature to adjourn forthwith. On July 4, said Redpath, "on the day when, everywhere, Americans were celebrating their liberty, the free-state legislature was broken up by force. This was the last drop of bitterness in the free-state cup and the culmination of Southern success, the date at once of the death and the resurrection of Freedom in Kansas."

The vacillating Governor Shannon, who by now was cracking under the pressure, decided to leave the Territory for ten days in late June. Before he left, he wrote Colonel Sumner that he feared disorders if the Topeka legislature met, and in view of the threat to the peace it "should be dispersed." Acting Governor Daniel Woodson issued a proclamation to that effect, and Sumner's own opinion was that this was a prudent policy to pursue. He came to Topeka with five companies of soldiers and two pieces of artillery. The free-state leaders asked if they could go through the formality of a meeting, and Sumner agreed.

Before noon, when the legislature was scheduled to convene, the troops ringed Constitutional Hall and Sumner entered the House of Representatives. A roll call did not produce a quorum and then after some activity by the sergeant-at-arms seventeen members responded to a second roll call. Colonel Sumner walked down the aisle and said, "Gentlemen, this is the most disagreeable duty of my whole life. My orders are to disperse the legislature, and I am here to tell you that it cannot meet. God knows I have no partisan feelings in the matter. I have just returned from the border where I have been driving out bands of Missourians. You must disperse. This body cannot be permitted to meet. Disperse."

The members got up and left. Sumner mounted his horse outside and rode off while an assembled crowd gave three cheers for the Republican candidate running for President that year, John C. Frémont, and three loud groans for President Pierce—who, though from New Hampshire, throughout the Kansas struggle had been as pro-southern as any southerner could have been. (When the streets of Topeka were named for Presidents, Pierce was omitted.)

This authoritarian action left a distinctly bad taste, even in South-dominated Washington. Sumner might at least have waited until after July 4 or until the legislature took some action that was objection-able. In late August, Secretary of War Jefferson Davis explained that his orders to Sumner had been misunderstood, that he had looked upon the members of the Topeka legislature as "men assembled with-out authority, men who could pass no law that should ever be put in execution, and in the meantime they might be considered as a mere town meeting."

Brown, after the legislature was chased away, left the farm in the environs of Topeka and took to the bush. His whereabouts until he reappeared in early August are a mystery. By this time, though he was moving much in secret, the name of "Old Brown" had become a synonym of terror in Kansas. A proslavery meeting back in Paola, with Brown far off, broke up when it heard that John Brown was on the way to "take out" some men.

The cause of a free Kansas flamed through the North after the Lawrence affair. Men such as Gerrit Smith who had been hitherto indifferent now became eager supporters. Thayer wrote: "The raid upon Lawrence and the blockade of the Missouri River added to the imprisonment of our leading men aroused the indignation of the North to such an extent that the freedom of Kansas was secured. From this time on no further effort was required to raise colonies. They raised themselves."

Abraham Lincoln, who watched the trend of public opinion very carefully, made his strongest anti-South pronouncement at Bloom-ington, Illinois, on May 29: "Let us draw a cordon, so to speak, around the slave states, and the hateful institution, like a reptile poisoning itself, will perish by its own infamy." The newly formed Republican party for the first time nominated a candidate for Presi-dent, John C. Frémont, and in its platform stated, "Kansas should be immediately admitted as a state of the Union with its present free constitution." More than that the platform pledged "condign punish-ment" for the President and others responsible for the Kansas mis-government. At every Republican rally a sure-fire way to make pulses throb was to read a message from Senator Charles Sumner apologizing that he could not be present because of the grievous wounds he had received and then detailing them, as the result of his beating by "Bully Boy" Brooks in the Senate on May 22 while delivering his speech on "The Crime Against Kansas."

A National Kansas Committee, coordinating auxiliaries in cities and towns all over the North, was formed in Buffalo in July. Money poured in. Ralph Waldo Emerson wrote in his journal, "I know people who are making haste to reduce their expenses and pay their debts, not with a view to new accumulations but in preparation to save and earn for the benefit of Kansas emigrants."

James H. Lane, self-elevated to General Lane, set about to raise a northern army which with Kansas settlers would flank the blockade of the Missouri River by going overland through Iowa and then into Nebraska and south into Kansas. He delivered a series of remarkably eloquent speeches in Chicago and elsewhere. Thomas Wentworth Higginson in awe recorded after hearing him: "Never did I hear such a speech, every sentence like a pistol bullet, such delicacy and light-ness of touch, such natural art . . . he had every nerve in his audience at the end of his muscles."

With his northern army of six hundred settlers in all, men, women, and children, including about a hundred and fifty fighting men, Lane after traversing Iowa arrived in Nebraska City in Nebraska on the Kansas border at the beginning of August.

John Brown came out of hiding to ride north to meet Lane's force. With him were members of his family who had decided to leave Kansas—Henry Thompson, wounded at Black Jack, Salmon, who after Black Jack had been badly kicked by a horse, Owen, who had suffered from a fever which had reduced him to a skeleton, and Oliver. Frederick also intended to leave but at the border turned back with his father, a decision that was shortly to cost him his life.

Samuel J. Reader, marching near Nemaha Falls, Nebraska, with some free-state men to join Lane's army, met Brown. From notes in his journal he gave his impressions:

Someone in front shouted, "There he is." Sure enough it was Brown . . . as we passed the old man on either side of the road, we rent the air with cheers. If John Brown ever delighted in the praises of men, his pleasure must have been gratified, as he walked along enveloped in our shouting column. But I feared that he looked on such as vainglorious, for if he responded by word or act, I failed to hear or see it. In passing I looked at him closely. He was rather tall and lean, with a tanned, weather-beaten aspect in general. He looked like a rough, hard-working old farmer. . . .

When Brown reached Lane's army at Nebraska City, he met the journalist Richard J. Hinton for the first time, and inquired of him where he could find William Thompson, the brother of Henry Thompson, who, he had been advised, was coming with Lane to join Brown. Thompson was not there. He had met the Brown boys going home and joined them. Hinton saw "a frame full of nervous power, but not impressing one especially with muscular vigor." He was struck by the expression in Brown's eyes, "one of steadfast alertness, keen, sharp observation—the look of the uncowed man in constant danger and always on the watch, in some respects, the 'hunted look.' "

Brown refurbished himself in Nebraska before returning to Kansas. Reader had seen him "dilapidated, dusty and soiled," but now he wore new white summer clothing and a large straw hat. Sanborn wrote: "He made a great impression on several of the company, who without knowing him at once declared that he must be a 'distinguished' man in disguise."

While at Nebraska City, Brown met a man who was destined to play an important part as his trusted lieutenant at Harper's Ferry. This was twenty-five-year-old Aaron D. Stevens, who was commanding a marauding free-state company under the name of Captain Charles Whipple. A court-martialed former member of the United States Army, he was an escapee from an army prison where he had been serving a three-year term at hard labor for assaulting an officer. Hinton was amused by the drill routine of the company. Whipple would call out, "What are you doing here, men?" The shout— "Holding town meeting." Whipple—"Where are your ballot boxes?" The shout—"Here," as each man brought his hand down with a clap on his Sharp's rifle.

Lane had expected to be designated as the official commanding general of the cause financed by the National Kansas Committee, but he was disappointed. He was met at Nebraska City by the committee's president, Thaddeus Hyatt, and the representative from Massachusetts (of whom we shall hear more), Dr. Samuel Gridley Howe. On meeting him the emissaries were filled with distrust since Lane appeared to be what he was, an adventurer, impulsive, unstable, and vainglorious. Dr. Howe wrote: "Various considerations conspired to create a well-grounded apprehension in our minds that by some hasty and ill-timed splurge he would defeat the object of the expedition." Lane, receiving no official commission, found it advisable to assume the name of General Joe Cook and as General Cook more or less commanded free-state forces for the following six weeks.

Brown, Lane, and Captain Samuel Walker went back together into Kansas. While Lane pushed on to Lawrence, Brown for his own reasons stopped at Topeka, and then alone went on to Lawrence. A series of vigorous assaults were conducted by free-state forces against proslavery positions, at New Georgia near Osawatomie on the Marais des Cygnes, on Franklin, and against a sturdy log-house near Lawrence named Fort Saunders. In all cases the proslavery men retreated, with little loss of life, but much loss of provisions, and of prestige.

Brown probably did not take part in these fights, though they were attributed to him by the proslavery side. In a manifesto by B. F. Stringfellow published in Lexington, Missouri, on August 16, asking for men to enlist to fight in Kansas, the outrages by the "notorious Brown" were listed. Jason Brown wrote to his sister Ruth, on August 13: "Old Capt. Brown can now be raised from every prairie and thicket." Owen wrote home on August 26, from near Topeka, having returned to Kansas, "Those who come through here say that Father is the most daring, courageous man in Kansas." Brown was referred to that month in the New York *Times* as "the terror of all Missouri."

Neither was Brown present in the attack on the log-blockhouse named Fort Titus for the commander Colonel H. T. Titus. It was a fierce fight in which there was death on both sides and many men wounded. The battle was won by free-state forces after some futile charges when the free-staters backed a wagon of burning hay against the blockhouse, thereby setting it afire.

When Captain Samuel Walker brought Titus in as a prisoner into Lawrence, Brown was on the spot demanding that Titus' life must be forfeited. Walker related: "Our arrival at Lawrence created intense excitement. The citizens swarmed around us, clamoring for the blood of our prisoner. The committee of safety had a meeting and decided that Titus should be hanged, John Brown and other distinguished men urging the measure strongly. At four o'clock in the evening I went before the committee and said that Titus had surrendered to me, that I had promised him his life and that I would defend it with my own." Walker left the room, went to the house where Titus was being guarded and routed a desperado who was about to shoot Titus.

"Captain Brown and Doctor Avery were outside haranguing the mob to hang Titus despite my objections. They said I had resisted the committee of safety and was, myself, therefore a public enemy. The crowd was terribly excited, but the sight of my three hundred solid bayonets held them in check."

The last act of Wilson Shannon as governor of the Territory was to go to Lawrence and effect the release of Titus in exchange for the freedom of five free-staters who had been arrested for sacking the town of Franklin. Both sides agreed in hailing Shannon's departure— good riddance. President Pierce refused to accept his resignation and fired him. Even his proslave friends had turned against him, and for his safety he had to stay clear of them in his exodus from Kansas. It had been a singularly vexing and thankless proconsulship for him. Every action or inaction on his part had somehow managed to make the situation in Kansas worse.

Brown was at Osawatomie on August 20, being far better out- fitted than he had been two months before when Redpath saw him in camp with his toes protruding from his boots. Now, as Bondi described, he arrived "with a spic and span four-mule team, the wagon loaded with provisions; besides he was well supplied with money and all contributed by the Northern friends of Free State Kansas, men like Thaddeus Hyatt."

He joined forces with raiding companies under Captain James B. Cline and James H. Holmes. His previous business experience had given him great respect for a contract, and he drew up for his thirty men, who were listed by name, "Bylaws of the Free-State Regular Volunteers under the command of John Brown." We have a copy of those bylaws.

There was provision for the booty taken:

Article 5th. All valuable property taken by honorable warfare from the enemy, shall be held as the property of the whole company or com- panies as the case may be equally, without distinction; to be used for the common benefit, or to be placed in the hands of responsible agents for sale, the proceeds to be divided as nearly equally among the company as may be.

Apparently only acts of major theft were permitted:

Article 15th. All acts of petty theft, needless waste of property of the members or of citizens is hereby declared disorderly. . . .

The company arrogated to itself governmental powers of punishment, including death:

Article 20th. No person after having first surrendered himself a prisoner shall be put to death or subjected to corporeal punishment, without first having had the benefit of an impartial trial.

The conduct of members had to be puritanical:

Article 14th. All uncivil, ungentlemanly, profane, vulgar talk or conversation shall be discountenanced.
Article 22nd. The ordinary use, or introduction into the camp of any intoxicating liquors as a beverage, is hereby declared disorderly.

We are not sure how much activity in the way of fighting this company carried on. We do have one stirring eyewitness account, by J. W. Winkley, of Cline's company: "They came swiftly up over the brow of the hill in full view with Brown at their head, and without halting or even slackening their speed swung into line of battle. Only thirty men! Yet they presented a truly formidable array. The line was formed two deep and stretched out to give the men full room for action. Brown sprang his horse in front of the ranks, waving his long broadsword, and on they came, sweeping down. . . ."

As it happened they were about to attack their allies, Cline's forces, and fortunately were intercepted in time. Such errors happen in warfare too often.

On August 25, Captain Cline made a sweep of Sugar Creek Valley, in Linn County, capturing twelve prisoners and some military equipment. E. P. Bridgman related that he watched Captain Brown going through the spoils of war piece by piece. For a long time he stared at the stock of one gun before setting it down. Bridgman, in curiosity, picked up that gun after Brown walked off and saw inscribed on its stock, "Made in Harper's Ferry, Virginia, United States Arsenal.

This may be fable, since a great deal of apocrypha grew up in later years. Luke Parsons in his account told how Brown read his Bible the last thing before going to sleep. Parsons once thumbed through his Bible and found it heavily underlined with comments written by Brown in the margins. Salmon Brown labeled this statement by Parsons as "all bosh." His father never had a Bible with him after the Pottawatomie affair. Moreover, said Salmon, there were no prayers except for grace before meals, and all stories that Brown made prisoners join in prayers were also "all bosh."

On August 26, Brown raided a proslavery settlement under the command of Captain John E. Brown (no relation—there seem to have been a lot of Browns in Kansas), and did more raiding the following two days. He was back at Osawatomie on the night of August 28 with a hundred and fifty head of cattle he had appropriated from the enemy.

A large force was mustered in Westport, Missouri, by Major General Atchison for an invasion of Kansas. The first column, a regiment of two hundred and fifty men under Brigadier General John W. Reid, was ordered to wipe out Osawatomie. At dawn on August 30, Reid circled the town on the south, wheeled north and then like the good military tactician, attacked from the unexpected direction, from the northwest.

A mile from the town, Rev. Martin White, who was in the advance guard and acting as guide, encountered Frederick Brown, who was completely unarmed, and another youth, David Garrison, who were standing by their horses. "Hello, boys," said White, "are you going to Lawrence today?" "No," replied Frederick, and then walking closer to the mounted White, "Don't I know you?"

"I know you," said White, "and you are my enemy." Thereupon he aimed his rifle at him and shot Frederick through the heart. The twenty-five-year-old boy, the first of the Browns to die in the cause, lay face down in the road in a pool of blood. David Garrison ran into the brush but was found and murdered.

Reporting the death of Frederick to his wife, Brown wrote, "Preacher White, I hear, boasts of having killed my son. Of course, he is quite a *lion*."

Instead of moving on to the town, Reid's force tarried on a ridge to eat breakfast. The news was brought to Osawatomie by twelve-year-old Charlie Adair, Brown's nephew, who rode his pony into town. "The border-ruffians are coming and they have killed cousin Frederick and Mr. Garrison." Brown, who was across the Marais des Cygnes, got the news by a messenger. "Men, come on!" he shouted. They made a crossing of the river and hurried the three miles to Osawatomie. On the way, Brown said to Luke Parsons, "We must save the women and children first, and then ourselves if we can. We will attract their attention, while the men get their families out of danger."

Then he asked Parsons, "Were you ever under fire?" Parsons re-

plied, "No, but tell me what to do and I will do it." Brown gave
him the stern admonition, "Take more pains to end life well than to
live long."

There was only a handful of free-staters to resist Reid's large
force. Brown said he had thirty men, a figure which is accepted. Captain Cline had a dozen, but he left the scene after a little fight, saying that he had run out of ammunition. Brown ordered Parsons and
a couple of men to hold the blockhouse. He would try to hold Reid's
large force at bay by taking the rest of the men into the trees and
brush along the Marais des Cygnes which was parallel to the road
along which Reid's men were marching and "annoy them from the
flank."

From the blockhouse, Parsons recounted, "I could see them advancing in two long lines, with a brass cannon in the center. Their
swords and guns glittered in the morning sun." In the brush,
Brown placed his men forty feet apart. "Keep behind stumps and
bushes. Keep out of sight. I don't want them to know our force.
Keep cool, take good aim, shoot low." Parsons found the fire much
too hot to hold the blockhouse and he and his men had to abandon it
and join Brown in the brush.

Brown's gallantry as usual was superb. Jason, though he disliked
bloodshed, had this fight thrust upon him and fought by his father's
side, giving a fine account of himself. Firing from the foliaged concealment, Brown and his men inflicted casualties on Reid's men, who
were all mounted, causing consternation among them. They retreated
and had to reform. Jason saw Major Buford beating them with his
sword. They brought up the brass cannon and started a barrage,
which was ineffective since they fired it too high, into the trees.

Brown thought he had been hit. He said to Parsons, "Do you see
anything on my back? Any blood? Something has hit me an awful
rap on that shoulder." Parsons saw nothing. "Well, I declare. I don't
intend to be shot in the back if I can help it." The next day there was
a black lump as big as an egg on his shoulder. Grape-shot had struck
a tree, and a little, glancing off, had struck his shoulder.

Reid ordered his men to dismount and march on foot into the
woods. There was no choice for Brown and his greatly outnumbered
troop but to run without standing upon the order of their going.
They filed down the bank of the river, and then jumped into it, wading across to find haven on the opposite bank. Brown, one man recalled, cut a "queer figure, in a broad straw hat and a white linen

duster, his old coattails floating outspread upon the water and a revolver held high in each hand over his head, while balls whistled around him." Some of his men were hit by bullet fire while making the crossing. Reid's men, now unmolested, burned and plundered thirty of the thirty-five houses in the town. Reid said this was flouting his instructions, but "I could not help it." The horses and cattle were driven off, including those which Brown and Cline had so industriously accumulated in the raids of the previous week.

In a report which Reid wrote that night, he said, "We killed about thirty of them, among the number, certain, a son of Old Brown, and almost certain, Brown himself." The death of the terrorist was for a time believed and rejoiced in. The St. Louis *Morning Herald*, announcing it, said the Pottawatomie affair was "by far the most atrocious and inexcusable outrage yet perpetrated in that distracted Territory . . . his death and the destruction of his family, would, for that reason, be less a matter of regret even with men of the humanest feelings."

Of his thirty men, Brown lost six killed in the battle and four wounded. Reid lost about the same number in killed, the bodies being buried in Paola that night, and he had many wounded. Reid claimed that it all had amounted only to "driving out a lot of quail," but the glory belonged to Brown who though overwhelmed in numbers, ten to one, had made it a contest, and had inflicted on the enemy an equal number of casualties. Brown was known thereafter in Kansas as "Osawatomie Brown." The Territory rang with the story of the battle. From prison in Lecompton, John Jr. wrote to his father on September 8: "Poor Frederick has perished in a good cause, the success of which cause will yet bring joy to millions. Considering the enemy's great loss, it is certainly a great victory for us, certainly a dear burning of the town for them. Every one I hear speaking of you are loud in their praise." In a later year, Senator John J. Ingalls said, "The battle of Osawatomie was the most brilliant and important episode of the Kansas war. It was the high divide of the contest. It was our Thermopylae. John Brown was our Leonidas with his Spartan band."

Near-anarchy prevailed in Kansas, but though in its worst phase it was happily also in its last phase before the iron fist of the United States government would clamp down. Thomas Wentworth Higginson, arriving in late summer on the last leg of his trip from Boston by stage over Iowa and Nebraska, wrote of the strange sensation he experienced on arrival in Kansas: "Never before in my life had I been distinctively and unequivocally, outside the world of human law—it had always been ready to protect me even when I disobeyed it. Here it had ceased to exist."

Acting Governor Woodson on August 25 issued a proclamation declaring Kansas "in a state of open insurrection and rebellion." He exceeded good judgment in asking that loyal citizens of Kansas help the legally constituted authorities to drive out "the large bodies of armed men, many of whom have just arrived from the States," which gave legal warrant for proslave groups to go after antislave, and vice versa. General Reid, who had by now backtracked into Missouri, claimed that in his Osawatomie attack he had commanded Kansas militia in support of the territorial government, as Woodson had requested.

General Lane, alias General Joe Cook, was darting here and there. He pursued General Reid but when close on his heels inexplicably turned about. He marched to Lecompton and made a demonstration there, demanding the release of political prisoners, including John Brown, Jr., but left when he was warned by Lieutenant-Colonel Cooke of the United States Second Dragoons that he faced a fight with federal troops if he tried to take over the town. He returned to Lawrence which was filling with refugees telling of outrages in the eastern border areas, particularly near Leavenworth where William Phillips, tarred and feathered in May, had been murdered on September 2.

While Lane was holding a council of war on September 7, Brown entered Lawrence riding a horse with a gun across his saddle, followed by a wagon carrying the wounded Luke Parsons. An eyewitness years later recalled that the cheering for Brown was loud, "but John Brown seemed not to hear it and paid not the slightest attention."

Lane's council of war deputized Colonel James A. Harvey to lead a punitive expedition against Leavenworth. He conducted some raids and appropriated proslavery property near Leavenworth but did not invade that town where he would, no doubt, have received a hot reception. The former Captain, now Colonel Charles Whipple, staged a highly successful raid on Osawkee, carrying off eighty proslavery horses.

The Administration in Washington made up its mind to pacify Kansas. A presidential campaign was in progress, and the chaos in

Kansas, seemingly sanctioned by Washington, threatened the election of James Buchanan and the continued rule of the Democratic party. Secretary of War Jefferson Davis wrote Acting Governor Woodson that the Sixth Regiment of Infantry was being sent to Kansas, and Woodson could also call on Illinois and Kentucky for two regiments of foot militia that President Pierce was ready to requisition from those states. Davis wanted to see the "rebellion" crushed, but the highest priority was peace.

A new territorial governor, John W. Geary, arrived in Lecompton on September 12. He later told how Kansas appeared at "the most gloomy hour of her history":

Desolation and ruin reigned on every hand; homes and firesides were deserted; the smoke of burning dwellings darkened the atmosphere; women and children, driven from their habitations, wandered over the prairies; the highways were infested with numerous predatory bands and the towns were fortified and garrisoned by armies of conflicting partisans, each excited almost to frenzy, and determined upon mutual extermination.

Geary arrived at a conciliatory moment. The political prisoners had been freed at Lecompton on September 10. John Brown, Jr., released on bail of $1,000, had a joyous reunion with his father at Lawrence. In front of General Lane's headquarters that night there was a meeting, pronounced as "the most enthusiastic and heart-cheering of any that has ever been held in Kansas." John Brown was among the speakers. The New York *Times* had Brown last on a list of six, which included the leaders Governor Robinson and General Lane.

Kansas could have an era of peace if old rancors were buried, Geary pleaded in his first address. He asked Kansans to "suspend fratricidal strife" and "look upon one another as the children of a common mother." Outside elements had tried "to array brother against brother" during this convulsive period. He announced that he would organize a new militia which would be composed of only those who were genuine residents of the Territory, thereby recognizing that Missourians had intruded in Kansas. As time went on, Geary would become more and more wedded to the free-state cause. He resigned on March 20, 1857, feeling that President Buchanan, just inaugurated, would be unsympathetic to his position.

Major General Atchison had planned to send several columns from Missouri into Kansas but now decided to pack them into one army for a knockout blow. The southern cause was tottering. The border-ruffians had been meeting their match in free-state ruffians of the stamp of John Brown and Colonel Whipple. However, if Kansas was to be pacified by Washington, then all would surely be lost in a contest decided by the ballot box. Free-state settlers were streaming in by the overland route through Iowa and then south from Nebraska.

Atchison, with his top aides, Reid, Whitfield, and Stringfellow, advanced on Lawrence on September 14, twenty-five hundred strong, infantry and cavalry, with a howitzer, a six-pounder battery. There was some desultory shooting at long range, and then Atchison's force retired to Franklin.

There had been two false alarms in Lawrence before the real military threat developed that afternoon. Earthworks and fortifications were hastily built; a main fortress was constructed on the debris of the Free State Hotel. Free-state men with their Sharp's rifles stood behind them ready for action.

John Brown was in Lawrence that night. James Redpath ran in his book an engaging interview Brown gave him—like the one given to William A. Phillips—while bivouacked under the heavens: "That night we lay down immediately within the breastworks with a stone for a pillow and a cloud for a covering." Captain Brown came along and asked if he could lie down beside Redpath and his companion.

"He then lay down by our side and told us of the trials, the wars he had passed through, that he had taken a claim in Lykins County and was attending peacefully to the duties of husbandry when the hordes of wild men came over from Missouri and took possession of all the ballot boxes, destroyed his corn, stole his horses and shot down his cattle and sheep and hogs and repeatedly threatened to shoot, hang him or burn him if he did not leave the Territory."

Now—it was altogether fitting that this discourse should have been delivered beneath the moon and stars since it was all moonshine and stardust. Brown had never been a settler, he had never entered a claim anywhere, he had never engaged in husbandry, the usurpation of the ballot boxes by the border-ruffians had occurred six months before he reached Kansas, he had never owned any livestock, and that owned by his sons had been carried off in revenge after the Pottawatomie massacre. But this is significant, historically. If it was fiction by Redpath, it illustrates how such nonsense about Brown was swallowed unquestionably by the reading public after his death. If it was fiction by Brown himself, it shows how, as time went on, he fantasized about his persecutions—and there is evidence that Brown did convince himself that his maltreatments had forced him to take up the sword, while the truth was that he had come to Kansas only to fight.

Redpath's imagination ran riot when he described the shooting at Lawrence the following night: "In a few moments the firing became general and in the darkness and otherwise stillness of the night, the continued flash, flash, flash of these engines of death along with the line of living fire presented a scene the appearance of which was at once not only terrible but sublimely beautiful."

There was no fighting in Lawrence, whatsoever. Under Governor Geary's orders, Lieutenant-Colonel Joseph E. Johnston put a large force of United States troops on Mount Oread and posted them at various other points around Lawrence. Geary rode out to meet with Atchison in the early morning of September 15. He headed off a Missouri force moving on Lawrence and was escorted to Franklin where he addressed the leaders of the pro-southern force, Atchison, Whitfield, Reid, and Titus. "Though held in a board house," he said magniloquently, "the present is the most important council since the days of the Revolution, as its issues involve the fate of the Union now formed." He appealed to them as members of the Democratic party not to injure its chances by attacking Lawrence, and made a vague promise that he would take proper care of the Abolitionists. Atchison took the only course open to him by agreeing to help Geary and said he would disband his army. Atchison's men did considerable burning and stealing in their retreat to Missouri, but the major pro-slave threat to Kansas was finished when Atchison dissolved his army.

How much did Brown have to do with saving Lawrence? Redpath and Sanborn claimed that he had been responsible for that. Villard was more modest in admitting that he was not in command but gave him a role. Brown, Villard said, went from one "fort" to another giving encouragement and made an address to the citizens of Lawrence, with advice based on his own battle experience: "Don't yell and make a great noise, but remain perfectly still and silent. Wait till they get within twenty-five yards of you, get a good object, be sure you see the hind sight of your gun, then fire. A great deal of powder and lead is wasted by shooting too high. You had better aim at their legs than at their heads."

However, there were some who claimed that Brown filled no role at all. Lieutenant-Colonel Joseph Cracklin, who seems to have been the ranking officer that day, wrote at a later date that "Redpath and other worshippers to the contrary notwithstanding," as far as he could recall, Brown did not do any more toward saving Lawrence "than the most obscure person in the town."

John Brown undoubtedly had a personal following and was considered a factor in the Kansas struggle. That he was allowed to be one of the speakers at the Lawrence celebration meeting on the night of September 10 along with Robinson and Lane demonstrates that.

Yet, there is abundant evidence (even giving weight to the fact that this evidence was produced in the 1880s when Brown was being drastically downgraded in Kansas) that he was regarded with distrust by the leaders and settlers. He was a firebrand who feasted on trouble, who sought to exacerbate the discord, while the majority wanted peace. His goal was to carry on the fight against the institution of slavery, while the majority were willing to endure fighting but only to found a state. He was regarded as destructive, not constructive. He was an extremist, while the majority were moderate, as manifested by their vote to exclude all Negroes from the Territory. Very importantly, they lacked confidence in him because he was thought to be deficient in sound judgment in making decisions, his chronic failing.

Here is an unflattering assessment given in 1884 by J. S. Avery, who said that he had served under Brown: "He struck us as a man poorly balanced in his conclusions and judgments. He made no impression of great strength of character but did seem restless, uneasy and not at all to heed greatly the counsels and opinions of others. The vast majority of the settlers of Douglas County [in which Lawrence was located] at that time regarded him as wild, visionary and wholly impracticable. . . . He was looked on as a creature of the times that were upon us." His favorite expression, said Avery, was "war in earnest," and he was an "irritant" factor.

There are other statements to the same effect from reliable free-state men. S. N. Wood said: "The truth is that Brown never had the confidence of the Free-State men of Kansas and no sensible man followed his lead." Colonel James Blood said, "John Brown was never called upon by the Kansas people to take part in any difficult or dangerous work."

The term of service of John Brown in 1856 in tumultuous Kansas was drawing to a close. There was no longer any place for a free-wheeling company such as his. As the crackdown by federal troops proceeded, men of Colonel Whipple's company were arrested and sentenced to terms at hard labor. Even immigrants arriving via Nebraska were arrested if they were found armed.

On September 13, Robinson had written to Brown from Lawrence asking him to come in for a chat. He assured him that he had talked with Governor Geary and, "There will be no attempt to arrest anyone for a few days, and I think no attempt to arrest you is contemplated." Brown saw Robinson on September 15 and, finding Robinson kindly disposed toward him, asked him for a blanket letter of thanks. Brown had a plan in mind for which this letter would be very useful. Robinson complied.

Lawrence, September 15, 1856

Capt. John Brown: My Dear Sir:—I take this opportunity to express to you my sincere gratification that the late report that you were among the killed at the battle of Osawatomie is incorrect.

Your course, as far as I have been informed, has been such as to merit the highest praise from every patriot, and I cheerfully accord to you my heartfelt thanks for your prompt, efficient and timely action against the invaders of our rights and the murderers of our citizens. History will give your name a proud place on her pages, and posterity will pay homage to your heroism in the cause of God and humanity.

Trusting that you will conclude to remain in Kansas and serve during the war for the cause you have done so much to sustain, and with earnest prayers for your health and protection from the shafts of Death that so thickly beset your path, I subscribe myself,

Very respectfully,
Your Ob't Servant
C. Robinson

This praise to the man who perpetrated the Pottawatomie massacre! John Brown, Jr., claimed that in their meeting Robinson asked his father to undertake some more violence à la Pottawatomie, and Brown answered him, "If you know of any job of that sort that needs to be done, I advise you to do it yourself." Robinson said this letter was a forgery. In October, 1884, John Brown, Jr., wrote Sanborn: "I can have no more doubt of its genuineness than I have that Robinson has either broken down mentally or is a contemptible scoundrel."

Between September 15 and 22, Brown was at the home of Augustus Wattles near Lawrence with John Brown, Jr., and his wife, Jason and his wife, and Owen, who after recovering from his illness in Iowa, had returned to Kansas. On October 1, he was near Osawatomie making preparations for his departure from Kansas. He said farewell to the members of his company, putting them under the command of James H. Holmes and enjoining them to carry on the antislavery fight, or, as he put it, "to carry the war into Africa."

Mrs. John Brown, Jr., and Mrs. Jason Brown with their children took the Missouri River route east by boat, since the blockade had now been lifted. The men left in a wagon, loaded with arms and ammunition, drawn by a four-mule team, and a one-horse covered wagon. They traveled to Topeka, crossed the river there, moved north to Nebraska and then east to Tabor, Iowa, which they reached on October 10. En route they narrowly escaped capture by United States troops who could have readily seized Brown in Lawrence during September if they had not been preoccupied. Lieutenant-Colonel Cooke from the Nebraska border reported on October 7: "I arrived here yesterday at noon. I just missed the arrest of the notorious Osawatomie outlaw, John Brown. The night before, having ascertained that after dark he had stopped for the night at a house six miles from the camp, I sent a party who found at 12 o'clock that he had gone."

John Brown would return to Kansas again, in 1857, 1858, and 1859.

Professor Leverett W. Spring wrote: "Whatever may be laid to his [Brown's] charge—whatever rashness, unwisdom, equivocation, bloodiness—no faintest stain of self-seeking stains his Kansas life." This is an unusual admission for a Kansas historian.

In after years, Brown was branded in Kansas not only as a murderer, which he was, but as a horse-thief, who was as much concerned with filling his pockets, and perhaps more so, as with the cause of a free Kansas.

In 1913 a vitriolic book was published by Hill Peebles Wilson, *John Brown: Soldier of Fortune*, which was built around this thesis. It was well received in the South and in certain quarters in Kansas. He said that Brown's "greatest or principal object was to get money and get it quickly." His indictment of Brown went to lengths that were incredible, such as that the Pottawatomie massacre was motivated by Brown's desire to acquire horses and that he killed five men to silence them (while flaunting his identity to seven other witnesses whom he did not kill). Sanborn commented on this book that his conception of Brown was "as faulty as if he had described him as a humped-back Hottentot from South America."

This book was dedicated to Mrs. Sara Robinson, the widow of Charles Robinson. A surprise came when Wilson sued the estate of Mrs. Robinson for $5,000, producing an agreement for literary prostitution recorded on February 22, 1911. The documents are in the Boyd B. Stutler collection. Wilson agreed to write a book of three hundred to four hundred pages "that will be an effective criticism of the life and character of John Brown. . . . I will endeavour to publish a highly creditable book, a work that will command the attention and respect of the cultured people of this cultured age. I will write the book in the hope that it will reverse the popular verdict recently secured by Oswald Garrison Villard in favor of his contention that the motives of John Brown while in Kansas were altruistic. I will do this for the sum of $5,000 to be paid to me or my assigns by Mrs. Sara Robinson." Mrs. Robinson signed the agreement. It appears that the estate first resisted the claim and later paid it.

As far as the stealing of horses and cattle is concerned—the chronicles of Bleeding Kansas show that it went on a massive scale on both sides as the accepted spoils of war. Higginson related that in the Kansas of 1856, "The parties were so defined that their labels attached even to dumb animals and people spoke of an 'anti-slavery colt,' or of a 'pro-slavery cow.'" The well-known operation was called on both sides, "impressing into the service."

The death toll in Kansas in 1855 and 1856 was relatively low in view of the turbulence, because the objective on both sides was to disable the enemy, and the most effective method was to strip him of his moveable wealth, which consisted of his cattle and even more vital his horses, which were his transport and agricultural machinery. In a strange twist, David C. Buffum, a free-stater, was killed near Franklin on September 16, 1856, because he refused to give up his horse with which he was plowing.

Stolen horses in Kansas are spoken of as if they were a treasure, but the going price for a horse there was only $10. Trying to sell stolen horses in Missouri was risking one's life for a free-stater, and there was only the black market in Kansas, in which the price was depressed by the supply from United States soldiers who sold government horses on the sly.

There is no evidence that Brown realized much money from his operations beyond supporting himself and his men and outfitting himself with new clothes and a buggy. Until his death in 1859 his family remained at a near-destitution level. This is evident from a letter of April 27, 1858, to North Elba, from Springdale, Iowa. He was sending a couple of barrels of flour home. Apparently freight charges then could be C.O.D., and he told his family, "If you have no money to pay the freight, sell some flour to the neighbors."

In Kansas, as throughout the history of our rough western frontier, there were no saints on either side. Professor Spring, in his account of 1856, wrote: "Free-state depredators, in larger or smaller gangs, scoured the region, filling the air with profanity, intimidating pro-slavery settlers, shooting at those who were not sufficiently docile, plundering right and left. A curious observer has chronicled the contents of a single foray-wagon: green corn in the ear, surmounted by a cooking-stove, a crib-cradle, a dining-table, clothing, bedding and a great variety of miscellaneous articles." In August, 1858, when there was a greater market for stolen horses, George W. Collamore wrote from Kansas to John A. Andrew, a leading citizen of Boston: "The whole country abounds in unprincipled men and especially does this remark apply to Lawrence, which place is a great rendezvous for rogues and horse-thieves, and not a suitable place for any decent person. Some of our principal men are charged with being connected with bands of horse-thieves."

A few months after Brown had departed, the Lawrence *Herald of Freedom*, on February 7, 1857, wrote wistfully about him. This was in an article concerning a tour of southeast Kansas in which the writer had reached the environs where the Browns had lived:

Old Captain Brown has been a man of distinction in the East. He was of the firm of Perkins & Brown in Ohio, which took the premiums at the World's Fair in London and also in New York for the finest and best wool. They were known throughout the country as importers of the best Spanish, French and Saxony sheep.

Noble-minded and generous men have ever been the mark of tyrants, and so here. The family of Browns, the most patriotic and enterprising of men, have been expelled from Kansas by the United States government, set on by the brutality of pro-slavery officials.

John Brown Sr. is a little past middle age, slightly gray, puritanic in his religion, and whatever he does, he does conscientiously from a sense of duty and as he expressed it from a fear and love of God. He is mild and gentle in his manners and fearless and uncompromising in his discharge of his duty.

Yet, in October, 1859, after Brown's capture at Harper's Ferry, the editor of the *Herald of Freedom*, G. W. Brown, was savagely attacking Brown as a fiend for his deeds in Kansas.

The change of opinion about Brown in Kansas is a curious phenomenon. Today he is a *popular* hero there. In the rotunda on the second floor of the state capitol building in Topeka there is a mural by John Steuart Curry showing a gigantic figure of Brown, bearded, with wild expression, holding a Bible in one hand and a rifle in the other, towering over free-soil and proslavery forces in Bleeding Kansas. Brown's visage adorns Kansas publications, state and private.

One cannot help wondering if it is the stain of Brown's criminality at Pottawatomie that makes him so offensive to the intellectual community in Kansas, which would rather not have him as a state symbol in a population of decent law-abiding Americans. There was a ruckus about the Curry murals in Kansas in 1941, and Curry left the state without signing them. There was objection raised to the blood on Brown's hand, and a state legislator denounced the "atrocity on the wall of horrors." That state "boosterism" is an important element is shown by the objections to the depiction of a Kansas prairie fire and tornado in the background of the Curry mural.

From the beginning, the reaction against the John Brown legend seems to have been excessive. The first essay in the literary field was an article by Reverend David Utter in the *North American Review* in November, 1883. Utter wrote: "His principles were those of the Russian Nihilists, first make a clean sweep of the present civilization and let the future build what it can." The Nihilists of that day wanted only representative government in the Duma. This raises a question—does John Brown enjoy the distinction of being the first American to be labeled a "Russian Red"?

The work of James C. Malin has given substantive tone to the Kansas revulsion. His research is impressive and I am indebted to it for uses in this book. But his bias seems excessive and he indicts Brown on all counts. He casts doubt on Brown's dedication to the slavery cause prior to his going to Kansas while there is a mass of evidence that Brown was sincere to the point of fanaticism on the slavery question. He holds Brown responsible for the reign of terror in Kansas in the summer of 1856 while stating that Brown was a minor factor in Kansas history. Reflecting, perhaps, that attitude of Kansas intellectuals, Joseph W. Snell, assistant state archivist of Kansas, who assisted me in my research, commented to me, "Had it not

been for Harper's Ferry, Brown would be as little remembered in
Kansas today as James Montgomery," the Kansas "jayhawker"
whom we shall meet later. Brown's influence on Kansas history seems
to me to have been incomparably greater.

Brown was quite ill when he left Kansas, from dysentery and chills,
and he lay on the floor of the wagon most of the time until it reached
Tabor in Iowa, not far from the Nebraska border. In this town in
which Abolitionist sentiment was very strong he recuperated between October 10 and October 18, when he left for Chicago by
stage. In Chicago, he went to the central headquarters of the National
Kansas Committee to consult with them about financial aid to enable
him to carry on further his Kansas crusade.

The committee asked Brown if he would escort a wagon train
under Dr. J. P. Root which was headed for Kansas. They wanted to
give this train armed protection since a previous wagon train with
arms had been hijacked by Missouri ruffians while crossing over
from Iowa to Nebraska. The Harper's Ferry raid was a long way off
in time, but as it happened, this train was carrying the two hundred
Sharp's rifles which Brown was destined to carry with him in 1859 in
that celebrated foray. Brown consented mainly because he wanted to
intercept his two sons, Salmon and Watson. On the North Elba farm,
when they heard the news about their brother Frederick's death, they
agreed, "Let's go to Kansas and kill Preacher White," and dropping
everything they made their way west. On the train to Chicago, they
bumped into Frederick Douglass who helped them out with $25.

Watson stopped at Tabor. Salmon went into Kansas and a little
south of Topeka heard the false news that White was dead and so he
rode back alone east to Ohio. Brown picked up his son Watson in
Tabor, and with a mule between them they traveled back to Chicago,
taking turns riding on the mule. In December, 1856, Brown had a
reunion in Ohio with all of his sons, except Oliver who was home at
North Elba.

The two hundred Sharp's rifles had not gone on to Kansas but
had been stored in the cellar of the Reverend John Todd's home in
Tabor, where Brown would find them in 1857.

CHAPTER FOUR

Boston–
The Cause and the Cult

❧

"WHAT WOULD JOHN BROWN have been without Boston?" asked rhetorically Wendell Phillips Garrison, son of the famed Abolitionist, William Lloyd Garrison. Most probably his antislavery career would have terminated after his 1856 Kansas exploits. From the beginning of 1857 Brown was kept afloat financially by a group of fanatical Abolitionists, which chose to label itself the Secret Six, and it was the members of this group who put up the money and supplied the arms which made possible his Harper's Ferry raid. Brown was to be, in Benét's words, a

> Cloudy apostle, whooped along to death
> By those who do no violence themselves
> But only buy the guns to have it done. . . .

These six men were from the eastern establishment. Five were from the cream of society in the Boston area, the other, living in New York State, was the nation's greatest landowner. Four were Harvard graduates. Of the six, one was the nation's leading philanthropist, another its leading humanitarian, and a third its leading preacher. It was quite an array of social standing, brains, character, and money.

Why did these men, predominantly idealists and reformers, adopt the rough hewn John Brown as their own and furnish the instruments for violence and bloodletting? For part of the answer we must examine the intellectual and moral climate in Boston, which was somewhat unique. Boston mentality is important for another facet of the John Brown story since it was in Boston that his canonization began with his execution in 1859, while the rest of the nation was divided and dazed about the Harper's Ferry affair.

It is understandable that the Puritan conscience with its obsession with sin should have regarded slavery as a sin. Moreover, the Puritan conscience was a busybody conscience which regarded it as sinful not to do everything possible and do it incessantly to turn others from sin. The first legislative assembly in New England enacted a law: "No bond slavery, villeinage, or captivitie, shall exist in the Massachusetts Colony."

The emotional fires of Puritanism had been banked when Jonathan Edwards initiated in 1734 the Great Awakening, a crusade continued by Reverend George Whitfield, who preached a hundred and seventy-five sermons in seventy-five days in New England. There was a new enthusiasm for religion and a new humanitarianism, as the common man was taught that he could demonstrate his election by God through his good works. Owen Brown, John Brown's father, recorded in his short memoir the great influence on his own thinking of a series of revival meetings he attended in New Canaan, Connecticut, in 1785.

When John Brown declared that he was "an instrument of God," it was no unique mental aberration, since, in the New Calvinism of the Awakening, anyone by his works could prove himself God's tool. Harriet Beecher Stowe said of her *Uncle Tom's Cabin* that "The Lord himself wrote it and I was but the humblest instrument." It is not surprising that Brown's thinking on slavery should have fitted in with the pattern of Puritan thinking since his origins were in New England; the Western Reserve Area of Ohio where he spent his formative years was an offshoot of Connecticut.

When Brown fused his religious belief and his antislavery belief, it was an authentic reflection of the character of the antislavery movement which started in upper New York State in the mid-1820s as a religious revival movement led by Charles G. Finney, who recruited that effective crusader Theodore D. Weld. It was consonant with its religious origin that abolitionism preached the doctrine that slavery was not an evil but a positive *sin*, the handiwork of Satan, and biblical quotations were ferreted out to prove it. Garrison in his paper, the *Liberator*, which he launched in Boston on New Year's Day of 1831, reveled in the castigation of slavery as a "sin against God." Mrs. Stowe said of Garrison that he had "the whole language of the Old Testament at his tongue's end, and a text from the old prophets ready like an arrow on a bow string." In that respect he and Brown were much alike, and they also agreed in becoming estranged from denominational churches because they would not denounce slavery.

To Finney and Weld, antislavery was only one part of an eclectic movement for the improvement of the human race. Their benevolent aims included establishment of Sunday schools, distribution of Bibles, salvation of sailors, temperance, and prison reform. Garrison, before his *Liberator* venture, had run papers to preach temperance and world peace, and he was strong on women's rights.

This cosmic concern was given impetus in New England by the transcendentalist movement launched by Emerson, Thoreau, and Hawthorne in 1836 in Boston. "What is man born for but to be a reformer?" asked Emerson. Transcendentalists believed in the perfectibility of man, or as Emerson put it, "The power which is at once spring and regulator in all efforts of reform is the conclusion that there is an infinite worthiness in man which will appear at the call of worth." Reform became a mania in Boston, which though a city of less than 150,000 population in 1850, was out to reform the human race. There were Brook Farm and Fourierism, Horace Mann, Margaret Fuller, and Orestes Brownson. There were Swedenborgians, Millerites, vegetarians, Grahamites, prohibitionists, feminists, nonresistants, Thomsonians, and Come-Outers of every shade.

While John Brown had a concentrated interest on one subject, slavery, his backers, the Secret Six, were diffused in their interests which were movements for general reforms, some of them remote and Utopian, and they were more or less conditioned to the attitude that the purity of motive, the striving was more important than the attainment of the goal. This explains in part the shock felt by the Six when the Harper's Ferry raid actually did come off.

Abolitionism, particularly that of the radical, shrieking Garrison, which demanded immediate, uncompensated emancipation of the slaves, made little headway in the North, nor did abolitionism of more moderate tone. Garrison personally opposed political participation, but others launched political action in 1840 with the Liberty party. Its candidate, James G. Birney, received 7,000 votes and in 1844 he received 62,000 votes out of a vote over 2,600,000. In 1848, the Free-Soil party, with moderate candidates, the former President Martin Van Buren and Charles Francis Adams as his running-mate, received only 10 percent of the vote. In 1852, the Democratic candidate, Franklin Pierce, running on a platform that pledged not to disturb slavery, carried all but four states, and this at a time when *Uncle Tom's Cabin* (priced at 37 1/2 cents per copy) had reached a sale of a million copies.

Despite the Puritan conscience, abolitionism, had been in disrepute even in Boston in the 1830s. There were epithets hurled at them, such as "obnoxious pests," "eternal whiners," and "indiscreet men and unsexed women." John Quincy Adams in his diary talked of the "plausible rascality" of Garrison's nonresistant abolitionism, classing it as a quackery, like phrenology.

On October 21, 1835, a mob, made up of solid Boston citizens, searched the *Liberator* offices for the visiting English Abolitionist, George Thompson, and not finding him, dragged Garrison himself out and through the streets of Boston by a rope around his waist. For his safety, the mayor put him in jail and then shipped him to Providence. The Boston *Evening Transcript* said: "In what terms of indignation can we speak of the man who by rancorous denunciation and his brawling, ferocious abuse, together with the disorganizing tendencies of his doctrines, has excited the people to such an ebullition of their deeply exasperated feelings."

Boston profited heavily from shipping trade with the South, and the merchant aristocracy of the city dominated public opinion. The Richmond *Whig* said: "They know too well which side their bread is buttered on to give up these advantages." As the years went on, in the 1840s and 1850s, an intellectual élite would emerge to assault slavery and win public support, labeling the values of the merchant class as sordid and immoral.

One of the first in the field (the first of the Secret Six, whom we shall meet in turn) was the Reverend Theodore Parker, the "Savonarola of the Transcendentalists," as Emerson characterized him. An intellectual gourmand, he was probably the most learned man of his time, having a knowledge of sixteen languages and a library of fifteen thousand volumes. His fame was world-wide. At the conclusion of his sermon in 1854 on the fugitive slave, Anthony Burns, he said, "To-morrow's sun shall carry my words to all America. They will be read on both sides of the Continent. They will cross the ocean," and he was not exaggerating. He was almost as well known in England and Germany as in the United States. When the English author, Thackeray, visited these shores, the first person he wanted to see was Parker. One of his most avid admirers was William M. Herndon of Springfield, Illinois, who used to supply his law partner with re-commended reading. He placed a Parker sermon, "The Effect of Slavery on the American People," on Abraham Lincoln's desk, un-derscoring the sentence, "Democracy is direct self-government, over all the people, for all the people, by all the people." In November, 1863, he realized that Lincoln had digested the passage.

Parker, who was born in 1810, was too poor to enter Harvard but he was allowed to take examinations through the course. He gradu-ated from Harvard Divinity School and became pastor of the Roxbury Unitarian Church, a pastorate that ended in May, 1842, when he delivered a discourse, "The Transient and Permanent in Christianity," in which he denied the special authority of the Bible, and the supernatural and divine mission of Christ. All pulpits were closed to him, and when he intensified his attack on slavery, he was, in his own words, "as much an outcast from society as if I were a convicted pirate."

He was not expelled from the Unitarian Church and did not with-draw. He started his own church services in the Meledeon of Boston which was packed to the rafters each Sunday with twenty-three hundred listeners, and then in 1852 he moved it to the larger Music Hall where five thousand heard him. Stocky, ungainly, with an almost-bald, Socrates-like head, he stood in the pulpit and preached, as he said, "like a Hebrew prophet." His mission, he felt, was to elevate the soul of man, and he preached a natural religion of ethics, discus-sing the secular evils, not only of slavery but of exploitation of work-ers and evils of the factory system. His audiences were spellbound and orthodox sects were demoralized by his influence. They set a special day of prayer in 1858 to invoke divine interference with this dissenter, one gospeller praying, "O Lord, put a hook in his jaw."

He articulated the "higher law" doctrine in a sermon on slavery at a ministerial conference in 1842: "Oh, my brethren, I am not afraid of men. I can offend them. I care nothing for their hate or their esteem. But I should not dare to violate the eternal law of God. I should not dare to violate His law, come what may." The doctrine was taken up by Abolitionists and became a standard theme.

Brown came to his concept of the "higher law" through the Great Awakening, which taught that each man had an inner light that could grasp God's will. At any rate, though no theoretician, Brown was a blood-brother to the intellectual Abolitionists of Boston in loyalty to "higher law," which, since it was undefined, meant that his conscience as an individual was more important than obeying the written laws of society.

The man of the cloth, said the Reverend Mr. Parker, must be an activist in achieving reform and progress, and Parker among other activities was a hyperactive member of the Vigilance Committee of Boston, which after the enactment of the fugitive slave law of 1850 helped to spirit fugitive slaves out of Boston before they fell into the clutches of the slaveholders. On October 15, 1850, two slavecatchers from the South got warrants in Boston for the arrest of William and Ellen Craft, a couple who had escaped to Boston two years earlier.

Having been notified by the secretary of the Vigilance Committee, Parker arrived at 6 A.M. at the United States Hotel where the slave-catchers had a room. In an interview with them, Parker told them that he was addressing them as if he were their best friend. Their lives were in danger; the popular indignation was spontaneous and deep and could not be allayed while they were in Boston. They took his advice and scurried to the depot to get on a train for New York. Then Parker legally married the Crafts who had been living together under the common law. He put a bowie knife in William's hand after he made them man and wife, charging him to use it only in extremity. "Nay, if you cannot use it without hating the man you strike, your action will not be without sin," a Cromwellian maxim that the righteous must love his enemy as his enemy and hate him only as God's enemy.

The secretary of the Vigilance Committee who had alerted Parker in the morning's early hours was the humanitarian, Dr. Samuel Gridley Howe. Of him, Senator Charles Sumner said, "He is the soul of disinterestedness. He has purged his soul from all considerations of self so far as mortals may do so, and his sympathies embrace all creatures." Born in 1801, he graduated from Harvard Medical School. Influenced by Byron he deserted his incipient practice to go to Greece to help in its struggle for freedom, where he served both as fighter and surgeon, in the latter capacity setting up hospitals. He returned to the United States, raised money for the relief of the Greeks and managed its distribution in Greece. While in Europe he organized, with Samuel F. B. Morse and James Fenimore Cooper, a committee to aid Polish political refugees and when he went to Berlin to distribute the funds, he was imprisoned by the Prussian government for six weeks of solitary confinement.

He returned to the United States to devote his life to mankind. He had been honored by the king of Greece by being made a chevalier of the Order of St. Saviour, and henceforth he was to be "Chev" to friends like Theodore Parker and to his new poetess-wife, Julia Ward Howe. On his hat tree there was always hung the plumed azure-colored helmet Byron had first worn in Greece.

He founded the school known as the New England Asylum for the Blind and later the Perkins Institution. A thrilling story, almost a miracle, was his pioneering and successful attempt to educate seven-year-old Laura Bridgman, who had been blind and deaf from an early year. The techniques that Anne Sullivan used to educate Helen Keller, particularly the touch-language, were invented by Howe, and Miss Sullivan learned them at Perkins. He put out editions of the Bible in raised type called Howe-type. The tireless Comet-Apostle had many other humanitarian interests, such as his collaboration with Dorothea Dix in decent care for the insane. When he died in 1871, Oliver Wendell Holmes wrote a poem about him:

> He touched the eyelids of the blind
> And lo! the veil withdrew,
> And o'er the midnight of the mind
> He led the light of dawn.
>
> No labored love, no sculptured art
> Such hallowed memory needs,
> His tablet is the human heart
> His record living deeds.

Howe became an enthusiast early in the antislavery movement. In 1846 he ran unsuccessfully for Congress on the Conscience Whig ticket. He was a subscriber to the "higher law" doctrine. "Nothing can truly become law, real law, that contravenes the principle of right."

In Syracuse, New York, in October, 1851, while the American Anti-Slavery Society was holding a convention, an alarm bell rang. A fugitive slave, Jerry McHenry, had been taken into custody. The members ran posthaste to the prison, battered down the door, put the Negro in a light carriage drawn by the fastest horses, and off he went to Canada and safety.

The philanthropist, Gerrit Smith, three years older than John Brown, from Peterboro, New York, took part in that rescue and every October 1 afterward he staged a commemorative event called the Jerry Rescue Meeting. "There can be no Christianity, no Christ, no God," he said "if that poor, innocent, bleeding brother had been plunged into the horrors and hell of slavery." Smith had started out as an African colonizationist but, concluding that this was only an evasion of the main problem, if not a southern decoy, had turned to abolitionism. He helped to form the Liberty party in 1840 and was named its candidate for President in 1848, but he bowed out. In 1852 he was elected to Congress and resigned before his term was over because he got nowhere with some of his pet schemes, such as the abolition of the United States post office.

Smith possessed a huge fortune. His father, Peter Smith, had built the nation's largest land empire, using the device of buying in tax-defaulted lands. Gerrit was undoubtedly a manic-depressive, swinging from acute melancholia and hypochrondia to fits of exaltation wherein he was impelled to become the nation's leading philanthropist, his name heading every subscription for a worthy cause. As we have previously noted, he gave away lands to Abolitionist Oberlin College and he donated 120,000 acres of land in the New York Adirondacks for settlement by as many as three thousand Negroes. His interests ran the widest gamut. He assisted the patriot and revolutionist Mazzini in Italy and the potato famine sufferers in Ireland. He campaigned not only against alcohol and tobacco but also against tea, coffee, meat, and, in fact, against almost everything that seemed to afford pleasure. He backed campaigns for Sunday schools, foreign missions, prison reforms, women's rights, abolition of capital punishment, and observance of the Sabbath on the seventh day of the week. After the Civil War, he was to go on the famous bail bond for Jefferson Davis with Horace Greeley and Cornelius Vanderbilt.

The effort in Boston to keep fugitive slaves free from the toils of the southerners, with which Smith was closely allied, had remarkable success. A fugitive slave, Fred Williams, was working as a waiter in Boston under the name of Shadrach since he had fled from the "fiery furnace" of southern slavery. He was arrested in February, 1851, and just after a hearing before a federal commissioner he was enveloped by friends, swept off, and escorted to Canada where he became a barber. Parker hailed it as "the noblest deed done in Boston since the destruction of tea in 1773." But the efforts of the Vigilance Committee failed in the case of Thomas Sims, who was seized in Boston in April of that year. A force of two hundred federal marshals guarded the federal courthouse. An ingenious would-be rescuer contrived a plan for Sims to jump from a window of his cell to the street, and on to mattresses below the cell. Unfortunately, the jailers stuck bars in the window before Sims could leap to freedom and he was conducted back to slavery.

The author of this thwarted plan was the Reverend Thomas Wentworth Higginson, minister, author, reformer, discoverer and friend of the poetess Emily Dickinson. He was a soldier, too, commanding the first regiment of freed-slaves in the Civil War, and about this he wrote an absorbing book, *Army Life in a Black Regiment*. He was born in 1823, the son of a wealthy shipowner and a descendant of an eminent colonial cleric. He graduated from Harvard at the age of seventeen, taught school for a while, and then attended the Harvard Divinity School. Tall and muscular, he enjoyed athletics and the strenuous life from his youth. He was a rower, skater, boxer, and amateur naturalist. After graduation from Harvard, he became pastor of the First Religious Society (Unitarian) of Newburyport, Massachusetts. By degrees he preached himself out of his pulpit. He espoused the antislavery cause strongly in a community that was at best lukewarm on the issue. He invited a fugitive slave to preach at his church and exchanged pulpits with Theodore Parker. He berated the long hours and low pay in factories in Newburyport. After the election of 1848, in his Thanksgiving Day sermon, he scorched his congregation for supporting slaveholder Zachary Taylor for President. His businessman parishioners may have won a protective tariff, but if that meant "the sacrifice of Freedom and the slave . . . from such protection God protect us!" Seats at his Sunday services emptied after that and the next year he decided to resign the pastorate.

In 1850 he ran unsuccessfully as a Free-Soil candidate for Congress, during which he declared that the fugitive slave law must yield to the "higher law." He became minister of the nonsectarian Free Church in Worcester which he made less a church than an ethical culture society, discussing besides slavery topics of the day, temperance, poverty, exploitation of labor, penal reform, and the like.

"Never did I hear of anything daredevil without wishing to leave all else and do it," Higginson said in a later year. In his work to rescue fugitive slaves he maintained a yacht in Boston harbor. While his efforts were unavailing in the case of Thomas Sims in 1851, a fresh opportunity came when Anthony Burns was arrested in Boston on May 24, 1854, as a fugitive slave and carried off to the federal courthouse, imprisoned in the same room that Sims had occupied three years earlier.

In a meeting at Faneuil Hall on the night of May 26, the Reverend Mr. Parker lashed the audience with savage rhetoric. "Fellowsubjects of Virginia," he called out. When there were cries of "NO," he continued, "Yes, we are the vassals of Virginia. It reaches its arm over the graves of our mothers and it kidnaps men in the city of the Puritans. Gentlemen, there is no Boston today. There was Boston once. Now this is a northern suburb to the city of Alexandria [Virginia]."

A crowd of five hundred gathered around the courthouse, throwing bricks. Then the Reverend Mr. Higginson and others, wielding a fourteen-foot beam, broke ajar the doors. Higginson and a Negro squirmed inside and were struck by guards with clubs and cutlasses. A shot from outside killed one of the guards, and Higginson, gashed on the face by a cutlass, and his companion escaped. Richard Henry Dana, Jr., noted in his journal: "I knew his ardor and courage, but I hardly expected a married man, a clergyman and a man of education to lead the mob." The next day, Burns, under heavy military protection, was taken to the docks and Dr. Howe wrote that among the spectators he "wept from sorrow, shame and indignation."

The cause was winning increasing support in Boston. The conservative industrialist, Amos Lawrence, had offered his help to the federal marshals in the Sims case, but in the Burns case three years later he said that he preferred to see the courthouse razed rather than see the fugitive returned. Abolitionism had been shunned like the plague before 1840 by proper Bostonians. Now, upper-class Boston was split on ideological lines, and members of one group would not consort with the other. Dr. John G. Palfrey, the Harvard theologian, told Higginson that what really hurt was "the attitude of men who have loved you and whom you have loved all your life, and who pass you by now on the streets without talking to you."

The enactment of the Kansas–Nebraska bill made the tocsin ring anew. In the Music Hall, Parker announced: "In the steady triumph of despotism, ten years more like the ten years past and it will be over with the liberties of the American people." Parker bade godspeed to forty men leaving for Kansas, and the man of the cloth observed with satisfaction that they were armed with "twenty copies of Sharp's Rights of the People of the new & improved edition."

The sacking of Lawrence and the brutal beating of Senator Sumner in May, 1856, raised a tempest in Boston. There were three meetings in less than two weeks, with Dr. Howe the invigorating spirit, and Julia Ward Howe wrote to her sister: "New England spunk seems to be pretty well up." On June 25 the Massachusetts Kansas Aid Committee was set up to aid settlers "directly," that is to furnish them with arms. In July, a National Kansas Committee was organized in Buffalo with Eli Thayer as its general agent to supervise liaison with state and local groups. In the list of names sent by the telegrapher from Buffalo of committee members, one from each state, was "Abram Lincoln of Springfield, Illinois," and it was printed that way in eastern papers. Although he had been considered for Vice President in the Republican National Convention of 1856, Lincoln was almost unknown outside of Illinois. In view of the fact that he had been selected as a Republican elector for Illinois and this unofficial Kansas duty was not consonant in his opinion with that official position, Lincoln withdrew from the Kansas Committee.

Dr. Howe decided to go out to Kansas himself with Thaddeus Hyatt to look over the situation and disburse $10,000 raised for the Kansas cause. Forced to take the overland route because the Missouri River was blockaded, he was infuriated by the sight of brave men toiling intrepidly over the plains in the summer heat because the river route could not be used. He wrote Senator Sumner: "How long will the North eat dirt & not turn sick?" When he reached Tabor eight miles east of the Missouri, which was a way-station for free-state settlers where they were fed and housed, he wrote back that it "fulfills the ideal of a town of true Cromwellian grit, praying, fighting Christians with a faith ever ardent & with 'powder always dry.'"

He and Hyatt conferred with General Lane and, as we have mentioned before, decided to entrust their funds to other persons who were more reliable. Howe traveled into northern Kansas before heading home. He had by now become intransigent on the Kansas issue. He would never hold out an olive branch since "Slavocracy would devour it, dove and all, as they have ever been disposed to, if now we waver & hesitate."

Higginson arrived a few weeks later as New England agent for the Massachusetts Kansas Aid Committee. He purchased Sharp's rifles and ammunition and escorted a group of settlers. He traveled overland six hundred miles over the prairies, for four days and nights, riding on top of a stagecoach. From Nebraska City to Topeka he trekked for six days in a twenty-wagon train. What he saw in Kansas made him fighting mad. He put no faith in the professions of Governor Geary, since "Geary's intention is to give them peace & bread at the price of obedience to the laws of the false legislature." He now saw no hope for the Union, which was a covenant with slaveholders, and agreed with Garrison that an "amputation" was necessary. "Disunion. . . . As God is in heaven our destiny and duty is to be found there. It is our only hope," and he presided in Worcester on January 15, 1857, at a Massachusetts Disunion Convention at which Garrison was a vice president.

Gerrit Smith had shifted in his attitude. In mid-1855 when asked to help buy guns for a boys' military company in Washington, he replied: "I am so afraid of war and patriotism that I dare not help boys buy one musket, not even a boy's little musket." But in a letter of May 31, 1856, to the Syracuse *Journal*, he wrote: "Hitherto I have been opposed to the bloody abolition of slavery. But when it begins to march its conquering bands into the Free State, I, as ten thousand other peace men, am not only ready to have them repulsed with violence but pursued even unto death with violence."

Emerson put down in his journal in 1856: "There is this peculiarity about the case of Kansas, that all the right is on one side. . . . We hear the screams of hunted wives and children answered by the howls of the butchers."

When the absolutist John Brown arrived in Boston in January, 1857, he was met by a group of men who matched him in absolutist conviction. The spirit of relativism, dissent, and compromise which were traditional in the American political conscience had vanished from their minds in this cause. Mere protest was not enough. The situation called for iron-willed action.

Higginson may have been the first of the Six to meet Brown. He had heard about him in Kansas and had a memory of meeting an outlaw under a false name in Lawrence. In the hurly-burly of the times, he could not remember the man clearly. Brown met Parker in Chicago. On October 26, 1856, Horace White, assistant secretary of the National Kansas Committee, wrote him: "Reverend Theodore Parker of Boston is at the Briggs House and wishes very much to see you." Afterward, Brown left for Tabor.

Back in Chicago, Brown found waiting for him a letter from George Luther Stearns, a wealthy Boston businessman who had talked with Parker. Stearns invited Brown to come to Boston and said he would pay his expenses.

Long-bearded Stearns, who was born in 1809, was the son of an obstetrician of the Boston suburb of Medford. His father had died when he was a boy and he started work at the age of fifteen. He launched his own business, producing linseed oil by a new process and flexible lead pipe under a new patent, and then branched into ship-chandlery. Though not in Gerrit Smith's income bracket, he was prosperous enough and was to be Brown's most generous sponsor.

He had early become interested in the antislavery cause and had worked for the Liberty party back in 1840. He married a niece of the noted Abolitionist, Lydia Maria Child, and got into the inner circle of zealots by friendships he made in the posh Bird Club with Charles Sumner and Dr. Howe. After the fugitive slave law he hid a Negro for a week under a bedroom floor of his home before shipping him to Canada and safety. As chairman of the Massachusetts Kansas Aid Committee he was an enthusiast, raising many small contributions by pleading for "someone who would go without dinner for Kansas."

Brown accepted by letter the invitation from Stearns. He traveled to Columbus, Ohio, where he saw Governor Salmon B. Chase and solicited a letter of endorsement. Chase wrote a cautious one, on December 20, basing it on hearsay: "Captain John Brown of Kansas Territory is commended to me by a highly respectable citizen of this state as a gentleman every way worthy of confidence." That citizen was probably Congressman Joshua R. Giddings. Chase then referred to the letter written by Charles Robinson. "Upon these testimonials, I cordially recommend him to the confidence and regard of all who desire to see Kansas free." Chase sweetened this letter by handing Brown $25.

The letters of commendation were sent by Brown to Gerrit Smith in Peterboro, New York. Smith had met him before in the dim past and might not recall him. Smith replied most enthusiastically: "Captain John Brown—you did not need to show me letters from Governor Chase and Governor Robinson to let me know who you are. I have known you for many years and have highly esteemed you as long as I have known you. I know your unshrinking bravery, your self-sacrificing benevolence, your devotion to the cause of freedom and have long known them. May Heaven preserve your life and health, and prosper your noble purpose!"

He visited Smith at Peterboro around Christmas time, and then went to Rochester to renew his friendship with Frederick Douglass. The content of the conversations at this time we do not know. Probably Brown revealed his experiences and accomplishments in saving Kansas.

He had not seen his wife and daughters since August, 1855, but he did not visit North Elba for some weeks. His work, his mission was foremost in his mind. He arrived in Boston on January 4, 1857.

The first person on whom Brown called was the secretary of the Massachusetts Kansas Aid Committee, to whom he had a personal letter of introduction, Franklin B. Sanborn of Concord, Massachusetts. He is the final member of the Secret Six whom we meet, Brown's biographer-to-be and vocally the most ardent hero-worshipper.

Sanborn was the youngest of the Six, at this time a month past his twenty-fifth birthday and only a year and a half out of Harvard. He was six feet three inches tall with fine, feminine features, a face described "like an early portrait of Raphael." The unfriendly New York *Herald* after Harper's Ferry described him as "one of the women-in-breeches poets of Boston." While at Harvard he had become an enthusiast about Theodore Parker, whom he went to hear often in Boston, and out of his slender savings he bought a copy of his sermons for the library of the Hasty Pudding Club. Even before graduation, he had become secretary of the Massachusetts Free Soil Society and a fund-raiser for the Massachusetts Emigrant Aid Company. He was a disciple of Emerson, who persuaded him, after he got his degree, to take on the job of principal of a coeducational school for children of aristocratic families at Concord. He was the chairman in 1856 of the local Kansas committee at Concord, and he raised more proportionately to the population than was raised anywhere else in Massachusetts.

He had had a long friendship with Ariana Walker, who was suffering from a strange neurological disease, and whom he married eight days before her death. He thereby acquired some money. The letter of introduction that Brown presented was from her brother, George Walker, an Abolitionist of Springfield.

Sanborn described the man from Kansas who appeared before him:

"His figure was tall, slender and commanding." Brown was five feet ten inches tall, and his figure spare as throughout his adult life, weighing about a hundred and fifty pounds. His skin was leathery and weather-beaten, like that of an old farmer. "His bearing was military and he gave a singular blending of the old soldier and the deacon." He wore a brown military overcoat with cape such as was to be popular in the Civil War and a fur cap with visor that he called "my Kansas cap." But his suit underneath, also brown, of broadcloth, was as sober and correct as that of a deacon. "His mien was serious and patient rather than cheerful; it betokened the 'sad, wise valor' which [George] Herbert praises." His sharp chin and sharp line of mouth conveyed the look of inner resolution, as Sanborn viewed him.

Brown was aging rapidly now. All who met him in Boston took him for a man in his sixties although he was five months short of fifty-seven. His figure was stooped and his thick, brown hair shot through with gray. His health had always been robust. His son, Owen, said that he could not recall his father ever having missed a meal from sickness. Now, the incessant grind was taking its toll. When he died at the age of fifty-nine, he would appear to be a man of seventy.

Sanborn was to be henceforth quasi-executive secretary of the Six, Brown's liaison man. To all and sundry, Sanborn announced, "Ecce homo." The deeds of this old warrior in saving Kansas bore witness for him. Sanborn escorted Brown to meetings with the Reverends Parker and Higginson, Dr. Howe, and Mr. Stearns. Contributions came in immediately. Higginson gave him $30 on January 10. Howe gave him two pistols and a rifle as tokens of his regard.

Howe's wife, Julia Ward Howe, told in her *Reminiscences* that her husband spoke to her of a remarkable man who "seemed to intend to devote his life to the redemption of the colored race as Christ had willingly offered his life for the salvation of mankind." One day, there was a knock on her door and when she opened it, there was a man standing there being drenched in the rain. She knew instantly he was the man her husband had mentioned, though he had not been described to her.

It was a strange destiny that her fame would be intertwined with that of Brown's. In late 1861, during the Civil War, Dr. Howe went to Washington to become a member of the United States Sanitary Commission. One afternoon, Julia Ward Howe went in a carriage with Governor Andrew of Massachusetts, Mrs. Andrew, and Dr. James Freeman Clarke, to Old Bailey's Crossing in Virginia to watch

an inspection of Union troops. On their return they were singing
soldier songs, and Dr. Clarke said to her, "That song, 'John Brown's
Body' seems to be a particular favorite, Mrs. Howe. Why don't you
write better words to the tune." She replied, "I wish I could." That
night she was seized by the fever of inspiration and wrote down the
words of the "Battle Hymn of the Republic." It was published in the
Atlantic Monthly in February, 1862, and was soon being sung to the
music of the John Brown song. Together, they would become great
songs in the history of the nation, and would span the oceans to stir
foreign peoples.

Brown was socially lionized, received in the best Boston homes
and met other figures in the cause. He encountered Garrison one
evening at Parker's home, and they had a debate on their divergent
approaches to attacking slavery, Brown urging attack by force on the
monstrous sin, Garrison, the nonresistant, urging moral force instead of "carnal weapons." The long debate consisted of each hurling
quotations from the Scriptures against the other, and the result was a
stand-off. Brown was also received in the home of the great Abolitionist orator, Wendell Phillips. The industrialist Amos Lawrence,
who was a moderate, noted in his diary on January 7, "Captain
Brown, the old partisan hero of Kansas warfare, came to see me. I
had a long talk with him. He is a calm, temperate and pious man, but
when roused he is a dreadful foe."

Lawrence would feel otherwise about Brown later on when he
learned more about him. It should be noted that Boston was ignorant
of Brown's connection with the Pottawatomie affair and probably of
the affair itself. Higginson had heard Brown's name associated with it
in Kansas but he apparently never brought it up.

George L. Stearns, his son, Frank P. Stearns, wrote in a biography
of his father, took to Brown immediately. They were both idealists
and practical businessmen. "They met like the iron and the magnet."
Stearns invited him out to his Medford home for dinner on the second Sunday of January. He asked Brown if he had an objection to a
visit on a Sunday, and Brown, who was developing a poetic form of
utterance, replied: "Mr. Stearns, I have a poor, little ewe that has fallen into the ditch, and I think the Sabbath is as good a day as any to
help her out."

Mrs. Stearns said of her first sight of Brown that evening:

When I entered the parlor, he was sitting near the hearth where glowed
a bright, open fire. He rose to greet me, stepping forward with such an

erect, military bearing, such fine courtesy of demeanor and grave earnestness, that he seemed to my instant thought some old Cromwellian hero suddenly dropped down before me, a suggestion that was presently strengthened by his saying (proceeding with the conversation my entrance had interrupted), "Gentlemen, I consider the Golden Rule and the Declaration of Independence one and inseparable, and it is better that a whole generation of men, women and children should be swept away than that this crime of slavery should exist one day longer." These words were uttered like rifle balls, in such emphatic tones and manner that our little Carl, not three years old, remembered it in manhood as one of his earliest recollections.

At dinner, Brown made a profound impression. He refused all dainties, even refusing butter, saying that he did not know what it was to eat for pleasure. He talked continuously of his year in Kansas, "watered by the tears and blood of my children," of his campaigns, of the barbarities inflicted on him, the burning of his home near Osawatomie and the stealing of his livestock, of the cruelties endured by John Brown, Jr.—and he had with him the very chains his son had dragged for seventy-two miles on that march—of the murder of his son Frederick. Then, like a fine actor, he relieved the tension with a highly humorous account of how he took Pate at the battle at Black Jack.

The tales of his tribulations and triumphs were delivered clipped and sharp. Stearns queried him: "I suppose, Captain, that if Judge Lecompte had fallen into your hands he would have fared rather hard." Brown turned around in his chair and said: "If the Lord had delivered Judge Lecompte into my hands, it would have required the Lord to have taken him out again."

It was after this dinner that the boy Henry Stearns pressed on him his pocket money for the poor of Kansas and asked him to tell about his boyhood, and we have earlier discussed this autobiography which Brown mailed him from Iowa several months later. The older Stearns was highly moved by Brown's "sagacity, courage and strong integrity," and his purse was open to Brown from then on.

Captain Brown fulfilled for the members of the Secret Six the image of the man they wanted. He was, they believed, of true Puritan stock, descended from Peter Brown of the *Mayflower*. (Social snobbery was strong in Boston.) They loved him for the sufferings and sacrifices he had undergone in Kansas and, what is more important, that he was willing to undergo further for them. They were acutely conscious, even guilt-ridden, that while they only raised money, cheered and wept from the sidelines, he was totally involved, foregoing the normal comforts of existence while staking his life. This man had the courage of their convictions.

They romanticized him as "Old Covenanter," "Border chieftain," and "Roundhead hero." These images surfaced from their recollections of the Waverly novels of Sir Walter Scott with which Higginson, Howe, and Sanborn had been stuffed in childhood. The scholarly Parker said that the Waverly novels were the only fiction he had ever read. Similes from Scott stick out in Higginson's reports. The romantic influence of Byronism was also strongly felt by these men.

Brown's objective in Boston was to raise money for the Kansas cause to be spent by him under his sole direction. "I think the little beggar children in the street are sufficiently interested to warrant their contribution." Specifically, he wanted $30,000 to arm and equip a company of a hundred men to fight for Kansas, but he would take less. This $30,000 figure would include the value of any arms that might be contributed.

The Massachusetts Kansas Aid Committee of which Stearns was chairman quickly voted to put into Brown's possession the two hundred Sharp's rifles that had been transported by Dr. Root the previous November to Tabor, Iowa, and stored in Reverend Todd's cellar. They also voted him 4,000 ball cartridges, 31,000 percussion caps, and four iron ladles. Since a Sharp's rifle cost $25, the guns alone were worth $5,000. The committee stipulated, however, that Brown must hold the rifles subject to the order of the committee.

For further assistance, Brown appeared before the National Kansas Committee which was meeting for a week-long session starting January 23 at the Astor House in New York City. A dispute had arisen between this National Committee and the Massachusetts Committee about the ownership of the two hundred Sharp's rifles, but this was cleared away when the National Committee voted to relinquish title to the Massachusetts Committee which was the donor.

Initially, the National Kansas Committee seemed favorably inclined to Brown's request for money to support a company of a hundred men, but then turned cold to the project. Their understanding had been that these hundred men were to be active settlers, scattered about the Territory, engaged in normal pursuits, and to be called out only to repel invasion or to protect the free-state settlers. When they found out that Brown intended them to operate full-time as a unit, under his command, they had grave doubts.

The secretary, H. B. Hurd, asked Brown: "If you get the arms and money you desire, will you invade Missouri or any slave territory?" Brown replied tartly: "I am no adventurer. You are acquainted with my history. You know what I have done in Kansas. I do not expose my plans. No one knows them but myself, except perhaps one. I will not be interrogated. If you wish to give me anything, I want you to give it freely."

The committee was reluctant to give him a blank check, and the most uneasy about Brown was the Illinois representative who had taken Lincoln's place, William F. M. Arny. The committee voted $5,000 "in aid of Captain John Brown in any *defensive* measure that may become necessary." It was stipulated that he could not draw any more than $500 at one time, and not even that until he demonstrated he intended to return to Kansas. He collected only $110, months later in August, when he reached Tabor. Brown was disappointed and felt that he had been used badly. On April 3, he wrote to a friend, William Barnes: "I am prepared to expect nothing but bad faith from the National Kansas Committee at Chicago, as I will show hereafter. This is for the present confidential."

After the adjournment of this session in New York, Brown, at the request of Horace White of the committee, furnished a list of articles by item needed by his projected company, together with their purchase cost at Lawrence. He gave a total tabulated cost of $1,774. Both James C. Malin and Hill Peebles Wilson have pointed out the discrepancy between this figure and $30,000, indicating that Brown must have aimed to pocket a large personal profit. In justice to Brown, this figure of $1,774 was for wagons, wagon horses, implements, tools, utensils, etc., for a company of fifty and not a hundred men. Arms and ammunition were not included on this list nor clothing for the men, and it covered the cost of provisions for men and horses for only two weeks. The figure of $400 for rent for horses was ridiculously low. The $30,000 figure may well have been exorbitant, but one cannot resist the conclusion that Brown in the $1,774 tabulation asked for a sum that he thought he might possibly collect. White wrote Brown that the committee would ship the articles he requisitioned. All Brown got in the end was fourteen boxes of clothing sufficient for sixty persons shipped in March to Tabor; in one box there were four small mills to grind wheat and corn for bread. The committee shipped Brown twenty-five Colt's Navy revolvers, but when he did not pick them up at Lawrence, they were turned over to the Free-State militia group, the Lawrence Stubbs.

Every device was used by Brown in his great money-hunt. Sanborn prepared a bill that was introduced in the Massachusetts legislature to appropriate $100,000 to relieve the distress of Kansas settlers. Brown appeared on February 18 before the Joint Committee on Federal Relations to which it had been referred. Sanborn introduced Brown as the sixth descendant of Peter Brown of the *Mayflower*, and said, "He has been in Kansas what Miles Standish was to the Plymouth Colony."

Brown, addressing the committee, made a case that he should be one of the prime beneficiaries of such a bill since merely in the defense of Lawrence, in December, 1855, the loss of wages for himself and his sons in the ruin of their winter work, amounted to $7,500, while their suffering could not be estimated in money terms. He described what he and the other Browns had endured. The captain, laying aside his paper, said that he had now at his hotel and would exhibit to the committee, if they so desired, the chains which one of his sons had worn when he was driven beneath the burning sun by federal troops to a distant prison on a charge of treason. Redpath wrote: "The cruelties he there endured, added to the anxieties and sufferings, incident to his position had rendered him, the old man said, as his eye flashed and his voice grew sterner, 'A maniac—yes, a MANIAC.' He paused a few seconds, wiped a tear from his eye and continued his narration." Brown had, one night in the preceding May, been indeed a MANIAC.

Further, he said, as his prepared manuscript reads: "It cost the U.S. more than half a million for a year past to harrass poor Free State settlers in Kansas, & to violate all law & all right, moral and Constitutional, for the sole & only purpose of forcing Slavery upon that Territory. I challenge this whole nation to prove before God or mankind to contrary." When asked about the type of immigrants needed in Kansas, Brown said crisply that men were needed "who fear God too much to fear anything human." They must act from their conscience not in hating slavery but in obeying the will of God.

All was in vain since the committee voted to shelve the bill, believing that Kansas was not the responsibility of the state of Massachusetts.

The effort to get money from a government source was not abandoned. A try was made to get the legislature in New York State to enact an appropriation for Kansas relief, and also, as Stearns put it in a letter to New York sponsors, "to organize a secret force, well-armed and under the control of the famous John Brown to repel Border Ruffian outrages. . . ." Stearns wrote that he knew Brown well, that he had the confidence of the free-state settlers. While he held true to the original principles of making Kansas free, "Many of the Free-State leaders, being engaged in speculations are willing to accept peace on any terms." In his conversations with Stearns, Brown had apparently succeeded in discrediting leaders like Robinson and Lane. The proposal did not win support in New York.

The Massachusetts Kansas Aid Committee, under the chairmanship of George L. Stearns, voted him $500 on January 9 and another $500 on April 11, and Brown collected this sum of $1,000 a week later. Presumably Stearns picked up the tabs for his living expenses in January and until mid-February, and he gave him another $100 as a personal gift. Amos Lawrence gave Brown a gift of $70.

On February 10 to 16, Brown returned to North Elba where he had a joyous reunion with his wife and daughters, whom he had not seen for a year and a half. Ellen, whom he had left in the cradle, was now old enough to be lifted in his arms and hear his favorite hymn, "Blow, Ye Trumpets, Blow." In March, he commenced a tour around the circuit in New England to raise money for himself. He wrote his friend William Barnes of Albany that he "could make no further sacrifice except to go about in the attitude of a beggar; & that I have done, humiliating as it is." He had no diffidence in making known the debt due him for his services, as circulars he had printed show:

This will introduce a friend who visits in order to secure means to sustain and secure the cause of Freedom in the U.S. and throughout the world.

In behalf of the cause, he has exhausted his limited means as to place his wife and three young daughters in circumstances of privation and dependent on the generosity of friends who have cared for them.

He has contributed the entire services of two strong sons for two years and his own services for three years.

During this time, they have undergone great hardship, exposure of health and other privations.

During much of the past three years he had with him in Kansas six sons and a son-in-law who together with him were all sick.

Two were made prisoners and subjected to the most barbarous treatment.

Two were severely wounded.

One was murdered.

During this time he figured with some success under the title of "Old Brown," often perilling his life.

He himself is endorsed as an earnest and steady-minded man and a True Descendant of Peter Brown of the *Mayflower* Pilgrims.

He visited Springfield and Worcester and Concord in Massachusetts, Hartford, New Haven, Canton, and Collinsville in Connecticut. He may have stopped off at other towns. When in Canton, he obtained the tombstone of his grandfather Captain John Brown, who died in the Revolutionary War, which he described in a letter to his wife as "Grandfather John Brown's old Granite Monument, about 80 years old; to be faced and inscribed in memory of our poor Fredk who sleeps in Kansas." It was shipped to North Elba. With added inscriptions for his sons, Oliver and Watson, killed at Harper's Ferry, and for himself, it would mark John Brown's grave.

On March 4, he published an appeal in the New York *Tribune* for funds to be sent to his treasurer, William H. D. Callender of Hartford. "It is with no little sacrifice of personal feeling that I appear in this manner before the public." We do not know how much this appeal netted, if anything. It was addressed to "THE FRIENDS OF FREEDOM," and the first paragraph read:

The undersigned, whose individual means were exceedingly limited when he first engaged in the struggle for Liberty in Kansas, being now more destitute and more anxious than in time past to continue the effort to sustain the cause, is induced to make this earnest appeal to the friends of Freedom throughout the United States, in the firm belief that his call will not go unheeded. I ask all honest lovers of Liberty and Human Rights, both male and female, to hold up my hands by contributions of pecuniary aid, either as counties, cities, towns, villages, societies, churches or individuals.

There was a significant event for the future John Brown legend when he met at Concord on March 11, Henry D. Thoreau and Ralph Waldo Emerson. These two intellectuals were to be the men who by their encomiums put the halo around Brown at the time of his execution in 1859. In his *Recollections of Seventy Years*, Sanborn, who lived in Concord, wrote that he took Brown with him at noon across the street to dine at Mrs. Thoreau's table, where Sanborn dined daily. At two o'clock he left Brown with Thoreau, discussing Kansas affairs. Brown narrated in detail to Thoreau the battle of Black Jack. While Brown sat there conversing in the early afternoon of a short winter's day, Emerson, who had just returned from his winter lecture tour, came in, as he often did, to call on Thoreau, and was introduced by him to John Brown. Emerson invited Brown to stay at his home on the second of his two days' visit to Concord.

"The three men, so celebrated, each in his own way," wrote Sanborn, "thus first met under the same roof and found they held the same opinion of what was uppermost in the mind of Brown." Thoreau gave his impressions of John Brown in this meeting in 1857: "A man of rare common-sense and directness of speech, as of action; a transcendentalist above all, a man of ideas and principles." In their talk, Brown had spoken of his experiences in Kansas "without even giving the least vent to his pent-up fire. It was a volcano with an ordinary chimney-flue."

In his speech that first night at Concord, Brown shook the reputed John Brown, Jr., chains and, according to Sanborn, "His words rose to a thrilling eloquence and made a wonderful impression on his audience." Emerson recorded in his diary that Brown "gave a good account of himself in the Town Hall last night." Emerson was charmed by Brown's description of his bucolic life in Ohio and noted it in his diary. Brown said he had three thousand sheep there, and knew them so well that he could detect instantly a strange sheep in his flock. He said that a cow by secret signals of the eye could tell its calf to run away, lie down, or hide itself. He always made friends with his horse and he could as readily sleep in the saddle as in his bed, the horse making a special effort not to give him a start.

Emerson said of Brown: "For himself, he is so transparent that all men see him through." Actually, Emerson and Thoreau did not grasp Brown at all. Giving his impression of Brown, Emerson wrote: "This is a Unionist. . . . He believes in the Union of the States and he conceives that the only obstruction to the Union is slavery and for that reason as a patriot he works for its abolition." Sanborn wrote the exact opposite to Higginson about Brown: "I believe he is the best Disunion champion you can find." With his hundred men, he could do more to split the Union than five thousand men in Higginson's Disunion Convention. Each believed what he wanted to believe, but Sanborn hit the truth.

Writing in the *Mississippi Valley Historical Review*, Gilman M.

Ostrander shows other ways in which there was no real meeting of the minds. When Brown said, "Better that a whole generation of men, women and children should be swept away than that this crime of slavery should exist one day longer," this seemed to Emerson to accord with his own statement that the whole population of South Carolina was not worth one hair of Senator Sumner's head. Emerson used this, however, as an eloquent literary convention, to honor Sumner and no more, and he could not grasp the fact that Brown meant it literally.

Sanborn gave another instance of this gap in thinking, an earthy one. Brown told Thoreau that on his European travels he found that the soil of England was rich and that of Germany poor because in England the peasantry lived on the soil they cultivated while in Germany they gathered into villages at night. This thought had a great appeal to the cloud-borne thinker Thoreau, as a Rousseauean concept of the union of man with nature. Actually, Brown had nothing abstract in mind; he only meant that in returning to their villages at night with their cattle and horses, the German peasantry took with them the natural manures which are needed for the soil.

There was a good deal of humbug and laughter in Brown. On April 16, he wrote to Eli Thayer from Springfield (Thayer at this time was his admirer and had given him a gift of arms): "One of the US Hounds is on my track; & I have kept myself hid for a few days to let my track get cold. I have no idea of being taken & *intend* (*if* '*God Will*';) to go back with Irons *in* rather than upon my hands."

He was referring to a residence in hiding in the home of Judge and Mrs. Thomas B. Russell in West Newton from April 6 to 15. He had been placed there by Parker after telling him that he was in imminent danger of arrest. Parker wrote Judge Russell that if he were in Brown's position he should shoot dead any man who attempted to arrest him for those alleged crimes. "Then I should be tried by a Massachusetts jury and be acquitted."

There is not a scintilla of evidence that anyone from Kansas was looking for Brown, but it was useful for him to dramatize himself as being in peril of his life.

He had a fine time in Judge Russell's home playing the part of the hunted desperado. He used to take out his two revolvers and a repeater every night before going to bed to make sure of their loads, announcing, "Here are eighteen lives!" He once said to Mrs. Russell,

"If you hear a noise at night, put the baby under the pillow. I should hate to spoil these carpets, too, but you know I cannot be taken."

Mrs. Russell recounted that Brown had the keenest sense of humor. He loved to imitate the talk of Negroes in long-winded, exaggerated, and magniloquent speeches. At the table, he would shock them by telling them how he had eaten joints and toes of crawling creatures they had never heard of. When he laughed, he did not make the slightest sound, not even a whisper or intake of breath but shook all over. "It was the most curious thing imaginable to see him, in utter silence rock and quake with mirth." No doubt, his spoof gave him endless, inward mirth.

While at Judge Russell's home, he came downstairs one morning with a written document, a lament over his plight. He read it aloud to Mrs. Russell:

Old Browns *Farewell*: to the Plymouth Rocks; Bunker Hill, Monuments; Charter Oaks; and Uncle Toms, Cabbins.

Has left for Kansas. Was trying since he came out of the territory to secure an outfit; or in other words *the means of arming and equiping thoroughly*; his regular minuet men: who are mixed up *with the people of Kansas*: and *he leaves the States*; with a DEEP FEELING OF SADNESS: that after having exhausted *his own small means*: and with his *family and his* BRAVE MEN: suffered hunger, nakedness, cold, sickness, (and some [of] them) imprisonment, with most barbarous, and cruel treatment: *wounds, and death*: that after lying on the ground for Months; in the most unwholesome *and* sickly; as well as uncomfortable *places*: with sick and wounded destitute of any shelter a part of the time; dependent (*in part*) on the care, and hospitality of the Indians: and hunted like Wolves: that after all this; in order to sustain a cause, which *every Citizen* of this "*Glorious Republic*," is under equal Moral obligation to do: (*and for the neglect of which* HE WILL *be held accountable* TO GOD:) in which *every Man, Woman, and Child of the entire human family*; has a *deep and awful interest*: that when *no wages* are *asked, or expected*: he cannot secure (amidst all the wealth, luxury, and extravagance of this "*Heaven exalted*" people;) even the necessary supplies, for a common soldier. "HOW ARE THE MIGHTY FALLEN?"

JOHN BROWN.

Boston, April, 1857.

He asked Mrs. Russell if she would be good enough to summon Mrs. Stearns from Medford. When Mrs. Stearns arrived, he read to her this *chef d'oeuvre.* He said: "Oh, if I could have the money that is smoked away in Boston during a single day, I could strike a blow that would make slavery totter from its foundations." He asked her advice about his sending it to the Reverend Mr. Parker as a subject for a Sunday sermon. She said no, would he give it to her so she could show it to Mr. Stearns, which is what Brown had undoubtedly planned all the while.

She was deeply moved by Old Brown's Farewell. The next morning, "The splendor of spring sunshine filled the room when I awoke." The luxury surrounding her made her wish "to comfort and aid Old John Brown. It seemed not too much to sell our estate and give the proceeds to him for his sublime purpose. What if another home were not so beautiful."

When her husband awoke, she told him her thoughts. He commended her, but said, "Would it be fair to our children to give up all we have?" Instead, he would make some other arrangement to help Old Brown. He rode out that morning to the Russell home and gave Brown a letter of credit for $7,000, but it had a condition attached to it—it could be used only for expenses when Brown was actually engaged anew in the struggle for Kansas with a hundred "volunteer-regulars" in the field.

Brown wrote to his son John Jr. on April 15 and "crowed" a little:

My collections I may safely put down at $13,000. I think I have got matters so much in train that it will soon reach $30,000. I have had a good deal of discouragement & have often felt quite depressed; but hitherto God hath helped me. About the last of last week I gave vent to those feelings in a short piece (which you may yet see in print) headed Old Brown's Farewell to the Plymouth Rocks, Bunker Hill Monuments, Charter Oaks and Uncle Toms Cabbin. The effect on a Boston merchant who saw the manuscript was that he immediately gave me a letter authorizing me to draw on him on sight for $7000 & others were also moved to be in earnest.

A theme Brown often struck was, "Help me now while I am alive since I will soon be walking into the jaws of death. I was told that the newspapers in a Certain city were dressed in mourning on hearing that I was killed & scalped in Kansas. Much good it did me. In the same place I met with a more cool reception than in any other place where I have stopped. If my friends will hold up my hands while I live, I will freely absolve them from any expence over me when I am dead."

He mentioned many times his concern about what would happen to his wife and small children if he were killed in Kansas. In a telegraph message to him, Amos Lawrence told him that in that dire event his family would be protected. On March 19, Brown wrote Lawrence: "The offer you so kindly made through the Telegraph some time since emboldens me to propose the following for your consideration. For One Thousand Dollars cash I am offered an improved piece of land which with a little improvement I now have might enable my family consisting of a Wife and Five minor children (the youngest not yet Three years old) to procure a Subsistence should I never return to them; my Wife being a good economist and real old fashioned business woman."

Lawrence replied that having donated $14,000 to Kansas he did not feel like spending more, but he reassured him that should he die for the cause, "The family of Captain Brown of Osawatomie will not be turned out to starve in this country, untill Liberty herself is driven out."

When Brown pressed this matter, a subscription for the $1,000 was pledged, Lawrence giving $310 and Stearns $260. The money was slow in coming in to fill the pledges, and in mid-May, before leaving for the West, Brown insisted that the sum be made up. He said that he had already contracted with his neighbors, the Thompsons, to buy a tract of land from them for $1,000. "I did not start the measure of getting up any subscription for me (although I was sufficiently needy as God knows)." It seems that the subscription was actually Brown's idea.

Brown wrote to Sanborn on May 15 from Gerrit Smith's home in Peterboro after he had left North Elba for the West. He put the case strongly since he knew Sanborn was unenthusiastic about the idea of giving extra emoluments to martyrs. "This, I think, is much the cheapest and most proper way to provide for them (my family), and far less humiliating to my wife, who though not above getting her bread over the washtub will never tell her trials or wants to the world." Then he deftly plucked the chord of guilt in the mind of those who merely gave money: "I would never utter a syllable in regard to it were I not conscious that I am performing a service which is equally the duty of millions who need not forgo a single hearty Dinner by the support they are called on to make."

The $1,000 was raised. Brown wanted a check to be sent for the $1,000 for the land being bought; instead, at the end of July, while

Brown was in the West, Sanborn himself went to North Elba to disburse the money.

The transaction was somewhat complicated, but it is clear that the situation was not exactly as Brown had represented it. He already owned a farm of 244 acres. The money was going for another 160-acre tract which he split and gave half to his daughter Ruth and her husband, Henry Thompson. The $1,000 was far in excess of the price of the land paid to Gerrit Smith, and $574 was paid to his in-laws, Franklin and Samuel Thompson, presumably for buildings on the farm, and the remainder was paid to Mrs. Brown, $25.45.

Sanborn passed it all off, writing to Stearns: "The subscription could not have been better bestowed and the small balance which I paid Mrs. Brown came very opportunely." Sanborn apparently felt in his own mind that he was called on to justify this subscription further and wrote again on August 27 to Stearns and Lawrence that the land was good, there were buildings on it, and it was covered with hardwood timber. "Both Mrs. Brown and Mrs. Thompson (her husband was wounded in the battle of Black Jack and who has two children) are hard-working, self-denying, devoted women, fully sensible of the greatness of the struggle in which Captain Brown is engaged and willing to bear their part of it. I can assure the subscribers to this fund that money was never better bestowed than in aiding these excellent women to maintain themselves."

In his biography, Sanborn made no editorial comment and drew no conclusion, but from his recital of the financial facts in detail it is clear what was running through his mind. It was a biographer's privilege of hyperbole when he summed up his hero: "The deed of his life sprang from a spirit as guileless, as pure, as true, and as unselfish as that of a child." Sanborn knew of Brown's human shortcomings, but these were overridden by his devotion to their cause.

Sending a Bible to his daughter Anne on October 1, 1859, soon before Harper's Ferry, Brown wrote her: "Anne, I want you first of all to become a sincere, humble and consistent Christian and then to acquire good and efficient business habits." The Christian crusade and money were intermingled. In one of his last letters to his family before the gallows, he interrupted his discourse with God to ask why he had not heard how the farm stock was doing. The historian Rhodes commented about Brown: "His intimate letters, a curious mixture of pious ejaculations and worldly details, of Scripture quotations and the price of farm products call to mind the Puritanical jargon of Cromwell's time."

Puritans tried to prosper in this life, and the Puritan conscience was always elastic on the subject of making money. In colonial times in Boston it countenanced making rum from West Indian molasses to buy Negroes on the African coast for shipment to the Western Hemisphere. Boston revolutionaries of the 1770s had been spurred by resentment about British interference with their smuggling activities. Higginson, for one, shrugged off precise knowledge he had that Brown was not a man of integrity in financial matters. Martin Stowell, who did Higginson's bookkeeping in Kansas for the Massachusetts Committee, wrote him in November, 1856, that he was crossing off the books a bad check of $100 he had cashed for John Brown. "You have doubtless heard of the hero of Osawatomie, the scourge of the Ruffians and terror of their accomplices, of his having his house destroyed and all effects stolen. . . . If you know him and his noble sacrifices, you will heartily approve of my course." This theft did not deter Higginson from sanctifying Brown in the *Liberator* of January 16, 1857, as "Old Captain Brown, the Ethan Allan, the Israel Putnam of today, who has prayers every morning and then sallies forth, with seven stalwart sons, wherever duty or danger calls, who swallows a Missourian whole, and says grace after the meat."

The Secret Six used Brown as he used them. They were aware of the fact that he made his living out of being an antislavery fighter. Brown believed he was grossly underpaid for his pain and risk—and he was right. As we have said before, he provided only a meager living for his family and the main focus for his funds was the cause. He did not line his pockets. His backers were not defrauded. In the end he performed, and performed beyond the hopes and expectations of his Boston circle of backers.

What is more relevant as to bad faith on Brown's part is the clear evidence that he never intended to do any or much fighting in Kansas. He had reached his peak there in 1856 and his mind now turned to plans of a more ambitious scope, some form of a direct assault on the South which would involve the freeing of slaves, to "carry the war into Africa." It was for this purpose that he was raising money.

Kansas at this time was tranquil. In March, 1857, the New York *Tribune* correspondent in Kansas reported: "Kansas will come in free, EASY." Brown tried to justify his projected Kansas company by saying that this might be the lull before the storm, like the peaceful Kansas winter of 1855–56, but conditions now were quite different. United States troops patrolled the Territory and the border-ruffian army was gone from the scene.

On March 2, the history of the pikes for the slaves, which showed up at Harper's Ferry, began. Charles Blair, a blacksmith and forge-master of Cantonville, Connecticut, who manufactured them for Brown, gave a detailed account in his testimony before the Mason Committee of the United States Senate which investigated Harper's Ferry.

The morning after he had delivered a lecture on Kansas at Canton-ville, Brown was at the village drug store and displayed a two-edged dirk with a blade eight inches long that Brown said he had taken from Captain Pate at Black Jack. Brown "remarked that if he had a lot of those things to attach to poles about six feet long, they would be a capital weapon of defense for the settlers of Kansas to keep in their log cabins to defend themselves against any sudden attack." Having learned that Blair, who was among the spectators, was engaged in the business of edge-tool making, he asked him what he would charge for making them. Blair said he could not commit himself offhand but he guessed $1.25 apiece for five hundred and $1 apiece for a thousand of them.

Later that day Blair was visited by Brown in his shop and he found that Brown was in earnest about his turning out a thousand pikes for $1,000. Blair said, "Mr. Brown, I am a laboring man and if I engaged in this contract with you, I shall want to know how I shall get my pay." Brown replied, "That is all right. It is just what you should, and I shall make it perfectly secure to you. I will give you one half the money, that is $500, within ten days. I will pay you the balance within thirty days, and give you ninety days to complete the contract." He wanted, however, to see a dozen samples, for which he would pay. Within a few weeks, Blair made them. Brown expressed his satisfaction, making some alteration in the type of malleable iron used, and specified that a screw should be put in so that the blade, to be eight inches long and two inches wide, could be detached.

They drew up on March 31 an informal contract on a half page of paper and Blair received $350 from Brown. Blair purchased materials, went to a handle-maker in Massachusetts to arrange for making a thousand wooden handles, purchased steel for the blades and set a man busy forging them. He received a letter dated April 2 from Springfield in which Brown said he had no further funds but hoped to have them soon, and in the next letter of April 25 from Springfield, Brown enclosed $200, making $550 or $50 more than the promised first payment. Brown now cut down on his order, saying, "If you do not hurry out but 500 of those articles it may perhaps be as well, until you hear again."

Blair wrote Brown that the handles made of ash wood were in a green state, and, unless they were seasoned, when the blades were put in they would shrink and the blades would come loose. On May 14, from Canastota, New York, Brown instructed Blair not to produce the first five hundred pikes until the wood was properly seasoned nor the remainder until he heard from him. In view of this letter and since Brown owed him another $450, Blair continued on the work only until June when he laid it all aside in an unfinished state, the handles put away in the storehouse, the steel which had been purchased and the few blades which had been forged laid away in boxes. He would not hear from Brown again until 1858.

Brown's statement that he wanted these knived-pikes for settlers in Kansas was pure nonsense. They would be useless, no match for revolvers and bowie knives. They could be a useful weapon for slaves who were unacquainted with the use of firearms, but who could wield these poles in overwhelming numbers against an enemy.

With a demonic drive, Brown pursued his long-range plan, which he held for now secret from his sponsors. His next move he adverted to in a letter to John Jr., who was in his confidence, on April 15, 1857: "Your remarks about the value & importance of discipline I fully appreciate; & I have been making arrangements to secure the assistance & instruction of a distinguished Scotch officer & author quite popular in this country. I am quite sanguine of my success in this matter."

This man was "Colonel" Hugh Forbes, with whom Brown was going to have a ton of trouble.

Forbes was forty-five years old, an Englishman, who had lived in Italy as a silk merchant in Siena. He has been described as a fly-by-night adventurer and even an imposter, but it seems that he was a man of a little substance. In *Garibaldi and the Making of Italy*, by George M. Trevelyan, Hugh Forbes is described as having shared the perils of Garibaldi's retreat from Rome to the Adriatic in 1849. *Compendio del Volontario Patriotico* by Colonello Ugo Forbes, published in Naples, was recommended by Garibaldi as a manual for Italian and other volunteers. This treatise on the art of war was composed in the

1849 retreat between Terni and Cesanatico. *The Manual of the Patriotic Volunteer* was published both in London and New York in 1855 and there are copies today in the Library of Congress. A series of four lectures by Hugh Forbes at New York University, on *Recent Events in Italy* was also published. After the events, to be recounted, of Forbes's involvement with John Brown, he returned to Italy in 1860 as a friend of Garibaldi. According to Trevelyan, Forbes recommended to Garibaldi that he raise a British legion, but Garibaldi declined to give him the command and left him behind as governor of Milazzo Castle.

After Garibaldi's failure in 1849, Forbes had moved to Paris and London. His wife and family remained in Paris while his daughter lived with him in New York. In New York City he eked out an existence, doing translating since he was an expert linguist, writing occasional articles for the New York *Tribune*, editing an Italian language newspaper, *The European*, and giving fencing lessons.

Brown met Forbes and was impressed with Forbes's military experience, his authorship of a book on warfare, and his supposed expertness on guerrilla warfare. He was impressed, too, by the suave, aristocratic manners of Forbes, and did not see the unstable, feckless adventurer, a character out of a Balzac novel. He hired Forbes for $100 a month and authorized him to draw $600 as advance pay from his treasurer, William H. D. Callender of Hartford. Forbes was to revise his *Manual of the Patriotic Volunteer* along lines that Brown wanted, a job that was to take six weeks, and was then to join Brown in Iowa, to act as drill instructor for men who, Forbes understood, were to fight to defend Kansas. Brown told him that the corps was to have a hundred men. Brown did not mention the hiring of Forbes to his backers.

In May, Brown obtained further arms. He was seeking two hundred revolvers and received a low bid of $1,300 for Maynard-primed revolvers from the Massachusetts Arms Company of Chicopee Falls, which said it was granting a discount of 50 percent from its normal price for "aiding in your project of protecting the free state settlers of Kansas." To Stearns he wrote: "Now if Rev. T Parker & other good people of Boston would make up that amount I might *at least be well armed.*" Stearns lent the money himself. Advising Brown that he would be supplied with the revolvers, he hinted that he should dally no longer in the East. "I think you ought to go to

Kansas as soon as possible and give Robinson and the rest some Backbone."

The two hundred Sharp's rifles in the Reverend Mr. Todd's cellar in Tabor, Iowa, pursue their labyrinthine course. The Massachusetts Kansas Aid Committee under the chairmanship of Mr. Stearns rescinded its previous action conveying them to Brown subject to the order of the committee and now assigned them to Mr. Stearns as security for the loan he had made to the committee to pay for these revolvers.

It was a blow to Brown that his sons refused to join him in any further Kansas enterprise. The death of Frederick, the memory of Pottawatomie, and the sufferings of John Brown, Jr., were enough for them for a lifetime. On March 31, he wrote to his wife from Springfield: "I have only to say as regards the resolution of the boys 'to learn & practice war no more' that it was not at my solicitation that they engaged in it at first & that while I feel no more love of the business than they do, still I think there may be possibly in their day what is more to be dreaded, if such things do not now exist." The great Civil War bore out this prediction.

He did not break the news to his backers that his sons would not join him in Kansas, for fear that it would impair his money-raising ventures.

He left North Elba for Kansas on May 12 but he did not arrive in Tabor until August 7. He traveled hither and yon on unknown errands. He was in Cleveland on May 22, in Milwaukee on June 16, in Chicago on June 22, and then backtracked to Ohio to be at Tallmadge on June 24.

He had to go west to make some motion for a free Kansas as a matter of trust to his sponsors. To promote his larger plan, he had to recruit men. But he seemed irresolute, facing the grim prospect of going out alone. There were recurrent spells of sickness and he was laid up at Hudson in Ohio from May 27 to June 12. He was in low spirits, and from Hudson wrote lugubriously to his wife: "If I should never return, it is my particular request that no other monument be used to keep me in remembrance than the same plain one that records the death of my grandfather and son, and that a short story like those already on it be told of John Brown the fifth. . . . I would be glad that my posterity should not only remember their parentage but also the cause they labored in." This request was carried out after his execution in 1859.

"I have talked about fighting for free Kansas for months. Now, what kind of a show can I put on in Kansas to satisfy my friends?" Brown must have pondered that question incessantly during these weeks.

There seemed no need for any "volunteer-regulars." Amos Lawrence wrote quizzically to Brown in July about any warlike plans: "We look on the great question as now settled and all political movements as having chiefly a local interest." Free-state settlers were pouring in. The new governor who followed Geary was the former Secretary of the Treasury and senator from Mississippi, Robert J. Walker, who suited both sides, the proslave because he came from the deep South, the free-staters because he promised honest elections and in a contest based on the ballot box the free-staters were sure to win. The free-state legislature met peacefully at Topeka for a four-day session on June 13 without hindrance. The only political homicide of 1857 was that of the proslave city recorder of Leavenworth by a free-state man.

If he showed his face in Kansas, Brown might be apprehended as a suspected murderer. John Brown, Jr., feared that his former friends would "hand you over." He wrote his father: "It seems as though if you return to Kansas this Spring I should never see you again. But I will not look on the dark side. You have gone safely through a thousand perils and hairbreadth escapes." Edmund B. Whitman, agent of the National Kansas Committee, assured Brown from Lawrence on June 30 that he need have no fear. "Your friends are desirous of seeing you. The danger that threatened the Territory and *individuals* have been removed in the shape of quashed indictments. Your furniture [meaning his arms] can be brought in and safely stored while you are looking for a location." He said he was sending young Richard Realf to Tabor with $150 of the committee's funds. Realf arrived there on July 6 and since Brown had not yet arrived he left for him a letter containing $110, deducting $40 for his expenses. We shall hear more of this Realf.

From Ohio, Brown wrote to friends in Kansas to get their assessment of the political temper in the Territory. He wrote in April to Augustus Wattles in Lawrence using the assumed name of Nelson Hawkins, and in June the name of James Smith. Brown would operate under fake names for the rest of his days, whether from necessity to conceal his identity, from expediency, or from the whimsy which was strong in his makeup. In the latter letter, he assured Wattles that he was on his way to Kansas and "Free-State men need have no fear of my *desertion*." Wattles' reply brimmed over with nonurgency: "Come as quickly as possible, or not come at present, as you choose." Brown wrote in early June in the same vein to the New York *Tribune* correspondent in Lawrence, William A. Phillips, who also answered rather frigidly that he saw no need for military measures at this juncture, he would not go to Tabor to confer with Brown, and he did not know anyone else who would. The prevailing atmosphere in Kansas was one in which the progress being made toward a free state might be impaired by the extremist, Brown, as the moderates saw it.

Shun the ballot box and the political apparatus, uproot the bogus proslave legislature by force. That was Brown's advice as expressed in choice language to Wattles. "I bless God that he has not left the free-state men of Kansas to pollute themselves by the foul and loathesome embrace of the old rotten whore. I have been trembling all along lest they might back down from the high and holy ground they had taken. . . . I would most gladly give my hand to all whose 'garments are not defiled' and I humbly trust that I shall soon again have the opportunity to rejoice (or suffer *further* if need be) with you, in the strife between Heaven and Hell."

Wattles and others, who did not want "strife," gave Brown the cold shoulder. He had arms and was for that reason welcomed by Whitman. The only other encouragement that Brown received was in a letter from his lieutenant in the 1856 raiding, James H. Holmes, who wrote that the secretary of state for the Territory, Frederick B. Stanton, had announced that the laws of the bogus legislature would be enforced. "There will be no voting; no paying of taxes; and I think the Free-State men will remove the Territorial Government and set up their own. Then we want you." That could be a long way off.

Encouraged or discouraged, Brown had to push on. His son Owen, probably the most attached to him of his sons, changed his mind about fighting "no more" and left North Elba to rejoin his father. The two with a hired teamster plodded across Iowa in two wagons. To save money, they "lived exclusively on herring, soda crackers & sweetened water for more than three weeks (sleeping every night in our waggons), except that twice we got a little milk and a few times some boiled eggs." So Brown recounted to Sanborn by letter. On

August 7, Brown arrived at Tabor where the precious Sharp's rifles, so vital to his plans, were stored in the Reverend Mr. Todd's cellar.

Two days after Brown reached Tabor, "Colonel" Hugh Forbes arrived there by a different route, having taken a boat on the Missouri River. Forbes was the first to learn of the Virginia expeditionary plan, apart from Brown's own family. John Brown, Jr. knew of it, and Brown discussed it with Owen en route to Tabor.

Forbes had been hard to handle in the very first weeks of his employment. The work of revising his book went on and on, and Forbes wanted more money. Joseph Bryant, Brown's friend, visited Forbes in New York, and Forbes told him he needed money to bring his wife and children over from Paris. "He thinks they will have to come in on the third-class passage which grieves him very much as his wife is not in good health." Brown was so irked that he wrote Bryant to request Forbes to refund the $600. Forbes told Bryant he had used up almost the entire amount. "I did not say anything about his refunding as he assured me in the most positive way he could that he would set out as soon as he got his book finished, which would be done in about a week." Forbes gave up the idea of sending for his family in Paris and instead shipped his daughter there to join her mother.

Finally, Forbes said he had finished the job. Bryant offered to find a publisher but the new manual remained in manuscript. Forbes now, before going west, set about to sponge up as much money as he could. He had free-lanced for the New York *Tribune*, and called on Horace Greeley in the *Tribune* offices. (Greeley in October, 1859, dredged up his memory of Forbes after the Forbes story appeared in print from documents Brown carried with him to Harper's Ferry.) He told Greeley that he was going to Kansas to fight for the cause. Greeley gave him $20 and other free-state sympathizers in New York contacted by Greeley made up about a $700 donation. Greeley recalled: "He went—was absent some weeks—came back. That was all I knew of his service to the free-state cause in any shape."

Forbes knew of and was highly impressed by Brown's top-echelon backers. On his own initiative, he visited Gerrit Smith at Peterboro, introduced himself as Brown's intimate associate and asked for money. He was a smooth salesman, and Smith gave him $150, writing to Thaddeus Hyatt that he thought Forbes would "prove very useful to our sacred work in Kansas."

When Forbes reached Tabor, Brown unburdened himself of his innermost thoughts about his Grand Design. They had an extensive debate about military tactics and objectives in the southern expedition, Forbes giving Brown the benefit of such experience as he had in warfare abroad, and a sober common-sense appraisal.

Into the fabric of this tale are woven strands that seem surrealist fantasy, such as this bizarre scene in an Iowa hamlet of two men putting their heads together to overthrow the curse of slavery afflicting the nation—one a middle-aged, penniless, European drifter living by his wits, and the other a man of fifty-seven who had led a life of failure, capped in 1856 by deeds of murder and violence for which responsible men in Kansas regarded him as a pariah, who had about $100 in his pocket and had serving under him only one man, his son. Yet this man, Brown, did manage to give the South the biggest scare it ever had.

One feature of Brown's plan, as he unveiled it to Forbes, was nothing short of diabolical. He had only contempt for state militia which he had fought at Black Jack and Osawatomie, but United States troops were another matter, and he realized that when he would "carry the war into Africa," he would come into conflict with them.

Brown had long pondered the problem. His answer was a bold one. He would repel the threat and augment his own force by persuading the United States soldier to desert his flag and join him, or as he put it, "to exchange the service of Satan for that of God." The material reward would be that the Army private would get from him an officer's commission to lead slaves. Beyond that, he would appeal above his oath of allegiance to the soldier's better instincts. The manual that Brown had assigned Forbes on guerrilla warfare was a minor matter. He wanted Forbes to prepare an appeal to the United States soldier to desert, which would be the major chapter in *The Manual of the Patriotic Volunteer*.

This is one of Brown's more interesting ideas, and we will dwell briefly on it. The following year this opus was enlarged by Brown's aide and literary amenuensis, John Henry Kagi, who had an intellect superior to that of Brown or Forbes. The chapter, "The Duty of a Soldier," was "Presented with respectful and kind feelings to the Officers and Soldiers of the United States Army in Kansas" (Brown was concealing his Virginia Plan). It proclaimed that there are two warring principles in the world, Right and Wrong, and there can be

no compromise between them. This was the absolutist Brown talking. He also wrote that "Right cannot alter though it may shine more
beautiful under persecution." Soldiers must not be "vile living machines and thus sustain Wrong against Right." In the draft Brown sent
Augustus Wattles in 1857 he added as a postscript that a citizen soldier must govern his actions, "*as though he was President of the
United States.*" In the 1858 version there is some deeper thinking,
obviously from Kagi's pen: "In ancient times the term soldier was
synonymous with freeman. Indeed, there are instances in ancient history in which the soldiery in camp was consulted on public affairs
and gave its vote on the great questions of Right against Wrong, and
in some cases the soldier was the first part of a nation to proclaim the
supremacy of Right."

Brown sent copies to Sanborn and Parker, together with requests
for money. Sanborn expressed disapproval of the crude attempt at
seduction of the soldier, saying that the attempted subversion of national authority would be futile. The unsophisticated Gerrit Smith,
who bubbled with enthusiasm, was delighted with the draft he received from Forbes and rewarded him with $25 for his starving
family.

Forbes would make his principal contribution, Brown advised him,
by setting up and supervising three military academies to train men
for fighting in Virginia—one in Iowa, another in northern Ohio, and
a third in Canada. At the moment, Forbes had only two men to drill,
Brown and his son Owen, who had a crippled right arm from childhood and therefore could not make much of a soldier. Brown wrote
his wife: "We are beginning to take Lessons & have (we think) a
very capable Teacher." Forbes became increasingly convinced that
Brown was an impractical dreamer. He asked him for more money
and Brown replied that he had paid him $600 until October 1. He
had arrived in Tabor with $30, he had found there the $110 left by
Richard Realf in July, and further funds were coming in driblets
from the East. Out of the little he had, he gave Forbes all he could
spare, $60. They parted company on November 3, not on the friend-
liest terms, Brown accompanying Forbes as far as Nebraska City,
where Forbes boarded a wagon headed eastward.

Brown took possession of the two hundred Sharp's rifles in the
Reverend Mr. Todd's cellar and moved them to a barn. He had been
authorized by the Massachusetts Kansas Aid Committee to take pos-

session of them subject to their order. Now, since they were assigned as security to Stearns by the Massachusetts Committee, he took them subject to Stearns' order. He found them, he told Sanborn, in "middling good order," and cleaned those that were rusted.

Taking inventory of the situation: Brown had no money, and after Forbes went East, he had no drillmaster—but then he had no men to drill.

On the other side of the balance sheet: Brown had possession, without title, of two hundred of the very best rifles. He owned the ammunition for them, he owned two hundred revolvers, and miscellaneous equipment. He had paid more than half the cost for a thousand pikes to arm slaves. From Tabor, for the first time, he informed Sanborn about the order for the pikes, asking him to trust his judgment as to their usefulness for Kansas settlers. They were "cheap but effectual weapons to place in the hands of entirely unskilful and impractical men which will not easily get out of order and require no ammunition . . . wise military men may ridicule the idea but *I* take the whole responsibility of the job."

On the plus side, too, Brown had rich and powerful friends on whom he could count if he did not lose their friendship. His nerve was as strong as it was in the early days in Pennsylvania when a worker in his employ said that, "for courage and determination Napoleon or General Jackson was never more than his equal." Then, too, over the years he had become more convinced that he was the Lord's anointed man of valor, his Gideon. *Nil desperandum*. He was well along on the road to Harper's Ferry.

In Tabor he faced a dilemma and he was to linger there motionless from August 7 to November 2, deliberating his course. If he made some foray into Kansas it could be remunerative since he could dip deeply into the $7,000 letter of credit from Stearns. He might cover himself with glory, enhance the respect his eastern friends had for him, and gain recruits. On the other hand, the risks were extremely high. He might be engaged by federal troops, lose his arms, be captured and even exterminated, which naturally would be the end of his plan to "carry the war into Africa."

The political situation since he had started in transit for Kansas was as unpromising for him as before. Free-state men had boycotted the election on June 15 of delegates to the constitutional convention at Lecompton, branding it as a rigged proslave maneuver. There was a free-state convention on July 15, presided over by Lane, which set elections on August 9 for officers in the free-state government of Kansas. This election took place two days after Brown's arrival in Tabor, and about 7,200 votes were cast as compared with only 2,200 votes for delegates to the Lecompton convention, showing a heavy preponderance of free-state men in Kansas.

The free-state men, following the course of the ballot box, ignored the advice of radicals like Brown not to "pollute themselves by the foul and loathesome embrace of the old, rotten whore." On August 21, Augustus Wattles wrote him that "those who had entertained the idea of resistance have entirely abandoned the idea." Only James H. Holmes, whom Brown in 1856 had dubbed his "little hornet" for his success in cattle-stealing, encouraged him to return. "Several times we have needed you very much." Holmes obviously yearned for a resumption of their old sport. He talked of the "business for which I believe you have a stock of material with you," and "If you wish other employments, I presume you will find just as *profitable* ones."

Brown's inclination to do nothing whatever in Tabor is indicated in a letter he wrote to his wife within ten days of his arrival. "Should no disturbance occur; we may possibly think it best to work back eastward. Cannot determine yet."

His letters to Sanborn show that he was preparing him and the others for a policy of inaction, while wondering how they would react to it. "I am still waiting here for company additional teams & means of paying expences or to know that I can make a diversion in favor of our friends in case they are involved in trouble." That was the only role he could see for himself, to "make a diversion." Then, significantly revealing his ultracautious intentions, he asked Sanborn to please tell Stearns that "provided I do not get into such a speculation as shall swallow up all the property I have been furnished with, I intend to keep it safe so that he may be remunerated in the end."

He prepared Stearns directly for indefinite delay. "I am now waiting further advice from Free State friends in Kansas with whom I have speedy private communications. I am at this moment unable to move very much from an injury of my back." Then another letter to Stearns. He was "in immediate want of from Five Hundred to One Thousand Dollars for *secret service and no questions asked.*" He expected "rather interesting times" in Kansas, "But no great excitement is reported. Our next advices may entirely change the aspect of things, I hope the friends of Freedom will respond to my call & 'prove me herewith.' "

A month after he set up residence in Tabor, Brown commenced a correspondence with James H. Lane that seems almost *opera bouffe*. Lane knew that Brown had a large supply of arms. He did not know that Brown held the rifles only for Stearns and subject to his order.

On September 7, Lane wrote Brown from Lawrence that he and others were perfecting an organization to protect the ballot box at the October 5 election for territorial delegate and members of the legislature—which was merely a pretense for his request. "We want you with *all the materials* you have. I see no objection to your coming to Kansas publicly. I can furnish you just such a force as you may deem necessary for your protection here & after you arrive." Brown had absolutely no intention of turning over his arms to Lane but apparently decided to play along to see what he could get out of it. He wrote back that he had a "strong desire" to see Lane, and "as to the job of work you enquire about I suppose that three good teams with well covered waggons & ten really ingenious, industrious men (not gassy) with about $110 in cash, could bring it about in the course of eight or ten days."

Lane's first letter was addressed, "Sir." His next letter of September 29 was addressed, "Dear General," since he had appointed Brown a "Brigadier-General 2nd Brigade 1st Division." He was enclosing all the cash he had, $50, and was dispatching "ten true men." He said that "it is *all important* to Kansas that your things should be in at the *earliest possible moment* & that you should be much nearer at hand than you are." The reply from Brown of September 30 said that he was returning the $50 by the emissary, "Gen'l Jamison." He explained that "it will be next to impossible in my poor state of health to go through on such very short notice, four days only remaining to get ready load up & go through. I think, considering all the uncertainties of the case want of teams etc. that I *should do wrong to set out. I am disappointed in the extreme.*"

The disappointment was about the small sum of money, as he wrote frankly to E. B. Whitman in Lawrence five days later. He was sending Charles P. Tidd, a youth who had just joined him, to Whitman for more money. "The fifty dollars Lane sent was only about enough to pay up my board bill here with all I had in hand. I need not say my disappointment has been extreme." On October 24, Whitman wrote that he was sending by Tidd $150 he had scraped up. "General Lane will send teams from Fall City so that you may get your guns all in. Make the Tabor people wait for what you owe them. They must."

Why Lane wanted the arms after the October 5 election was over is a mystery. Robinson later speculated that half-crazy Lane intended an armed assault on the Lecompton convention, which was drafting a proslave constitution for Kansas. At any rate, from Fall City on October 30, Lane wrote Brown: "I trust this money will be used to get the guns to Kansas or as near as possible. If you will get them to this point we will try to get them on in some way. The probability is that Kansas will never need the guns. One thing is certain, if they are to do any good, it will be in the next few days."

Brown filched the money. He did enter Kansas immediately there-after but alone and without any guns except his own revolver. On November 5 he arrived at the home of E. B. Whitman. He received money, tents, and bedding from Whitman, and then after staying with him for two days he disappeared. The exasperated Whitman wrote to Stearns: "Brown then left, declining to tell me or anyone where he was going or where he could be found, pledging himself, however, that if difficulties should occur he would be on hand and pledging his life to redeem Kansas from slavery. Since then nothing has been heard of him and I know of no one, not even his most intimate friends, who know where he is."

By now, Brown had accurately gauged the temper of his eastern friends. He would not lose their favor by not entering the field against the foe. They would be just as happy if he did nothing. They were concerned with salving their conscience by good works and good intentions and getting an "E" for effort. This is abundantly clear from a letter Stearns sent him on November 7: "In my opinion the Free State party should wait for the Border-ruffian moves and checkmate them as they are developed. Don't attack them, but if they attack you, 'Give them Jessie' and Frémont besides." (The reference was to Jessie Frémont.) Brown disposed of his entire Kansas mission of 1857 and Mr. Whitman by writing to Stearns: "I find matters quite unsettled; but am decidedly of the opinion that there will be no use for the Arms or ammunition here before another Spring. I have them all safe & together unbroken & mean to keep them so until I can see how the matter will be finally terminated. I have many calls upon me for their distribution, but shall do no such thing until I am satisfied they are really needed."

For many weeks Brown had been truly perplexed about his course.

He had no motive to dissemble with his sister and brother-in-law, the Adairs, and to them he wrote on October 5, "*How to act now*; I do not know." His quandary had been finally dissolved, and free from doubts he set in motion his Virginia plan, which he scheduled for the following year, 1858. He would recruit men now in earnest. The assembling of the Harper's Ferry men begins.

Owen Brown, unmarried, was the second oldest of John Brown's men in the raid. At this time he was thirty-three years old. He would be one of the five to make good their escape and he was to live to 1889, outliving all other participants in the raid.

Charles Plummer Tidd, who was now working for Brown, would be another of the five who escaped, but three years later he gave his life for the Union cause in the Civil War. He was twenty-three years old at this time. A native of Maine, he had little education and had come to Kansas in 1856. He was described as conveying the impression of "a clever, handy mechanic."

Brown was operating quietly now as he recruited men. He wrote the Adairs: "I do not wish to have any noise about me at present as I do not mean to 'trouble Israel.'" While at Whitman's home on November 5, Brown sent for John Cook who had joined him in June, 1856, after the battle of Black Jack, and left after the company was dispersed by Colonel Sumner. Brown told Cook vaguely that he was organizing a force "for stopping the aggressions of the pro-slavery men," and Cook volunteered his services.

John Edwin Cook, now twenty-seven years old, was to escape from Harper's Ferry but was captured near Chambersburg, Pennsylvania, and was returned to Virginia under circumstances of very bad luck. He was tried and executed at Charlestown on December 16, 1859. While the attention of the outside world was focused on Brown, the people living in Harper's Ferry were far more interested in Cook—all of which will be explained later.

Alexander K. McClure, who was hired as Cook's lawyer when he was brought to Chambersburg, recorded his astonishment when he met him. Could this be Cook, one of the most ferocious of John Brown's men? He was short, not more than five feet five inches tall. He had long, silky-blond hair, curled about his neck, and effeminate, white skin, "his deep, blue eyes were gentle in expression as a woman's." In a conversation with him, McClure thought he was "in the library of some romantic lover of literature and the fine arts."

Cook came from a fine family in Haddam, Connecticut. He attended Yale and studied law in New York. At the time of the Harper's Ferry event, his sister was the wife of the governor of Indiana, Ashbel P. Willard.

He was impulsive, fervid, and eloquent. Salmon Brown, who got to know Cook in Kansas and Ohio, was fascinated with him. "Cook was more than high-strung—he was highly erratic and not overly stocked with morality. He was the best pistol-shot I ever saw. When the ducks and geese flew over us on the road, he would always bring one down. He was just as much of an expert in getting into the good graces of the girls wherever we stopped. He would have a girl in a corner telling them stories or repeating to them poetry in such a high-faluting manner that they would laugh to kill thunder."

Cook recommended Luke F. Parsons and Richard Realf, who joined Brown. Neither one would participate in the Harper's Ferry raid. Realf is particularly interesting. He was a talented poet and his poems have appeared in volumes and singly in various anthologies. He was born in Sussex County, England, in 1834, the son of a rural constable, which put him socially one step higher than an agricultural laborer. As a boy he revealed promising talent as a poet, and various of the local gentry showed interest in him. He became a protégé of Lady Byron, the poet's widow. A book of his poems, *Guesses at the Beautiful*, was published when he was sixteen, and he was regarded by some, such as the poet Leigh Hunt, as a new Shelley. While staying at the home of one of Lady Byron's cousins in Leicestershire he seduced his host's young daughter and fled in the scandal. He became a vagabond, Villon-style, at Brighton and Southhampton, singing his ballads in the streets, living on pennies thrown to him. His relatives gave him money to go to New York; he worked at a settlement house, and then drifted to Kansas where he became wrapped up in the free-state movement. Brown was to hold him in high regard and affection.

Accompanied by Cook, Realf, and Parsons, Brown came to Topeka on November 14, and there he lined up the two most important members of his corps. The first was Aaron Dwight Stevens, then twenty-six years old, who would be seriously wounded at Harper's Ferry, tried, and executed at Charlestown on March 16, 1860. He stands out as the strongest and most attractive of the personalities clustered around Brown. George B. Gill, who would soon enlist, recalled in 1893: "Stevens—how gloriously he sang! He was the noblest soul I ever knew . . . one of nature's noble men if ever there was one. Generous and brave, impulsive and loving, one cannot speak too well or too kindly of him."

He was born in New London County, Connecticut, of fine New England stock, his great-grandfather having been an officer in the Revolutionary War. At the age of sixteen, he ran away and joined the Massachusetts Volunteer Regiment in the Mexican War and was honorably discharged. He went home to Connecticut but yearning for more excitement he enlisted as a bugler in a United States dragoon regiment serving in the far West, and took part in fighting Navaho and Apache in New Mexico. While the regiment was marching back to Fort Leavenworth, he saw a major club a private for disobeying a petty order. Stevens in a rage fell on the major, beating his bugle out of shape on his head. He dragged a ball and chain across the plains to Fort Leavenworth where he was tried by court-martial and sentenced to be shot. President Pierce, on a plea for clemency by some officers, commuted the sentence to three years' hard labor in the guardhouse.

He escaped in January, 1856, hiding among the Indians on the Kaw River. He then appeared in the free-state cause and as a good soldier formed several mounted companies into the Second Regiment of Free-State Volunteers, which he commanded as Captain and later Colonel Charles Whipple. The regiment saw action at Indianola, Osawkee, Tecumseh, Fort Titus, and other points and protected the emigrant route south from Nebraska.

He was striking-looking, Hinton describing him as "handsome and active as a young, Greek gladiator." He was six feet, two inches tall in his stockinged feet and had a powerful though graceful frame. He was the only one of the participants at Harper's Ferry (aside from the black men) whose hair was not light. He had raven-black, curly hair and a full beard from the time of his appearance in Kansas in 1856. His father and elder brothers had taught singing; he had been a choirboy, and he regaled the company at night with his rich, baritone voice.

Stevens' skill in the use of the saber was remarkable, and when he joined Brown he became drillmaster of the company, taking the place of the vanished Forbes. Brown cited him as an example of a United States soldier who had "exchanged the service of Satan for that of God," but the change had not been voluntary on Stevens' part.

John Henry Kagi, who threw in his lot with that of Brown's, was to be Brown's right-hand man. He was then twenty-two years old and was to die at Harper's Ferry on October 17, 1859. He was mentally the best endowed of the company. George Gill recalled: "His fertility of resources made him a tower of strength to John Brown. He was a logician of more than ordinary ability. He was full of wonderful vitality and all things were fit food for his brain." He was born in Bristolville, Ohio, of Swiss descent; his father was the village blacksmith. Kagi was largely self-taught and knew Latin and French well enough to teach them.

He taught school in Hawkinstown, Virginia, when he was nineteen, and became an Abolitionist from seeing slavery at first hand. After voicing his views, he lost his job and left the state. He went west and was admitted to the bar in Nebraska City when he turned twenty-one. His talents were manifold. He could make money as a court stenographer or shorthand reporter. He was a correspondent for several eastern papers, and Brown termed him "our Horace Greeley."

He was infuriated on seeing Colonel Sumner's dispersion of the free-state legislature at Topeka on July 4, 1856, and joined Colonel Whipple's regiment on the spot. Federal forces took him prisoner in November and he was in jail for four months before being released on bail.

He resumed reporting for eastern papers. Judge Rush Elmore had been notified by President Buchanan that he would not be reappointed to the bench in Kansas. In a report, Kagi told of a court ruling that Elmore had made and added that Buchanan needed no excuse to fire an incompetent judge like that. One morning Elmore encountered Kagi outside the building in Tecumseh, not far from Topeka, where Elmore was holding court. Elmore charged into Kagi, wielding his gold-plated cane. Blood streamed from Kagi's head as he pursued the judge, revolver in hand, while Elmore darted from pillar to pillar, firing his own revolver at Kagi. Finally, he disabled Elmore with a shot in the groin. A bullet fired by Elmore had struck Kagi in the breast but had been deflected by a book in his breastpocket so that it bounced harmlessly into a rib where it was cut out with a penknife. Kagi would say ever after: "Don't ever believe that books don't have value. I owe my life to one."

Kagi was recovering from his headwounds from the match with Elmore when he joined Brown. He was stringy-tall and his features were angular. He slouched around unkempt and unshaven and he was as unimpressive in appearance as Stevens was impressive. His temperament was serene and he was imperturbable in the face of the worst rebuff.

Brown left Topeka and headed northward toward Nebraska City with these young activists who were thrilled to serve under Osawatomie Brown. While in camp on a prairie, Brown informed them that they were leaving Kansas to attend a military school for the winter. The party split up and they met in Tabor in the last week of November. John Brown's force which assembled there included his son Owen, Cook, Stevens, Kagi, Tidd, Realf, a black man, Richard Richardson, who was a fugitive slave from Kentucky, Parsons, and Charles Moffet.

Another was one who was destined to be a participant at Harper's Ferry, and the youngest member, William H. Leeman. At the tender age of twenty he would die at Harper's Ferry on October 17, 1859. He came from Maine, had little education, having gone to work in a shoe factory at Haverhill, Massachusetts, when he was fourteen. He had joined John Brown's Volunteer Regulars in September, 1856, and he had fought under him at Osawatomie.

In his confession in his last days, Cook wrote: "We stopped some days at Tabor, making preparations to start. *Here we found that Captain Brown's ultimate destination was the state of Virginia.*"

The news that they were Virginia-bound, to be hurled against the strongest slave state, was greeted with doubts and protests. Parsons and Realf actually resigned but then returned to the fold. The men had no money and nothing else in view—Brown had a plan and now had money. He had received almost $600 from Sanborn in response to his request for money *"for secret service and no questions asked."* They left Tabor for the East, thinking that the war college would be set up in Ashtabula, Ohio. The wagons were heavily loaded with arms, including the Sharp's rifles which had been stored in Tabor, and so the men walked.

As they went onward to the East, their spirits rose. John Brown and his tremendous will-power exerted a magnetic influence over his flock who, with the exception of Owen Brown, were in years mere boys and waifs of society. When twenty-four-year-old Edwin Coppoc, captured at Harper's Ferry, was asked why he had participated in the raid despite the grave misgivings he said that he had about the target chosen by Brown, he replied, "Ah, Gentlemen, you don't know Captain Brown. When he wants a man to do a thing, the man does it."

Brown rhapsodized on his great purpose, according to Parsons' account, telling them that he had been created by God to be the deliverer of the slaves as Moses had delivered the children of Israel. They would be privileged to share in this historic work. As time went on, they became increasingly excited, tasting the same intoxicant wildroot as had Brown and like him they dreamed of glory and conquest. Centuries ago, Aristotle wrote, "Youth is easily deceived because it is quick to hope." The expanding vistas of their thought is indicated by an entry in a diary kept by Owen Brown. On December 8, only four days after leaving Tabor, on a very cold, snowy night with prairie wolves howling around them, they had a "hot discussion upon the Bible and war . . . warm argument upon the effects of the abolition of slavery upon the Southern States, Northern States, commerce and manufacture, also upon the British provinces and the civilized world; whence came our civilization and origin?"

G. W. Brown of the Lawrence *Herald of Freedom* said that Socrates had been condemned on perjured evidence for corrupting the youth of Athens, but it required no perjured evidence to convict Brown not only of corrupting fine youths but of inciting them to horrible crime and sending them to early deaths.

Brown knew well how to play on the aspirations of these directionless youths. If they followed him their lives would take on meaning, they would turn from unpersons to persons. He himself, he said, had been an unperson until he embraced the antislavery cause, deserting all else in life. He would shower on them high offices in a phantom government and commissions in a nonexistent army. But it was not all his doing. Kansas had corrupted these boys. They had smelled blood there. Their above-the-law, adventure-filled lives had made them restless and spoiled them for normal quietude.

The troop passed through Marengo on Christmas Day, went fifteen miles beyond Iowa City to a Quaker settlement known as the Pedes settlement. They had trudged two hundred and fifty miles over the dreary landscape of Iowa. Some took quarters in an inn known as Traveller's Rest in West Branch. (In this town the Quaker Herbert Hoover was born seventeen years later.) Others moved into the house of John H. Painter at Springdale.

The Quakers were friendly to the man they were aware was

Osawatomie Brown. They were confirmed Abolitionists, though of the nonresistant type. Rumors about the Pottawatomie massacre and Brown's connection with it had penetrated here. A leading citizen said to Brown right after his arrival, "Thou art welcome to tarry among us, but we have no use for thy guns."

To North Elba, Brown wrote on December 30 that the trip across Iowa was hard, since they had to camp out every night but one. "The persons I have with me are mostly well-tried men. Some of them have acted with me before; & all of them are pledged to stand by the work."

During Christmas Week, Brown's backers in Boston were jolted and perplexed by abusive letters written by "Colonel" Hugh Forbes.

Forbes had been dazzled by the prestigious names listed by Brown to him as his financial sponsors, the "humanitarians," as Forbes dubbed them. The fizzle of his visit to Brown at Tabor had been a blow to his hopes of cashing in, and worse, Brown, after giving him a mere $60, had apparently given him the sack. There was no doubt, however, that Brown did hold the confidence of these important men, and desperate as he was, Forbes would try to squeeze money out of them.

Brown had given Forbes when he returned from Tabor a letter to Frederick Douglass in Rochester. Douglass was unfavorably impressed, but since Brown had asked him to help out as he could, he put Forbes up in a hotel and paid his board. Affected by the story of the plight of Forbes's family in Paris, Douglass gave him some money, and introduced him to a German lady in New York City who introduced Forbes to her German friends. Douglass said Forbes "soon wore them out by endless begging." Forbes paid a visit to Horace Greeley at the New York *Tribune*, and ranted to him that he had been "deceived, misled, swindled, beggared, his family in Paris turned into the streets to starve." Greeley tried to ascertain who had deceived him, what promises had been made to him, but with no success. Forbes clammed up and would say only it was "someone."

With his European background, Forbes identified the plans he heard from Brown as the standard secret conspiracy and the Boston circle as the secret council behind the revolutionary plot. There might be gold for him by threatening to expose it. He wrote two letters to Senator Charles Sumner in Washington saying that he had been grossly abused by John Brown who was carrying out a plan (he did not define it) at the behest of Boston men, naming Sanborn as one of them. Sumner forwarded the letters to Sanborn, who had himself received a letter along the same line from Forbes, with an unmistakable threat to disclose something or other.

Sanborn, not having a glint of knowledge of Brown's Virginia plan, was mystified. Sanborn informed Parker of these letters. "Now, if it were not for his wife and children, who are undoubtedly in suffering, the man might be hanged for all me, for his whole style towards me is a combination of insult and lunacy." Yet, Sanborn feared there was something to this, that there had been some form of agreement between Brown and Forbes though Brown had told him nothing of it.

Sanborn wrote Forbes that he personally had nothing to fear from his threats. "You are at liberty to speak, write or publish what you please about me, only be careful to keep within the limits of your knowledge." It was true he had helped Brown in his work for a free-Kansas and he would continue to help Brown at any sacrifice. Sanborn sent Forbes $10, saying, "I can excuse much to one who has so much reason for anxiety as you have in the distress of your family."

As this year of 1857 drew to a close, Sanborn was filled with a great uneasiness. The news from Brown about the $550 spent for the pikes had been a surprise to him. Now Forbes must be alluding to some plan of a new dimension. What was this all about? He wrote urgently to Brown asking him to enlighten his friends concerning his arrangement with Forbes.

He would soon see Brown who would tell him all—or rather, all Sanborn needed to know. Abandoning his intention to go on to Ohio, Brown established his war college at Springdale, and leaving the boys there, he departed from Springdale alone on January 15 for the eastern seaboard and his friends.

CHAPTER FIVE

Conspiracy for "Mighty Conquest"

I believe when you come to look at the *ample field* I labour in & the rich harvest which (not only in this entire country, but) the whole world during the present and future generations *may reap* from its cultivation: you will feel that you are out of your element unless you are in it; an entire Unit. . . . And then how little we can possibly loose? Certainly the cause is enough to live for; if not to [omitted word] for. I have only had this one opportunity in a life of nearly Sixty years & could I be continued Ten times as long again, I might not again have another equal opportunity.

I expect nothing but to "endure hardness": but I expect to effect a mighty conquest even though it be like the last victory of Samson. I felt for a number of years in earlier life a steady, strong desire; to die: but since I saw a prospect of becoming a "reaper" in the great harvest I have not only felt quite willing to live; but have enjoyed life much & am now rather anxious to live for a few years more.

This is from a letter Brown sent to Sanborn from Peterboro, New York, on February 24, 1858, in which he invited Sanborn to join as a member of his Virginia expedition, the plan for which he had revealed to him two days before. Sanborn must have felt a stab of pain when he came to this letter in his biography. "I listened in vain through months of doubt and anxiety for a clear and certain call." Nonetheless, he had not lacked the courage to raise money, so that, while he had not missed a "single hearty Dinner," John Brown could go on to suffering and death.

"Till I follow my noble friend to the other world on which his hopes were fixed, I can never read this letter without emotion." When he first read it, it had removed all lingering doubts in his mind. "We saw this lonely and obscure old man, choosing poverty before wealth, renouncing the ties of affection, throwing away his ease, his reputation and his life for the sake of a despised race. . . . It was revealed to me that no confidence could be too great, no trust or affection too extreme toward this aged, poor man whom the Lord had chosen as his Champion."

Beside his blood-sacrifice, what complaint could be made about the methods used by Brown? As Brown was now inveigling impressionable youths to follow him, he was sucking in the wise men of Boston. With inexorable determination, he was bending weaker wills to his purpose. In 1857 he had obtained money and arms to fight in Kansas, which he had never intended to waste there. Now, in 1858, he asked for more money to stage a foray into the South, but he was not frank as to the nature and scope of the expedition he had in mind. From letters he wrote long after the Harper's Ferry raid, it is clear that Sanborn felt that he and his associates had been duped. But on what higher ground could they stand to cast reproach on Brown since they had hired a mercenary to do their work?

On his way east, Brown stopped off at West Andover in Ohio to visit with his son John Brown, Jr. On January 28 he arrived at the home of Frederick Douglass in Rochester where he would stay until February 17 working on his great plan. He insisted on paying his board to Douglass, and Douglass, who wanted him under his roof, charged him $3 a week.

We can be reasonably certain as was Sanborn that it was at this time and not in 1847, as Douglass wrote in his autobiography, that Brown discussed his Virginia project. Sanborn and others of the Six never set down in detail what Brown laid before them, but it undoubtedly was a repeat of what he told Douglass, who, in his autobiography, gave a detailed report.

Brown said he did not contemplate an uprising of the slaves since an insurrection would only defeat his purpose, but he did propose the creation of an armed force which would operate in the very heart of the South. He would place them in the mountains of the Great Black Way of the Appalachians which was the route of runaway slaves through the Carolinas and Virginia to southern Ohio. "These mountains are the basis of my plan," he said. "God has given the strength of the hills to Freedom. They were placed here for the emancipation of the Negro race." He knew these mountains well. They were full of good hiding-places and natural forts where one man could fight off a hundred.

He planned to run off slaves from the South. He would start with a force of twenty-five and expand it to a hundred. Those who were of judicious temperament and had persuasive tongues would go down into the fields and ask men to escape, choosing the most daring bucks. The slaves whom he would not incorporate into his hundred-man force he would assist to get to the free states of the North and from there to Canada. By this method, the institution of slavery would be gradually undermined and unsettled by making it insecure and masters would have to sell their slaves to plantations farther and farther south. Douglass pointed to weaknesses in his plan. How could he prevent the enemy from cutting off his supplies, and then how could he deal with armed posses bringing along bloodhounds? Brown assured him that the mountains were full of inaccessible glens and ravines where the hunters would never to able to find him.

Douglass approved the plan on basic economics, since slaveholders would not invest their money in a species of property "likely to take legs and walk off with itself." His enthusiasm was probably moderate, and Brown might have exaggerated the response when he wrote to John Jr. on February 4, of Douglass: "He has promised me $50 and what I value vastly more he seems to appreciate my theories and my labours."

This description is very much different from the Harper's Ferry raid that eventuated. The Douglass account coincides with Sanborn's brief version of what Brown explained to him in February, 1858—that from fortified mountain fastnesses his soldiers would sally forth to emancipate slaves. He would settle in the South if that was possible, and retreat through the North, if necessary. Sanborn summarized that from the time he first discussed it there were changes to the final dénouement, "amounting at last to an entire modification of the scheme."

While in Douglass' home Brown attended to some important matters by correspondence. There was the serious problem of Forbes, who was engaged in blackmail, threatening to expose the plan unless he was paid off. In a letter Forbes sent to John Jr., to be forwarded to his father, he insisted that he had been engaged for a period of one-year minimum, and he wanted another $600. Brown realized that if he paid Forbes $600, it might merely whet the appetite of the blackmailer.

The father wrote to the son in Akron. He would like to draw Forbes out further, keep him a little encouraged "and avoid an open rupture," for a few weeks at any rate. His instructions to John Jr. show his guile, sharper than ever. John Jr. must pretend that he had never sent the letter to him and he must reply to Forbes that he was returning his letter, "as I am unwilling that my father should, with all his other cares, difficulties and travails, be vexed with what I am apprehensive he will accept as highly offensive and insulting." Then, as a warning not to goad his father, he should say that he feared Père Brown would not take kindly to being told that he had hired Forbes for a year since it was a lie. "Again, I suspect you have greatly mistaken the man, if you suppose he will take it kindly in *you, or any living man*, to assume to instruct him how he should conduct his own business and correspondence"—a most revealing view of the inner man who alone shaped his iron will.

A small money bait should be held out to the rogue. John Jr. must say that he pities the plight of his family in Paris and is willing to send him $40, but first he would like to hear further about his intentions. We will see if we can chase Forbes off this way, said the father. Forbes made no reply, and a month later Brown wrote the son from Philadelphia, "I mean to avoid him untill I have a better account of him."

Brown wrote to Charles Blair in Collinsville about his pikes. The preceding August he had heard from Blair: "I very well know that when a man is depending upon the public for money he is very liable to be disappointed." However, no more money, no more work. Brown wrote him that he had just returned to the United States from abroad and wondered about the state of the matter. Blair reported that the situation was exactly the same. He was busy on other work, and the unfinished pikes were in storage pending full payment by Brown. He received a letter from Brown the following month from Philadelphia to the effect that he would surely complete the contract.

Blair would not hear again from Brown until June of the next year when Brown would appear in person at his shop in Collinsville.

From Rochester, Brown prepared the ground for his presentation to his wealthy friends. He used the *nom de plume* of Nelson Hawkins in his letters, though there was no need at all for secrecy, since all indictments in faraway Kansas had been quashed. Brown developed in his judgment of human beings and his cool calculation as to how to "play" them. He understood the psychology of Gerrit Smith and the Bostonians. He did not tender a word of explanation as to why he had done nothing for Kansas when he was in the West in the preceding months and there was not a word uttered by them in question. They were men engaged in a juvenile game. They enjoyed the idea that they were promoting illegal action, whether it came off or not. They reveled in the trappings of conspiracy, the Drama of Danger. Clandestine committee meetings, names and messages in code intrigued them.

He wrote to Gerrit Smith, saying simply that he would visit him on February 18. To the others he invested himself in deep mystery and danger. He wrote to Stearns asking him to come to Peterboro so that he could talk with him. Brown could not risk going to Boston since he was supposed to be hiding in Kansas. (He had appeared openly and recently in Lawrence and Topeka.) "It would be almost impossible for me to pass through Albany, Springfield or any of these points on my way to Boston; & not have it known: & my reasons for keeping it quiet were such that when I left Kansas: I kept it from *every friend* there." For that reason he could not even visit his own family.

To the Reverend Mr. Parker, he wrote that he was out of Kansas and in concealment, "but for very different reasons than those I had for doing so at Boston last spring," reasons he had not revealed to Parker then. For the same and identical object for which he had asked money of Parker in September for *"secret service no questions asked,"* he had now nearly perfected the arrangements for carrying out a plan "in which the world has a deep interest as well as Kansas." He needed $500 to $800. Did Parker think his Garrisonian friends could be induced to supply a little "straw" if he would be absolutely sure to make the "bricks"? Would Parker reply to Nelson Hawkins in Rochester through a secret intermediary?

Higginson, of the Six, had the loosest ties with Brown. They had met only in a group. Now Brown acted to bind Higginson to him with a hoop of steel. He wrote him on February 2. He was concealing his whereabouts in Rochester for good reasons but not connected with any anxiety for his personal safety. "I have been told that you are both a true *man* and a true *abolitionist* and 'I partly believe' the whole story." ("Partly Believe" was current newspaper slang from Paul's First Epistle to the Corinthians.)

His letter went on, "I now want to get for the perfecting of BY FAR the most important undertaking of my whole life: from $500 to $800 within the next Sixty days. I have written Reverend Theodore Parker, George L. Stearns and F. B. Sanborn Esqur on the subject; but do not know as either Mr. Stearns or Mr. Sanborn are abolitionists." It was a studied technique by Brown, to play one man against the other to maximize his return. He could hardly have meant this seriously since Sanborn was his most active and Stearns his most generous supporter.

He asked Higginson to raise money for him in Worcester. Higginson sounded a tentative note as if he wanted specifics. "I am always ready to invest money in treason, but at present have none to invest. . . . But I'll raise something if only $5 and send it on." Money was really tight in Boston as a result of a financial panic in August, 1857, which complicated Brown's task. Replying, Brown, with caution, said he could divulge only that "Rail Road business on a *somewhat extended* scale is the *identical* object for which I have been trying to get means. I have been connected with that business as *commonly conducted* from boyhood and never let an opportunity slip. I have been opperating to some purpose the past season but I now have a measure on foot that I feel *sure* would awaken in you more than *common interest* if you could understand it."

Sanborn received a similar cryptic letter. Edwin Morton, Sanborn's Harvard classmate, was a tutor in Gerrit Smith's household and relayed to Sanborn what he had read in a Brown letter. "This is news—he expects to overthrow slavery in a large part of the country." Sanborn, on the basis of this information, advised Higginson: "I should not wonder if his plan contemplated an uprising of slaves—though he has not said as much to me," and in his youthful enthusiasm he added, "The Union is evidently on its last legs and Buchanan is laboring to tear it into pieces. Treason will not be treason much longer but patriotism."

It was with a sense of great expectancy that Sanborn arrived on

February 22, Washington's birthday, to meet Brown at Gerrit Smith's manor in Peterboro.

"Our old and noble friend, Captain John Brown of Kansas, arrives this evening" is the entry in Gerrit Smith's diary for February 18.

The warmest hospitality was extended in the Peterboro manor house. Edwin Morton, at Brown's request, often played the piano. When he played for him Schubert's "Serenade," Brown unashamedly wept. Brown discussed his plan with Smith before Sanborn's arrival and got his endorsement. This appears from a letter he wrote on February 20 to John Brown, Jr., that Smith was "ready to go in for a share of the whole trade. I will say (in the language of another) in regard to this most encouraging fact, 'My soul doth magnify the Lord,'" and in another note, "Mr. Smith & family go *all* lengths with me."

Sanborn was the vital link, and he arrived on the late afternoon of February 22, drawn by sled from the nearest railroad station. They all had an enjoyable dinner that night and in the late hours went up to a room on the third story where Sanborn, Morton, Smith, and Brown conversed at great length.

Although Sanborn was not unprepared, Brown's plan did startle him. After all, southerners were in control in the federal government. The Democratic President, Buchanan, was their tool, the Virginian John B. Floyd was Secretary of War, Jefferson Davis of Mississippi and James M. Mason of Virginia were dominant members of the "inner club" of the United States Senate. And here was a plan to strike at slavery at its very heart by "a poor, obscure old man, uncertain at best of another ten years lease of life and yet calmly proposing an enterprise which, if successful, might require a whole generation to accomplish." From his words, it is crystal-clear that Sanborn interpreted Brown to mean that he would hack away at slavery over a long time by trying to run off slaves in a series of stabs. This was far removed from the "do-or-die" Harper's Ferry raid of 1859.

All objections that were raised by the others were answered by Brown with fact and logic and by a favorite scriptural text of John Calvin, "If God be for us, who can be against us." The meeting adjourned after midnight and they resumed the discussion the next morning. Late that afternoon, Sanborn and Smith walked for an hour in the snow through fields and woods. Brown, left behind, was discussing theology with an old soldier of Wellington's army at Waterloo, Charles Stuart. As the sun was setting, Smith turned to Sanborn and said, "You see how it is. Our dear friend has made up his mind on this course and cannot be turned from it. We cannot give him up to die alone. We must support him. I will raise so many hundred dollars for him; you must lay the case before your friends in Massachusetts and ask them to do as much. I see no other way." Sanborn said that he had come to the same conclusion: "We must either stand by him or leave him to dash himself alone against the fortress he is determined to assault."

Sanborn returned to Boston the next day and reported to the other four what he had heard. All were favorably inclined. Dr. Howe said that on the basis of his military experience the plan was absolutely feasible, since he had seen a few Greeks repulsing hordes of Turks in the mountains of Macedonia. Parker said he was not too sanguine, but many such "experiments" would have to be tried before slavery could be toppled.

That the Six believed that they were committing themselves to a military operation of limited scope is confirmed by Higginson's re-collection supplied later in his book, *Cheerful Yesterdays*. When he quizzed Brown soon afterward in Boston, Brown said to him that he would be governed by events. "If he could establish them perma-nently in their fortresses like the Maroons of Jamaica, so much the better. If not, he would make a break from time to time and take parties to Canada by paths already familiar to him."

They were comforted by Brown's assurance that he did not intend any slave insurrection. They were ingenuous. If runaway slaves de-fended themselves from being recaptured, that would be interpreted in the South as insurrection.

Brown mentioned Harper's Ferry only once throughout 1858 and 1859, and to only one member of the Six. Sitting one evening before a coal fire in the American House in Boston, two weeks after the Peterboro launch, Brown casually mentioned to Sanborn that Har-per's Ferry might be one of his objectives. Sanborn asked what he had in mind, and Brown replied that it would strike terror in the slaveholding class to find that an armed force had seized a place so important and so near Washington. Sanborn regarded this as a va-grant thought of Brown's and he attached no importance to it since Brown never brought it up again. The incident came back to San-born's mind only after the dreadful news in October, 1859.

The overwhelming probability is that Brown meant to strike at

Harper's Ferry from the very inception of his plan. Douglass recalled that, while at his home, Brown said that with a few resolute men he could capture Harper's Ferry and supply himself with government arms. "It was, however, very evidently passing in his mind as a thing he might do, and I paid but little attention to such remarks." The strongest evidence is recorded without comment by Sanborn. On February 4, Brown wrote to John Jr. that he was thinking that he would like him to make a trip to Bedford, Chambersburg, Gettysburg, and Uniontown in Pennsylvania, traveling slowly, and finding out about the families of the "Right Stripe" and getting acquainted. "When you look at the location of those places, you will readily perceive the advantage." Then, on March 4, he wrote his son, again urging the trip. "Hunt out friends . . . even at *Harper's Ferry.*"

Sanborn did not realize that in his letter of February 24 when Brown said he intended "mighty conquest," Brown meant it literally.

In retrospect, it is amazing that Brown could have disclosed his plan to so many people and that it should not have been betrayed and nipped in the bud. As we shall see, only one letter reached Secretary of War Floyd, in 1859. The many black people he communicated with breathed not a word. He wrote to James W. Loguen, of the Zion Church in Syracuse, and other prominent Negroes. Leaving Peterboro, he went to Brooklyn to the home of Dr. and Mrs. J. N. Gloucester, who had considerable money. In March he was in Philadelphia with John Jr. at the home of a rich Negro lumber merchant and philanthropist for aged Negroes, Stephen Smith, and met there with the gifted preacher, Henry Highland Garnet, William Still, and leading Negroes of Philadelphia.

All this time his thoughts were on more recruits. He wrote to his daughter Ruth asking for the services of her stalwart husband, Henry Thompson, who had served him so well in Kansas. "I have a PARTICULAR & VERY IMPORTANT; (but not dangerous) place for HIM to *fill*; in the 'school' & I know of NO MAN *living* so well adapted to fill it." He was better than a "hundred average schollars." Ruth replied that her father was rating too highly Henry's "qualifications as a scholar." She was devoted to the cause, would follow her husband anywhere in the world but they had to think of their two children.

While Henry did not join because of Ruth's veto, his two brothers on the North Elba Farm read the letter and on their own initia-

tive enlisted in 1859 in the expeditionary force. They both died at
Harper's Ferry. William Thompson, who was twenty-six at his
death, on October 17, 1859, had gone to join Brown in Kansas in
1856, but had met the Brown boys in Iowa while they were headed
east. Together with them he went home and he felt cheated of their
great adventure. His brother, Dauphin Thompson, died on October
18, 1859, while fighting in the engine-house beside John Brown. He
was only twenty-one years old.

Parker wrote Brown that he wanted to consult with him in Boston,
and Brown was in the city at the American House from March 5 to 8,
meeting with members who now had assumed the name, the Secret
Six—Sanborn, Parker, Howe, Higginson, Smith and Stearns. Sanborn
made an official notation for the members of their decision, that, while
"Hawkins goes to prepare agencies for his business," which they referred to intramurally as a speculation in wool, they would raise
$1,000 for him, of which each would donate at least $100.

Brown asked for nonmonetary assistance, too. In February he
asked Sanborn to solicit books for the use of his boys in school at
Springdale, including Plutarch's *Lives* and the best book on Napoleon. He now wanted Parker to lend his literary talents to his appeals.
He asked him to work over the section on the *Manual of the Patriotic
Volunteer* which he had designed to seduce United States soldiers
to desert to him. "It should be, in short, a most earnest and powerful
appeal to man's sense of right, and to their feelings of humanity." He
also wanted him to turn out a short address "intended for all persons,
old and young, male and female, slaveholding and non-slaveholding,
to be sent out broadcast over the entire nation." It was to be read by
his prisoners when in confinement and after their release. He intended
to win by kindness southern prisoners who had expected to be
"slaughtered like vile reptiles." He wrote Parker: "Females are sus-
ceptible of being carried away entirely by the kindness of an intrepid
and magnanimous soldier, even when his bare name was but a terror
the day previous."

If Parker had applied the most elementary common sense, he would
have realized that Brown had in mind something far more majestic
than a petty operation in the mountains. He had no taste for the
literary assignment from Brown. As overworked as he was, he did
not intend to waste his time and brainpower in an endeavor to sub-
vert the United States soldier, which would be incriminating as well
as futile. He sent to Brown an innocuous and irrelevant report on the

armies of Europe, written by Captain George B. McClellan, who had a first-hand knowledge of the subject which included a tour of duty as an observer in the Crimean War.

Why did these distinguished men—men who led sheltered and sedentary lives, men of words or of money, none of whom, with the possible exception of Higginson, could have wielded a weapon in anger—totally embrace this wild and incendiary scheme so sketchily put before them?

As we have noted, they were soft-soaped by Brown and were unaware of the magnitude of his scheme, though Parker, at least, got a clear signal. They loved the secret plot, they were inflated with a sense of self-importance and good works, and probably not overly concerned with results.

Brown's magnetic influence in personal contact must not be underrated as a factor. Those who would consider Brown mad must overlook the fact that men of perception who were acquainted with him over many months found Brown a man who could be carried away by enthusiasm so that an occasional idea of his might be out of line, such as the appeal to the United States soldier, but basically a highly rational and commanding personality.

The sensitive Ralph Waldo Emerson was impressed with Brown as a man of mind and character. Sanborn in later years insisted that Brown in the flesh measured up in every way to the hero-image built up after his death. Dr. Howe, introducing Brown to the Boston businessman, John M. Forbes, in 1859, wrote: "I think I know him well. He is of the Puritan militant order. He is an enthusiast, yet cool, keen and cautious."

Higginson had close contact with Brown during his March visit at the American House:

In his thin, worn face there were the signs of a fire which might wear him out, and practically did so, but nothing of pettiness or baseness, and his talk was calm, persuasive and coherent. He was simply a high-minded, unselfish, belated Covenanter, a man whom Sir Walter Scott might have drawn but whom such writers as Nicolay and Hay have utterly failed to delineate. To describe him in their words as "clean but coarse" is curiously wide of the mark: he had no more of coarseness than was to be found in Habakkuk Muckleworth or in George Eliot's Adam Bede; he had, on the contrary, that religious elevation which is itself a kind of refinement, the quality one may see expressed in many a venerable Quaker face at yearly meetings.

On the religious plane, the aid of these men to Brown accorded with Calvinist theology in which the idea of vicariousness, Christ's death for mankind, was deeply inbedded. John Jay Chapman stated in his essay on Howe: "John Brown was the living embodiment of an idea with which the anti-slavery mind was always darkly battling, the idea of atonement, of vicarious suffering. Howe and his associates somehow felt that they would be untrue to themselves, false to God, if they did not help John Brown." They were willing to suffer and bleed for the holy cause provided Brown did it for them.

The New York *Herald* said editorially in 1852 of Abolitionists: "The gentlemen are men of peace. They would not handle daggers. No, not they! They would not handle them, but they speak them, they write them. Like the apocalyptic monster, they have horns like a lamb but they speak like a dragon."

These men, in theory, remote from their own lives, were all apostles of violence and bloodshed, even the two Christian ministers. The Reverend Mr. Higginson was a Disunionist who craved a full-scale conflict between North and South and regretted that it had not developed out of the Kansas struggle. He wanted to see the slaves revolt. "A single insurrection, with decent temporary success, would do more than anything else to explode our present political platforms." The Reverend Mr. Parker talked revolution, and wrote a friend in 1858: "I would like of all things to see an insurrection of the slaves . . . it would do good even if it failed." A month after Brown had been his guest at Peterboro, Gerrit Smith gloated in a letter to Congressman Joshua R. Giddings: "The slaves will be delivered by the shedding of blood and the signs are multiplying that the deliverance is at hand." It is psychologically relevant that all six, clerics and laymen, were steeped since childhood in the Old Testament and continually had snuffed up the odor of blood righteously shed by the Chosen People, as Joshua shed blood in the slaughter of the infidels at Jericho.

They had given up hope that the issue might be resolved by the ballot box. In June, 1858, Parker declared that every President caters to the South. "The temperature may stand at twenty degrees below zero, Mississippi may be frozen over clear down to Natchez, Hellgate may be impassable for ice, and the winds of Labrador blow for months across the Continent—and still he cannot believe there is a North."

What if Brown failed? He might precipitate the war that would end slavery. Suppose he died? Then he would die holily, in a good cause. After all, his life was only an accident in the cause.

Introducing Brown in 1859 to John Forbes, Dr. Howe said that, "He has a martyr's spirit." It is probably more accurate to say that Brown appeared to the Six as a potential martyr than to say that he looked like Robert Bruce or William Tell, as Stearns described him before the Mason Committee in 1860. This martyr-image psychology is highly interesting, not only for the support given to Brown by his New England friends but for his future apotheosis. The observations which follow I have taken from an excellent study by Hazel Catherine Wolf entitled, *On Freedom's Altar; The Martyr Complex in the Abolition Movement.*

Abolitionism was a church militant and Tertullian had said, "The blood of the martyrs is the seed of the Church." In many Protestant homes, John Foxe's *Book of Martyrs* stood on a shelf beside the Bible. The English clergyman had described how a thousand martyrs marched to horrible deaths, some in vats of burning lime or boiling pitch or thrown to ravenous beasts, or suffering the tortures of the rack. Many screamed prayers of forgiveness for their tormentors before they died.

Abolitionist crusaders who left their homes and endured contumely in their travels pleaded with Americans to see the parallel with those enshrined in Foxe's *Book of Martyrs*. The crown of thorns was worn lovingly by leading Abolitionists. Garrison, in October, 1835, when pulled by a rope around his body through the streets of Boston was uplifted by the thought that he was going to martyrdom. He said, "That some of us will be assassinated or abducted seems more than probable. There is a whole eternity of consolation in this assurance that he who loses his life for Christ's sake shall find it." Theodore Weld in a church pulpit in Troy, New York, in 1836 was assaulted with sticks, stones, eggs, and pieces of brick, but, glorying in it, intoned, "Blessed are they who die in the harness and are buried in the field or bleach there."

The man who risked martyrdom was familiar in Abolitionist ideology, and there was more to it than that. Abolitionism *needed* martyrs. In 1836, William Ellery Channing said, "One kidnapped, murdered Abolitionist would do more for the violent destruction of slavery than a thousand societies." The canonization of John Brown after his execution was not entirely novel. In 1837 when Elijah Lovejoy, the editor of an Abolitionist paper, was murdered by a mob in Alton,

Illinois, not only did Abolitionist papers feast on him but poems about his martyrdom appeared all over, even in non-Abolitionist papers, and his sacrifice was a favorite topic for sermons. Abolitionists had a two-year field day with Charles T. Torrey, sentenced to eight years in Baltimore, Maryland, for helping slaves to escape and who died in jail in 1846.

While in Boston, Brown paid a visit to the current Abolitionist martyr, Senator Charles Sumner. James Redpath and Reverend James Freeman Clarke accompanied him. Sumner, recuperating from his wounds, was lying in his bed. Brown said to him, "Do you have the coat you were wearing when you were attacked by Brooks?" Sumner said, "Yes, it is in the closet. Do you want to see it?" Redpath wrote: "I recall the scene vividly, Sumner standing slightly bent, supporting himself by keeping his hand on the bed, Brown, erect as a pillar, holding up the blood-besmirched coat in his right hand and examining it intently. The old man said nothing, I believe, but I remember that his lips compressed, and his eyes shone like polished steel."

From Boston, on March 6, he wrote John Jr.: "My call has met with a most hearty response so that I feel assured of at least tolerable success." Indefatigably, with his remarkable endurance, he continued with his whirlwind tour. He looked up friends and possible donors in Philadelphia, New Haven, and New York City. Not until March 2, more than seven weeks after he had arrived in New York State, did he visit his family at North Elba. On April 2, he visited Gerrit Smith again at Peterboro and then spent four days with Frederick Douglass in Rochester. On April 8 he crossed Lake Erie and was in St. Catherines in Canada with James W. Loguen.

There was a considerable Negro colony in Canada, at least sixty thousand persons. It dated back to 1829 when there were riots against Negroes in Cincinnati in which several were killed in the streets and they had to barricade themselves in their homes. The governor of upper Canada sent a message that Canada would extend to Negroes a royal welcome. "Tell the republicans on your side of the line that we royalists do not know men of their color. Should you come to us you will be entitled to all the privileges of the rest of His Majesty's subjects." Two thousand Negroes on receipt of this welcome went to Canada and founded Wilberforce. Toronto now had a few thousand; there was at Elgin a model colony for escaped slaves; and at Chatham in Western Ontario there was a flourishing settlement of prosperous farmers, mechanics, and educators.

At St. Catherines he had long talks with Harriet Tubman, who, he wrote John Jr., "hooked on his (sic) whole team at once. He (sic) is the most of a man, naturally that I ever met with." This heroine, the "Moses of her people," a full-blooded African, was born a slave in 1821 on the eastern shore of Maryland. In her teens her skull was dented by a two-pound weight thrown at her by an overseer. She escaped in 1849, and instead of going to a safe haven, washed dishes in Philadelphia and Cape May, New Jersey, to save money. She returned one night to Maryland to rescue her sister and two children, and was back a few months later to save her brother and two other slaves. From there on, she became the Dark Ghost of the Underground Railroad, enabling more than three hundred slaves to escape, eluding capture although there were rewards posted as high as $12,-000 for her.

"There is the most abundant material, and of the right quality, in this quarter, beyond all doubt," Brown advised John Jr. from Canada. From St. Catherines he visited Toronto, Ingersoll, Hamilton, and Chatham. He paid a visit at the Chatham home of the black physician and activist for his race, Dr. Martin R. Delaney. Brown told the doctor that he had come to Chatham expressly to see him. He had a great project in mind which must be approved by a general council or convention, and he could not effect it in the United States, but had been advised that Delaney could accomplish it at once.

When Delaney expressed his astonishment that he had to come all the way to Canada, Brown replied, "Why should you be surprised? Sir, the people of the Northern states are cowards. Slavery has made cowards of the whites. You can effect nothing among such people." Delaney asked if a convention was all he wanted. "That is all, but that is a great deal to me," Brown answered. "It is men, I want, not money; money I can get plentiful enough, but no men. Men are afraid of identification with me, though they favor my measures. They are cowards, sir cowards!" He disclosed the plans for his Virginia expedition and Delaney said he would arrange the convention Brown wanted.

He was back in the States in Chicago on April 25, having spent seventeen days in Canada. He was en route to Springdale, Iowa, to retrieve his flock whom he had left there on January 15.

While he had been gone, his war college had been going full blast. The men had moved to the large house of William Maxson, northeast of Springdale, believed to have been the first cement house built in Iowa, where they were charged a dollar and a half per week for board, "not including Washing nor extra lights." In the meadows and hill slopes they were drilled by Stevens with rough hickory swords, they fought sham battles, advanced and retreated from hill to hill, practiced maneuvers, such as cutting zigzag trenches to dislodge the enemy from a hilltop.

In the morning, from six to ten, before drilling began, there were classroom discussions. These student militants were taking a psychedelic "trip" as the drug Brown had injected was coursing through their systems. They established a curriculum of their own on subjects for reform of the nation, as they discussed besides abolitionism, free college education, equal rights for women, prohibitory laws on sale of liquor, and they also took in mechanics, theology, spiritualism, and natural philosophy. It is a poignant picture of these youths in their flight of fancy preparing to be rulers of a new order when in fact many were fated for death at Harper's Ferry. On Tuesday and Friday evenings they would form themselves into a mock legislature in the village schoolhouse and under approved parliamentary procedures they would debate and pass laws. Kagi, Cook, and Realf were outstanding as debaters, and townsmen attended these sessions with pleasure.

Two Springdale boys took part in these legislative debates. They fraternized with the men of the Brown company, and when Brown returned they told him they wanted to join up. They left Springdale to do so in July, 1859. They were brothers, both Quaker idealists. The younger, Barclay Coppoc, was twenty years old at the time of the Harper's Ferry raid and was one of the five who escaped; he gave his life for the Union cause in the Civil War. The older, Edwin Coppoc, was twenty-four at the time of the raid, and was captured. He was cleancut and religiously sincere. Governor Henry A. Wise, of Virginia, said that Coppoc alone of those captured he would have spared had he the power. He was executed at Charlestown on December 16, 1859.

George B. Gill, the son of Dr. Henry C. Gill, one of the founders of Springdale, was a youth in his early twenties. He had a good education and had dabbled in literary endeavors in Canada. He decided to join up with Brown. A Canadian friend, Stewart Taylor, stopped off to see Gill on his way to Kansas and remained in Springdale. Both Gill and Taylor left Springdale with Brown and went to Chatham with him. Taylor was to take part in the Harper's Ferry raid and died on October 17, 1859, when he was twenty-three years old. He was the only one of John Brown's men who was not an American by birth.

The Quakers, being nonresistants, did not approve of the military drill, but as Abolitionists they warmed to the idea of training men to protect a free Kansas, which they thought was the purpose of all the training. To a very few, Brown confided that he had a larger purpose, that he had been called by Almighty God to save the American nation from slavery. The Friends who heard this could not doubt him. With their own belief in the Inner Light, that of God in Everyman, the Quakers expected man's conduct to be in accord with his inner conviction or revelation.

Brown ordered the evacuation of Springdale on April 27. At the farewell meeting the night before there was not a dry eye in the crowd. It had been an exhilarating sojourn for the men. In addition to work they had enjoyed the feminine company, and attachments had been formed that lasted for some time. Cook dutifully kissed all the girls at the farewell party.

John H. Painter said to Brown, "Friend, I cannot give thee money to buy powder, but here is $20 towards thy expenses." Thomas James cautioned him, "Thee must be careful or thee will get a rope around thy neck."

They were in Chicago the next day and in Detroit the day after that. The hotel where they stopped in Detroit refused to serve the black man, Richard Richardson, and so they moved to another. On April 30, they were in Chatham in Canada.

The men were by now on fire for the cause, eager for the confrontation. To a young lady in Springdale, Cook, who was fond of melodramatizing himself, wrote: "Through the dark gloom of the future I can almost see the dawning light of Freedom. . . . I almost hear the swelling anthem of Liberty rising from the millions who have just cast aside the fetters and shackles that bound them. But ere that day arrives, I fear that we shall hear the crash of the battle shock and see the red gleaming of the cannon's lightning." Stevens wrote to his sister Aimee, with whom he maintained a continuous correspondence: "I am ready to give up my life for the oppressed if need be." Realf wrote to a friend in Springdale that Captain Brown had arranged all, they would stay in Chatham for ten days to two weeks, "after which we will start for *China*."

On Saturday, May 8, the constitutional convention was called to order at 10 A.M. in a school building on Princess Street. The inhabitants were led to believe that a meeting was being held to organize a Masonic Lodge of white and black. The presiding officer was the pastor of a Negro church in Detroit, William Charles Munroe, and the secretary was John Henry Kagi. There were twelve white men present—Brown, his son Owen, Kagi, Stevens (who still used the name of Whipple), Cook, Realf, Gill, Tidd, Leeman, Moffet, Parsons, and Taylor. There were thirty-three black men present, including Richard Richardson of Brown's company. They came from as far away as Ohio and Pennsylvania. None of the American Negro leaders, such as Douglass, Loguen, or Stephen Smith, was in attendance. Only one of these black representatives was to take part in the Harper's Ferry raid, Osborn P. Anderson. He was a free-born mulatto from Pennsylvania, a printer by trade. At the time of the raid he was twenty-nine years old and would be one of the five to escape. He went to Canada to live, and there wrote an account of the great event, which was less accurate than impressionistic.

From the standpoint of recruitment, the meeting was a disappointment. "Nelson Hawkins" had written Sanborn that he had expected to attract "several good men for shepherds."

Reverend Munroe introduced Brown to the convention, and the would-be liberator made an address. Realf, who soon would run out on Brown, described it in detail in his testimony in 1860 before the Mason Committee of the Senate.

Brown had nurtured his purpose, he said, for twenty or thirty years. In 1851, he had gone to London on wool business and while in Europe he had made a tour of the Continent in which he inspected fortifications and earth-work forts with a view to adapting this knowledge to mountain warfare in the United States. The truth was that while Brown may have visited the battlefields of Waterloo, Jena, and Leipzig he had no time to get to Austria or Switzerland which might have provided lessons in mountain warfare.

There is no reason to doubt Brown's further statement to the convention that he had read extensively of Roman warfare, of the way the Circassian chief Schamyl had resisted the Russians, and had studied the life of Toussaint L'Ouverture. Brown's notebooks for the year 1857 indicate that he had given some study to guerrilla warfare:

Circassia has about 550,000.
Switzerland 2,037,000.
Guerilla warfare See Life of Lord Wellington Page 71 to Page 75 (Mina) See also Page 102 some reliable hints in same Book. See also Page 196 some most important instructions to officers. See also same Book Page 235 these words Deep and narrow defiles where 300 men would suffise to check an *army*. See also Page 236 on top of Page.

The book he had read was a biography of Wellington, by Joachim Hayward Stocqueler, published in 1852, and Mina was a Spanish chief who defeated Napoleon's men in the Spanish mountains.

Continuing with the Brown address: he proposed to establish himself in the southern Appalachians, running from Virginia down through the Carolinas, from Tennessee down through Alabama. Slaves would flock to his standard. He would operate on the plantations lying in the plains on each side of the mountains. He would defeat state militia sent against him, and United States troops, too, in Realf's words, "if it were possible." An area would be carved out in the mountains where the blacks would be organized under his constitution, where schools for them would be established and they would be taught useful and mechanical arts. A keynote speech at a convention is by custom an exaggerated "puff" and "pep talk," but even with this caveat it is evident that Brown's mind was fixed on "mighty conquest."

After concluding his address, Brown presented his constitution for consideration. The preamble stated the philosophy he had operated on in Kansas, that slavery itself was an insurrection against basic American principles and was a state of war in which the oppressed had to take up arms in self-defense.

Whereas, Slavery, throughout its entire existence in the United States is none other than a most barbarous, unprovoked, and unjustifiable War of one portion of its citizens upon another portion; the only conditions of which are perpetual imprisonment, and hopeless servitude or absolute extermination; in utter disregard and violation of those eternal and self-evident truths set forth in our Declaration of Independence: *Therefore,* we CITIZENS of the UNITED STATES, and the OPPRESSED PEOPLE, who, by a RECENT DECISION of the SUPREME COURT ARE DECLARED to have NO RIGHTS WHICH the WHITE MAN is BOUND to RESPECT; TOGETHER WITH ALL OTHER PEOPLE DEGRADED by the LAWS THEREOF, DO, for the TIME BEING ORDAIN and ESTABLISH for OURSELVES the FOLLOWING PROVISIONAL CONSTITUTION and ORDINANCES, the

BETTER to PROTECT our PERSONS, PROPERTY, LIVES and LIBERTIES: and to GOVERN our ACTIONS.

The constitution had forty-eight articles. The first forty-five were accepted without demurrer, but there was objection to the forty-sixth. "The foregoing articles shall not be construed so as in any way to encourage the overthrow of any State Government or the General Government of the United States, and look to no dissolution of the Union, but simply to Amendment and Repeal, and our flag shall be the same that our fathers fought under during the Revolution."

J. G. Reynolds, a coppersmith from Sandusky, Ohio, and a leader in the Underground Railroad objected. He did not want to swear allegiance to a nation that had subjected his people to cruelty and humiliation. Brown, Kagi, and Dr. Delaney urged adoption, and the convention overwhelmingly overruled Reynolds' objection.

This provision was absurd, since the preceding articles contemplated the establishment of a new state. It was Brown's technique of the brazen falsehood and a sop he threw to the timid. This soft-soap was successful, and it was not until they were actually engaged at Harper's Ferry that some of the men realized that they had embarked on treason—which Brown was candid in admitting to them at that time.

There would be an elected Congress of from five to ten members and a Supreme Court of five. A president and a vice president would also be elected, but the commander-in-chief was to be selected by the elected officials. The commander-in-chief would have a veto power over all laws for the first three years, and thus it would be in effect a military dictatorship.

"The entire and real property of all persons known to be acting either directly or indirectly with or for the enemy or found in arms with them or found wilfully holding slaves shall be confiscated and taken, whenever or wherever it may be found, in either free or slave states." It would be held as communal property. On the other hand, in order to get the support of poor-whites, personal property of non-slaveholders would be registered in the books and they could hold it as neutrals.

Prisoners were to be given fair treatment, given fair trials before execution, and anyone on his side who violated a female forcibly would be executed.

It was to be a Puritanical state: "The marriage relation shall be at all time respected, and families kept together, as far as possible; and broken families encouraged to reunite, and intelligence offices established for that purpose." Men must be good, or Brown would make them good, as Calvin did in his City of God.

On late Saturday afternoon the constitution was signed. When James M. Jones, an Oberlin graduate, came up to the desk Brown said to him, "Now, friend Jones, give us John Hancock bold and strong." A Declaration of Independence was also adopted, to be published on July 4, 1858, after the blow was struck. It was a paraphrase of the American 1776 Declaration and used similar phraseology, such as: "that the Slaves are, & of right ought to be free & as independent as the unchangeable Law of God requires that All Men Shall be. That they are absolved from all allegiance to those Tyrants etc."

After congratulatory remarks, the constitutional convention adjourned. In the evening a new body assembled, legally speaking, to elect officers on an interim basis. After the southern states at some future time recognized the freedom of the area carved out by the Liberator, these offices would become vacant and popular elections would be held. Balloting for the offices (which were unsalaried) took place on this Saturday evening and the following Monday when the meeting was held in another building, the First Baptist Church. John Brown was elected commander-in-chief, Richard Realf, secretary of state, George B. Gill, secretary of the treasury, and John Henry Kagi, secretary of war. None of these last three was over twenty-four years old. Two black men, Alfred M. Ellsworth and Osborn P. Anderson, were elected to the Congress. A committee of fifteen with Brown as chairman was appointed to fill other vacancies. As far we know, the vacancies were never filled. So concluded the Chatham meetings.

How shall we look at this strange Chatham affair? It seems weird in retrospect, but it may seem so only because John Brown failed. The bickerings in London prior to the First World War among a group of straggly Russian exiles, which were mere coffee-room hassles, in which Bolshevism won out over Menshevism and thereby the stamp of Lenin Bolshevism was put on the Russian Revolution, are not regarded as farcical only because the 1917 revolution in Russia was successful.

Brown liked to formalize everything, even the operations of his guerrilla band in Kansas. The constitution stated clearly his aims in his southern expedition, and the loose framework of government, Sanborn concluded, was well suited for guerrilla bands operating in the mountains. Nonetheless, Villard interrupted his panegyric on Brown to describe this as a "temporary aberration" of his mind, and quoted Dr. Herman Von Holst, a distinguished German law professor, who in his 1892 work on Brown called it a "piece of insanity in the literal sense of the word."

Consulting Von Holst's work, I find that his verdict was a mixed one. He wrote: "This document was a confused medley of absurd, because absolutely inapplicable forms and of measures well calculated for the end in view, of sound common sense and of absurd systematizing, of cool computation and of inconceivable overestimate of the resources at hand, of true, keen-sighted humanity and of reckless severity." It was absurd for a little band of Negroes and whites to create a new constitution, but it was entirely rational to form a strong organization to break the chains of slavery. It was absurd for a corporal's guard with no troops to copy the federal Constitution, but it was sensible to appoint a supreme commander-in-chief.

Van Holst goes on: "The plan was probably intended for the moral effect on emancipated slaves, to hold them under some restraint during confusion. It was a piece of insanity in the literal sense of the word to create such a government and to want to carry on such a war, and yet to declare that there was no intention of overthrowing the state or federal government."

No harm to his plan could emanate from the Chatham meeting, and Brown could see potential dividends all along the line.

He was now formally elected interim commander-in-chief. He flattered his young followers with high offices. He flattered the black contingent by his attentions, and he expected them to furnish many recruits and possibly money. He could assure Sanborn *et al.* that under his constitution with its strict controls the freed slaves would not be guilty of excesses, such as had occurred in San Domingo, and this was a genuine fear, even among Abolitionists. Moreover, it had great propaganda uses, and for this reason Brown had his constitution printed and brought many copies with him to Harper's Ferry. It advertised to both North and South that John Brown was not an irresponsible man leading a band of ruffians and cutthroats, but an extremist-constitutionalist (if such a genus exists). He aimed at conquest but at clemency, and after pacification his aims were reasonable and benevolent.

While Brown cannot be faulted for holding the Chatham meetings, the basic flaw, which foredoomed his Harper's Ferry plan, came up for criticism at Chatham. There is a pattern in his life. In his business career his projects all failed not for lack of ingenuity and perseverence in executing them but because his basic judgment was wrong. Just as he obstinately persisted in his belief that he alone could grade wool properly, in his great antislavery plan he persisted in a basic theory that others insisted to him was in error.

The skeptics at Chatham were the black members who told Brown he was wrong in thinking that the slaves would rally to his standard as soon as he raised it in the South. James Jones, the Oberlin graduate, told Brown bluntly from the floor that they would not, since they were not sufficiently informed or led. Brown could not legitimately argue from the San Domingo experience, he said, since the blacks there were not overawed by the whites, and French Revolutionary ferment had done its work. Brown must have thought that he was making an impression on some of the members, if not on himself, since he rose and cut him off, "Friend Jones, you will please say no more on that side. There will be plenty to defend on that side of the question." There was general laughter.

But the matter was not dropped. A black delegate said that Brown's plan should be delayed until the United States was embroiled in war with another first-class power, since his plan would be sure to fail under circumstances of peace. This idea had seconders. Brown acted as if this were a challenge to his honor. He rose slowly to his full height and said, "I would be the last one to take advantage of my country in the face of a foreign foe."

After the Chatham meeting was over, Dr. Delaney discounted his keynote address and chose to believe that all Brown had in mind was some improved system of the Underground Railroad to terminate in Kansas. Jones, who could not swallow the proposition of a slave uprising, thought that Brown intended to sacrifice himself and some white followers to rouse the people of the North from their stupor on the slavery subject, much as Arnold Winkelreid, the Swiss chieftain, threw himself on the Austrian spearmen, crying, "Make way for Liberty."

Other black friends remonstrated with Brown. On February 19 of that year, Dr. Gloucester in a letter in gentle vein from Philadelphia expressed his doubts to his "Most Esteemed Friend," writing that although his commendable measure to deliver the slaves had his support, "You speak in your letter of the people. I fear there is little to be done in the masses. The masses suffer from the want of intelligence and it is difficult to reach them in a matter like you propose as far as it is necessary to secure their cooperation. The colored people are impulsive, but they need sagacity, sagacity to distinguish the proper course. They are like a bark at sea without a commander or rudder."

There were white men, to whom Brown confided, who told him he was in tragic error. Hugh Forbes, in a letter he wrote to Dr. Howe in May, 1858, said that he had argued with Brown in Tabor that since no advance publicity could be spread among the slaves about his coming, there would be no response or at best a feeble one, "unless they were already in a state of agitation." The New York *Tribune* correspondent, William A. Phillips, with whom Brown had a discussion in Kansas in late 1858, made the objection that the American Negroes were "a peaceful, domestic, inoffensive race; in all their sufferings they seem to be incapable of resentment or reprisal."

The Reverend Theodore Parker was troubled that it was through docility and the lack of desire of natural vengeance that the Negroes remained in bondage. Take the case of Santa Cruz in the Canary Islands, with its barbarous laws before the revolt. If a slave excited others to run away, the plantation master without applying to any court could inflict punishment. The slave was laid down on a log and his right leg cut off with an axe and the stump plunged into boiling pitch to stanch the wound. It was common for owners to beat slaves with tamarind rods, thick-set with ugly thorns, and when the beating was over, the lacerated back was washed with a concoction of the machineel, a poison tree which made the wounds fester and remain long open. Yet, when 25,000 slaves revolted in 1846 and had 3,000 whites at their mercy they were content to settle for their freedom and did not harm a hair of a white man's head. Reverend Mr. Parker asked, suppose 25,000 Americans had been held in bondage this way, "How many of the 3,000 would see the next sun go down?"

Brown could not be shaken from his belief. To Hugh Forbes, he said he was sure he would get up to five hundred slaves the first day. To Phillips he replied hotly, "You have not studied them right and you have not studied them long enough. Human nature is the same everywhere, among white and black."

His reasoning process, though fallible, was entirely human. In a letter of 1787, Thomas Jefferson wrote to a friend: "The moment a person forms a theory, his imagination sees in every object only the traits which favor the theory." Brown reasoned from his first-hand knowledge of escaped slaves he had talked with in the North— largely in the Western Reserve area of Ohio—overlooking the fact that they were not typical. They were bolder and more resourceful than the others and therefore had taken the risk of escaping and had made it. (The United States Central Intelligence Agency made the same error in recommending support for the Bay of Pigs invasion of Castro Cuba in 1961, reasoning that the temper of the Cuban people was the same as that of the Miami refugees who had been extensively interviewed.)

Kagi, whom Brown regarded as an expert on Virginia, but who was *not*, had told him that the Virginia Negroes were particularly intelligent and likely to respond since most of them were half-brothers to their masters, and Brown accepted this ingenious thesis whole.

Brown was greatly influenced by the Abolition press and credo, which depicted the slaves as yearning to revolt. A North Carolinian, Randolph Abbott Shotwell, at the time of the raid, wrote that Brown had been swindled by a cult delusion: "The Abolitionists had so often rehearsed the falsehood that at length they deceived themselves into believing that the Southern slaves were groaning under the cruel yoke, brutally oppressed, subjected daily to the blood-cutting lash, to starvation, lust and all manner of ill-usage, that made it certain they would spring with wild shouts of joy to meet the first opening of the door to freedom."

Brown's trump argument was: "The slaves *have* revolted in past." He always cited San Domingo, which was, in truth, a special case. Aside from the French Revolutionary influence, the revolt there was set off by the mulatto *affranchis* who were semiliberated. The lot of the full-blooded Negro slaves there was far worse, in part due to absentee ownership, than it was in the case of American slaves. There was a heavy concentration of them within a small area, and they were homogeneous, preponderantly field hands, with few household workers.

There had been slave revolts in the American South, Brown pointed out, so there must be no lack of gumption. There was the revolt of "General" Gabriel in 1800, the year of his birth. In 1822 there was the plot engineered by Denmark Vesey, enlisting slaves in a radius of forty-five miles of Charleston, South Carolina. The arsenal near Charleston was to be broken into and the arms distributed, the city was to be fired in every quarter and the white population slaughtered. It was said that as many as six hundred slaves had been enlisted, and once the attack on Charleston commenced it was expected that all the blacks there would join and there would be an easy victory. The scheme was divulged to a loyal house-servant who told his master, and the leaders were captured and executed.

It was the revolt of Nat Turner, born in the same year as John Brown, which had made the strongest impression on Brown's mind. To Richard Hinton in Kansas later in this year of 1858 he said: "Nat Turner with fifty men held Virginia five weeks. The same number, well-organized and well-armed, can shake the system out of the State." He added, "Give a slave a pike and you make him a man. Deprive him of the means of resistance and you keep him down."

Turner was an eccentric fieldhand in Southampton County, in the southeastern corner of Virginia. His indulgent master allowed him to become a preacher and travel around. He saw visions, "And about this time I had a vision and I saw white spirits and black spirits engaged in battle, and the sun was darkened—the thunder rolled in the heavens and blood flowed in streams." There was another vision. An angel visited him and informed him, "The time is fast approaching when the 'first shall be the last and the last first.'" On August 22, 1831, he struck near Jerusalem Court House, Virginia. To his lieutenants he made an appropriate sermon, "Our race is to be delivered from slavery, and God has appointed us as the men to do his bidding, and let us be worthy of our calling."

Their strategy was to slaughter all whites in the county, without regard to age and sex. They first attacked a home where they killed mother, father and three children. Then they went from plantation to plantation, dealing death blows to every white man, woman, and child they found. On one farm, they dispatched a woman and ten children. The carnage lasted forty hours and fifty-seven whites were dead, the bloodiest slave insurrection ever in the South.

Troops were rushed from Richmond, Petersburg, Portsmouth, and Southampton. Negroes were massacred indiscriminantly until it was pointed out that valuable property was being destroyed. Weeks later, the half-starved Turner and his followers were rounded up, and he with sixteen followers went stoically to the gallows.

In telling Hinton that Nat Turner "held Virginia five weeks," Brown erred. Except for the first two days, Turner was on the run and in hiding. The memory of the Turner revolt remained stark and clear in Brown's day, and it had resulted in a traumatic dread over-hanging the land. "The night bell never tolled for fire in Richmond that the mother did not hug her infant more closely to her bosom." A Nat Turner-style revolt would be far more difficult in 1859 than it had been in 1831. The South was on the alert, an armed camp, and it had become more so as the tide of abolitionism had risen. Roads were heavily patrolled, slaves moving about were questioned, laws prohibited Negroes from carrying a weapon of any kind, and Negro assemblies in most states were banned.

Lincoln in early 1860 said that as a practical matter, even granted the willingness of the slaves to revolt, any insurrection of a general or extensive character was out of the question. "The indispensable concert of action cannot be attained. The slaves have no means of rapid communication and freemen, black or white, cannot supply it." Moreover, there were no "indispensable communicating trains" for conveying arms and ammunition. The Turner revolt was a freak outbreak, and entirely local.

Consider the magnitude of Brown's misjudgment. With himself he had twenty-two men at Harper's Ferry. He brought with him 200 Sharp's rifles, 200 revolvers, 950 knived pikes, 15 sabers, and 52 bay-onets. He attacked Harper's Ferry in order to get additional arms from the government arsenal there. And not one slave voluntarily joined him!

Matters had taken a turn for the worse for Brown while he was at Chatham. The less serious side because it was chronic was that he was out of money. He had received $600 of the $1,000 pledged from Sanborn by April 20, but it had all vanished. He had to pay for transporting his men from Springdale and boarding them, and ap-parently he had paid for traveling expenses and board for many of the black delegates in Canada. At any rate, he was so deeply in debt with unpaid bills that he could not even leave Chatham for the States.

The more serious side was that the viper Forbes was on his worst rampage yet, and had thrown a monkey-wrench into the works. He was making most violent threats to explode the plot, and Brown's backers had become so upset that they wanted to postpone the ex-pedition indefinitely, if not to cancel it. Such was the tenor of ad-vices Brown received from Sanborn.

Brown told his men that a temporary snag had developed in the financing of his campaign against Africa and that they must go to Ohio and get jobs for a while to support themselves. To Richard Realf he confided a special mission, which Realf described in his 1860 testimony before the Mason Committee. Brown told him that while he had been careful not to put things down in writing, he had indiscreetly given Forbes two documents that disclosed his plan for the Virginia invasion. He was afraid that Forbes would show these to Secretary of War Floyd and that would be the end. Realf was a fellow-Englishman. He must go to New York, insinuate himself into the good graces of Forbes and get hold of those documents, somehow, before everything was blasted to bits. Realf said he would try.

The number of men who had been directly informed of the plot now was in the dozens and the Lord only knew how many others had heard it indirectly. When Realf reached Cleveland and boarded for a few days with the men, the mushrooming number of those who knew of the conspiracy gave him the jitters, as he wrote his uncle in England. The black delegate at Chatham, J. G. Reynolds, he had learned, "has disclosed its objects to the members of a Secret Society (colored) calling itself the 'American Mysteries,' or some other confounded humbug. I suppose it is likely that these people are good men enough but to make a sort of wholesale divulgement of matters at hazard is too steep even for me, who are not by any means over-cautious."

Then, too, there was that exhibitionist, John Cook, who was making himself conspicuous by going around proclaiming that he had just come back from Kansas where he had killed five men, saying that he was now ready to launch a secret antislavery expedition, and the rest of the men at the boarding house were under his orders.

Realf went on to New York City, but he learned Forbes had gone to Washington and had not returned. He whiled away his time reading, and came across a book which had a great impact on his thinking. It was by the president of Brown college, Francis Wayland, entitled *The Limitations of Human Responsibility*. Wayland said, regarding the evil of slavery, that the only responsibility of decent men was to set the truth before the masters, but not to take measures the natural result of which would be to excite the slaves to insubordination or civil war. Although Wayland regarded slavery as a sin, yet no man is called on to discharge every duty to his fellow man in this life.

Wayland had something to say on the subject of the Puritan fanatic which Realf thought might apply to Old Brown. Such a man devotes himself to "the purpose to which he is urged by the voice of God speaking in his bosom. But if unfortunately he has misinterpreted the voice, the whole power of the man is enlisted in the work of mischief."

A highly nervous Richard Realf had a conversation in New York City with William F. M. Arny. We have met Arny before as the Illinois member of the National Kansas Committee who had a great distrust for Brown. Realf had spoken with Arny in Kansas. He wanted to go to England and deliver a series of lectures on Kansas which might raise funds for a free Kansas, and Arny had lent him money for his voyage to his homeland. Now, Arny asked Realf why he had not carried through with his plans. Realf replied that he was in deep water, and he wanted Arny's advice as a friend. He was involved in a "secret arrangement in which this Brown was a leader by which they proposed to make slavery insecure in the slave states," and it would have been in progress by this time if it had not been for Hugh Forbes who threatened to betray them. Realf could not divulge more.

Arny said he heard enough. As an older man, he would give the youth sound advice. The idea was outlandish and dangerous and he had better sever himself from it immediately, go to England, deliver his lectures, marry an American girl to whom he was paying attentions and settle down. Realf replied that he felt under some obligation to the "association in Canada." He would leave for England if Arny would do him a slight favor. His mission in New York was to track down Forbes, who, he had found out, had gone to Washington. Brown was fearful that Forbes was going to betray his plans to Secretary of War Floyd. Since Arny was about to go to Washington, while he was there would he find out whether or not Forbes had been in communication with Secretary Floyd? Would he let Captain Brown know the score? Arny said, "Yes."

Realf sailed for England. Brown never heard from him again, and Realf thereby probably prolonged his life. He had told Brown that he might lecture in England to raise money for him, and he did lecture there but entirely for the benefit of Richard Realf. Arny went on to Washington, and, regarding the activities of Hugh Forbes as none of his business, never performed the trust Realf had assigned to him.

Realf was found in Texas in early 1860 and testified before the Mason Committee. He denounced Brown for having committed "an intellectual error which had precipitated him upon a cruel and wicked deed." After the Civil War he wrote an ode glorifying Brown. It began, "Thank God for freedom's martyr." He had much financial and marital misery in his life and killed himself in a shabby hotel room in Oakland, California, in 1878 when he was forty-four years old. The poet, Richard Realf, who had been John Brown's secretary of state-designate was a tormented soul, as he said in one of his poems, "Born unto singing/ And a burthen lay mightily on him." His sole importance in life was John Brown's affection for him, and he had deserted Brown without a word and later had borne witness against him. That was part of the burden that lay on him until the grave.

Forbes did not visit or communicate with Secretary Floyd. He raised a fuss among United States senators in Washington. One Saturday morning, in the beginning of May, Senator Henry Wilson of Massachusetts was at his desk in the Senate, which was out of session, franking letters and doing some writing. Forbes, who "was a very nervous man and seemed to be in a passion," came up to him and poured out a story of how he had been deceived by John Brown. He had given up his business of teaching fencing in New York to drill men in the West and Brown had not paid him. His family was starving. The ground for the quarrel was not clear to Wilson, but Brown's purpose, which was financially backed by Sanborn and Dr. Howe in Boston as Wilson gathered, was one of military preparation for a strike into Missouri as a retaliation for Missourian interference in Kansas.

The leading Republican of the nation, Senator William H. Seward of New York, in his testimony before the Mason Committee, said that Forbes came to his home and he listened to him, assuming that he was soliciting charity. "I found his story very incoherent, very erratic and thought him a man of unsound mind." Forbes was a foreigner and showed him as proof of his importance a book he had got up, "strange and absurd," on the art of exciting military revolutions. He had been hired to go out to Kansas to train free-state men to defend themselves against an armed invasion expected from the slave states, he had been promised $1,200 but John Brown, when he joined him in Kansas, refused to pay him, and this Brown "was a very bad man who would not keep his word, was a reckless man, an unreliable man, a vicious man." His family in Paris was out on the streets starving as a result of Brown's nonpayment under the contract.

Forbes did not inform Seward of the Virginia expeditionary plan. He said that Brown proposed an attack on the border states to induce slaves to rise up, and the planned invasion of Kansas from the slave states would be foiled since the South would have enough trouble on its hands. Seward related that after he had given Forbes a fair hearing, he told him he could find no grounds for giving him private charity, and escorted him to the door.

Forbes had been subjecting Sanborn to a barrage of letters, and their general tenor had changed. He continued to say, "I have been grossly defrauded in the name of Humanity and Antislavery," but he did not emphasize money. Now he wanted the Boston revolutionary council to entrust the command of the expedition to him instead of to Brown who was much too rash, whose judgment was basically faulty, and who was out for personal gain. He would inject a higher moral tone into it. He wrote to Sanborn: "No cause can be benefited by the adhesion of a multitude of men scrambling for spoils and cheating each other. The greater the number of such men, the greater the evil. On the other hand, much can be accomplished by a mere handful if they be reliable and feel that they can depend on each other."

In early May, Dr. Howe received letters from Forbes explaining why, on the basis of his conversations with Brown in Tabor, which he detailed, they should not rely on a reckless and impractical general like Brown. Five men of the Secret Six quaked in their boots with fright. Their identity might be publicly disclosed by the "madman or villain," as Sanborn described Forbes. They had been willing to subsidize Brown but they were not willing to stick their necks out for the cause. Gerrit Smith, who had been ecstatic about Brown's plan in February, was now in deep gloom and told Sanborn, "I never was convinced of the wisdom of the scheme. But as things stand it seems to me madness to attempt to execute it." Sanborn wrote to Higginson that it looked as if the project would have to be deferred. Forbes's letter to Howe indicated he knew the details of the plan and the names of the backers. "How he got this knowledge is a mystery. He demands that Hawkins be dismissed and *himself* or some other be put in his place, threatening otherwise to make the business public."

Higginson protested with all his might against any delay. If Forbes did not succeed in blocking the project, then, as he told Parker, "Any betrayal afterward will only increase the *panic* which is one element in the speculation." Parker replied, "You are a better soldier than I but I think I'm right in the matter." To Sanborn, Higginson said he regretted that he did not have the money to "buy out the other stockholders." To Jason Brown in Ohio he sent a message to be relayed to his father in Chatham that he, Higginson, alone was protesting against the postponement. "If the thing is postponed, it is postponed for ever—for H.F. can do as much harm next year as this. His malice must be in some way put down or outwitted—& after the move is *once begun*, his plots will be of little importance."

The question of delay was settled for good by a letter of May 9 from Senator Wilson in Washington to Dr. Howe, which Dr. Howe concluded had been inspired by a visit from Forbes. Wilson was writing him in confidence that Howe and his friends should get the arms given to Old Brown for the defense of Kansas out of his hands. "If they should be used for other purposes, as rumor says they may be, it might be of disadvantage to the men who were induced to contribute to that very foolish movement."

The Secret Six did not know from Senator Wilson's guarded words that he had received no intimation whatever from Forbes of an invasion of Virginia but that Wilson thought that the arms were to be used in a punitive expedition against Missouri, which would escalate the Kansas fighting. Dr. Howe replied to the senator: "Prompt measures have been taken and will resolutely be followed up to prevent any such monstrous perversion of a trust." He assured Senator Wilson that "no countenance has been given" to Brown for any operations outside of Kansas. On May 14, Stearns wrote to Brown at Chatham that it had become his duty as chairman of the Massachusetts Kansas Aid Committee to warn Brown not to use the arms "for any other purpose and to hold them subject to my order as chairman of said committee."

In Chatham, Brown sat helpless because fundless, while his fate was being thrashed out in the East. When it became clear that his Virginia expedition would have to be delayed, he had to cope with the problem of adjusting his restless, young followers to a siege of prolonged inactivity. They were psychologically unhinged. Their thoughts had been lifted into the stratosphere at Springdale and Chatham, and they found it difficult to make a landing on earth, even temporarily, to a humdrum work-life when they had been prepared to remake the nation. Cook, in fact, wanted to stage a southern expedition on his own, preferring the risk of death to everyday work.

Brown exhorted them as best he could: "Suppose we do have to defer our direct efforts? Shall great and noble minds either indulge in useless complaint or fold their arms in discouragement, or sit in idleness, when we may at least avoid losing ground." These were the times that try men's souls. "It is in such times that men mark themselves. 'He that endureth unto the end,' the same shall get his reward in one of the noblest enterprises in which men were ever engaged."

He wrote to Stearns that he needed $300 immediately to pay his bills. He promised to hold everything in abeyance pending further instructions from his sponsors. "None of our friends need have any fears in relation to rash steps being taken by us. As Knowledge is said to be Power, we propose to become possessed of more Knowledge. We have many reasons for begging our eastern friends to keep clear of F. [Forbes] personally unless he throws himself upon them. We have those who are thoroughly posted up to put on his track and we humbly beg to be allowed to do so."

Action was taken by the Secret Six to escape from the dilemma posed by Forbes. Dr. Howe wrote Forbes a stern letter. Howe had decided to take cognizance of him, he said, only in the hope, "though perhaps the vain one, of disabusing your mind of certain errors which seem to be growing into insane belief." Forbes' railings at "New England humanitarians" did not bother him because he did not make any pretension "to humanitarianism *par excellence*." He had confidence in the integrity and ability of Captain Brown—but he was not responsible for Captain Brown's acts. "I have confidence in the integrity and ability of scores and hundreds of men for whose words and acts I am in no wise responsible. . . . I infer from your language that you have obtained (in confidence) some information respecting an expedition which you think to be commendable, provided you could manage it, but you will betray and denounce it if he does not give it up. You are, sir, the guardian of your own honor! but I trust that for your children's sake at least you will never let your passions lead you to a course that might make them blush!"

This classic of casuistry, of which Howe was justifiably proud, he wound up by saying that he would dispel any false notions about Captain Brown's true intentions by disclosing that Brown was about to set off for Kansas to give his aid to the free-staters in the coming elections. Were Forbes to write him less vituperatively he would consider helping out his starving family in Paris, but he would throw into the trash-can further letters of the kind he had been receiving.

Forbes replied to Howe acidly that "the caprice of refusing to read anything distasteful is so like a pouting, spoilt child that I should not be surprised at your being so easily hoodwinked by anyone who was to approach you with flattery and a pleasing story," and his disclaimer of responsibility for Brown was "cowardly shirking." Forbes had no doubt but that the "New England humanitarians" were plotting this thing so that, when war between North and South broke out, industrialists like Amos Lawrence would make a fortune in speculations, such as by buying up cotton in advance. And that was the last Howe heard from "Colonel" Hugh Forbes.

Having dug themselves into a safe, fortified bunker by their denials, Brown's friends adopted a new strategy for action. Gerrit Smith came to Boston and in his room in the Revere House on May 23 the Secret Six met—except for Higginson, who was boiling with indignation that Brown's foray had been put off, not because the plan was in jeopardy but because his backers feared for their skin. At this meeting, the five present decided that Brown must delay his Virginia plan until the next year of 1859. To mislead anyone who credited Forbes, Brown must execute a feint or "blind" by going to Kansas post-haste. They would sweeten the deal to mollify Brown. They would give Brown another $500 immediately, and would undertake to raise another $2,000 to $3,000 in 1859 to defray the cost of the postponed mission. This agreement was ratified by another meeting in the American House on May 31 of the Secret Six *in toto* since a reconciled Higginson attended.

And now a breathtaking piece of duplicity! Howe had assured Senator Wilson that there would be no "monstrous perversion of a trust" by allowing arms for Kansas to be used by Brown elsewhere. Yet, within days, Brown was given full title to the two hundred Sharp's rifles when Stearns foreclosed on them, since they were security for his loan. Stearns then donated them to Brown without any strings attached. Writing of this in 1885, Sanborn said: "It is a little difficult to explain this transaction without leaving the suspicion that there was somewhere a breach of trust." The fact of the matter is that it was a crass swindle of those who had donated their nickels and dimes for Kansas aid to divert this money for Sharp's rifles to be carried by John Brown to Harper's Ferry.

The Puritan conscience, we have commented before, was exceptionally elastic when it came to business matters. Let us recapitulate this feat of financial legerdemain:

First step. Thousands of people contribute money to the Massachusetts Kansas Aid Committee, and it buys two hundred Sharp's rifles at a cost of $5,000 which are transported west by Dr. J. P. Root in 1856 and stored in Tabor in the Reverend Mr. Todd's cellar pending distribution in Kansas.

Second step. The Massachusetts Committee, of which George L. Stearns is chairman, buys two hundred revolvers costing $1,200 for John Brown with money lent to it by George L. Stearns, a private citizen. The Massachusetts Committee under the chairmanship of Mr. Stearns assigns the two hundred rifles to Mr. Stearns as security for his loan.

Third step. The Massachusetts Committee, again with Mr. Stearns as chairman, votes to default on the loan to Mr. Stearns, private citizen, and then Mr. Stearns forecloses on the two hundred rifles and owns them, having acquired $5,000 worth of property for his loan of $1,200. He then gives the rifles to John Brown as a gift from a private admirer.

A retreat in fear followed by chicanery was now crowned with hypocrisy. Stearns and Gerrit Smith proposed that, while they would aid Brown further, they should have no guilty knowledge thereafter of Brown's plans, or as Sanborn put it, responsibility "should no longer fetter his friends in aiding his design." He was not to inform them of his plans in any detail or burden them with knowledge since it was "needless and inconvenient." They did not want him to report progress except by action. On July 26, Gerrit Smith gave another $100 for Brown, writing to Sanborn in confirmation of the understanding: "Whenever he shall embark on another of these contests, I shall again stand ready to help him. I do not want to know Captain Brown's plans. I hope he will keep them to himself." The beneficiary of their gifts was to be responsible only to himself.

Stearns sent money to pay his Chatham bills and Brown arrived in Boston from Chatham on June 1. He was told of the new arrangement. Dr. Howe said that when he received the $500 in gold he left in "good spirits." He had reason to be pleased. When he sprang the plan initially at Peterboro in February he had said that he needed $800 and would consider himself fortunate to have $1,000. He had now received far over $1,000, and was promised thousands of dollars more. The rifles were now his, a huge bonanza.

While in Boston for three days, Brown had a tête-á-tête with Higginson, of which Higginson made a memorandum immediately.

Brown said that Forbes' betrayal might have hurt his campaign since he wanted his opponents to underrate him. Higginson suggested that the increased terror generated by a leakage of his plan might have counterbalanced this. Brown switched and agreed with Higginson that the operation should not have been delayed, but Smith was a timid man and Stearns and Parker did not abound in courage.

Higginson was his soul-brother. "The sly, old veteran," Higginson noted, acquiesced to the others, but Brown confided to him he had had no choice since "it was essential that they shd. not think him reckless, & as they held the purse he was powerless without them, having spent every thing received this far. . . ." Higginson did not consider the possibility that the "sly, old veteran" might be catering to his vanity as he did to each of the others.

In truth, this elegant, well-bred intellectual from Cambridge was a soul-brother of the rude, self-taught frontiersman. Higginson was totally and without compunction committed to the extirpation of the curse of slavery and had none of the ambivalent feelings arising from considerations of personal safety that the others of the Six had. He was totally convinced that slavery would end in blood as it had begun in blood. Like Brown, he was convinced that the slaves would answer the call as soon as the Liberator appeared on southern soil. "We forget the heroes of Santo Domingo," he said in a speech in that month of May, 1858, in refuting the argument that slaves would not fight. He said in that same speech that on the occasions when he had been shaved by a Negro, he had marveled "at the patience of the Negro shaving the white man for many years, and yet kept the razor outside of his throat."

Higginson, straight as a die in his Abolitionist credo, would be the only one of the Six to stand up courageously for John Brown after the fiasco at Harper's Ferry.

Patience, patience—that is the lesson that I, who have so few years ahead of me, must teach the young, who have so many years to live. Brown said this to Richard Hinton later in the year in Kansas. The "blind" of going to Kansas was to be successful. Frederick Douglass commented that as a result of the new strategy, "No one believed Forbes, though the scoundrel told the truth" about Brown's intention to open up a new front with the money supplied by a Boston élite.

Brown's trip west to Kansas, unlike the one in 1857, would have to be fruitful. Higginson had expressed his doubts to him that the others of the Six, being infirm in purpose, would carry through with their promised aid to him in 1859. Brown would have to enthuse them, somehow.

He had only ten days to enjoy with his wife and family in North Elba before setting out for Kansas. He wrote:

The *cries* of my poor *sorrowstricken despairing Children* whoose *"tears on their cheeks"* are *ever* in my *Eye*; & whose *sighs* are *ever* in my Ears; may however prevent my enjoying the happiness I so much desire. But *courage, courage, Courage* the great work of my life (the unseen Hand that "girded me; & who has *indeed* holden *my right* hand may hold it still;) *though* I have not known Him;" at all *as I ought*:) I may yet see accomplished; (*God helping*;) & be permitted to return, *& rest* at Evening.

On this trip east, Brown was well pleased to find himself something of a celebrity. In fact, he contemplated writing a book about himself, which he was sure would be a best-seller. It would be a "narative of most *thrilling interest*," he wrote John Jr. "I am certain that from the manner in which I have been pressed to narate & the greedy swallowing everywhere of what I have told & complaints of my backwardness to gratify the public that the book would find a ready sale." Brown did prepare a few fragments before he dropped the project, such as his account of his journey across Missouri to Kansas in 1855.

There is another personal note to make here. When he appeared in Boston he was no longer clean-shaven; he was growing the beard which would be of patriarchal length in 1859 when he reappeared in Boston. Beards were not common at the time—they became popular in the Civil War and after. Brown had often expressed admiration for Stearns' majestic beard, which Stearns said he had grown on doctor's orders as a chest-covering since he suffered from chronic bronchitis.

The bearded John Brown, which is so much a part of the legend, existed only for one year. As a means of disguise, he scissored off his beard at North Elba in June, 1859, before he left to establish his base in Maryland for his Harper's Ferry foray, and when he appeared there his beard was only an inch and a half long.

CHAPTER SIX

"*Kansas,*
I Bid Thee Farewell"

KANSAS EXPERIENCED little violence from the time it had been pacified by Governor Geary and federal troops in the autumn months of 1856, until early 1858 when, in the counties bordering Missouri, Bourbon, and Linn counties, proslavery and free-state bands clashed. Before Brown departed for Kansas, the North had been shocked by the news of a massacre of free-state men near the border in Linn County. It became celebrated under the name of the Marais des Cygnes Massacre, though it happened a distance from that river.

Charles A. Hamelton was a native of Georgia from a fine family, and had attended the University of Georgia. He came to Kansas in 1855 and became a border-ruffian, planning "to vote and shoot in Kansas but for safety to sleep in Missouri." His dedication and leadership attracted followers and his band at one time numbered in the hundreds. In early 1858, he and his men had established themselves in quarters in Kansas.

On the opposing free-state side, there had emerged a leader who was one of the more interesting personalities in Kansas history. James Montgomery had been born in 1814 in Astabula County, Ohio, in the Western Reserve. His antecedents were fine, New England stock, both his grandparents having fought at Bunker Hill. He migrated to slave Kentucky and then to Pike County in Missouri in 1852. He settled in Kansas in 1856 and adopted the free-state cause, organizing in 1857 the Self-Protective Company.

Sanborn related his great surprise when he made the acquaintance of this border-chieftain in 1860: "He had an air of elegance and distinction which I hardly expected. He was a slender, courteous person with a gentle, cultivated voice and the manner of a French chevalier." He was, like Brown, highly religious and from youth had been a Campbellite preacher. Like Higginson, he was to command a Negro regiment in the Civil War. In the Kansas border-warfare he was a daring and indomitable leader. He had married an almost illiterate farmgirl of Kentucky whose fearlessness equalled his own, and she was quoted after one skirmish, "I do get plumb tired of being shot at, but I won't be druv out of my cabin."

Montgomery and his "jayhawkers" rode into the Hamelton stronghold of Trading Post, seized barrels of their corn whiskey, dumped them on the road, and gave an ultimatum to Hamelton to get out of Kansas. Hamelton evacuated and sent word from Missouri to his Kansas proslave friends "to come out of the territory at once as we are coming up there to kill snakes, and will treat all we find there as snakes." He was to keep his word.

On May 19, 1859, Hamelton and a mounted gang of thirty rode from West Point, Missouri, across the border, and arrived at Trading Post at 9 A.M. where they took into custody John F. Campbell, a clerk in a store. A half-mile from Trading Post they took prisoner a Baptist missionary well known to Hamelton, Reverend B. L. Reed, and two Kansas residents with whom the Reverend Mr. Reed was conversing, William A. Stilwell and Patrick Ross. Further up the road they invaded the cabin of Amos C. Hall and pulled him out of his sickbed. Next Charles Colpetzer was plucked from his home. Then Michael Robinson and Charles Snyder were hauled in and, farther north, two more men who were working in the cornfields, William and Asa Hairgrove. William Hairgrove was a native of Georgia and had known Hamelton very well there. Next, Hamelton came upon Austin W. Hall, a brother of Amos Hall, already in tow, who was returning with his horses from a blacksmith shop, and he joined the prisoners.

None of the eleven men bore arms when they were taken, none had taken any part in the factional fighting. Most knew Hamelton personally to some degree and did not think he meant bodily harm to them. They were hustled along and marched into a defile surrounded by the mounds which characterize the area a half-mile from the border. After they were herded into line, Hamelton's men on their horses formed another line on the side of the ravine. William Hairgrove, aware now that these preparations meant murder, said calmly, "Gentlemen, if you are going to shoot, take good aim."

Hamelton barked the orders, "Make ready, take aim." Before he could say, "Fire," one of the worst blackguards of his crew, W. B. Brockett, who had been Pate's lieutenant at Black Jack, turned his horse away. Hamelton shouted, "Brockett, goddamn you, why don't you wheel into line?" Brockett shouted back, "I'll be damned if I have anything to do with a goddamn piece of business like this. If it was in a fight, I would fire." Hamelton took out his revolver and fired at the prisoners, barking the order, "Fire," at the same time. The victims fell. Then a firing squad went down the line to finish the men off, but did not do a complete job.

Five of the men died on the spot: Campbell, Colpetzer, Robinson, Ross, and Stilwell. Five were seriously wounded. One, Austin Hall, miraculously escaped being hit at all, and feigning death fell to the ground with the others. Hamelton's men scooted off to Missouri. A hue and cry was quickly raised and they were pursued by two hundred Kansans, some of them led by Montgomery, to West Point, Missouri, where the trail grew cold. Hamelton returned to Georgia, served in the Civil War and was elected to the Georgia legislature in 1878. One man paid with his life for the crime. William Griffith was arrested in the spring of 1863 and executed in October at Mound City. The rope was adjusted around his neck by one of the intended victims, William Hairgrove.

Unlike Brown's Pottawatomie murders, this horror was widely publicized and roused wrathful indignation. In the *Atlantic Monthly* for September, 1858, a poem by John Greenleaf Whittier was published, "Les Marais du Cygnes." Some of the verses follow:

> From the hearths of their cabins,
>   The fields of their corn,
> Unwarned and unweaponed,
>   The victims were torn.
> By the whirlwind of murder
>   Swooped up and swept on
> To the low, reedy fen-lands,
>   The marsh of the swans.

John Brown in Kansas in 1856. The photograph is an ambrotype taken in Osawatomie early that year. *Library of Congress*

The earliest photograph of John Brown, a da-
guerreotype taken around 1850 when he was
engaged in the wool business in Springfield,
Massachusetts. The facial features have been
slightly retouched to make them more distinct.
Ohio Historical Society Library

Owen Brown, father of John
Brown. An ardent Abolitionist,
he strongly influenced his son.
Ohio Historical Society Library

Mrs. John Brown with daughters Ellen and Sarah. This was probably taken soon after
the execution of her husband. *Library of Congress*

John Brown, Jr. Operating in Ohio, he acted as forwarding agent and liaison man for his father in the Harper's Ferry raid. *Library of Congress*

Owen Brown, then thirty-five, was one of the five who made good his escape from Harper's Ferry. *Library of Congress*

Oliver Brown with wife Martha. At the age of twenty, he was killed at Harper's Ferry. By his father's side, he had been an executioner at the Pottawatomie massacre in Kansas in 1856. Martha kept house for John Brown's men at the Kennedy farm in the summer of 1859. *Library of Congress*

Watson Brown. He was killed at Harper's Ferry at the age of twenty-four. *Library of Congress*

Jason Brown in his old age. Although he did not take part in the Harper's Ferry raid, he fought by his father's side in the battle of Osawatomie in Kansas in 1856. *Library of Congress*

Salmon Brown in his old age. He did not take part in the Harper's Ferry raid, but by his father's side, he had been an executioner at the Pottawatomie massacre in Kansas in 1856. *Library of Congress*

John Brown in the spring of 1859. An unretouched photograph taken in New York City. Soon thereafter he cropped his beard which was only an inch and a half long when he appeared at Harper's Ferry. *Library of Congress*

The Secret Six

George L. Stearns, wealthy industrialist living in Boston. *Library of Congress*

Gerrit Smith was the nation's largest landowner and its leading philanthropist. *Library of Congress*

Dr. Samuel Gridley Howe, one of the nation's leading humanitarians, principally in the care of the blind. His wife was Julia Ward Howe. *Library of Congress*

Franklin B. Sanborn, a disciple of Ralph Waldo Emerson in Concord, Massachusetts. He was later John Brown's biographer.

The Reverend Thomas Wentworth Higginson. He was also an author and reformer and, in the Civil War, the colonel of a Negro regiment. *Library of Congress*

The Reverend Theodore Parker, internationally famous preacher. A maverick Unitarian, he articulated the "higher-law" doctrine. *Library of Congress*

Leading members of John Brown's company

John Henry Kagi, John Brown's right-hand man. The gifted Kagi was a lawyer, journalist, and schoolteacher. At the age of twenty-four, he was killed at Harper's Ferry. *Library of Congress*

Aaron D. Stevens. A court-martialed United States soldier who escaped from prison, he was John Brown's drillmaster. He was severely wounded at Harper's Ferry and later executed at Charlestown, Virginia, at the age of twenty-nine. *Library of Congress*

John Edwin Cook, a well-educated member of a fine Connecticut family. He escaped from Harper's Ferry but was returned by Pennsylvania and executed at Charlestown, Virginia, at the age of twenty-nine. *Library of Congress*

Edwin Coppoc, a Quaker idealist from Iowa. He was executed at Charlestown, Virginia, at the age of twenty-four. *Library of Congress*

Richard Realf, the poet. Brown's secretary of state-designate, he deserted John Brown in the summer of 1858. *Library of Congress*

Harper's Ferry after the Civil War. The Potomac River is in the foreground, the Shenandoah River is on the right. Maryland Heights is on the left, Loudoun Heights to which Brown planned to retreat is on the right. The empty space along the railroad tracks was occupied by the armory buildings. *Library of Congress*

The Kennedy farm in Maryland six miles from the Potomac bridge, which was the base for the Harper's Ferry raid. *Library of Congress*

Four blacks who participated in the Harper's Ferry raid

Dangerfield Newby, son of a Scotch plantation master. He was killed at Harper's Ferry at the age of forty-four. *Library of Congress*

Lewis S. Leary. He was a saddler and harness-maker from Oberlin, Ohio. He was killed at Harper's Ferry at the age of twenty-four. *Library of Congress*

John A. Copeland, Jr. He came from Oberlin College where he had been a student. He was executed at Charlestown, Virginia, at the age of twenty-five. *Library of Congress*

Osborn P. Anderson. He was a printer in Canada. He was one of the five who made good their escape from Harper's Ferry and later wrote an account of the raid. *Library of Congress*

The storming of the engine-house by United States Marines as sketched by an artist for *Frank Leslie's Illustrated Newspaper. Library of Congress*

The engine-house on exhibit at the Chicago World's Fair in 1893. It has been moved many times and is now in Harper's Ferry on the bank of the Shenandoah River. *Library of Congress*

The courthouse, which is standing today in Charles Town, West Virginia (formerly Charlestown, Virginia), where John Brown was tried. *Library of Congress*

Governor Henry A. Wise of Virginia, who managed carefully the trial and execution of John Brown and his comrades. *Library of Congress*

John Brown soon after his capture and under interrogation in the paymaster's office. Sketched on the spot by the artist known as Porte Crayon for *Harper's Weekly. Library of Congress*

John Brown before the court, Judge Richard Parker presiding, as sketched for *Frank Leslie's Illustrated Newspaper*. *Library of Congress*

John Brown ascending the scaffold, as sketched for *Frank Leslie's Illustrated Newspaper*. *Library of Congress*

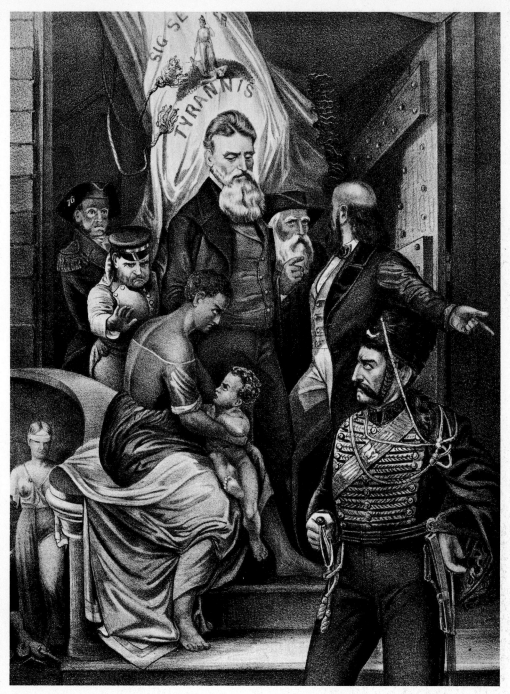

The mythical scene of John Brown meeting the slave mother on the way to the scaffold. A Currier & Ives lithograph of 1863. *Library of Congress*

The mythical scene of John Brown kissing the slave child on the way to the scaffold. A painting by Thomas Hovenden in 1883. *Metropolitan Museum of Art*

John Brown's farmhouse in North Elba, New York, where he is buried with the remains of many of his gallant comrades at Harper's Ferry. *Library of Congress*

With a vain plea for mercy
   No stout knee was crooked,
In the mouths of the rifles
   Right manly they looked,
How paled the May sunshine,
   Green Marais du Cygnes
When the death-smoke blew over
   The lonely ravine!

Strong man of the prairies,
   Mourn bitter and wild!
Wail, desolate woman!
   Wail, fatherless child!
But, the grain of God springs up
   From ashes beneath,
And the crown of His harvest
   Is life out of death.

Brown, after leaving his family at North Elba, showed none of the irresolution that had characterized his movements to the West the year before. He met his men in Cleveland on June 20 and explained to them why he had to go to Kansas in furtherance of the main design, which was postponed until the spring of 1859. Kagi, ever versatile and resourceful, had gone to Hamilton, Canada, gotten a job as a printer, and had managed to print copies of the Chatham constitution which he and Brown had co-authored. Brown, while in Cleveland, paid the printing bill. Kagi and Tidd accompanied Brown to Kansas. The others temporarily scattered. Stevens and Gill had girl friends in Springdale and went there before they joined Brown in Kansas. Parsons spent the summer on the farm of E. A. Fobes in Ohio, the brother-in-law of John Brown, Jr. Cook, after staying a while in Ohio, was assigned to go to Harper's Ferry where he was to take abode, work and become an espionage agent, reporting fully to Brown intelligence on that area. On July 23, John Jr. wrote his father in Kansas that Moffet and Parsons were working and doing well, Leeman was indolent, a "damage to any cause," and Cook, Parsons and Moffet talked much too much, "*entirely too communicative* of business matters."

The delay of a year was to cost five men for the expedition: Parsons, Moffet, Gill, Realf, and Richard Richardson who remained in Canada. The defections probably did not affect the success or failure of the Harper's Ferry raid a whit, and considerably lengthened these men's lives.

On June 26, Brown was in Lawrence, Kansas, with Kagi and Tidd. Two days later, he wrote his "Dear Friends at Boston, Worcester and Peterboro," informing them that he had arrived, and was on his way to "the neighborhood of late troubles." He did not intend to let them forget him and their commitment to him. "I do hope you will be in earnest now to carry out *as soon as possible* the measure proposed in Mr. Sanborn's letter inviting me to Boston this last Spring. I hope there will be *no delay* of that matter." In the proper mystery, there was no signature after "Yours in Truth," and all mail for him was to be sent in a sealed envelope to the Reverend Mr. Adair.

Hinton met Brown for the second time in a hotel in Lawrence. He found that Brown had aged far more than time required. "I venture to say that in 1858, John Brown looked to me as a 'Prophet' might have done; in 1856, he certainly embodied the 'fighter.' Under no circumstances could he ever have appeared commonplace."

On July 1, Brown was on the scene of the infamous massacre, and arranged to buy land near the ravine from a blacksmith, Eli Snyder. To North Elba from Trading Post, he wrote: "Considerable excitement still exists on both sides [of the border], some plundering and every few days some new murder is committed. The Free State men are at present in the abundant deserted houses. Farms lie in all directions. Some belong to Free State men who have fled through fear but the greater part are places deserted by Proslavery men & many of these were a few weeks since occupied by the murderers of their own neighbours," who had been identified by the survivors. Everything was in "a state of uncertainty and constant fear. We are at all hours on the alert." Old William Hairgrove was with him recovering from his grave wounds, and also a Missourian who had fled to Kansas for fear of his life after reporting to an eastern newsman the whereabouts of the killers.

Brown did not exaggerate the terror created by the Hamelton massacre. The New York *Times* correspondent, William Hutchinson, reported: "The people on my route were in arms as far as they dared to be. No farm work was thought of but men and women were gathered together in groups for protection in cabins that furnished the best defense."

In a jovial mood, Brown on July 9 told John Jr. of a guest from Missouri who had wandered into his lair. Brown apprized him "that notwithstanding he was in a perfect *nest* of the most ultra abolitionists not a hair would fall from his head 'so long as we knew of no mischief he had been engaged in.' " This visitor was greatly agitated. "I told him the Missouri people might have perfect quiet if they honestly desired it & further that if they chose war they would soon have all they might *any of them* care for. I gave him the most powerful abolition lecture of which I am capable; I having an unusual gift of utterance. . . . I presume he will not soon forget the old abolitionist 'mit de' white beard."

Brown had visited the cabin of James Montgomery and had found the "notorious Captain . . . a very brave and talented officer and what is infinitely more, a kind, gentlemanly and most excellent man and lover of Freedom."

Few would agree with all of that praise. Montgomery was widely regarded by the free-staters as a man of principle who acted harshly because of what he felt to be stern necessity, but as the historian Andreas stated, "He did many things which, when judged outside of their immediate and remote causes and connections, would not stand the test of the moral code," and like all gang leaders he could not restrain his men. Whether he had justification or not, his actions could be violent enough to make him a border-chieftain after Brown's own heart. On January 4, 1858, in the election for governor under the proslave Lecompton constitution, Montgomery's men stole ballot boxes and threw the ballots to the winds. On April 21, he attacked from cover a company of United States Cavalry which was about to overtake him, killed a soldier, and wounded two more. The federal troops fled, a disgrace that forced their captain to resign from the service. Governor James W. Denver reported to Buchanan's aged Secretary of State, Lewis Cass, that in the thirty miles from Fort Scott to the Marais des Cygnes, "we passed through a country almost depopulated by the depredations of the predatory bands under Montgomery, presenting a scene of desolation such as I never expected to have witnessed in any country inhabited by American citizens."

Brown's first action in Kansas smacked of the theatrical. He built a fort on the land he had acquired from Snyder, and broadcast defiance to Hamelton or other border-ruffians to come and get him. It was eighteen feet by fourteen feet, two stories high, walled with logs, had portholes on each floor, water from a spring ran through the house and into a pit on the southwest corner, and as an added protection from small arms fire it was banked with dirt and rocks to a height of four feet.

Needless to say, no one assaulted his Maginot Line. Brown did not make the agreed-upon payments to Snyder, who proceeded to sell the land to a friend of Brown, Charles C. Hadsall. Brown told Hadsall that the sale was agreeable to him if he would permit him the privilege of military occupation on his small lot, and Hadsall agreed.

Brown was no longer Nelson Hawkins but had a new picturesque name, Shubel Morgan. Why did he assume a fictitious name since everyone in Kansas knew who he was? Why did he take this useless security measure while he had been utterly reckless in wholesale divulgement of his plan for rebellion and treason? Was this pixyish humor on his part, or did he want to impress the conspirators in the East? We can only speculate about the answers.

With his penchant for formal organization, Articles of Agreement for Shubel Morgan's Company, in the handwriting of his draftsman, John Henry Kagi, were drawn up in July, 1858. They followed roughly the rules for his Kansas volunteer-regular company in August, 1856—strict deportment for members, fair trials for prisoners before punishment, and equal distribution among members of all booty. The list of members was fifteen but it was inflated. It had the names of James Montgomery, old William Hairgrove, recovering from wounds, and his friend Augustus Wattles, a peaceful farmer.

Nothing was happening, but, in a letter to Sanborn, Shubel Morgan conveyed the sense of impending crisis and his personal danger. The residents "watch every appearance of persons moveing about with anxious jealousy; & vigilance. . . . A constant fear of new troubles seems to prevail on both sides of the line; & on both sides are companies of armed men. Any little affair may open the quarrel afresh. . . . I have concealed the fact of my presence pretty much; lest it should create excitement; but it is getting leaked out; & will soon be known to all. As I am not here to *seek* or *secure revenge*; I do not mean to be the first to reopen the quarrel." As always, the theme of more money was sounded to Sanborn. He would need some very soon as his men could not work for wages.

Political developments were taking place which would move Kansas steadily on to statehood. The Lecompton constitution was framed by men who had been elected only by the proslave element in the Territory. This constitution was submitted to a vote of Kansas on December 21, 1857, and there were only two choices allowed, both unpalatable to the free-staters. They could vote for it "with slavery," or if they voted for it "without slavery," nonetheless, slaves were declared property and those in the Territory and their offspring would be perpetuated as slaves. The Democratic governor, Denver, declared it a "vile fraud, a base counterfeit and a wretched device." The free-state men boycotted the referendum, and the constitution "with slavery" was adopted. The situation became slightly less snarled-up when both factions voted for a territorial legislature which was captured by the free-staters, so there was now one legislature, instead of two.

The constitution was dumped in the lap of Congress in February, 1858. The author of the Kansas–Nebraska Act and the friend of the South, Senator Stephen A. Douglas, could not stomach the Lecompton constitution and he denounced it as a "trick, a fraud upon the rights of the people." Despite his opposition the Senate voted to accept it. The excitement in the House was intense, and in one all-night session thirty members from North and South engaged in a fistfight and brawl in the well of the House. In the end there was a compromise, the English bill, which submitted the Lecompton constitution to a vote of the people with an unprecedented bribe of public lands if Kansas accepted. The referendum on the bill took place on August 2, when 11,300 of 13,188 votes were cast against the constitution. Kansas was not yet in the Union, but it was now inevitable that when it entered it would be as a free state.

Such progress on the political plane failed to interest Brown one iota. He had a talk with Governor Robinson in Lawrence and said to him, "You have succeeded in what you undertook. You aimed to make Kansas a free state and your plans were skilfully laid for that purpose. But I had another object in view. I meant to strike a blow at slavery."

On August 9, he reported to John Jr. that as a result of his establishing himself on the border, "confidence seems to be greatly restored amongst the Free-State men." As for a trivial matter, "The Election of the 2nd Inst. passed off quietly on this part of the Line." Osawatomie Brown was the cynosure of all eyes, that is, among those who knew he was there. "Our going onto the line was done with the utmost quiet & so far as I am concerned under an assumed name to avoid creating any excitement." But the awesome news could not be kept a secret very long. "In Missouri the fact was pretty well understood, & the idea of having such a neighbour improving a Claim (as was the case) right on a conspicuous place and in full view for miles around in Missouri produced a ferment there which you can better imagine than I can describe. Which of the passions most predominated, fear or rage, I do not pretend to say."

He told his son that he planned to publish his book serially, with Augustus Wattles acting as agent, and it would be not only about himself but about the whole clan of Browns. His tentative title was "A Brief History of John Brown; otherwise (old B) and his family; as connected with Kansas; By one who knows."

No one from Missouri molested the old warrior. During these summer weeks, he had spells of sickness. On July 23, he took ill with the "ague," as he always called it, and stayed a few days with Wattles until he recovered. On August 23, he was more seriously ill and remained in the Reverend Adair's cabin near Osawatomie for three weeks. On September 9, he informed his son John that he had had "Ague and Chill fever. Was never more sick."

These illnesses returned with increasing frequency to the once altogether healthy and sickness-free Brown. Although he was attended by a physician while at the Adairs, we have no medical report on the symptoms and nature of the sickness. Was the "ague" malarial fever? There is no indication in the numerous bouts he had from now on that he ever again was treated by a doctor.

In the intervals between these indispositions, we know of some of his activities in this summer of 1858, and one most vital to him was the raising of funds. George L. Stearns sent him from Boston a bundle of promissory notes that Kansas settlers had given the National Kansas Committee in return for food, clothing, seed, etc. Stearns had been given these notes by the Massachusetts Kansas Aid Committee as security for advances made by him, under the same arrangement as in the case of the two hundred revolvers furnished to Brown. There was another jurisdictional mixup, since the Massachusetts Committee claimed that it had been the chief source of the funds for the National Committee, and that the notes therefore properly belonged to it. Brown went further and rested his title as endorsee of these notes on what he considered unimpeachable legal grounds— the National Kansas Committee in New York City on January 24, 1857 had voted him $5,000 in assistance and what it could provide in equipment for a hundred men and all he had collected was a couple of hundred dollars and fourteen boxes of clothing, so there was a huge sum owing him.

The dispute became acrimonious. The secretary of the National

Kansas Committee, H. B. Hurd, wrote to its agent (who was also the agent of the Massachusetts Committee), E. B. Whitman, that "Capt. John Brown has no authority to take, receive, collect or transfer any notes or accounts belonging to the National Kansas Committee nor has he ever had. Nor will any such dealing be recognized or sanctioned by the Committee." Nevertheless, Brown went ahead and collected several hundred dollars from settlers, demanding the money after he gave public notice that he was the agent of the National Kansas Committee, and Sanborn backed him up fully. Thus, money contributed for a free Kansas was again diverted to sustain the Harper's Ferry plan in the works.

During the summer, Eli Snyder related that he, Brown, Kagi, and Tidd made an unarmed excursion into Missouri. Kagi and Tidd went by road to Butler, pretending to be looking for jobs teaching school. Brown and Snyder pretended to be surveyors, and Brown took along his surveyor's compass and chain. They met at Pattenville and then agreed to part company and meet again on top of a hill under a clump of trees. The party looked down from the hill and saw a half-mile to the east the house of the Reverend Martin White. Through a telescope, they could see White clearly, sitting under the shade of a tree, reading a book. Snyder proposed a visit by Brown and himself. "I won't do that," was Brown's reply. Kagi said he would go with Snyder. Brown said, "Go if you wish but don't hurt a hair of his head." Kagi said that he would go but only if he had no instructions. And that was the end of the matter.

To James Hanway, Brown said, "I would not hurt one hair of White's head. I would not go an inch to take his life. I do not harbor the feelings of revenge. I act only from a principle, to restore human rights."

By the close of the summer, Brown had abandoned his fort. There was no action and no hope for action. Stevens and Gill had joined him from Springdale where they had spent a good summer. Kagi and Gill became his boon companions. "Knowledge is Power" was his favorite saying, and Brown liked brainy young men. Though he put great reliance on Stevens' stout right arm and his military expertise to train men he did not regard him as "clever."

"The Captain has shown that he can be in the Territory without making war," Kagi wrote in a short piece for the New York *Tribune*. But inactivity was not serving Brown's purpose. He wanted to do something with éclat while not risking his neck and the great invasion of Africa scheduled for the following year. He apparently considered throwing up Kansas work entirely, since on October 11 he wrote from Osawatomie to his wife that he was in better health but still quite weak. "I can now see no good reason why I should not be located nearer home as soon as I can collect the means for expences."

His mind was on his great mission. To Sanborn, he wrote on September 10: "I am most anxious about that and want you to name the earliest possible date when you can have your matters gathered up. *Dear friends do be in earnest.* The harvest we shall reap if you are only up and doing." He had frank conversations with the correspondents William A. Phillips and Richard Hinton. To Phillips, he discoursed on the history of slavery and denounced the politicians of the South as propagandists and those of the North as trimmers. Armageddon was close at hand. "We have reached a point where nothing but war can settle the question. Had they [the Southerners] succeeded in Kansas, they would have gained a power that would have given them permanently the upper hand, and it would have been the death knell of republicanism in America. They are checked, but not beaten. They never intend to relinquish the machinery of this government into the hands of the opponents of slavery. It has taken them more than a half century to get it and they know its significance too well to give it up."

He went on: "For my part, I drew my sword in Kansas when they attacked us. I will never sheathe it until this war is over."

They argued about the willingness of the American slaves to rise up against their masters on the southern plantations (a discussion mentioned previously). Brown cited the case of Spartacus and his slave rebellion against Rome. Phillips reminded him that these slaves for Rome had been warlike people in the countries from which they had been taken and had been trained to use arms. Brown answered with a shrug.

Hinton, talking with Brown again at the Adair cabin, found him more impatient and nervous in his manner than he had ever seen him before. He railed against the free-state leaders of Kansas, "They acted up to their instincts as politicians. They thought every man wanted to lead, and therefore supposed I might be in the way of their schemes." Hinton, who was opposed to moderation and shared Brown's desire for a drastic collision on the slavery issue between the two factions, remarked that the free-state policy had been an abortion. Brown looked at him with a peculiar glint in his eyes and mused, "Abortion? Yes, that's the word!"

Kagi, to whom Brown seemed to have confided his innermost thoughts, was quite frank to Hinton about the aims of the Virginia expedition to be launched in 1859, and Brown confirmed them. "The hour is near at hand." Several ringing sentences of Brown's clung in Hinton's mind. "Any resistance, however bloody, is better than the system which makes every seventh woman a concubine." "A ravine is better than a plain. Woods and mountain sides can be held by resolute men against ten times their number." "A few men in the right and knowing they are right, can overturn a king."

Conversing alone with Kagi, Hinton expressed his fear that many of the young men in this coming offensive would lose their lives. "Ah, yes, Hinton, but the result will be worth the sacrifice," said Kagi, who would give his young life as a sacrifice at Harper's Ferry.

"Captain Brown will now, if necessary, take the field in aid of Captain Montgomery," Kagi notified the New York *Tribune* in October. To Hinton, Brown expressed his admiration for Montgomery. "Captain Montgomery is the only soldier I have met among the prominent Kansas men. He understands my system of warfare exactly." That gentleman was taking direct action in his own fashion. In mid-October his company invaded Fort Scott where the worst border-ruffians were holed up. He took possession of the courthouse, dispersed a grand jury in session and destroyed its papers. He then roamed the area committing depredations on proslave property.

On the night of October 30, a volley of shots were fired into Montgomery's cabin, but Montgomery, his wife, and children were unharmed. Brown proposed to him that he would convert the cabin of his mother-in-law at Little Sugar Creek into a fort, and Montgomery assented. This work occupied Brown, Stevens, Kagi, and Tidd all November.

It was a time of good fellowship and good cheer, as Gill related. Brown cooked for the company. He had not drunk tea or coffee in early life and now drank tea only, so the men had to drink tea if they wanted any hot drink. They worked, they fished, sometimes "we took the prairie for our bed with the blue arch for our covering." Stevens' glorious voice pealed through the night as he sang the songs

Brown loved, "The Slave Has Seen the Northern Star" and "From Greenland's Icy Mountains."

Despite his professions of admiration for Montgomery, Gill stated that Brown had an acute jealousy of him and did not propose to follow another. The only occasion when he cooperated with Montgomery was on a march to the town of Paris on November 13 where Montgomery had just been indicted for destroying ballot boxes the previous January. Montgomery ransacked the town in vain to find the indictment and warrants of arrest. The acting territorial governor, Hugh S. Walsh, wrote to Secretary of State Cass in Washington proposing that "a reward of $300 for Montgomery and $500 for old John Brown and their delivery at Fort Scott would secure their persons and break up their organizations and drive them from the Territory." Preventive measures were necessary since they were plotting "some infernal diabolical act."

On November 30, a sheriff's posse went to capture Brown at the Montgomery fort, but the captain, unaware of the visit to be paid him, had gone to Osawatomie with Gill. The posse was met outside the fort by Stevens who told them to "Begone." Sheriff McDaniel said, "But you can't resist. Look at our force opposed to you." Raising his right arm, Stevens replied, "Believing we are right before God, we will resist if the whole Universe is against us!" Such was the dread of Old Brown that the posse disintegrated. The next day Montgomery's men sallied out and captured the sheriff on his way home, deprived him of his guns and after giving him a lecture released him.

Brown, absent during this affair at Osawatomie, wrote his family on December 2 that while the rest of the Territory was "comparatively undisturbed," the "worst feeling" continued to exist in the border areas which gave little prospect of quiet. "The Winter may be supposed to have fairly set in which may compel parties to defer hostilities."

The postscript is significant for what was uppermost in his mind. "Am still preparing for my other journey."

Returning to the scene of the frictions, Brown took on an unaccustomed role, that of a peacemaker, when he worked out for Montgomery and his opponents a peace agreement at Sugar Mound in Linn County. All criminal processes against free-state men were to be dropped and all prisoners released. All proslavery men forcibly expelled for being criminally active were to stay expelled. "All parties shall hereafter in good faith discontinue and thoroughly discontinue acts of robbery, theft or violence against others on account of their political differences."

No sooner was the ink dry on this agreement, inaugurating an era of sweetness and light, than it became a dead letter as Montgomery's men resumed their "jawhawking." Montgomery organized a force of a hundred men to attack Fort Scott claiming that the proslave faction had violated the peace agreement by not releasing Benjamin Rice, who had been taken to prison there in November. Outside Fort Scott, the night before the attack, there was a conclave concerning the top command, and since Montgomery insisted that he must lead, Brown would not participate, though Stevens and Kagi took part. Montgomery later said he was glad Brown dropped out since Brown was determined to burn the fort to the ground.

Montgomery succeeded in releasing young Rice who was imprisoned on the third floor in the Fort Scott hotel. The door had to be battered down with an axe, and Rice was there chained down with a heavy log. Across the street from the hotel, the owner of a store, J. H. Little, poured a load of buckshot into the breast of Kagi whose life was saved again by his outer clothing, this time the heavy overcoat into which the buckshot lodged. Then Little was cut down by bullets and his store looted of $7,000 worth of merchandise. The eastern press as usual gave a misreport of the news. The New York *Tribune* on January 3 said that a former deputy U.S. marshal, J. H. Little, was hanged. "It seems that he was officious still in the matter of taking and holding Free-State prisoners."

When Montgomery met Brown at the appointed rendezvous, he brought along a prisoner. In Gill's presence, Brown arraigned Montgomery bitterly for bothering to carry a prisoner along when he could have shot him on the spot or along the way.

For Brown, alias Shubel Morgan, this Kansas visit of 1858 had been somewhat stale and altogether unprofitable. Then, lo, an opportunity to "carry the war into Africa" with little risk presented itself, opening one of the more dramatic episodes of his career. Gill recalled, Brown "was just waiting for something to turn up, or in his way of thinking, was expecting or hoping that 'God would provide him a basis of action.' When this came he hailed it as heavensent."

While Gill was scouting down the line of the border he ran into a fine-looking mulatto named Jim Daniels, who told him that he was in the business of selling brooms. However, after he found Gill a sympathetic soul, he told him that he was actually looking for help. He lived in Missouri, and his wife, two children, himself, and another slave were soon to be sold to the highest bidder at an administrator's sale of an estate.

Gill brought Daniels to Brown who decided without hesitation that he would organize the rescue of Daniels and his family from thralldom and at the same time free slaves on neighboring plantations. Two parties were organized. Under Brown there were Gill, Kagi, a horse-thief named Pickles, Jeremiah Anderson, and four others. Under the command of Stevens were Tidd, Albert Hazlett, and five others.

Brown had now picked up two more men who were to participate in the Harper's Ferry raid. Both had served under Montgomery and had seen action under him. Jeremiah Anderson, then twenty-five years old, would die at Harper's Ferry on October 18, 1859. The grandson of southern slaveholders, he had been born in Indiana where he had average schooling and had worked at dull jobs before removing himself to Kansas and adventure in 1857.

Albert Hazlett, then twenty-one years old, would escape from Harper's Ferry. He was apprehended in his native state of Pennsylvania and was tried and executed at Charlestown on March 16, 1860. He was the closest thing to a "roughneck" among the Brown men. Joseph Barry of Harper's Ferry, who watched him at his trial, said he was "a man of about five feet and eleven inches in height, raw-boned and muscular. His hair was red and his eyes were of a muddy brown color and of a very unpleasant expression. In every sense of the word he looked like an 'ugly customer.'"

On a bitterly cold Monday, December 20, the night after Brown first talked with Daniels, the two bands entered Missouri and separated. Brown and his party made their way to the home of Harvey G. Hicklan who was holding the Daniels family and another slave temporarily before the sale. With drawn revolvers they entered the home and plundered it while freeing the five slaves. According to Brown's admission, they took "certain property" belonging to the estate. Gill offered the excuse that the party included some strange new men who were "mere adventurers, ready to take from friend or foe as opportunity offered," and they stuffed their pockets with watches or anything else they could find. On the other hand, Hicklan said it was an organized robbery under Brown's approving eye, that

Brown watched the men ransack the house, that as he left, "he defied us and the whole United States to follow him." He wanted Hicklan to be sure who he was, Old Brown, Osawatomie Brown, and "all heads follow me at the owners' risk."

Less than a mile away from the Hicklan house, the Brown party entered the house of John B. Larue. Brown stated his business to him: "We have come after your Negroes and their property. Will you surrender or fight?" Five slaves were liberated here. The portable loot from the two houses included six horses, oxen, a wagon, provisions such as bacon, flour, meal, etc., bedding, and the best clothing and boots.

The Stevens party visited the home of wealthy David Cruise where they wanted to take to freedom a woman slave who was a friend of the Daniels family. The sixty-year-old Cruise lived on a farm of several hundred acres. An unfortunate incident occurred here. As Stevens told it, Cruise opened the door, slipped behind him, locked the door, and then Stevens detected his reaching for his gun. Stevens drew first and shot him dead. It was too painful, even to think about. "You might call it a case of self-defense. Or you might also say that I had no business there." The loot here was extensive according to the authorities—two horses, eleven mules, a yoke of oxen, and a wagonload of provisions.

Stevens gallantly took the blame for the crime of another. Cruise really had been murdered in cold blood by Hazlett. Years later, in the St. Louis *Democrat* of April 15, 1888, Rufus Cruise, who was thirteen at the time, told of the murder. They were awakened at midnight of the bitterly cold night by shouts outside. "Hello, we want to stay all night." Cruise put his head out of the bedroom window and said, "Who are you?" The reply was, "We are Missourians from Bates County. We have been to Fort Scott on business with the court and are on the way home. We can't cross the Osage till daylight. We are very cold and will pay you if you let us sleep on the floor." Cruise said, "Well, gentlemen, these are squally times and a man can't be too careful, but I can't turn a dog away on a night like this." "Oh, you needn't worry," someone sang out, "we aren't Kansas men."

Father and son went downstairs in their nightshirts, without weapons of any kind, opened the door, and the party entered. Cruise went toward the fireplace and Hazlett shot him through the heart for no apparent reason. The men then scoured the house for money and jewelry, even forcing the stricken widow at the point of a gun to open up all the closets.

With wagons fully loaded with the eleven slaves and loot, the Brown and Stevens parties joined up and moved back to Kansas. The Negroes were deliriously happy after learning that they were bound for Canada, "Canaan's happy land." Though it was a very cold night the contraband were warm under blankets and laughter rippled through the air. One woman sang out, "Pity poor marsa! He's in a bad fix; corn not shucked, hogs not killed and niggers all gone!" Brown took along with him as hostages John B. Larue and two other men. The next morning he released them in Kansas saying that they could follow him if they wished. One of them replied, "I'll follow home. That is just what I'm going to do."

Exhilarated members of the squads used the opportunity to do some free-wheeling stealing on their own account while in Missouri. Hazlett stole a fine stallion; Brown very much admired it and later acquired it from him in exchange for a warrant for forty acres of land which Gerrit Smith had sent as a Christmas gift to Brown.

The daylight hours of the day following the raids were spent in a deep ravine in Kansas, distant from any road; the journey resumed that night and continued through the next day. At Wednesday midnight, they reached the home of Augustus Wattles where Montgomery and some of his men were bunked, sleeping in the loft.

Montgomery, awakened by the noise, put his head down the stairway and said, "How is this, Captain Brown? Whom have you here?" Brown exultantly waved his hat around in a circle, "Allow me to introduce to you a *part* of my family. Observe, I have carried the war into Africa."

There was a general buffet supper for all, white and black, and then the black men went back to the wagons to sleep while the women and children slept in the home of Wattles' son nearby. The next morning all were packed into a wagon drawn by oxen, driven by some unnamed man (Brown went temporarily his own way), and on Christmas Eve they reached the Adair cabin outside of Osawatomie. Though the Adairs had qualms about hiding stolen property, Florilla said, "I cannot turn them away." They were kept in her back kitchen through Christmas Day.

In the darkness of the early hours of the morning after Christmas, they were lodged in an abandoned cabin on the Pottawatomie, which a settler had put up hastily of unhewn hickory logs, the cabin having neither a floor nor even a door. The freed men and women were nevertheless in ecstacy and quickly built improvements which made it liveable quarters. They were fed and watched over by friendly neighbors. The area was scoured by search parties of Missourians, but they were not molested during their residence in that cabin, though it lay open and unprotected from view by brush or timber.

Brown looked on his feat of liberation as a glorious epic. The backlash of criticism stunned him.

The howl from Missouri was predictable. Newspapers denounced the robber and assassin, Old Brown, and called for terrible retribution for his infamy. The governor, E. W. Stewart, offered a reward of $3,000 for the capture of Brown and President Buchanan added $250. From this time until his capture at Harper's Ferry, John Brown would be a man with a price on his head.

It was the near-unanimous excoriation in Kansas that took Brown by surprise. "He thinketh that the end being good and necessary, the necessary means can not be bad." In other eyes this was heinous; it was a wilful violation of man-made law and the Ten Commandments to forcibly expropriate property, albeit slave property, rob homes, and murder. A clergyman in Moneka denounced Brown as one who pretended to be a good Christian and to be guided by "the teachings of the Prince of Peace," and yet without apology he committed murder and lived on plunder. "If this is Christianity, anything is preferable to it." The correspondent of the Missouri *Democrat* probably did not overstate it when he reported: "I have yet to see the first free State man in or around Osawatomie who did not condemn this action."

From the start of his antislavery crusade, up to and including Harper's Ferry, Brown, fanatically convinced of the rightness of his cause, was governed by subjective ethical considerations while blind to over-all political effects, since he regarded the political process as an appeasement of Satan. On the other hand, to the settlers of Kansas, the political consideration was paramount. The laborious march to free statehood was now imperiled since they might all be crushed by an invasion from Missouri and murderous activities of border-ruffians might now be licensed. Fears that a massacre was imminent were set off when a posse of five hundred men set out from Fort Scott. Brown wrote to Montgomery to be in readiness to fight, but there were no clashes.

George A. Crawford had an interview with Brown near Trading Post on January 3 and took him to task in these terms: Brown was not a Kansas settler. He would leave the Territory and the retaliatory blow would fall on the bona fide Kansas settlers. The border-ruffian Brockett had announced his way of thinking to him: "When a snake bites me, I don't go hunting for that particular snake, I kill the first snake I meet." Kansas was at peace with Missouri, and no one should take the law into his own hands since even in the border counties of Bourbon and Linn, the free-staters were in the majority and had elected their own law-enforcement officers.

Brown gave the gruff retort: "It is no pleasure to me, an old man, to be living in the saddle, away from home and family, exposing my life, and if the Free State men of Kansas feel that they no longer need me, I will be glad to go."

The new territorial governor, Samuel Medary, offered a reward of $250 each for the apprehension of Montgomery and Brown—making a total of $3,500 for Brown. General James H. Lane requested Medary to give him an official commission to lead an army to disperse the two bands and take into custody the two miscreant captains. The offer of that untrustworthy gentleman was declined. The revulsion of feeling was so intense that even Montgomery publicly disowned Brown. "For Brown's doings in Missouri, I am not responsible. I know nothing of either his plans or intentions. Brown keeps his own counsel and acts on his own responsibility."

Captain Samuel Walker, delegated by the governor to report on the situation around Osawatomie, wrote to him that he met everywhere men who sustained Montgomery in the past who felt they could do so no longer. Yet, when Montgomery decided to turn himself in, he got a rousing greeting. On January 18 he walked into the territorial court in Lawrence and he was freed on $4,000 bail for the only indictment pending against him, for robbing a post office. The New York *Times* correspondent, Randolph, reported that the territorial legislature was in session, and when he entered, "Scores were pressing to grasp him by the hand while he 'looked down' upon the heads of those who but a few days before were branding him as the arch-robber. Firm, fearless, erect, he now stood in the same hall where his name had been traduced and vilified. This must have been to him one· of the strange vicissitudes of human life." Montgomery, indeed, had personal magnetism.

Brown was at Wattles' home on January 7. While Montgomery

and Kagi were discussing the implications of the Missouri raid, Brown silently worked on a manuscript, and then, raising his head, said, "Gentlemen, I would like to have your attention for a few minutes. I usually leave the newspaper work to Kagi, but this time I have something to say on my own." He then read to them a letter to the New York *Tribune*, his "Parallels." It was published in the *Tribune* (with some abbreviaton) on January 22:

> Trading Post, Kansas, Jany. 1859
>
> Gents: You will greatly oblige a humble friend by allowing the use of your colums while I briefly state two parallels, in my poor way. Not One year ago Eleven quiet citizens of this neighborhood (viz) Wm Robertson, Wm Colpetzer, Amos Hall, Austin Hall, John Campbell, Asa Snyder, Thos Stilwell, Wm Hairgrove, Asa Hairgrove, Patrick Ross, and B. L. Reed—were gathered up from their work, & their homes by an armed force (under One *Hamilton*) & without trial; or opportunity to speak in own defence were formed into a line & all but one shot, Five killed & Five wounded. One fell unharmed, pretending to be dead. All were left for dead. The only crime charged against them was that of being Free-State men. Now, I inquire what action has ever, since the occurrence in May last, been taken by either the President of the United States; the Governor of Missouri, or the Governor of Kansas, or any of their tools; or by any proslavery or *administration man*? to ferret out and punish the perpetrators of this crime?
>
> Now for the other parallel. On Sunday the 19th of December a negro called Jim came over to the Osage settlement from Missouri & stated that he together with his Wife, Two Children, & another Negro man were to be sold within a day or Two & beged for help to get away. On Monday (the following) night, Two small companies were made up to go to Missouri & forcibly liberate the Five slaves *together with other slaves*. One of these companies I assumed to direct. We proceeded to the place surrounded the buildings liberated the slaves & also took certain property supposed to belong to the estate. We however learned before leaveing that a portion of the articles we had taken belonged to a man living on the plantation as a tenant, & who was supposed to have no interest in the estate. We promptly returned to him *all we had taken* so far I believe. We then went to another plantation, where we freed Five more slaves, took some property; & Two *white* men. We moved all slowly away into the Territory for some distance, & then sent the White men back, telling them to follow us as soon as they chose to do so. The other company freed One female slave, took some property; &, as I am informed, killed One White man (the master), who fought against the liberation. Now for a comparison. Eleven persons are forcibly restored

to their *natural; & inalienable rights*, with but one man killed; & all "Hell is stirred from beneath." It is currently reported that the Governor of Missouri has made a requisition upon the Governor of Kansas for the delivery of all such as were concerned in the last-named "dreadful outrage." The Marshal of Kansas is said to be collecting a *possee* of Missouri (not Kansas) men at West Point in Missouri a little town about Ten miles distant, to "enforce the laws," & all pro-slavery conservative Free-State, and dough-faced men & Administration tools are filled with holy horror.

Consider the two cases, and the action of the Administration party.

Respectfully yours,
John Brown

This document is certainly evidence of Brown's eloquence and his cogent reasoning power. Like any lawyer's brief, it emphasized only his side of the case. It did not suit his purpose to draw the true parallel, between the Pottawatomie massacre and the Hamelton massacre—in both cases five innocent men were slaughtered. Then, we should note that Brown minimized the theft of property by his men and excused the murder of Cruise on self-defense grounds. He was assuredly on firm ground in arguing that a lot more furor had been churned up about his one killing in Missouri than Hamelton's five in Kansas, and no move had been made by state or federal authorities to apprehend those wanton murderers. The pro-southerners, with their obsessive insecurity complex about slavery, were always more sensitive about the theft of slaves than they were about mayhem, even against white citizens.

It was the censure of his staunch friend, Augustus Wattles, that hurt Brown most. Wattles described their last conversation. Brown defended himself and his extremist methods: "I have been at your abolition meetings. Your schemes are perfectly futile. You will not release five slaves in a century. Peaceful emancipation is impossible. The thing has gone beyond that point."

There was no more to be said or done. "I considered the matter well. You will probably have no more attacks from Missouri. I shall now leave Kansas and probably you will never see me again. I consider it my duty to draw the scene of the excitement to some other part of the country."

It was farewell forever to Kansas! In a later year, Charles Robinson made the acid comment that forced by popular protest to leave Kansas, "He went to Harper's Ferry, where, no 'dastard politician' being in the way, he displayed his wonderful generalship by committing suicide."

The hegira from Kansas which started from Garnett on January 20 with Gill as Brown's companion and with twelve Negroes in their wagon was one of Brown's boldest adventures. We say twelve, because a woman had just borne a girl to whom the Christian name Captain John Brown was given. In the dead of winter, Sanborn wrote in wonder, "Brown pushed ahead, regardless of warnings and threats, but relying on the mercy of God and his own stout heart." He had a price on his head of $3,500, and though a committee of the territorial legislature had advised Governor Medary that anyone who turned him in "would sink into the grave of an Arnold or Judas," it was a fortune for those times. He could be easily spotted since the fugitives had been advertised the nation over, the wagon was odd-looking and drawn by the oxen stolen from Hicklan. The wagon rolled over frozen ground or through mud. Whether the loot he had taken had been exaggerated or whether it could not be disposed of, Brown and Gill had no money in their pockets. When they reached Major J. B. Abbott's cabin outside of Lawrence, four days later, riding by night and resting by day, Gill's feet were frozen and Brown's fingers, nose, and ears were frozen.

Brown had written ahead to his friend M. F. Conway at Lawrence asking him to obtain money from the agent of the National Kansas Committee, E. B. Whitman, but there was bad news for Brown from Conway. "I am of the opinion that you will not be able to get any funds from him. He expressed himself to me since his return from the East as dissatisfied at your proceedings in Lawrence when you were here before." Brown exchanged his ox-team for horses and got some money, perhaps selling some of his possessions in the wagon, and left Lawrence on January 25. Two miles north of Lawrence the young Gill said he was exhausted and remained at a cabin to recuperate while Stevens, who had been at Topeka to line up provisions, took his place beside the indomitable old man.

A short distance from Topeka they stayed at the Sheridan cabin. Jacob Willetts was summoned by Brown from Topeka, and when told that the black people Brown was conducting to freedom had no shoes and little to eat, Willetts went to stores in Topeka and brought back shoes, food, and some money he had raised. While they were riding in the wagon he noticed that Brown was shivering and that his legs trembled a good deal. He suspected something, and reaching down felt his trousers which were of cotton and suited to summer and not winter weather.

"Mr. Brown, have you no drawers?" he asked. Brown replied that he had none. Willetts said, "Well, there is no time to go to the store now, but I have on a pair that was new today and if you will take them you are welcome." After a few words, they got down beside the wagon, Willetts took his drawers off and Brown put them on.

The wagon reached Holton, north of Topeka, on January 28 in a blinding snowstorm, and the next day they were at Spring Creek six miles away in the cabin of Abram Fuller. The news of their presence was well circulated in the neighborhood. One of the slaves, Samuel Harper, related that a few men approached the cabin, nosing about. Stevens greeted them and said, "Gentlemen, you look as if you were looking for somebody or something." The leader responded, "Yes, we think you have some slaves up in that house." Stevens said, "Is that so? Well, come on with me and see." The slaves quivered for fear that they were being turned in. When they came to the cabin, Stevens opened the door long enough to grab a double-barreled gun, and pointed it at them. "You want to see your slaves, do you? Well, just look up those barrels and see if you can find them." The men fled. Gill, who had rejoined Brown, confirmed this story. "Three ran. One had to drop, as a 'bead' was drawn upon him."

These men were the vanguard of a posse of eighty men under A. P. Wood who were mobilized to capture Brown. Governor Medary dispatched an exultant message to President Buchanan that Brown's capture was imminent. Learning of the enemy presence, Brown had sent a call for help to Topeka and reinforcements arrived. With the male slaves, Brown had twenty-six able-bodied men to oppose eighty. The posse was lined up across the Fuller ford, in a strong position, Gill said, strong enough to defeat a thousand men.

One of his men said to Brown, "Captain, what do you propose to do?" He responded, "Cross the creek and move north." There was a suggestion diplomatically couched, "But, Captain, the water is high and I doubt if we can get through. There is a much better ford five miles up the creek." The quick reply was, "I intend to travel it straight through and there is no use to talk of turning aside. Those who are afraid may go back. The Lord has marked out a path for me and I intend to follow it. We are ready to move."

Thus opened the Battle of the Spurs. Brown placed them in double file in front of the wagons and said, "Now go straight at 'em, boys. They'll be sure to run." The closer the dreaded Old Brown and his mighty host came to the ford, the higher the terror mounted among the men entrenched across the ford. They had expected to attack, not to be attacked. Even before the crossing began, they started to flee. They jumped on their mounts, or two on a mount, and one man left the battlefield in most disgraceful fashion, dragged by the tail of a horse of a comrade which he had grabbed. "The scene was ridiculous beyond description," Gill recalled. The crossing was made and ropes dragged the wagons across the ford. The enemy was gone. Those of Brown's men who had horses pursued the posse and brought back four prisoners and five horses.

Brown told his prisoners that he could not give them mounts lest they should escape and bring a fresh party of attack, but to show them he meant no unkindness, he would walk along with them. They cursed terribly their bad luck in being captured and Brown addressed them: "Gentlemen, you do very wrong in thus taking the name of God in vain. Besides, it is very foolish, for if there is a God you gain nothing by profanity and if there is no God, how foolish it is to ask God's curses on anything." The men were released after three days and reported that they were well treated, sharing the common fare, but it went against the grain to eat with and be guarded by "damned niggers."

On their return home the men blustered against Brown. The pro-slave Leavenworth *Herald* in a reluctant tribute to Brown said that their epithets including the word "coward" might better be applied to their own party. "Old Captain Brown is not to be taken by 'boys' and he cordially invites all proslavery men to try their hands at arresting him."

February 1 was Brown's last day in Kansas. Though the Nemaha River was too high to cross, the weather was bitterly cold so that it might freeze over at night. Brown went over the Nebraska line and spent the night at the Sac and Fox Reservation at the home of a half-breed Indian. The following morning he found the ice strong enough to bear a man but not a team and so the wagon was taken apart and pushed across in pieces, and a bridge was constructed of poles with rails, bushes, and boards on them and over this the horses were led. Three days later, somehow eluding another posse of forty men, he crossed over the Missouri River into Iowa and a day later he was in the familiar precincts of Tabor. On February 10, he wrote his family for the first time since January 11, announcing that through "the mercy of God" he had arrived in Iowa.

This modern Anabasis against great odds helps to explain the confidence with which men followed Brown into the trap at Harper's Ferry. Those who saw Brown walk untouched over impassable barriers and through enemies and dangers, seemingly in an armor of invulnerability, acquired a superstitious belief in the man. For Brown himself, the experience was important. One who believes himself the bearer of a special destiny ordained by cosmic forces looks for omens and signs. This ordeal from which he emerged unscathed was further proof to him that he was truly anointed by the Lord for his great mission.

"I suppose you get the common news," Brown wrote home. He had evidently learned that his Missouri exploit had been given good coverage in the eastern press. No doubt, his "Parallels" had been designed by him less to justify himself than to insure that when published in the New York *Tribune* it would give him publicity where it would do him the most good.

It was the favorable reaction of his eastern backers that was vital to Brown, not that of men of Kansas. It was the men who held the money-bags whom he wished to galvanize with enthusiasm, and from that standpoint the Missouri foray was a success. He had staged a socko-spectacular. That manic-enthusiast, Gerrit Smith, wrote his wife on January 10: "Do you hear the news from Kansas? Our dear John Brown is invading Missouri and pursuing the policy which he intended to pursue *elsewhere*." On January 22, from Peterboro, he sent Sanborn $25 to be forwarded to Brown. "The topography of Missouri is unfavorable. Would that a spur of the Allegheny extended from the East to the West borders of the state!"

On January 3, the New York *Tribune* reported that a gang of Jayhawkers under Captain Brown had entered Bates County, Missouri, stolen four horses from Jerome Jackson and burned his home. On January 6, there were more accurate details in a lead story captioned OLD BROWN INVADES MISSOURI. It stated that Captain Brown had entered Missouri to give confidence to the people of Kansas and teach the Missourians the necessity of remaining at home. In the same issue Horace Greeley editorialized, "Captain Brown, who had cooperated with Montgomery and whose property had been destroyed and his son murdered in the former wars, did not wait for invasion.

He led a party into Bates County, who retorted on the slaveholders of the vicinity the same system of plunder which the Free State people of Kansas have suffered during the recent invasion."

The *Tribune* had by far the best in-depth reporting from Kansas. Other newspapers reported it mistakenly as a joint foray by Montgomery and Brown. The New York *Times* on January 11 said: "Brown especially has suffered wrongs enough at the hands of Missouri invaders to almost steel his heart against every sentiment of humanity. To avenge the death of his murdered son and the long list of outrages perpetrated upon him during the Kansas struggle he considers almost a religious duty."

On January 22, the *Tribune* correspondent in Lawrence summed up the affair: "Some bad may have grown out of the movement, but I have yet to see what it is. Much good has come of it. The bluster of Missouri has lessened. While hundreds of the non-slaveholding whites express great indignation at the invasion of their state, and boil over with patriotism in public, they privately laugh at the idea of their defending a species of property that is a curse to them, and rejoice that certain lordly slaveholders have 'come down to their level.'"

At Tabor, Brown got an unexpected reception from his former friends which set him back on his heels. At the Sunday morning service he sent to the pulpit a petition for "public thanksgiving to Almighty God in behalf of himself, & company; and of their rescued captives . . . & his signal delivery of all out of the hand of the wicked, hitherto." The Reverend Dr. H. D. King in the pulpit with the Reverend John Todd said to him it was his church and his decision, but advised him not to make this prayer without further consideration, "inasmuch it is said they have destroyed life and stolen horses." A public meeting was announced from the pulpit for Monday night.

The next night, Brown started the meeting off with a recital of his trip into Missouri and, while talking, he saw a Dr. Brown of St. Joseph, Missouri, a slaveholder, entering a pew. Brown interrupted his remarks to say that one had just entered whom he did not want there and he requested him to withdraw. The sense of the meeting was that Dr. Brown should stay and so Brown said he was leaving. As he walked out, he said to Tidd, "There are some there who would give us a halter for our pains. We had best look to our arms and horses." There was too much sanctimony in Tabor.

Stevens announced to the meeting: "So help me God, I will never sit in a council with one who has brought and sold human flesh," and he walked out, too. The meeting debated a resolution that while they sympathized with those who fought for human freedom, "We have no sympathy with those who go to slave states to entice away slaves and take property or life when necessary to attain that end." Kagi, who remained in the meeting, drew up a resolution, which was offered by a Taborite, "That we, the citizens of Tabor, repudiate his conduct and theirs, and will hereupon take them into custody and hold them to await the action of the Missouri authorities." The meeting evaded this caustic test of its sincerity.

Filled with disgust, Brown left Tabor on February 11, and the caravan moved eastward. With no attempt whatever at concealment of his identity, Brown was in Des Moines on the eighteenth, and Kagi paid a visit to the editor of the Des Moines *Register*, John Teesdale, to give him a good story for his readers, which Brown amplified in a letter to him the following month.

Two days later they reached the town of Grinnell, the home of Josiah Busnell Grinnell, a leading Abolitionist of the state. This man was the founder of two cities, the organizer and first president of the college bearing his name, prohibitionist, director and promoter of railroads, founder of banks, lawyer, preacher, and member of the Civil War congress.

In his *Men and Events of Forty Years*, Grinnell related that Brown knocked on his door and introduced himself as a friend of his father in Springfield. He was invited in. Brown said, "This cannot be a social visit. I am that terrible Brown of whom you have heard." It was Saturday, and Brown said he made it a rule not to travel on the Sabbath unless necessary. He needed a place for the slaves to stay. Grinnell threw open the door of his parlor, which he henceforth called the Liberty Room. He said, "This room is at your service and you can occupy the stalls at the barn which are not taken. Our hotel will be as safe as any place for part of your company."

The honors and attentions heaped on him at Grinnell touched Brown deeply, and he sent back to Tabor with withering scorn this report:

RECEPTION OF BROWN & PARTY AT GRINNELL, IOWA
1st. Whole party & teams kept for Two days free of cost.
2d Sundry articles of clothing given to captives.
3d Bread, Meat, Cakes, Pies, etc. prepared for our journey.

4th Full houses for Two Nights in succession at which meetings Brown and Kagi spoke and were loudly cheered; & fully indorsed. Three Congregational Clergymen attended the meeting on Sabbath evening (notice of which was given out from the Pulpit). All of them took part in justifying our course & in urging contributions in our behalf & there was no dissenting speaker present at either meeting. Mr. Grinnell spoke at length & has since laboured to procure us a free and safe conveyance to Chicago: & effected it.

5th Contributions in cash amounting to $26.50 Twenty Six Dollars & Fifty cents.

6th Last but not least Public thanksgiving to All-mighty God offered up by Mr. Grinnell in the behalf of the whole company for His great mercy; & protecting care, with prayers for a continuance of those blessings.

As the action of Tabor friends has been published in the newspapers by some of her people (as I suppose), would not friend Gaston or some other friend give publicity to all the above.

> Respectfully your friend
> John Brown
> Springdale, Iowa 26th Feby 1859

P.S.

our reception among the Quaker friends here has been most cordial.

> Yours truly,
> J. B.

On February 25, the Brown party was in Springdale for a reunion with the Quakers, who were more uneasy about their presence than they had been the year before. Nonetheless, they extended warm hospitality until the leave-taking on March 9. George B. Gill remained behind in Springdale, which was his home, and Brown was never to see him again. He complained of an inflammation of a joint which prevented him from going on.

Grinnell, with the cooperation of William Penn Clarke, an Abolitionist of Iowa City, rented a freight car from West Liberty, Iowa, to Chicago. The rental was rescinded by the Rock Island Railroad when it was too late, and John F. Tracy, the superintendent of the road, refused to accept the $50 rental payment since "we might be held for the value of every one of those niggers."

The party spent the night at a steammill at West Liberty. Early the next morning, a passing train from Iowa City, the western terminus of the road, dropped off a boxcar, which was pushed to a siding. At noon, the express train arrived en route to Chicago. The locked boxcar with the slaves in it was attached to the engine and Brown with Kagi and Stevens sat in the coach. The six-hundred-mile trip by wagon from Missouri was over and the remaining five hundred miles would be by railroad to "Canaan's happy land."

Half a mile from the depot in Chicago early next morning, the train stopped and the boxcar was detached and pushed onto a siding and the slaves released, all in good shape and spirits. Brown looked up Allan Pinkerton, a Scotsman who was starting his detective agency and who was a firm friend of the cause. He was addressing a meeting of the Cook County Bar Association that afternoon and he undertook to raise money, which he did to the amount of $400.

Pinkerton arranged to get a boxcar from the superintendant of the Michigan Central Railroad, C. G. Hammond who not only donated the car but saw to it personally that it was well stocked with water and provisions. Brown went ahead to Detroit to be sure to meet up with Frederick Douglass who was there, and Kagi took charge. On March 12, the grueling grind which had commenced on the night of December 20 was over as Brown saw the former slaves, now assured of freedom, and with money in their pockets, take the ferry from Detroit to Windsor in Canada, to start a new life. Brown's last words to them were, "Lord, permit Thy servant to die in peace, for mine eyes have seen Thy salvation! The arm of Jehovah protected us."

CHAPTER SEVEN

Conspiracy for "Mighty Conquest," Resumed

"WE DO NOT HAVE IDEAS," said Heine. "The Idea has us and enslaves us and scourges us and drives us into the arena to fight for it like gladiators who combat whether they will or no."

William Hutchison, the correspondent for the New York *Times* in Kansas, interviewed Brown at the home of Augustus Wattles on December 30 after his return from the Missouri raid. He slept with him that night and later recalled the experience:

Our bed was a mattress made of hay, laid upon the floor of the second story. Sleep seemed to be a secondary matter with him. I am sure he talked on that night till the small hours, and his all absorbing theme was "My work," "my great duty," "my mission" etc., meaning, of course, the liberation of the slaves. He seemed to have no other object in life, no other hope or ambition.

The Idea was temporarily stymied by the too-familiar sensation of running "like a toad under the harrow," due to the fact that he was out of money. Most pressing was the need to send something to his family in North Elba. From Tabor, he promised his wife on February 10 that he would send "something besides my good wishes," and he did later forward a draft from Springdale through John H.

Painter. The source of the funds was the stolen mules and loot which Painter sold. On March 3 he wrote to Dr. Jesse Bowen in Iowa City saying that he had left there a little cannon (undoubtedly the one donated to him in 1857 by Eli Thayer). "Could you, or any one induce the inhabitants of your city to make up something for it: & buy it either to keep as an old relic; or for the sake of helping me a little? I am certainly quite needy; and have moreover quite a family to look after." It was purchased and for many years was at the library of the University of Iowa in Iowa City.

The company reached Cleveland on March 15. He made a hurried trip by himself to Boston to see his rich backer, George L. Stearns and Sanborn. The only record we have of this trip is a letter of Mrs. Mary Stearns to her father of March 18. John Brown had arrived at her home that morning. No doubt, her father had heard how Brown had liberated twenty-three slaves in Missouri. He had saved Lawrence from destruction. "His name is to the border-ruffians what the name Black Douglas is to the Scotch, a terror beyond all other names. He passed last night with Ralph Waldo Emerson at Concord and came from there this morning with Mr. Sanborn of Concord who has given his whole time the last three months in Kansas service, a noble and refreshing specimen of manhood." Mary Stearns evidently had not been entrusted by her husband with the southern expeditionary plan. "You are aware, I suppose, that there is a dreadful time at hand in Kansas. Mr. Brown thinks that within the year the bloody struggle for freedom there will be chronicled."

He arrived back in Cleveland on March 20. This city on Lake Erie, a terminus of the Underground Railroad, only thirty miles from his home town of Hudson, was a hotbed of abolitionism. Brown openly flaunted his presence in Cleveland, although there were posters prominently displayed announcing the reward of $250 offered for his detention by President Buchanan, and the United States marshal had his office only four blocks from the City Hotel where he stayed. This bravado was all that was needed to convince wavering members that Brown was veritably the Moses for whom the Red Sea parted to allow his passage.

An auctioneer sold two horses and a mule for Brown while Brown, standing in front of him, announced they came from Kansas and there was a defect in title. They brought good prices. Brown wrote a certification to A. F. Lindsley of Cleveland that a stallion was taken near Fort Scott in the border fighting in November, 1858. Lindsley asked Brown jokingly what he should do if the owner came after him, to which he got the reply, "I don't know about the owner, but I can assure you of this much. The man I got him from will never come after him."

Cleveland was burning with excitement about the "Oberlin rescue case." The Negro population in the Western Reserve had doubled between 1850 and 1860 and a southerner was quoted, "You might as well hunt a devil there as hunt a nigger." Nonetheless, some Kentuckians had tried to arrest a slave named Price under the fugitive slave law, an attempt foiled when the whole university town of Oberlin joined to wrest Price from the slavecatchers and spirit him to freedom across Lake Erie to Canada. Federal warrants were sworn against twenty-two residents of Oberlin and Wellington who refused bail, preferring to be martyrs for the cause—and they were martyrized.

Delegations came from all over the state to honor the prisoners. State politicians tried to outdo each other in praising the prisoners. The city editor, not yet twenty-five, of the Cleveland *Plain Dealer,* Charles Farrar Browne, who was gaining a reputation as a humorist under the pseudonym of Artemus Ward, commented that the nub of the affair was that "some are defendants and some are not—and those who are not are apparently sorry that they ain't." Delegations marched with banners around the prison. One day, there was a mass meeting of twelve thousand outside the prison, addressed by Governor Chase and Congressman Giddings, and the prisoners themselves delivered speeches from behind the wall or from cell windows. This unique event might well have been attended by John D. Rockefeller, a young commission merchant of Cleveland who was a red-hot Abolitionist and a personal friend of Charles Browne's.

Kagi reported the case for eastern papers, and he and Tidd laid plans for a rescue of the prisoners. The need for that was averted when the Kentuckian slavecatchers came to Cleveland to testify at the trial and the state of Ohio arrested them on the ground that the apprehension of Price was a kidnapping in violation of state law. They fled the state, thus disposing of the case. A few of the twenty-two arrested in the Oberlin case were Negroes and again their courage deeply impressed Brown as to their fighting potential and again he failed to realize that they were not representative of southern slaves.

Two more recruits for Harper's Ferry were lined up from Oberlin.

John Anthony Copeland, Jr., born in North Carolina, was a free black man, a mulatto who had been an Oberlin student and was one of the defendants in the Oberlin rescue case. He was executed at Charlestown, Virginia, on December 16, 1859, when he was twenty-five years of age. The prosecutor, Andrew Hunter, said that if he had had the power to pardon any one of the prisoners he would have picked Copeland, and the presiding judge Richard Parker said, "Copeland had been educated and there was a dignity about him that I could not help liking."

Lewis S. Leary was, according to available information, Copeland's uncle although seven months younger, and Leary recruited Copeland after he had decided to join Brown. He was killed at Harper's Ferry on October 17, 1859, leaving at Oberlin a wife and six-month-old daughter, who was educated by the help of Redpath and Wendell Phillips. His wife did not know what his mission was when he took leave of her. He had been a saddler and harnessmaker at Oberlin for two years. He was a quadroon, his great-grandfather having been Irish, Jeremiah O'Leary, who fought under General Nathaniel Greene in the Revolutionary War and who married a woman of mixed Negro and Indian blood.

Leary had listened with interest to a lecture by Brown in Cleveland and then talked with Kagi about becoming a comrade-in-arms. This lecture with a quarter admission charge took place on March 21. The attendance was only fifty although it was well advertised by the two Cleveland papers, and the press gave it good coverage.

Artemus Ward who reported it for the *Plain Dealer* looked with wonder and admiration at this man from nearby Hudson who at an age when he should have been sitting by the hearth rocking his grandchildren had gone roughing it and fighting in Kansas and had earned some national fame. "He is a medium-sized, compactly built and wiry man, and as quick as a cat in his movements. His hair is of a salt and pepper hue and as stiff as bristles. He has a long, waving, milk-white goatee, which gives him a somewhat patriarchal appearance. His eyes are gray and sharp. A man of pluck is Brown. You may bet on that. He shows it in his walk, talk and actions. He must be rising sixty and yet we believe he could lick a yard full of wild cats before breakfast and without taking off his coat." Brown's story of his excursion into Missouri was so "refreshingly cool," that Browne suggested that "he would make his jolly fortune by letting himself out as an Ice Cream Freezer."

The main speaker was preceded by Kagi, who impressed Browne as a "melancholy brigand," some of whose statements were "no doubt false and some shamefully true." Brown's lecture was not about Kansas but all about himself, a paean to John Brown with some bombast. Artemus Ward's humorous treatment was more fitting than the Cleveland *Leader*'s straight report, which included these items: if anybody tried to take him to get the reward, Captain Brown said he would settle the question on the spot. President Buchanan had offered $250 for him, and he offered $2.50 for the safe delivery of the body of James Buchanan in any jail of the free states. He had never driven proslavery men from Kansas but if occasion demanded he would drive them into the ground like fence stakes where they would remain permanent settlers. He had never killed anybody although on some occasions he had shown young men how some things might be done as well as others.

Brown was highly honored by an invitation from Congressman Joshua R. Giddings to come to Jefferson and speak in the Congregational church there. After the death of John Quincy Adams, Giddings had become the leader of the antislavery forces in the House of Representatives. Brown undoubtedly saw that the friendship of Giddings might be important to him if he became deeply involved with proslavery troops, including United States troops, when he launched his Virginia expedition. Giddings later related that "all listened to his story with attention . . . every Democrat as well as Republican present gave something." Giddings himself donated $3. After the lecture, Brown was a guest at the Giddings home where he had tea with his family. This link with Giddings alone made his visit to Cleveland a success.

While in the Western Reserve, Brown had a talk with John Brown, Jr., who had possession of the arms, the two hundred Sharp's rifles and the two hundred revolvers with ammunition. They had been shipped to him from Springdale as "carpenters' tools" by John H. Painter in February, 1858. John Jr. concealed them in the village of Cherry Valley in a furniture warehouse under coffins that were ready for sale. In June, Brown, having become increasingly nervous about Hugh Forbes, wrote his son: "I wish you as soon as you can with perfect quiet to remove the tools to where they will be safe and dry & where neither my friends or men or any one but the Keeper & you will know where to find them." So John Jr. moved part of them into a secret room in the haymow of a farmer, William Coleman, in the township of Wayne and the remainder into the sugar-house of his brother-in-law E. A. Fobes. He had cleaned and oiled them regularly, and his father told him to hold himself in readiness for the signal for final shipment.

Brown stopped off at the home of Frederick Douglass in Rochester and informed him that Der Tag was close at hand; he did not tell him that Harper's Ferry was the chosen target. He was disappointed that Douglass had no money for him. Brown met a full-blooded Negro, Shields Green, who was living with Douglass as a servant and clothes-cleaner. "Green was a man of few words and his speech was singularly broken," recalled Douglass, "but his courage and self-respect made him quite a dignified character." He had been a slave in South Carolina and after the death of his wife he had escaped by sailing ship from Charleston, leaving a son in slavery. A small man in stature, he sometimes called himself Emperor Green. He was twenty-three years old when he took part in the Harper's Ferry raid and was executed at Charlestown on December 16, 1859. He was the only full-blooded Negro among Brown's men.

From February, Brown had been laying the groundwork with the Secret Six for collecting the final $2,000 to $3,000 promised him in June, 1858, to effectuate the project. It appears from the correspondence that Higginson was correct in his judgment that the other five of the Six were infirm in their purpose. If Brown had not fired them with his Missouri "spectacular," they might well have run out on him. A letter of March 4 from Sanborn to Higginson stated that Brown had written Gerrit Smith that with some new men he is ready "to set his mill in operation," is coming east for the purpose, and, "As a reward for what he has done, perhaps money might be raised for him." What if Brown had done nothing during the autumn and winter?

The Reverend Mr. Parker would maintain his keen interest in Brown and his venture to the end, but he had dropped out as far as monetary contributions were concerned. He was seriously ill, probably from consumption. Unable to withstand the rigors of a New England winter, he had prevailed on Dr. Howe to accompany him to Cuba in December and January. He would soon leave the United States for Rome, where he would die in 1860 at the age of fifty.

Dr. Howe on the return trip stopped off in South Carolina and enjoyed southern hospitality at the beautiful plantation home of Wade Hampton. He told Sanborn that he had become less enthused about Brown's plan when he envisaged the prospect that he might be responsible for burning a lovely home like that and endangering the lives of gracious people like the Hamptons. Brown was counting on him, and on March 1 sent a letter to him, "To effect a good seasons work one ought to begin early; & all that I know of to hinder our doing so is the want of a trifling sum for an outfit." Howe gave nothing but moral support that spring.

Higginson hung back. The attitude of Brown's soul-brother of the year before is enigmatic. In his book, *Cheerful Yesterdays*, he explained, "It had all begun to seem rather chimerical," and to Sanborn he said, of the latter's plea to raise money in Worcester, "It is hard for me to solicit money for *another* retreat." From his correspondence with Boston lawyer Lysander Spooner, it would appear that Higginson, the superactivist, was thinking in terms of a gigantic bloodbath in the South, and Brown's professed aim to run off slaves seemed too minor. Sanborn tried to arouse his enthusiasm: "I think we may look for great results from this spark of fire," but Higginson gave only $20 that spring of 1859.

The amount Brown finally raised before D-Day was far in excess of the $2,000 fund promised the year before. Among the contributions, Gerrit Smith gave $750 and George L. Stearns something over $1,200.

Brown was at Peterboro for three days after his visit with Douglass. He addressed a small meeting attended by Smith, Edwin Morton, and a few friends. Brown was "tremendous," Morton informed Sanborn, and at times so eloquent that Mr. and Mrs. Smith were in tears. Morton said he had been in doubt about Brown's course before, but he no longer had any doubts. "*L'experience demontre, avec tout l'evidence possible, que c'est la société qui prépare le crime*," and the instrument is not culpable. Smith hailed Brown during this meeting. "If I were to point out, and I will say it in his presence, the man in all this world I think most truly a Christian, I would point out John Brown." On the spot, he wrote down a pledge of $400. Sending Brown a draft of $100 some weeks later, Smith assured him, "You live in our hearts, and our prayer to God is that you may have strength to continue in your Kansas work. My wife joins me in affectionate regard to you, dear John." ("Kansas work" was an agreed-upon code for his operations thereafter in the slave states.)

Brown was with his family at North Elba from April 19 to May 5, before launching the last fund-raising drive from Boston. For most of the time at North Elba he was down with the "ague," as he wrote Kagi on May 16, "so much so as to disqualify me for everything, nearly."

His last sojourn in the Boston area was almost a month in duration, from May 7 to June 2. The fund-raising, Brown wrote Kagi in Ohio, was "a delicate and very difficult matter," made a harder grind by the fact that he had not recovered from his illness. On May 19, he sent the good news to his wife that he had not had "the shake" for five days and his hearing was improving.

His reception was not all as "cheering" as he advised Kagi it had become. He first went to Concord to see Sanborn and he delivered an address at the Town Hall attended by the Concord intellectuals, Emerson, Thoreau, and Bronson Alcott. Alcott recorded in his diary that he understood that Captain Brown was on his way south to run off slaves and render the peculiar institution insecure. "I think him equal to anything he dares—the man to do the deed, if it must be done, and with the martyr's temper and purpose." The flowing beard gave him "the port of an apostle. I think him the manliest man I have ever seen—the type and synonym of the Just."

His speech did not go down too well with the law-abiding citizenry of Concord. Many were waking up for the first time to the sanguinary capacities of the man. He described his Missouri raid, and when he went on to assert that it was right to repeat such incursions and to take property and even life in the process, Sanborn said that his audience winced. He drew good applause but only a small contribution to encourage a repetition of such activity.

In Boston, Brown got a frigid reception when he called on Amos Lawrence who had given generously to buy the farm for his family in 1857. He had a bodyguard along with him in Boston, young Jeremiah Anderson, and Lawrence wrote in his diary: "He has been stealing negroes and running them off from Missouri. He has a monomania on that subject, I think, and would be hanged if he were taken in a slave state. . . . He and his companion both have the fever and ague, somewhat, probably, a righteous visitation for their fanaticism." Rumors about the Pottawatomie affair had reached Boston by this time, and Sanborn either individually or in a group asked Brown about it. Brown denied responsibility while saying he had approved it.

With his rustic dress and flowing beard he attracted a great deal of attention. With Anderson by his side, he walked down Court Street unconscious of the stares of pedestrians as he peeled an apple with his jackknife. He conferred with Howe and Stearns. After a meeting at his home, Dr. Howe told Sanborn, "He is a character, I assure you."

Under the compact arranged the previous June, Brown did not provide any further enlightenment as to his plans to any member of the Six who preferred to remain unenlightened.

Several prominent men furnished their recollections of Brown's closing days in Boston. Wendell Phillips said that the last time he saw Brown was when he brought to his home Harriet Tubman, the "Moses of her people," and said to him, "Mr. Phillips, I bring to you one of the best and bravest persons on this Continent."

Senator Henry Wilson, who had warned Dr. Howe in the spring of 1858 not to entrust guns to the irresponsible Brown, met him at a dinner at the Bird Club where Brown was in the company of Stearns and Howe. Brown said to him in a calm and firm tone that he understood that Wilson did not approve of his course. Wilson, assuming that he was referring to the invasion of Missouri, replied that he did not and, if it had happened two years before, Kansas would have been invaded from Missouri and there would have been great bloodshed. Brown replied in a flinty tone that he thought he had acted right and that his foray had exercised a good influence.

John Murray Forbes, a businessman who had grown wealthy from clipper trade with China and had gone into railroad-building, had been introduced to Brown by Howe. He invited him with Dr. Howe to his home in Milton for tea. Forbes said later that he detected a "little touch of insanity" in Brown's eyes when he declared that the contest between North and South could be settled now only with bayonets and bullets. There were several friends of Forbes's there and Brown "held them with his glittering eye" till past midnight. Forbes gave him $100, for his "past EXTRAVAGANCES, and none for his future."

John A. Andrew, who was elected governor of Massachusetts in 1860, met Brown at a friend's house on a Sunday evening. He gave him $25 because he was ashamed that he had given nothing to one who had sacrificed and suffered so much for the cause. Brown had fought, "while I had been quiet at home earning my money and supporting my family in Boston under my own vine and fig tree with nobody to molest me or make me afraid." He noticed that "the old gentleman in conversation scarcely regarded other people, was entirely self-possessed and appeared to have no emotion of any sort but was entirely absorbed in an idea which pre-occupied him and put him in a position transcending ordinary thought and ordinary reason."

Brown left Boston on June 4, Sanborn advised Higginson, with at least $2,000 he knew about in his pocket, the major share from Stearns, who was a man "who having put his hand to the plow, turneth not back."

Sanborn added, "Now is the time to help in the movement, if ever, for within the next two months the experiment will be made." Two of Brown's sons would participate with him. Brown had wanted to go to Canada to recruit from among the fugitive slaves there since he had gotten commitments from some in 1858, but he could not go since he did not have the time. Sanborn could not go because "my school will not let me." Would Higginson go there with Harriet Tubman and do this work? Higginson declined, perhaps because Brown had not solicited his aid, and Higginson felt he had been slighted since Brown had left for Kansas in 1858.

On June 3, at 6 P.M., Charles Blair got a start when an old, bearded gentleman appeared at his shop in Collinsville, and reminded him he was John Brown. "I have been unable, sir, to fulfill my contract with you up to this time for the pikes. I have met with various disappointments." Blair: "Mr. Brown, the contract I considered forfeited, and I have business of a different kind now. I do not see how I can do it." Brown: "Well, I want to make you perfectly good in the matter. I do not want you to lose a cent." Blair: "Why not take the steel and handles just as they are?" Brown: "No, they are not good for anything as they are." Blair: "What good can they be when they are finished? Kansas matters are all settled." Brown: "They might be of some use if they are finished up. I might be able to dispose of them." Blair: "Very well. If you pay me the remaining $450, I will find a man in the vicinity to do the work."

Brown spent the night at an inn, and he called the next morning at seven. He gave Blair $50 in bills and a check for $100. On June 7, he sent a check for $300 from Troy, New York. In July, while Blair was in the West, his son received a letter to send the "goods" when completed to J. Smith & Sons in Chambersburg, Pennsylvania. At the end of August Blair packed the finished blades in boxes and the handles in bundles and shipped them. He received a letter, dated September 15, signed J. Smith & Sons, that the "freight" had arrived. For some unexplained reason, Brown received only 950 instead of 1,000 pikes.

He had his last earthly reunion with wife and family at North Elba in the week beginning June 9. Before he left, he cut off his beard. He was at West Andover, Ohio, with John Jr. on June 18 where he recorded in a diary that he had borrowed John's compass and his "Jacob staff." He arranged to communicate with him through an intermediary. He was taking precautions such as that to conceal personal identities while he was shouting to acquaintances with no regard for secrecy that he was on the way to Virginia to free the slaves. From Akron, he wrote to North Elba that he was now on his way to the "Ohio River. . . . My best wishes for you all is that you may truly love God and his commandments."

Going east by rail, he went through Pittsburgh and arrived on June 27 in Chambersburg, Pennsylvania, fifty miles north of Harper's Ferry. The following notification was sent to Ohio to John Henrie (for John Henry Kagi) from Brown, who was no longer Nelson Hawkins or Shubel Morgan, but as it suited his humor, his very common name, Brown, had been dropped for the most common name of all, Smith.

Chambersburg, Pa. 30th June, 1859

John Henrie Esqur
   Dear Sir
   We leave here to day for Harpers Ferry; (via) Hagerstown. When you get there you had best look on the Hotel register for I. Smith & Sons without making much inquiry. We shall be looking for cheap lands near the Rail Road in all probability. You can write I. Smith & Sons at Harpers Ferry should you *need* to do so.

Yours in truth
I Smith

Brown, his sons Owen and Oliver, and Jeremiah Anderson spent that night in an inn at Hagerstown, Maryland. On July 3, they were at Harper's Ferry, where John E. Cook had been living for months. On Independence Day the four men started to reconnoiter the battle zone, and at 8 A.M., while strolling on the Maryland side on a road running parallel with the Potomac, they ran into John C. Unseld, a fifty-four-year-old mechanic who had a Maryland farm near Harper's Ferry. He testified before the Mason Committee about his encounter with Isaac Smith.

Smith was with three other men. Smith told him he wanted to buy land and asked its price. Unseld said it ranged from $15 to $30 an acre. Smith said he had hoped he could get land for a dollar or two. Unseld told him he would have to go to Kansas to buy land for that price. Smith said perhaps he could rent land for a while. He claimed he was a farmer from northern New York State but the frost had ruined his crops there, and so he had sold his land and was going to farm farther south. Unseld suggested that he try to rent a farm five miles west along the Potomac road running at the foot of the mountain. It was owned by the heirs of Dr. Kennedy.

A week later he again met Smith who told him that he had rented the Kennedy farm till next March 1 for $35, the two houses on it, pasture for a cow and horse, and firewood. Unseld visited Isaac Smith every ten days from then on, never accepting the invitation to go inside, but conversing while seated on his horse. Smith did not cultivate the land; he had purchased one cow, one horse, a small wagon, and three hogs. He did not tell Unseld much about himself except that he had done surveying and mining prospecting. "I own a little instrument that I carry in my hand the size of a small bucket. It has a magnet that will tell me where there is iron-ore. It has a needle to it and if the iron ore is in front of me it points to it and when I come there it will spin around." Since Smith had bought picks and shovels in Harper's Ferry, Unseld concluded that mineral prospecting was the business of the newcomer.

On November 28, a few days before the execution, Unseld visited Brown in prison. "Captain Brown," he said, "what did you have in mind when you made your attack on Harper's Ferry?" Brown answered, "I knew there were a great many guns there that would be of service to me, and if I could conquer Virginia, the balance of the southern states would nearly conquer themselves, there being such a large number of slaves in them."

This is as authoritative a summary as can be given of his purpose. He had discussed his strategy only with his adjutant, John Henry Kagi, who was killed on the first day of the raid. We, therefore, do not know the details of the plan, though its general contour is plain.

> O Thou Great Being above, whose hands but Thine
> could have created so much sublimity and grandeur?

These words were set down by Robert Harper on his first view of the site which would bear his name. Born in Oxford, England, in 1703, Harper had emigrated to Philadelphia where he was an architect and millwright. In 1747 he agreed to build a meetinghouse for Quakers at the site of what is now Winchester, Virginia. He stopped one night at an inn near Frederick, Maryland, and in conversation he was told there was a short route to his destination called "The Hole," where, moreover, he would be treated to beautiful scenery such as he had never seen before. Harper reached there the next day and decided that this would be his home.

One can readily believe that John Brown, who was moved by deep emotions of religious belief, was uplifted when he saw Harper's Ferry for the first time and that he associated in his thought the work of the Creator with his own work.

Harper's Ferry is a neck of land in West Virginia, at the time, Virginia, bounded by the Shenandoah and Potomac rivers and jutting out in their confluence. The two rivers cut through steep wooded cliffs of the Blue Ridge Mountains. On the Maryland side of the Potomac there is Maryland Heights, which rises to a height of thirteen hundred feet. On the Virginia side of the Shenandoah there is Loudoun Heights rising even more perpendicularly to eight hundred feet. Behind the town of Harper's Ferry, which nestles precariously on the banks of the rivers, rises the craggy Bolivar Heights. Between these lofty ramparts lies the gorge made by the meeting of the two rivers. The hills on which the town was built are so steep that a journalist wrote, "The natives must propagate children and chickens with one short leg to maintain the town's equilibrium."

Sitting on a high rock in Harper's Ferry, now named Jefferson Rock, Thomas Jefferson in 1783 recorded his impression of awe: "The passage of the Patowmac through the Blue Ridge is perhaps one of the most stupendous scenes in nature. . . . In the moment of their junction they [the rivers] rush together against the mountains, rend it asunder and pass off into the sea." As a Deist, he explained it from natural causes. The mountains had formed first and then the rivers had made an interior sea which burst through, forcing a passage. "The piles of rock on each hand but particularly on the Shenandoah, the evident marks of their disruptions and avulsions from their beds by the most powerful agents in nature, corroborate the impression [of] a war between rivers and mountains which must have shaken the earth itself to its center." Jefferson said, "This scene is worth a voyage across the Atlantic."

Mr. Harper found a trader, Peter Stephens, squatting on this land as he had for the previous fourteen years, and Harper bought him

out for fifty British guineas. The ownership of the land was in Lord
Fairfax's name and Harper visited him the next year at his residence,
Greenway, and bought a patent for the lands. Harper established a
ferry at the junction of the two rivers, and thereby the place acquired
its name.

George Washington was familiar with this locality. He had surveyed lands here for Lord Fairfax; two of his Revolutionary War
generals, Horatio Gates and Charles Lee, came from this area; the
Jefferson County seat, Charlestown, was named for his brother,
Charles. In 1796, President Washington recommended to Congress
that a 125-acre tract be purchased from Harper's heirs for a gun factory. "It is the most eligible spot on the river, in my opinion."

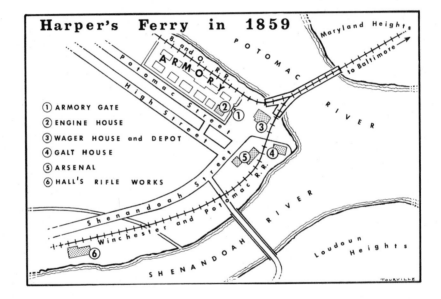

There was water power, and, in the mountains, timber and deposits
of iron ore for the forges. The first guns were completed in 1801 and
by 1810 production had increased to ten thousand muskets a year.
The Hall Rifle Works, established under government contract in
1819, turned out one thousand breech-loading flintlock rifles that
year under John Hall's own invention, using interchangeable parts. In
1859 the Hall Rifle Works was located a half-mile up the Shenandoah
from the junction of the two rivers, situated on a small island, Vir-
ginius Island, made by a canal.

The town became a bustling community. The Chesapeake and

Ohio Company bought up rights originally belonging to George Washington and built a canal on the Maryland side of the Potomac, extending from Washington, fifty-eight miles away, which was operational in 1833. In 1859, barges ninety-feet long and fourteen-feet wide plied this canal carrying heavy freight such as pig iron at low cost. In 1834, the Baltimore and Ohio Railroad extended its line from Baltimore, eighty-one miles away, to the Potomac side, and by this miracle of technology the journey from Baltimore was reduced to a mere six hours. A timber bridge was built across the Potomac in 1836, replaced in 1852 by a single suspension truss bridge of wrought iron, regarded everywhere by engineers as a remarkable feat. Harper's Ferry became a vital railroad link between the East and the Ohio Valley. The bridge, for both railroad and highway, in 1859 was a covered bridge, and close to the Virginia side it was Y-shaped, the Baltimore and Ohio swinging sharply along the Potomac to its right while the Winchester and Potomac Railroad at a right angle went along the Shenandoah.

In 1859, Harper's Ferry had a population of about thirty-five hundred, a good many of them mechanics from the North who worked in the United States armory works, which consisted of twenty buildings along the Potomac. They were paid princely wages of $2 a day and the town was prosperous. At The Point, the junction of the rivers, there was a thriving hotel and eating house, the Wager House, and Galt House, a saloon. On the Shenandoah bank, the government arsenal was located and there the guns were stored. Harper's Ferry turned out fifteen hundred to two thousand guns a month.

John Cook had lived in Harper's Ferry since August, 1858, supporting himself as a teacher, book salesman, and lock-tender on the canal. He married Mary V. Kennedy of Harper's Ferry on April 18, 1859; six months later, during the raid, she had her baby with her at Chambersburg. Cook was a popular young fellow, known throughout Harper's Ferry as a fabulous shot. He would hit half-dollars at a long pistol range. One of his feats was to attach a tape loosely to a tree with tacks and drive the tacks in with bullets. Cook told Brown accurately that the residents of Harper's Ferry had no guns. Beyond that, Cook provided Brown with information about the area, which was mostly misinformation, concocted out of his fervid imagination.

In choosing Harper's Ferry as the spearhead of his assault on the South, Brown turned the original plan, as far as it was grasped by his Boston sponsors, upside down. This was not a mountain fastness, but was the very opposite, a pit surrounded by high mountains. This was not an inaccessible spot, but on the contrary was on a main communication link with the great city of Baltimore, eighty-one miles away. He had said that he would try to avoid a bloody confrontation, but at the very outset he planned to take by force a vital southern town, and worse than that, he would take on as an adversary the federal government by his forcible possession of its armory and arsenal.

The about-face might be put this way—his backers thought he intended to play a hand of poker, but Brown was "going for broke." They thought that in a sortie or two he would seek to corral slaves, spread fear, and unsettle the institution of slavery. Instead, Brown aimed for "mighty conquest"; he would try to overthrow slavery or die. From the beginning of his career to the end, Brown was the reckless speculator and optimist, playing for the biggest stakes.

Brown must never have contemplated retreat, which would be an admission of failure. An inspection of the area around Harper's Ferry makes it evident that there was no place adapted for retreat. Save for Maryland Heights, there are no mountains on the Maryland side for thirty miles, no chasms, no cliffs. A topographical report of the area a few years later said: "So far from being wild and uninhabitable, it contains some of the finest roads and most desirable farms, most of the region being characterized by hills of moderate height whose rounded summits are covered with verdure." He would have been snared immediately in Maryland if he had tried to transport slaves to freedom.

Alexander R. Boteler, the congressman representing Harper's Ferry, was an eyewitness of the raid, and in 1883 gave a graphic and convincing account. If the assumption were correct that the slaves were ready to rise up, said Boteler, Harper's Ferry was a logical and not an illogical starting-point. Within the angle of the land formed by the confluence of the two rivers, there were many slaves. The figure has been set at twenty-two thousand within a radius of thirty miles of whom five thousand were able-bodied males. There were thousands of stands of guns periodically in the arsenal and Harper's Ferry was a gateway to the southern mountains by Loudoun Heights.

Brown was not at all sure that the slaves would rise up if he first established a stronghold in the mountains. How would the slaves learn about him, and how many would be moved to join before he was surrounded and wiped out? He felt that he had to start out with a "bang." Hugh Forbes's advice to him had made an impression. "Unless they were already in a state of agitation," the response would be at best a feeble one. Brown told Frederick Douglass just before the raid that he saw the bold move on Harper's Ferry as indispensable. "It will serve notice to the slaves that their friends had come and will be a trumpet to rally them to our standard." This news of the arrival of the Liberator by taking the important United States government works at Harper's Ferry would spread like wildfire.

By a combination of terror and leniency and use of hostages he figured he could hold Harper's Ferry for as long as two days while the slaves gathered to his standard. Then the army of a thousand men or more would cross the bridge over the Shenandoah and ascend Loudoun Heights, a climb of an hour. It was too steep for wagons, but the men would carry or drag the arms, equipment, and provisions up. The army of liberation would then move south. The Heights dip down a little for the first three miles and then rise to fifteen hundred feet, a level which is maintained for twenty-five miles below Harper's Ferry, "where the mountains broaden to a dense and labyrinthical wilderness and rise to a height of 2,000 or more feet." This is Fauquier County, where there were 10,000 slaves and 650 free Negroes according to the 1850 census compared to 9,875 whites. From there to the southern border of Virginia there were counties with a majority of slaves containing at least 200,000 Negroes. Thence the mountains reach like fingers as far south as Alabama.

In September, 1858, in Kansas, Kagi discussed the plan with Hinton, who reported in the Boston *Traveller* after the catastrophe what Kagi had told him: "No intention was expressed of gathering a large body of slaves and removing them to Canada. On the contrary, Kagi clearly stated in answer to my inquiries that the design was to make the fight in the mountains of Virginia, extending it to North Carolina and Tennessee and also to the swamps of South Carolina, if possible. Their purpose was not the *extradition* of one or a thousand slaves but their liberation in the states wherein they were held in bondage." Again, he emphasized that Kagi told him: "We will retreat *southward*." They intended to operate on the plantations on the eastern side of the mountains, enlisting slaves and foraging for food, horses, and supplies from the plantations. Brown's army would grow and grow, and so would panic in the South.

The provisional constitution adopted at Chatham was to be proclaimed in effect. One of the purposes, said Kagi, was to "alarm the Southern Oligarchy by discipline and the show of organization. In their terror they would imagine the whole North was upon them pell-mell, as well as their slaves."

Brown's plan was by no means impossible of execution if it had had some slave support initially. This is the opinion of persons familiar with the mountain terrain. A factor that militated against its success was that October 16 was fairly close to winter and it would have required much clothing and shelter to prevent all, white and black, from being frozen in the mountains. This is one of the conditions distinguishing this operation from the success of the Maroons in Jamaica in holing themselves up for years in the mountains, a favorite theme in Abolitionist literature. Again, the plan resembles Fidel Castro's feat of building up a force in the Sierra Maestra mountains of Cuba and foraging on neighboring plantations. But Castro had the benefit of help from sympathizing peasants. Brown most probably would have found the poor-whites, on whom he counted, solidly arrayed against him.

In a state of turmoil, anything might happen, but the probability was that even if Brown and a substantial number of his men and liberated slaves had escaped to the mountains, the United States Army would have squelched the attempted coup and the baptism of fire might have had a salutary effect, since it might have given both North and South some second thoughts before plunging themselves into the full fury of Civil War.

Brown told Hugh Forbes that he had identified himself in the Bible. He was another Gideon, selected by the Lord to save Israel. His life had been miraculously preserved in the Kansas fighting so that he could accomplish His work—thirty times men had taken direct aim and fired at him and the only result was that his hair had once been singed. Like Gideon, his men were few in numbers but with his faith in himself, his God, and his destiny, he did not reckon the odds.

Sanborn had pondered incessantly the mind of John Brown, and in 1909, five decades after the raid, he wrote: "In Kansas his bold policy had succeeded against the pro-slavery administration headed in its military department by Jefferson Davis. Brown hoped it might also succeed in the slave states." The demon had lodged itself in his mind since that night in May, 1856, when he had struck down without mercy the enemies of God. By the Pottawatomie murders, Brown had succeeded in promoting a collision between the two factions, North and South, which leaped at each other's throat while Brown walked unscathed through the fire. Brown felt sure that if, under his plan, he managed to get a foothold in the South, so great would be sympathy for him in the North that he could similarly cause a precipitation of North–South conflict, this time on a national scale.

One day at the Kennedy farm, soon before the assault, Owen Brown mused, "If we succeed, some day there will be a United States flag flying over this house. If we do not, it will be considered a den of land pirates and thieves."

He was correct in making ultimate success or failure the touchstone for judging adventures of this sort. As it happened, because his father's attempt did not succeed, John Brown in later years was to be often described as a madman. No treatment of Brown can ignore the considerable body of opinion that he was mad. This is a treacherous field in which there are no established norms or demarcation lines and all judgments must be highly qualitative ones. Nonetheless, we must explore the evidence.

This school of thought about Brown's madness came into being at the time of his trial in Virginia, not as a canard of his enemies but as the warm-hearted attempt of his friends to save his life. Not until the Scottsboro Boys' case in the 1930s was there such a frantic effort in one section of the nation to save a life from the penalty of the law in another section. Nineteen affidavits were presented to Governor Henry A. Wise of Virginia, almost all from his friends in the Western Reserve of Ohio, claiming that Brown was mad. Governor Wise gave these affidavits short shrift, expressing his belief publicly that Brown was the sanest man he had ever met. In after years, the John Brown madness was considerably embellished by his detractors, and historians in modern times have inclined to the theory.

This author believes that Brown's alleged insanity has been overdone, and that he had the possession of his mental faculties which we label "sane," though he was certainly a strange animal, driven as he was by overweening egotism and ambition, a compound of extreme sentiment and extreme cruelty, and sustained by abnormal endurance which was a form of demonic fury. He impresses me not as one who was out of his mind, but as the common garden-variety of fanatic, one whose mind is concentrated on a single object, who has a driving passion to accomplish it, who twists what he sees to fit into his concept, and is particularly prone to wishful thinking. Without such men there would be no organized religion and few, if any, "causes."

The Harper's Ferry raid cannot be branded as per se insane. In the roll call of weird conspiracies in Western nations of the last few centuries, including such as the Guy Fawkes Gunpowder Plot and the John Wilkes Booth conspiracy, John Brown must be given a high rating for rationality. Audacity beyond ordinary reason is the hallmark of all conspiracies against states, and is an essential ingredient for success. Harper's Ferry made more sense than, say, Hitler's Beerhall Putsch or Fidel Castro's attack on the Moncado Fortress in Santiago de Cuba on July 26, 1953. Brown's delusion that the slaves would rise up was shared by Abolitionists, and he was not as "insane" in that belief as was John Cook, who had lived in Harper's Ferry for more than a year, who made spot surveys for Brown, and assured him that not only would the slaves rebel against their masters but that he would get the active support of hundreds of the white residents.

By the McNaghten's rule, Brown was assuredly legally sane at Harper's Ferry since he understood the nature of his act and knew that it was wrong. He was not psychotic, as was Nat Turner, since he did not have and was not guided by visions and was acutely aware of reality. He was sane in the sense that his actions were rationally and purposively directed to his end. I note that Samuel Eliot Morrison in his *Oxford History of the American People* describes Brown as a "madman with a method." This phrase is a Shakespearean inversion or conceit, not a scientific category, since madmen are characteristically erratic in connecting means and ends. More than that, Brown showed evidence of a healthy mind in the self-discipline required to carry through a plan through severe obstacles over a period of years.

From first to last, Brown's letters seem sound, logical, and coherent, with every thought as sharp and clear as his clear and vigorous script. Higginson related that when he told Brown's wife of the affidavits, "She spoke of it with surprise, and said that if her husband were insane, he had been consistent in his insanity from the very first moment she knew him." Brown's letters do reflect the same man throughout.

If he was mad why was it not detected and commented on by those who were close to him? There were no such suspicions expressed. Certainly, the highly educated members of the Boston circle should have recognized signs. The distinguished physician, Dr. Howe, who was involved in the care of the insane, far from considering Brown unhinged, in later years maintained that although he was taken by surprise by the attack on Harper's Ferry, after much thought he regarded Brown's plan as an able one and its failure could not have been taken for granted. Sanborn repeatedly condemned talk of Brown's insanity as nonsense. In 1909, he said: "It is easy to show by comparison that the few score slaveholders who misled their countrymen into the abject and defeated folly of Disunion in 1860–1861 were far more insane and out of their reasonable minds than John Brown could possibly have been." Higginson in 1859 condemned the affidavits from his friends as a "most shallow charge . . . most cruel kindness." Higginson has been quoted as having said in later years that the "delicate balance" of Brown's mind had been "disturbed." In the full context of the statement in his *Cheerful Yesterdays*, Higginson was placing the blame for the fiasco on the other members of the Six who had overruled him, and insisted on the postponement from 1858 to 1859. He said that as a result "indeed it became obvious that this longer postponement had somewhat disturbed the delicate balance of the zealot's mind and had made him at the very outset defy the whole power of the United States government," by choosing Harper's Ferry as his target.

Undeniably, there was insanity in Brown's family. There was his son Frederick. His spells were periodic and the Reverend S. L. Adair left a paper that Frederick was for the most part an "intelligent and judicious" youth, citing the fact that Frederick had been elected a delegate to the Topeka constitutional convention in the fall of 1855. The props under John Brown, Jr.'s mind were none too strong and they gave way after the Pottawatomie murders. He suffered from "gloomy turns of mind." In 1859 he told his father that he could not take part in the Virginia invasion since he had a "Depressed state of mind," which disqualified him from anything "engrossing in its nature." He lived a normal life until his death in 1895. The mother of these two men was Brown's first wife, Dianthe Lusk, and Villard said: "There was a mental weakness in the Lusk family which manifested itself early in her married life, as it did in her two sisters." Statements from four persons were cited by Villard in support of this.

The original affidavits presented to Governor Wise in 1859 re Brown's alleged insanity are in the Library of Congress. It is surprising that historians have put much faith in these *ex parte* statements. Louis Ruchames found them weak and unconvincing, and so did this author in examining them.

There is one solid statement. O. C. Kendrick, the superintendant of the Northern Ohio Lunatic Asylum, wrote that the brother of Brown's mother, Andrew L. Mills, was now an inmate, and two of his children, George H. Mills and Florilla B. Edwards, had had attacks that caused temporary confinement there. There was no doubt insanity in his mother's family.

For the rest, allegations are piled on, one on top of another, which are loose and unsubstantiated and, far from constituting legal or juridical proof, they do not even have journalistic merit. What trust can be given to a statement: "I knew two cousins and an aunt and they were all mad"? Relatives are pulled in wholesale. Thus E. N. Sale said in his affidavit: "His father was a most excellent but very peculiar man." This is the charge regarding his grandmother: Jonathan Metcalf said, "My wife was personally acquainted with Brown's grandmother and I have heard her say she was insane." His brother Salmon Brown was listed as insane, while in fact he was a distinguished figure of New Orleans and there was nothing mentally ailing with him, except that he took on in political combat the formidable General Andrew Jackson. Relatives have been added by historians to the list, including Brown's mother. There is no statement at all in the affidavits relating to her.

His friends, one and all, declared Brown a "monomaniac," by which they probably meant that having fastened on the one subject of slavery his mind had become deranged on it. The strongest statement rendered as evidence of his lunacy is in the affidavit by J. N. Goodall of Cleveland. In 1857 he had a conversation with Brown in a railroad car between Cleveland and Columbus. Having returned from Kansas, Brown started to talk about slavery, "at which I attempted to point out what seemed a more conservative course, remarking very kindly to him that Kentucky would, in my opinion, have been a free state had it not been for the excitement and prejudice engendered by the ultra-Abolitionists of Ohio. At this remark he sprang to his feet with clenched fist and eyes rolling like an insane man (as he most assuredly was) and remarked that the South would become free within one year were it not that there were too many scoundrels as myself to rivet the chains of slavery." The others in the car agreed with Goodall that Brown was insane.

On the subject of the iniquity of slavery, Brown was no more demented than Garrison or Wendell Phillips, who might have behaved the same way.

What is most surprising in reviewing the so-called "proofs" of Brown's insanity is not that they are so many, but that they are so few and fragile, although there was an effort in later years to dig some up. Here is a list:

His half-brother Jeremiah said that Brown had given up his business and left his family to fight against slavery. This proved he was insane.

Aaron Erickson wrote Governor Wise about his "insane obsession" about grading wool in his Springfield business and the consequent mammoth loss. (If everybody who made "boners" in business were declared insane, there would be more cooped up than at liberty.)

Captain Samuel Walker said that one morning in the summer of 1856 he went to wake Brown who was leaning across a tree, with a rifle across his knees. "I put my hand on his shoulder; that moment he was on his feet, his rifle at my breast. I pushed the muzzle up and the ball grazed my shoulder. Thereafter, I never approached Brown when he was asleep as it seemed to be his most wakeful time." Walker said this convinced him Brown was insane.

On June 24, 1857, Brown attended at Tallmadge, Ohio, a celebration of the semicentennial of Tallmadge's founding. The Reverend Leonard Bacon delivered an address, and when he concluded he received a message from John Brown in the audience that he would like to make a talk about Kansas. Bacon sent back word that it would be "entirely inconsistent with the character of the occasion." The Reverend Bacon wrote Governor Wise that this convinced him that Brown was insane.

A letter from one N. Eggleston in the *North American Review* was given wide publicity in 1883. "I knew the old scoundrel long before Kansas was known. He tried to blow up his stepmother in an outhouse with gunpowder." John Brown, Jr., asked his aunt, Mrs. Marian Hand, if she knew what this was all about. She said this must have reference to an incident when her brother Salmon tried to blow up with gunpowder a privy which had outlived its usefulness, and all the neighbors gathered to watch the experiment. Her mother was certainly not in the privy at the time.

In 1858 and 1859, Brown was crippled repeatedly by bouts with the "ague." Amos Lawrence wrote to Governor Wise in his plea for clemency, "It is natural enough that the hardships and excitements of the past three years together with fever and ague from which he now suffers should have broken the health of one of his age and that with this, the action of his mind should have become so irregular as to make him a monomaniac."

Lawrence's comment does have some relevance to those last days of September and October, 1859. The Harper's Ferry plan, however, took shape earlier, in 1857. With the huge burdens he bore and his frequent illnesses, it is quite possible that Brown's mind lost its resiliency and he could not cope with the complex problems posed by the invasion. This may account for the fact that his tactics at Harper's Ferry seem impulsive rather than the result of preplanning and ratiocination.

Brown had expected to launch the attack by September 1, which would have allowed plenty of time before the onset of winter, but the problems of logistics proved to be greater than he anticipated. He set up three headquarters. The Kennedy farm would be the springboard. Chambersburg would be the staging area, in charge of John Henrie (Kagi), and all communications to Isaac Smith at Harper's Ferry had to go through Henrie. John Brown, Jr., at West Andover, Ohio, though he excused himself from direct participation on account of mental depression, would play an important part. Under the name of John Smith he would be the forwarding agent, not only for the arms that he held, but for other supplies. He would also be the contact agent with the outside world.

Kagi took living quarters at the boarding house of Mrs. Ritner, where Isaac Smith stayed for a day or two when he was in Chambersburg. It was understood in the boarding house that Dr. Smith had extensive mining properties in Virginia that necessitated his absence for long periods of time. John Henrie was known as a reserved young man growing a flowing beard who read books all the time. He showed great *sangfroid*. Mrs. Ritner complained of a wild dog that marauded on her premises. One day she exclaimed, "There he is!" The window was open, and Henrie, sitting and reading at a table, took out his revolver, shot the dog cleanly between the eyes though it was a long way off, and returned to his book, as unruffled as if he had brushed off a fly.

On July 5, the day after he had talked with Unseld, Brown wrote to his wife, saying that he had sent son Oliver back to North Elba. He needed some females with him. The Kennedy farm, stocked with males, but with no women there to keep house, would stick out like a sore thumb in the neighborhood. Would she come? "It will be likely to prove the most valuable service you can ever render to the world." If not, would his daughter Annie and Oliver's wife, Martha, come?

Three days later he wrote John Jr., enclosing $100. This letter which is reproduced on the following page by courtesy of the Ohio Historical Society shows the preciseness with which the commander-in-chief planned all details, and on his shoulders rested everything, raising money, disbursing it, recruitment, strategy, and tactics. He wanted his son to hold back "Whipple & Co." meaning Aaron D. Stevens and the others, until he settled the problem of "board," meaning the setting up of the Kennedy farm as a permanent abode. He wanted his son to be "in readiness to make the journey through the country Northward." He had been promised recruits from the black people of Canada, and wanted to dispatch John Jr. there in August, but he later changed that plan.

Mrs. Brown informed her husband that she was not well enough to join him, but Annie and Martha would go. On July 22, Brown wrote home that "Oliver, Martha and Anne all got in safe on Saturday of the week they set out." Annie was sixteen years old. Oliver, twenty years old, had been with Brown in Kansas and had taken part in the Pottawatomie massacre. His wife, Martha, seventeen years old, was pregnant, and she and her child would die in the spring of 1860. The shock of Oliver's death at Harper's Ferry no doubt contributed to that added tragedy.

With the arrival of the girls, the men moved into the Kennedy farm. The main building, three hundred yards from the road, had a kitchen and storeroom in the basement, living room, dining room, and bedrooms on the main floor, and an attic that could be used for sleeping quarters. Three hundred yards from the other side of the road there was a small cabin that could be used as a storeroom and also as a dormitory.

On July 23, John Smith (John Brown, Jr.), in West Andover, Ohio, wrote John Henrie in Chambersburg: "Please say to Esq Smith that I yesterday forwarded to canal at Hartstown, Pa. 11 Boxes Hardware & Castings . . . By R.Rd. Via Pittsburg & Harrisburg." The arms were now on their way to Harper's Ferry.

The order to report for duty was sent by mail to all the followers. The disappointments began for Brown. He was dismayed by the reluctance of George B. Gill to leave Springdale, which was an apparent defection. Gill, his secretary of the treasury-designate, was second only to Kagi in Brown's affection and respect. Gill's only contribution was to be this inspirational message found at the Kennedy farm: "At the right hour, by all you deem sacred, remember me." Brown wrote Kagi: "I hope George G. will so far redeem himself as to try; & do his duty after all. I shall rejoice over 'one that

repenteth.'" In after years, Gill was profuse with explanations, such as this: "I was on my way to Harper's Ferry at the time of the premature blow and apparent failure. I had been in correspondence with Kagi and knew the exact time to be on hand and was on my way to the cars when the thrilling news came that the blow had been struck. Of course, I went no further."

Charles Moffet and Luke Parsons also defected. Moffet's explanation for their absence was the same as that of Gill. He said that Kagi's letter summoning them and the news of Harper's Ferry arrived on the same day. "I know positively of my own knowledge and from men's mouths that there were from one to five hundred men on the road when the news burst."

Many of the men answered the call immediately—Tidd, Hazlett, Leeman. The greatest anxiety of the twenty-three-year-old Canadian, Stewart Taylor, who would die at Harper's Ferry, was that he might be left out. On July 3 he wrote to Kagi reminding him of his availability: "It is my chief desire to add fuel to the flames. The amount may be small but every little helps. My ardent passion for the gold fields is my thought by day and my dream by night. I often think that I am with you bringing it forth in masses that will surprise the world."

At Springdale, the Quaker idealists Edwin and Barclay Coppoc broke the news to their mother that they were leaving for Ohio. It was bitter news to her—she was widowed, and had lost three of her six children and additionally was going blind. "Ohio? I believe thou art going with Old Brown. When thou gettest a halter round thy neck, wilt thou think of me?" Barclay replied, "Mother, we cannot die in a better cause."

The letter from Brown of July 27 on the following page, from the files of the Ohio Historical Society, delaying the departure of Watson Brown and "D.," meaning Dauphin Thompson, in order to allow more time for haying, shows that Brown was managing his farm as well as managing the removal of the national curse of slavery. Then, on August 2 he sent the marching orders: "Watson and D. should set out soon after getting this. They will avoid saying anything on the road. Persons who do not talk much are seldom questioned much." William Thompson followed two weeks later. Watson Brown, who was twenty-four years old, was the only one of the Brown boys who had not fought with their father in Kansas. He was married to a Thompson girl, Isabella Thompson, and was the father of a boy who was born just before he left for his rendezvous with death at Harper's Ferry.

Brown had $2,500-plus in the exchequer to start with. At the beginning of August he wrote John Jr.: "I begin to feel almost certain that I can squeeze through with that amount. I have endeavoured to economize in every possible way and I will not ask for a dollar until I am driven to do so." However, a few days later when he had to pay an $85 freight bill for the arms shipped by John Brown, Jr., he felt "apprehensive of getting into a tight spot. It is terribly humiliating to me to begin soliciting of friends again; but as the harvest opens before me with increasing encouragements, I may not allow a feeling of delicacy to deter me from asking the little further aid I expect to need."

Instead of going to Canada to gather up promised recruits, John

Brown, Jr., was ordered by his father to head for Boston to raise more money.

From Rochester, John Jr. reported he had a day-long visit with Frederick Douglass, who would go South to meet with his father. It might be possible for Douglass to bring along Harriet Tubman. "If alive and well, you will see him ere long. I found him in rather low spirits, I left him in high." Douglass apparently found the prospect pleasing. It appears that Douglass had made a pledge to be by Brown's side during the operation.

From there, John Jr. went on to Boston, and reported on August 17. He had first called on "Dr. H." (Howe) who received him most cordially. Next he saw "the man who does business on Milk

Street," meaning Stearns, who invited him out to Medford for dinner. Stearns gave the son a message for his father: "Tell friend Isaac that we have the fullest confidence in his endevour whatever may be the result." John Jr., in turn, had the highest praise for Stearns. "I have met no man on whom I think more implicit reliance may be placed." "The friend at Concord," meaning Sanborn, was not at home, but the others said they would give him the message. John Jr. concluded by saying that he was very glad he had gone to Boston, since all were eager to have the news about friend Isaac, who, they were afraid, "was in another part of the world, if not in another sphere. Our cause is *their* cause, in the fullest sense of the word."

His mission was successful. Sanborn was away on a brief vacation and when he returned he wrote Brown on August 27 that he was cranking up the money-raising machinery again to guarantee him an additional $300. "I conclude that your operations will not be delayed if the money reaches you in the course of the next fortnight if you are sure of having it then." Sanborn was not aware of the fact that Brown was at Harper's Ferry, and he directed all mail for him to John Henrie at Chambersburg.

Dr. Howe was the first to chip in. A letter to Brown signed only "Doctor" read, "I begin the investment with $50 and will try to do more through friends." Stearns gave $200 to Sanborn to forward. Higginson gave only $20. He had grown skeptical about Brown, and Sanborn bucked him up: "Have we seen so little fruit from the agent's labors that we should distrust his Fabian valor? Who saved Kansas in '56 and invaded Missouri in '58?"

The Reverend Mr. Parker, dying in Rome, asked Sanborn to keep him up to date. "I wish I had something to drop in the hat at the end. How goes our little speculation in wool and what dividend accrues therefrom?"

Gerrit Smith gave $150. The advice from Sanborn that the operation would soon be launched sent him into ecstacy. He wrote a remarkable letter to the Syracuse *Herald* on August 29 announcing that he would not preside at the Jerry Rescue meeting that year since it was a hollow farce. Jerry had been forgotten and humanitarianism was dead, inasmuch as Jerry Rescuers voted men into public office who bowed to laws recognizing slavery. "Indeed, always exempting an anniversary of the New York State Temperance Society, I do not know of a greater or more shameless or more pernicious hypocrisy than an Anniversary of the Rescue of Jerry."

It was too late for slavery to be ended by peaceable means, he added. Only an insurrection would accomplish it. "For insurrection we may look any year, any month, any day. A terrible remedy for a terrible wrong." It might well succeed. "Will telegraphs and railroads be too swift for the swiftest insurrections? Remember that telegraphs and railroads can be rendered useless in an hour. Remember, too, that many who would be glad to face the insurgents would be busy in transporting their wives and daughters from the worst fate that wives and daughters can face."

His imagination had been fired by the impending move by John Brown. But they were words and only words for Gerrit Smith. The deed at Harper's Ferry, as we shall see, gave him a most terrible shock.

Frederick Douglass met Brown on August 19 near Chambersburg in an abandoned stone quarry. Harriet Tubman was ill and could not come. He was accompanied by his servant, Shields Green, and Kagi was along with Brown, who carried a fishing-tackle in his hand as if he had been fishing nearby. Douglass thought that he looked in every way like a man of the neighborhood, and as much at home as any of the farmers around there. His face looked to him "much worn by thought and exposure."

The four sat among the rocks on that Saturday afternoon and talked over the enterprise. Brown confided to Douglass for the first time that the taking of Harper's Ferry was his settled objective. Douglass was vehement in his objections. This was an attack on the federal government and would rouse the whole nation. Moreover, "You are walking into a perfect steel-trap and you will never get out alive." Douglass had been in favor of a plan for drawing off slaves from plantations to a mountain hideout, but he would not lift a finger for this plan.

Brown countered that it was a necessary measure to rouse the slaves, and as far as he was concerned, it would be a fine thing if it did rouse the whole nation. He pleaded with Douglass to weigh his argument and rely on his judgment. The discussion was resumed on Sunday morning. Neither Douglass nor Brown could be budged after the hours of debate. At the very end, Brown put his arms tight around Douglass and said, "Come with me, Douglass. I will defend you with my life. I want you for a special purpose. When I strike, the bees will begin to swarm, and I shall want you to help me hive them."

Douglass, adamant, said that since the plan had been entirely changed, he was returning to Rochester. He asked Shields Green if he wanted to go back with him. To his great surprise, the young Negro, who had listened to the entire debate, said, "I b'lieve I'll go wid de ole man." So Green accompanied Brown on the return trip to the Kennedy farm.

Douglass' severance from the project was a grave setback to Brown's hopes. His towering prestige would have attracted Negro support before the launch, and his presence was certain, Brown thought, to bring many slaves flocking to him when the banner of freedom was raised. It is interesting that the African Negroes are generally regarded as ruled by savage passions, but it was they and not the whites who were the skeptics about Brown's intention from the time of the Chatham convention; it was they and not the whites who were unblinded by passion, who were clear-minded and level-headed about the prospects of success of a slave insurrection. Brown had anticipated an equal number of whites and blacks in his force but he had only five Negroes at the end. He had expected to gather up many Negroes from Canada but he had only one, Osborn Anderson.

A new Negro recruit joined the ranks at the Kennedy farm in August. This was the oldest member, forty-four-year-old Dangerfield Newby, who would die at Harper's Ferry on October 17. A huge man, six feet two inches tall, he was the son of his master, a Scotchman who had freed on his death all his mulatto children. Newby's wife and seven children were being held by a new master in slavery at Warrenton, Virginia, and he was fighting to free them. In a letter his wife begged him to buy her "as soon as possible, for if you do not get me, somebody else will. Oh, dear Dangerfield, come this fall, without fail, money or no money, I want to see you so much, that is the one bright hope I have before me."

The company of men at the Kennedy farm learned that they were slated to attack Harper's Ferry only a few days before the conference with Douglass. They had come thinking that they were merely going to repeat the Missouri raid, this time on a larger scale. On a trip by wagon to Chambersburg, Brown informed his son Owen of the real intent, and Owen tried to dissuade his father from this course: "You are walking straight into the arms of the enemies as Napoleon did when he entered Moscow." Brown was chagrined by Owen's opposition; he said Kagi agreed wholeheartedly with him, but if the men felt the opposite way, he would be willing to abandon the enterprise. "We have gone too far for that," said Owen, "we must go ahead."

On their return from Chambersburg there was a meeting of the men at the farm. All those who knew and understood the site and significance of Harper's Ferry—the newly arrived black men did not —were opposed to the scheme, with the sole exception of Cook. It was suicide, they all said. Brown answered, "We have only one life to live and once to die, and if we lose our lives, it will perhaps do more for the cause than any other way." But they must trust his military judgment, and he did not mean to die there. Some of the men vowed they would never go against Harper's Ferry. Brown resigned as commander-in-chief. There was a sulk for two days. Edwin Coppoc considered going home. Tidd left the farm and stayed with Cook in the town. Then they all gave in. They had no choice since most had no place to go and no money. Owen Brown handed his father a letter signed, "Your friend, Owen Smith," which stated, "Dear Sir, We have all agreed to sustain your decisions, until you have proved incompetent, & many of us will adhere to your decisions as long as you will."

The weeks at the Kennedy farm from July 19 to October 16 were a wearisome ordeal for the high-spirited youths confined there. Most had arrived by mid-August. By September 25, all were there except for the two Oberlin recruits, John Copeland and Lewis Leary. They were virtually penned in the house. Under no circumstances, Brown ordered, was a black man to go outside the house in daylight hours. As for the white men, they might individually take a little exercise about the house, or one man at a time might go to the post office or visit a store to buy some provisions for the house. Cook, of course, had the freedom of the town of Harper's Ferry and as a salesman of maps was touring the environs constantly.

Brown was extremely active, appearing openly with his son Owen by his side. He was often in Harper's Ferry, where Cook introduced him as his good friend, Dr. Smith. At the depot there he received boxes that he said contained mining equipment. Owen talked for hours with railroad men on the topography of the countryside, the number of slaves, and even about the best guns in the arsenal. Brown and Owen on Sundays attended a little Dunker chapel near the farm, and there were open-air Dunker meetings in a nearby grove. The Dunker sect were nonresistant Abolitionists.

There is a record of eight trips Brown made by wagon to Chambersburg, and on September 27 he and Kagi went to Philadelphia for three days. He supervised the transport to the farm of the hundreds of pikes and the arms and ammunition from Chambersburg to the farm, most of which was done by a young Pennsylvania Dutchman who carried on this business with his own freight wagon. Annie recounted: "The rifles were in boxes called 'furniture' and were used to sit on and kept standing against the walls in the dining room, one box of pistols being in a bedroom near Martha's bed. She used it for a table or dressing case. I had to tell people who called that my mother was coming soon and that she was very particular and had requested us not to unpack her furniture until she arrived."

The men did the housework, cleaning the house and washing clothes so that the girls would have the burden only of the cooking. They played cards and checkers, sang, read magazines and the Baltimore *Sun*, to which Brown subscribed, studied military tactics under Stevens. Brown encouraged debate and discussions on all subjects including religious ones and often joined in the debates. Stevens had a copy of Tom Paine's *Age of Reason*, which provided material for discussion between believers and nonbelievers. Cook had obtained from the arsenal the official directions for browning and coloring guns, and the men spent time applying these to the guns in the house.

That they felt pent-up is abundantly demonstrated by this recollection supplied by Annie: "When there was a thunderstorm, they would jump about and play, making all kinds of noise to rest themselves, as they thought no one could hear them then." These caged young lions felt equal to any action when they sprang out on October 16.

Detection was a constant anxiety of Brown's in those long weeks, and there was good reason for it, with a house packed with a dozen and then a score of men doing nothing, and with wagons going between Chambersburg and the farm carrying arms and supplies. Cook was his greatest worry, he told his daughter Annie. His loose tongue, his impulsiveness, and indiscretion might well betray the plot. Brown was appalled by Cook's proposal that he circulate among the slaves to tell them that the Liberator was on the way. As it was, Cook linked Brown to an interest in local slaves by taking a census of slaves along the Charlestown road, telling everybody that it was to settle a bet he made with his friend Isaac Smith. He never concealed the fact that he had fought for the free-state cause in Kansas.

Annie was fearful of a neighbor's dropping in unexpectedly, and kept a constant lookout, even when serving the food. She was particularly worried by a little barefooted woman neighbor with her four little children, Mrs. Huffmaster, "the little hen and chickens," who was a "worse plague than the fleas." Mrs. Huffmaster noticed the large amount of the washing. "Your men folks have a right smart lot of shirts." Annie would call out when she saw Mrs. Huffmaster on the way with her brood, and if the men were eating they would pick up the table cloth and dishes and scurry up to the attic, but she was sure that Mrs. Huffmaster had once seen the Negro, Shields Green, in the house, and that was a serious matter. Dauphin Thompson wrote home that Shields had been seen by a neighbor-woman. "It is rather a bad job but it can't be helped as we are not ready to begin operations yet." This is in a letter of September 4.

Brown's other worry besides Cook was the letters that the men were writing. He could not censor their mail, and he realized that they were at a high emotional peak and needed an outlet. But they were certainly blurting out information that might raise suspicions. He unburdened himself to Kagi on August 11, writing him from the Kennedy farm: "If everyone must write some girl; or some other extra friend telling or shoing our location; & telling (as some have done) all about our matters; we might as well get the whole published at once in the New York Herald. Any person is a *stupid Fool* who expects his friends to keep for him that which he cannot keep himself. All our friends have each got *their special friends*; and they again have theirs; and it would not be right to lay the burden of keeping a secret on any one; at the end of a long string."

He had belatedly realized the need for security while over the past two years he had broadcast his intention widely. He was assuredly justified in his fears at this time. Richard Hinton said he had collected copies of twenty letters written by the men while at the Kennedy farm that disclosed that some plan to attack slavery by force was afoot. The twenty-year-old lad, Willy Leeman, wrote his mother in Maine: "Yes, mother, I am waring with Slavery the greatest Curse that ever infested America. For three years I have been Engaged in a Secret Association of as gallant fellows as ever pulled a trigger with the sole purpose of the Extermination of Slavery." He told her that action was imminent. "I am now in a Southern Slave State, and before I leave it, it will be a *free state, Mother*." This letter was in an envelope with a Harper's Ferry postmark.

One warning did reach Secretary of War John B. Floyd:

Cincinnati, August 20

Sir: I have lately received information of a movement of so great importance that I feel it my duty to impart it to you without delay.

I have discovered the existence of a secret association, having for its object the liberation of the slaves of the South by a general insurrection. The leader of the movement is *"Old John Brown,"* late of Kansas. He has been in Canada during the winter, drilling the negroes there, and they are only waiting his word to start for the South to assist the slaves. They have one of their leading men (a white man) in an armory in Maryland—where it is situated I have not been able to learn. As soon as everything is ready, those of their number who are in the Northern States and Canada are to come in small companies to their rendezvous, which is in the mountains in Virginia. They will pass down through Pennsylvania and Maryland, and enter Virginia at Harper's Ferry. Brown left the North about three or four weeks ago, and will arm the negroes and strike the blow in a few weeks; so that whatever is done must be done at once. They have a large quantity of arms at their rendezvous, and are probably distributing them already.

As I am not fully in their confidence, this is all the information I can give you. I dare not sign my name to this, but trust you will not disregard the warnings on that account.

Floyd pigeonholed the letter. He explained why before the Mason Committee. There was an error in the letter. The federal government had no armory in Maryland. "I supposed therefore that it had gone into detail for the purpose of exciting the alarms of the Secretary of War and to have a parade about that for nothing. Besides, I was satisfied in my own mind that a scheme of such wickedness and outrage could not be entertained by any citizens of the United States." Yet, he was impressed enough that he kept the letter, while he generally threw away anonymous letters.

The author of this letter was a young man, David J. Gue. He visited Springdale in August, 1859, with his brother and learned of the plan from a Quaker there, Moses Varney, who knew of it because of Brown's indiscretion. Varney felt that it was doomed to failure and something should be done to head it off and save the lives of Brown and his gallant comrades. Gue wrote this letter hoping that the Secretary of War would increase the guard around the government installations at Harper's Ferry and thereby induce Brown, when warned by Cook, to abandon the conspiracy. The letter was an effort to save Brown, not to destroy him.

There is no clear proof that any suspicion other than this letter attached to Brown before the fatal day. As a matter of fact, newspapers published reports that John Brown was back in Kansas. On September 8, John Brown, Jr., wrote Kagi:

By the way, I notice through the Cleveland Leader that Old Brown is again figuring in Kansas. Well, every dog must have his day and he will no doubt find the end of his tether. Did you ever know of such a high-handed piece of business? However, it is just like him. The Black Republicans, some of them, may wink at such things, but I tell you, friend Henrie, he is too salt a dose for many of them to swallow and I can already see symptoms of division in their ranks. We are bound to roll up a good stiff majority for our side this fall.

On September 8, Brown wrote to North Elba: "Martha and Anne on way home in course of this month." Then this poignant statement: "I do not know what to advise about the spotted cow as much will depend on what you have to feed her."

During September he collected all the money from Boston that he expected. The recruits did not come from Canada, and apparently they would not come. On September 29, Martha and Annie left for home and they were accompanied as far as Troy by Oliver Brown. On October 8 he wrote his last letter home before the confrontation at Harper's Ferry. "I want Bell [Isabella] and Martha both to feel that they have a home with you untill we return. We shall do all in our power to provide for the wants of the whole as one family till that time."

John Brown did not attack Harper's Ferry with a feeling that he was going to perish. Far from that, he was committing himself to send money home to care for the family until he and the boys set foot again on the soil of North Elba. Although he was realistically aware of the very high risk, in his characteristically positive mode of thinking, he had faith in his survival.

If there was to be much time before winter, the campaign had to start soon. On October 1, in his last letter to John Jr., Brown said that he was not sure that anything reaching him after October 6 would do much good. He wrote Sanborn, fixing the day as October 15. On October 10, Kagi wrote John Jr. from Chambersburg that his father had left the day before and he himself was leaving for good that very afternoon. They had used up all their money and had not $5 left. Cook had sent his wife and child to Mrs. Ritner's boarding house for the duration. John Jr. must not try to send any further supplies and if he had any more recruits he must hold them in Ohio and find work for them "until we open the way clear," from the South to the Mason and Dixon line.

Kagi explained:

This is just the right time. The year's crops have been good and they are now perfectly housed, and in the best condition for use. The moon is just right. Slaves are discontented at this season more than at any other, the reasons for which reflection will show you. We can't live longer without money—we couldn't get along much longer without being exposed. A great religious revival is going on, and has its advantages. Under its influence, people who are commonly barely *unfavorable* to Slavery, under religious excitement in meetings speak boldly against it. In addition to this and as a stimulant to the religious feeling, a fine slave man near our headquarters, hung himself a few days ago because his master sold his wife away from him. This also arouses the slaves. There are more reasons which I could give, but I have not time.

Secretary of War Floyd, during his tenure, pursued a policy of stocking heavily southern armories, which helped the Confederacy considerably through its early months in 1861. Cook stated that the date of Brown's attack had to be set before October 20, on which date, he had heard in Harper's Ferry, there was to be a heavy shipment of arms out of the arsenal, almost stripping it bare.

The provisional government was proclaimed in being on October 10 when the commander-in-chief issued General Order No. 1. Battalions of the army would be made up of four companies of seventy-two men each, making 288 men in a battalion. Each company was divided into "bands" of seven men, each under a corporal, and every two "bands" was a "section" under a sergeant.

Commissions were handed out in this hypothetical army. Oliver, Watson, and Owen Brown were made captains. Other captains were Stevens, Tidd, Cook, William Thompson, and Jeremiah Anderson. Lieutenants commissioned were Edwin Coppoc, Dauphin Thompson, and Leeman. None of the five black members was commissioned an officer, since white officers were to lead an army made up of freed slaves.

The document following reproduced from the files of the Ohio Historical Society, is the commission making Edwin Coppoc a lieutenant. It is a printed form signed by Brown as commander-in-chief and Kagi as secretary of war. The arc of peculiar letters at the top is GREETING. The writing underneath it on the right is "Near Harper's Ferry, Maryland."

There was another bizarre note in the closing days of the preparation, the enlistment of the final recruit.

Francis Jackson Meriam was a month shy of being twenty-two years old. He was the nephew of the Abolitionist Francis Jackson, of Boston, and he had inherited some family money. He looked frail and erratic and he most certainly was. He was scrawny, his face was blotched and he had a glass eye. He was one of the five to make good their escape from Harper's Ferry, and Owen Brown who led the party said that Meriam had a perfect disguise by taking out his glass eye, which contorted his features.

He was a fanatical Abolitionist and for long had talked of going down South and helping slaves to escape north, a task for which he was obviously unsuited and for which he got little encouragement. On December 23, 1858, he wrote to Brown in Kansas offering his services: "Mr. Redpath and Mr. Hinton have told me of your contemplated action in which I earnestly wish to join you. Is there anything it would be well for me to study meanwhile? Of course I shall pay my own expenses and shall acquire the use of the proper tools for the work." Brown for an unexplained reason never replied. Perhaps someone had described Meriam to him.

Now, in those last days, on the streets of Boston, Meriam met a Negro, Lewis Hayden, who told Meriam that Brown was ready to make the plunge. Meriam wanted to take part. Hayden directed him to Sanborn who sent him to Higginson in Worcester, with a note, "Perhaps you will have a message for the Shepherd." They were startled by his appearance, but even more startled by the intelligence that he had $600 in gold which he was willing to donate to Brown, whose appetite for funds were endless.

Sanborn speeded Meriam to Chambersburg. Kagi had left but Meriam obtained John Henrie's new address. He had his will drawn out by A. K. McClure in which he left his money to the Abolitionist cause. He went to Philadelphia and then to Baltimore. Edward K. Shaffer, who had a store in Baltimore, testified that Meriam came in on October 13 and wanted to buy forty thousand to fifty thousand percussion caps. Shaffer had a smaller quantity which he sold for $45. The youth paid in three $20 gold pieces but was so nervous that he left the $15 in change behind and had to be called back. Meriam arrived at Harper's Ferry two days before the raid, stayed overnight at the Wager House, and was brought to the Kennedy farm the day before the onslaught.

He carried with him almost $550 in gold. This was manna from Heaven, and Brown must have looked on Meriam as the final proof that God was interested in the success of his venture. He grabbed the money, had Meriam take the oath, and then assigned him guard duty for the arms at the Kennedy farm. Brown had been so hard up

O. S. A. H. S.

NOV 7 1945

No.

HEAD-QUARTERS WAR-DEPARTMENT,

WHEREAS, *Edwin Coppoc* has been nominated a *Lieutenant of Company* in the Army established under the PROVISIONAL CONSTITUTION; NOW, THEREFORE, In pursuance of the authority vested in Us by said CONSTITUTION, We do hereby Appoint and Commission the said *Edwin Coppoc* Lieutenant

Given at the Office of the Secretary of War, this day, *Oct. 15th, 1859*

John Brown COMMANDER IN CHIEF.

SECRETARY OF WAR.

522

(From Western Reserve Historical Society)

for money that he had been compelled to borrow $40 from Edwin Coppoc. When he was captured at Harper's Ferry he had $260 in gold on his person. It is not clear what happened to the rest of the money. He probably stocked up with various supplies purchased at nearby general stores. (He did not repay Coppoc and on the day of his execution he apologized to him for being unable to discharge the debt.)

Higginson by letter expressed his surprise to Sanborn that he had sent Brown this pathetic specimen, who struck him as mentally unbalanced. Sanborn replied, "I consider him about as fit in this enterprise as the Devil is to keep a powder house, but everything has its use & must be put to it if possible."

Sanborn's patience might have been worn thin by Higginson's continual carping. After all, this youth, Meriam, was not only willing to give much money but to risk his neck. In his reply to Higginson, he burst out with what was undoubtedly intended as a rebuke to those, including himself, who sat comfortably, far from the firing line, and merely gave money. It is a fitting summation of the activities of the Secret Six:

'Tis a virtue posted in numbskulls to give money freely. . . . Out of the mouths of babes and sucklings come dollars by the hundred, and what is wisdom compared to that? I do not expect much of anybody. "Tis a vile world, my masters."

On Saturday the complement of men was complete at the Kennedy farm, twenty-two with Brown, fewer than he had hoped for but they would have to do. Meriam had arrived in the morning, and Cook moved in that night. He had spent the day before feverishly molding bullets, and when asked by his mother-in-law what they were for, he answered, "For the Indians in Kansas."

On Sunday morning, the sixteenth, Brown held prayer service. He read a chapter from the Bible about the enslavement of the children of Israel in Egypt, and then offered a prayer for the liberation of the slaves. Osborn Anderson said, "The service was impressive beyond expression. Every man there assembled seemed to respond from the depths of his soul." Stevens read the provisional constitution again, and administered oaths to new arrivals like Meriam. Kagi filled out officers' commissions for those who had not received them.

In the afternoon, Brown gave out assignments of duties for the occupation of Harper's Ferry. According to Anderson, he instructed them to be careful before shooting: "And now, gentlemen, let me impress one thing upon your mind. You all know how dear your life is to you and to your friends. Remembering that, consider that the lives of others is as dear to them as life is to you."

They had supper and after nine o'clock Brown called out, "Men, get on your arms. We will proceed to the Ferry." He put on his old "Kansas cap" and got on a wagon that was loaded with twenty pikes, some wooden torches or flambeaus made of hickory to retain the fire and covered with pine to ignite the hickory, a sledgehammer, and a crowbar. Three men were left behind to guard the arms, Owen Brown, Meriam, and Barclay Coppoc. The brothers Coppoc embraced. They would never see each other again—Barclay would escape and Edwin would be captured and executed.

One or another of the men took turns sitting in the wagon beside Brown. The others of the eighteen, in ranks two by two, trudged beside or behind the wagon, long, gray shawls around their shoulders, beneath which were slung Sharp's rifles.

As the men marched the five and a half miles down the road in a dim moonlight, what were their thoughts? Certainly they felt exuberant and relieved that they had been released from confinement. They had a sense of self-importance that they were embarked on a great, perhaps historic, mission. They were exalted by a belief that their purpose was a noble one.

Their last letters reflect this idealism. Stevens wrote to his sweetheart, Jennie Dunbar: "What happiness there is in thinking and knowing that we are doing the best we can for the good of humanity." Watson Brown wrote to his wife, Isabella: "I do want to see you and the little fellow very much but must wait. There was a slave near where we live whose wife was sold to go South the other day and he was found hanging in Thomas Kennedy's orchard, dead, the next morning. I cannot come home as long as such things are done here."

Stewart Taylor, a "spiritualist," was certain that he was going to die, that it was a fate he could not escape. Annie Brown wrote: "He predicted his own death which really came true. He talked as coolly about it as if he were going into another room." Watson Brown had a presentiment of his death, writing Bell: "I sometimes think perhaps we shall not meet again."

The overwhelming number of these young men were confident that they would somehow come out alive, though none was unaware of the high danger. In his last letter to his sister in Nebraska, Kagi wrote: "Things could not be more cheerful and more certain of success than they are. We have worked hard and suffered much, but the hardest is down now and a glorious success is in sight." Dauphin Thompson informed his family in North Elba: "I suppose that folks think we are fools, but they will find out we know what we are about."

Jeremiah Anderson wrote to his brother in Iowa: "We go in to win at all hazards. So if you should hear of failure, it will be after a desperate struggle and a loss of equipment on both sides. But this is the last of our thoughts. Everything seems to work to our hands and victory will surely perch upon our banner. The old man has had this in view for twenty years, and last winter was just a hint and trial of what could be done."

This expression was typical. The confidence of the men rested ultimately on a mystique wrapped about Brown, that he had triumphed against odds in the past and would do so again. Having surrendered their judgment about invading Harper's Ferry, they surrendered completely. Brown once told Ralph Waldo Emerson of his tremendous will-power. Without moving, he could force a dog or cat in a room to leave merely by the power of his eye. His will-power could work on human beings, too, and it had drained out the will-power of these young men who had become mere projections of his own will. There is no evidence that Brown was ever asked to explain to anyone of them what he planned to do after taking possession of Harper's Ferry, and he did not take anyone except Kagi into his confidence.

Brown believed in himself, and the others believed in Brown. It was in that faith that they advanced on Harper's Ferry.

CHAPTER EIGHT

At Harper's Ferry

THE FOLLOWING DISPATCHES were received by the Associated Press office in Washington, D.C., on the morning of October 17, 1859:

Baltimore, 7:45 A.M.

A dispatch just received from Frederick dated this morning states that an insurrection has broken out at Harper's Ferry where an armed band of Abolitionists has full possession of the government arsenal. The express train going east was twice fired into and one of the railroad hands and a Negro killed, while they were trying to get the train through the town. The insurrectionists arrested two men who had come to town with a load of wheat, and seizing their wagons loaded them with rifles and sent them into Maryland. The insurrectionists number about 250 whites and are aided by a gang of Negroes. At last accounts fighting was going on.

The above is given as it was received. It seems very improbable and should be received with caution.

Baltimore, 10 o'clock

It is apprehended that the affair at Harper's Ferry is more serious than our citizens believe. The telegraph wires are cut and we have no communication beyond Monocacy Station. The southern train due here at an early hour has not arrived. It is rumored that there is a stampede of Negroes from this state. There are many other unconfirmed rumors.

Another account received by train says the bridge across the Potomac was filled with insurgents all armed. Every light in the town was extinguished and the hotels closed. Men were seen in every quarter with muskets, who arrested citizens and impressed them into service, including Negroes. The United States arsenal and government payhouse and all other public works were seized. During the night the mob made a demand on the Wager House for provisions and enforced the claim with armed men. The citizens are in terrible alarm and the insurgents threaten to burn the town.

The following message was sent at 7 A.M. by Andrew Phelps from Monocacy Junction, Maryland, to William Prescott Smith, Master of Transportation for the Baltimore and Ohio Railroad:

Express train bound east under my charge was stopped this morning at Harper's Ferry by armed Abolitionists. They have possession of the bridge and the arms and armory of the U.S. The leader of the men requested me to say to you that this is the last train that shall pass east or west. If it is attempted it will be at the peril of those having them in charge.

At the next stop, Ellicott Mills, there was a message to Phelps from Smith:

Your dispatch is evidently exaggerated and written under excitement. Why should our train be stopped by Abolitionists and how do you know they are such? Let me know at once before we proceed to extremities.

The reply from Phelps to Smith:

My dispatch is not exaggerated. I have not made it half as bad as it is. The captain expects a reinforcement of 1500 men to liberate the slaves.

Smith was second in command of the B. & O. RR. The president, John W. Garrett, on being notified, telegraphed to President Buchanan a full statement of what he had learned, and added: "This is a moment of greatest peril."

Elijah Avey was a sixteen-year-old boy learning the watchmaking trade in Charlestown, the county seat of Jefferson County, eight miles from Harper's Ferry. He was awakened at 6:30 A.M. on October 17 by the noise of bells, the long roll of drums, and the strident notes of the fife calling assembly. He dressed hurriedly and rushed outside. He saw men of two companies of militia, the Botts Grays and Captain Rowan's company, forming ranks before the courthouse. He asked Sheriff Moore, who was preparing to mount his horse, what it was all about. "Harper's Ferry is in the hands of unknown men and that's where we're going."

Alexander R. Boteler, the congressman representing Jefferson County, lived in Shepherdstown, ten miles from Harper's Ferry. News of an outbreak of some kind reached there early in the morning. He set out in a carriage. On the way, on Bolivar Heights, he met an old Negro, with bandied legs and a crooked stick, running. "Well, uncle, which way are you going?" "I'se only gwine a piece in de country for ter git away from de Ferry." "You seem to be in a hurry." "Yes, sah, I'se dat. It's 'bout time ter be in a hurry when dey gits ter shooting' sho' nuff bullets at yer." "Anyone been shooting at you?" "No, not exactly at me, bless de Lord, 'cause I don't give 'em a chance 'ter."

In Washington, at noon, Chief Clerk Walsh of the Navy Department drove rapidly into the Washington Navy Yard and asked Lieutenant Israel Green how many Marines were there. He said ninety. Walsh said they must leave at once for Harper's Ferry where there was a disturbance. They left the Washington depot for Baltimore at 3:30 P.M. with two howitzers.

First Lieutenant J. E. B. Stuart of the First United States Cavalry was in the War Department: His account states: "The dispatches received by the President were kept very secret for fear of a rise in Washington. It was, however, whispered very cautiously through the different bureaus of the Department. I heard it accidentally and although scarcely anything was known except that the Harper's Ferry armory was in the possession of a mob of rumor said over 3,000 men, still it was pretty well surmised that it was a servile insurrection."

Brevet-Colonel Robert E. Lee was summoned from his home in Arlington across the Potomac. In civilian clothes, he had a conference with President Buchanan and Secretary of War Floyd at the White House. The President gave him a hurriedly written proclamation ordering the insurgents to disperse. Lieutenant Stuart, whom Lee did not know at the time (he wrote his name in his report as Stewart), offered his services which Lee accepted. Lee had been at Fort Monroe, Virginia, at the time of the Nat Turner rebellion and believed this was similar, a slave insurrection with white assistance.

At 6:30 P.M. Lee and Stuart reached the Relay House, eight miles before Baltimore, and found that the Marines had already taken a train for Harper's Ferry. Lee was told that the railroad would furnish him a special locomotive to get him there. He wired Lieutenant

Green to wait for him at Sandy Hook, and then wired Secretary Floyd that from the latest advices it appeared that the insurgents numbered five hundred men. The locomotive left at 8 P.M. and they arrived at Sandy Hook at 10 P.M. There he learned that the number of insurgents had been greatly exaggerated and they were now surrounded in the armory yard. Their leader was a man of the neighborhood named Smith. They crossed the Potomac bridge at 11 P.M. and the Marines took stations in the armory yard. Lee learned than that the leader was Osawatomie Brown, the ruffian from Kansas.

In Charlestown, prominent lawyer Andrew Hunter feared the attack on Harper's Ferry might be a ruse to draw all able-bodied men away from Charlestown. He organized all men and boys left behind into patrols and gave them what few weapons were available. At midnight came a dispatch that the invading band was modest in numbers and was led by John Brown of Kansas fame. Elijah Avey recalled, "The veil had been lifted. The intense feeling of fear of an unknown and dreadful enemy was dissipated."

Alexander M. Ross, an Abolitionist and friend of Brown's, was in Richmond. He recalled: "Crowds of rough, excited men filled with whiskey and wickedness stood for hours together through the night in front of the offices of the Enquirer listening to reports as they were announced from within. When the news of Brown's defeat and capture was read from the window, the vast crowd set up a demonic yell of delight, which to me sounded like a death-knell to all my hopes for the freedom of the enslaved."

Hours before Lee arrived on the scene, a chapter in history had been written. John Brown had failed—and failed miserably. Kagi was dead. Dangerfield Newby, William Thompson, and Billy Leeman had died foul deaths. Leary was in his last hours. Stevens, badly wounded, was a prisoner. Brown with a remnant of his force was penned up in the fire-engine-house in the front of the armory grounds with nine hostages. His two sons, Watson and Oliver, were in the fire-engine-house with him, both mortally wounded.

Brown later told his trial counsel, George H. Hoyt, that while his men had displayed superb valor, from a professional standpoint their performance was sadly wanting, since "Stevens was the only real soldier." Brown's performance as the general was also sadly wanting. Perhaps because the burdens he bore proved too great for one man, and an aging, ailing man at that, he had done no careful planning beforehand. He had intended to improvise his tactics and be guided by events. However, he lost his options within hours because the basic intelligence governing his over-all strategy was wrong, staggeringly wrong, on two counts.

Brown had expected the slaves to flock to him. He had told Frederick Douglass, "When I strike, the bees will begin to swarm." He "liberated" about a dozen slaves and put pikes in their hands—they were only confused and most immediately threw them away. Authors Du Bois and Hinton to the contrary notwithstanding, there is no evidence that a single slave joined Brown voluntarily.

If he had tried, he could hardly have picked a better area of the South for a demonstration of slave loyalty. There were no cotton, sugar, or rice plantations in this area. Most of the farms in the immediate vicinity were run by gentleman farmers who did not even grow enough to make a living from their crops. Most slaves were household servants; those who were field hands were comfortably boarded, and held under such loose rein that many were away from home all that night gathering chestnuts, since it was chestnutting season. The New York *Herald* on November 13 had an item that the news came to the Annual Fair of the Lynchburg, Virginia, Agricultural Society and one farmer pooh-poohed it, saying, "If there were any danger at all, I would go to my plantation for a bodyguard of my slaves."

Harper's Weekly, which was strongly pro-Union, sentimentally depicted on its front page some planters arming slaves to protect them. It ran a drawing headed "A Premature Movement," showing Brown handing a pike to a slave. He says, "Take this. My name is Brown, follow me," and the slave replies, "Please God, Mr. Brown, dat is onpossible. We ain't done seedin' yit at our house." There was also a drawing showing two elegant black gentlemen in conversation, Caesar and Pompey. "Was you interrupted, Pompey?" "I 'lieve not. I allows dem was ignorant pussuns, onadquainted wid de neighborhood of Harper's Ferry." "Dat I always knew'd before I ever heard of 'em."

If it had all not been so tragic, it would have been farcical.

Brown's second great mistake was that he believed that he could cow the local populace and control Harper's Ferry and the bridges of egress across the Potomac and Shenandoah for two days while slaves swarmed to him and he prepared to move, preferably to the South. He held control for only a little more than half a day. He believed that there were few or no guns in the town and the residents were unorganized and divided in their sympathies. However, he underestimated the sons of Virginia in the surrounding countryside who were armed and had been ready for a generation for another Nat Turner. Whatever discreditable conduct can be charged to the local militia, the basic fact must not be clouded that within a few hours of the news, with resoluteness and numbers, they rushed in and sprang the trap around Brown.

Colonel Lee's report to President Buchanan detailed the mobilization. By 11 A.M. the Jefferson Guards had arrived from Charlestown under Captain J. W. Rowan. Then came the Hamtramck Guards under Captain V. M. Butler. Next to arrive were the Shepherdstown Troop under Captain Jacob Rienahart. Later in the afternoon came the Captain Alburtis Company from Martinsburg. After sunset, more troops arrived. There was Captain B. B. Washington's company from Winchester, the first men in uniform, followed by three companies from Frederick, Maryland, under Colonel Shriver. These were followed by companies from Baltimore under General Charles C. Edgerton. All these were on hand before the United States Marines under Colonel Lee marched over the bridge into Harper's Ferry.

The expedition began when Cook and Tidd cut the telegraph lines on the Maryland side of the Potomac and the caravan led by Brown in the wagon crossed the covered bridge. As they approached the Virginia side, the watchman, William Williams, recognized Brown and Cook and in puzzlement greeted them. Stevens and Kagi prodded the muzzles of their rifles against him and said he was a prisoner. Watson Brown and Taylor were left to guard the bridge and the rest marched to the armory gate, sixty yards from the bridge.

The watchman there, Daniel Whelan, was ordered to open the gate. He said he did not have the key. A crowbar and sledgehammer were gotten from the wagon and the gate was opened. Whelan was "nearly scared to death," as a man said to him, "Make no noise or we will put you into eternity." Then Brown said to him, "I came here from Kansas and this is a slave state. I have possession of the United States armory and if the citizens interfere with me, I must burn the town and I will have blood."

Edwin Coppoc and Hazlett were sent across Shenandoah Street to break into the United States arsenal which stood within another enclosure where there was no guard. Oliver Brown and William

Thompson guarded the bridge over the Shenandoah. A detachment went to the Hall's Rifle Works and captured it. Kagi and Copeland were assigned to guard it and they were reenforced later by Leary.

At 11:45 P.M., Patrick Higgins, the night watchman, arrived at the Potomac side of the bridge to relieve Williams. He wondered why the bridge was all in darkness with the lamps all extinguished. Halfway across the bridge, two men put guns to his breast and told him he was a prisoner. One escorted him toward the armory but close to the armory gate Higgins managed to give his guard a terrific blow above his ear. He disregarded the shout, "Halt," and ran for cover to the Wager House, which was connected to the railroad station. A bullet creased his scalp with little damage. He braced himself at the bar with a few drinks. Like the other watchmen, he was confounded by the events, not knowing what to make of them. At any rate, he could not go to his job until further notice.

At 1:15 A.M. the B. & O. train from Cincinnati and Wheeling arrived. It stopped when shots were fired at it ahead from the bridge, and the conductor, Andy Phelps, went forward to investigate. He was told by armed men on the bridge that he could not proceed. "What do you want?" he said, and one replied, "We want liberty and we want it now."

Shephard Hayward was a free Negro employed by the B. & O. as the baggagemaster, and when the station agent, Fontaine Beckham, was absent, he took charge, even selling tickets. Hayward in the railroad office wondered about the halted train and about Patrick Higgins who had not dropped in on him as was his custom. He walked around the depot and then walked onto the bridge where he was accosted. He ran back toward his office. A shot went through him, slightly below his heart. "Captain, I am shot," he shouted to Phelps. He dragged himself in agony into the railroad office, where he died fourteen hours later.

It was a tragic irony that the first man to be shot in the attack was a free Negro, not one of the southern enemy. Why was he shot? Benét wrote in his poem, ". . . his face gray with pain and puzzled at sudden death/ Stares at us through the bookworm dust of the years/ With an uncomprehending wonder, blind with surprise." Apparently there was a reason. From a later conversation, which we shall relate, it seems that he was shot as punishment by Oliver Brown because he refused to join in with the raiders. This is the sense, too, of a marker to Hayward at Harper's Ferry, erected by the Sons and Daughters of the Confederacy, "exemplifying the character and faithfulness of thousands of Negroes, who under many temptations throughout subsequent years of war so conducted themselves that no stain was left upon a record which is the peculiar heritage of the American people."

John D. Starry, a thirty-five-year-old physician, was the first resident of Harper's Ferry to grasp the situation. He had a room opposite the railroad station and was awakened at 1:30 A.M. by shots. He looked out the window, saw the halted locomotive chugging at the station, saw the confusion around the train and armed men milling around, carrying rifles. He went down to the street. Higgins called out to him that Shephard Hayward was wounded. The doctor went into the railroad office and found Hayward lying on a plank between two chairs. He examined the wound and saw that it was mortal. He told Hayward that he would return to him with a sedative. Higgins told him what he had experienced. "Now, I didn't know what 'Halt' mint than any more than a hog knows about a holiday, and so I ran." Starry dressed his scalp wound.

He walked over to the armory gate and asked a man guarding it what this incursion meant. "Never mind, you will know in a day or two." Starry said to him, "Do you expect to stay a day or two?" he got no answer. The time had come for action. Starry routed out three boys he knew from their homes. He sent one to Charlestown to Captain Rowan, one to Shepherdstown, and a third to stop all Baltimore and Ohio trains coming east. All carried the message that Harper's Ferry had been seized by a band of armed men. The doctor went to the home of A. M. Kitzmiller, who was in charge of the government works in the absence of the superintendant. Then he ordered the Lutheran church bell to be rung. He visited friends and stopped men in the street to find out how many guns were available in Harper's Ferry. He was told that there were only one or two squirrel guns and a few shotguns in the possession of citizens. All the guns were in the arsenal which the invaders held.

At 6:30 A.M., as it was getting light, Dr. Starry decided that the best contribution he could make was to ride to Charlestown himself to make sure that Captain Rowan and his men were on their way to Harper's Ferry. Soon after he left, a well-to-do grocer, Tom Boerly, was wounded. At the corner of High and Shenandoah streets, Boerly fired a shotgun at a man at the arsenal gate. A return shot, fired from behind the arsenal fence, penetrated his groin, and he died from the ghastly wound in two hours.

One of the distinguished residents of the area, living five miles from Harper's Ferry by the road on Bolivar Heights, was Colonel Lewis W. Washington, a great-grandnephew of the first President. (The colonelcy was honorary—from the governor.) He was forty-six years old, "handsome, of medium height, slow and grave of speech and rather like Trumbull's portrait of Washington." At 1:30 A.M. on October 17 he was awakened from a deep dream of peace by what he thought at first an apparition. There were five men standing at the entrance to his bedchamber which was on the ground floor in the front of his mansion. One of the five held a flaming flambeau in one hand and a revolver in the other. The other four held rifles. Each had two revolvers sticking in his belt in front.

It was real enough when he recognized one of the men, John Cook of Harper's Ferry. The leader of the party, he later learned, was Stevens, and others were Tidd, Taylor, and the Negro, Green, the last always addressed respectfully as "Emperor." Cook had made Washington's acquaintance in Harper's Ferry and asked if he could call on him some day to inspect the relics in his home. He had called three weeks before and had examined with interest the pistol that Lafayette had presented to General Washington and also a sword that was a gift from Frederick the Great, which General Washington had used as a dress sword. Cook said he came from Kansas where he was a member of a hunting party that shot buffaloes for their hides and showed him two revolvers he always carried. They went outside and engaged in a shooting match which Cook permitted Washington to win, and he said to him, "You are the best shot I ever met."

To the housebreakers, Washington said, "You are a very bold-looking set of fellows but I doubt your courage. You have too many arms to take one man. I believe with a popgun I could take any one of you." Stevens said, "Colonel Washington, you are our prisoner." Washington was alone in the house, his daughter having left the day before. "Possibly you will have the courtesy to tell me what this means. It is really a myth to me." Stevens replied, "We have come here for the purpose of liberating all the slaves of the South and we are prepared to do so."

As Washington was dressing, Stevens said to him, "I presume that you have heard of Osawatomie Brown." Washington said he had not. "Then you have paid very little attention to Kansas matters." Washington answered, "I have become so much disgusted with Kansas that whenever I see 'Kansas' at the head of a column in a newspaper, I turn the page." Stevens, "speaking apparently with great glorification," said that he would be able to see Osawatomie Brown himself that very morning.

Stevens wanted his money and his watch. (This confiscation of slaveholders' property was perfectly legal under the Chatham provisional constitution.) Washington said they would have to take them by force. "I am going to speak very plainly. You told me your purpose was philanthropic, but you did not mention at the same time that it was robbery and rascality." Cook appropriated a very handsome gun that he had seen on his previous visit and they took also a shotgun, a rifle, and an old pistol of Harper's Ferry make of 1806 which Colonel Washington kept as a curiosity. Stevens carried off the silverware, but then dropped it, thinking it might be just plated silver.

They took his most precious possession, the sword from Frederick the Great. Cook apologized to Washington, saying that he was sorry that he had to rob him after having enjoyed his hospitality. Washington replied with disgust that he could save his apologies. "Just make certain that I get that sword back."

They "liberated" all the slaves on his premises, only three in number, since the rest were on French leave that night, and put them in one of Washington's farm wagons drawn by four horses. They also took Washington's carriage in which he sat on the back seat with Cook.

They drove up to the house of Mrs. Henderson, the widow of Richard Henderson. Washington said, "There is only the mother here and the five daughters who have just lost their father. It would be an infamous shame to wake them up at this hour." They heeded Washington, and went on. Next they came to the home of John H. Allstadt, where they made their entrance by crashing a fence rail against the front door. "Get up quick or we will burn you up," they shouted. Two women put their heads out of a bedroom window and cried, "Murder!" They were told to shut up or they would have their heads blown off. Allstadt said he would give them money if they would go away, but Stevens said they wanted him and his eighteen-year-old boy and their slaves. They picked up six slaves here, one belonging to Washington, packed them into the wagon and from there went on to Harper's Ferry and the armory yard where they arrived at 4:30 A.M.

When Washington arrived at the armory yard he realized that this was something more serious than he had believed. The headquarters was the engine-house near the armory gate, behind which for a third of a mile loomed the buildings of the armory, such as the rolling mill, forging shop, stocking shop, machine shop, and component departments. The building was thirty-two by thirty feet, divided into two rooms; the fire-engine-house proper was twenty-two feet long, facing the armory gate, while the watch-house, separated by a wall from the engine-house, was about ten feet long. It was the watch-house into which Washington was escorted and where he met the leader, Osawatomie Brown.

"I presume that you are Mr. Washington. You will find a fire in here, sir. It is rather cool this morning. I think after a while, possibly, I shall be enabled to release you, but only on condition of getting your friends to send in a Negro man as a ransom. We must put an end to this thing, this evil. I wanted you particularly for the moral effect it would give our cause to have one of your name as prisoner. I shall be very attentive to you, sir, for I may get the worst of it in my first encounter, and if so, your life is worth as much as mine." As for the sword from Frederick the Great, "I will return it to you on your release." Brown carried it around in the morning hours. In the afternoon he discarded it for a gun.

The train had spent the whole night at Harper's Ferry. Twice Brown had sent messages to conductor Phelps that he could move on, but Phelps refused. At 6 A.M. Brown went out to converse with Phelps who said he was afraid to move the train because he didn't know the condition of the bridge. Brown said, "You need have no fears. I will walk ahead of you just ahead of the engine." And so the two men walked across the bridge while the train followed at a slow crawl. On the Potomac side, Brown bade Phelps good-bye. "There will soon be hundreds of slaves here and there must be no more trains through Harper's Ferry, east or west."

Brown's men were gobbling up men from the streets, mostly armorers on their way to work. John E. P. Daingerfield, a clerk in the armory, was stopped by two men in an alley who said, "We have taken possession of the government works." Daingerfield said, "You talk like crazy men," and got the rough answer, "Not so crazy as you think, as you will soon see." He was led to a man named Captain Smith who told him he was a prisoner. "I have come to free the slaves of Virginia and by twelve o'clock I will have fifteen hundred of them."

There were soon as many hostages and freed slaves as could be handled, forty at least, and Brown sent a message to the Wager House by a bartender he had nabbed, "Watty" Kemp, that he wanted breakfasts for fifty. The food was carried to the engine-house, but was almost untouched. Brown's men feared that the food had been poisoned and the prisoners shunned the food from the same fear.

Daniel J. Young, a chief machinist, approached the gate and was denied permission to enter by a man who said they were holding possession by authority of the Great Jehovah. Young replied, "If you derive your authority from the Almighty, I must yield as I get my right to enter from an earthly power, the government of the United States. I warn you, however, that, before this day's sun shall have set, you and your companions will be corpses." Unmolested, he departed.

All during those morning hours not a single slave came to join Brown. Surely, if Harriet Tubman or some other knowledgeable black had with him he would have been advised that no slaves were coming at all and he had better flee over one of the bridges, while he was able to do so, taking his hostages with him as a shield and for bargaining. Why did he remain? Brown would never give a satisfactory answer. Von Holst wrote, "It is as though during those decisive hours a thick veil had fallen over the eyes that were wont to see so clearly."

Kagi, at the Hall Rifle Works in the late morning, read it clearly when no slaves showed up. He sent a frantic message to Brown through Leary as messenger: "Get over the bridge and into hills. Do not delay. Our purpose is accomplished. The blacks will respond. Pray you not remain here." He received a message given to Leary by Stevens: "Tell Kagi to remain firm."

After depositing Colonel Washington, the Allstadts, and the slaves at the armory, Cook was sent in the wagon drawn by the four horses across the Potomac to move arms from the Kennedy farm closer to Harper's Ferry. Under Cook there were Tidd, Leeman, and two of the slaves.

As they were going along the road on the Potomac side they encountered Terence Byrne on horseback on his way to the Ferry and Byrne jovially greeted his friend Cook, who ordered him to stop. "I am sorry to inform you that you are my prisoner." Byrne said, "You are certainly joking, John." Cook said, "No, I am not." Byrne saw a gun-barrel protruding from his coat. Tidd, walking behind the wagon, approached Byrne and said, "No parley here or I will put a ball through you."

They went to the Byrne farm. Cook said when they arrived, "We want your slaves." Byrne laughed and said, "If you want them, you will have to do the same thing we would have to do, look for them. They went away on Saturday night and they haven't returned yet." So loose were the bonds of slavery in that area.

Cook, grateful for an audience, launched into what Byrne, testifying before the Mason Committee, described as a "higher-law" speech, along this line: "We are operating under a higher law than that of Virginia. We are obeying a power which for centuries has been proclaimed by the philosophers and statesmen and jurists of the United States and Europe. The law of nature. Wherever a human soul exists, that law applies. The meanest slave has the same right to live and attain knowledge that you and I possess." The Byrne family listened wide-eyed. A lady, a cousin who was visiting, was unimpressed and said, "Terence, why have you not cowhided these ruffians out of this house?"

Tidd returned from the Kennedy farm with boxes of arms in the wagon. Leeman was detailed to conduct Byrne to the armory grounds. It had begun to rain and so Byrne took an umbrella under which both huddled as they walked. They passed William Thompson on the road and Leeman asked him how the people at Harper's Ferry were taking it all. Thompson said, "Pretty well. They're more frightened than hurt," and he passed on. They crossed the bridge and Brown greeted them at the engine-house. Byrne came just in time to hear a short speech by Brown to all his prisoners: "Gentlemen, if you knew my history, you would not blame me for being here. I went to Kansas as a peaceable man and I was hunted down like a wolf by proslavery men and I lost a son. And now I am here."

Cook, Tidd, and the Negroes drove the wagon to a schoolhouse about two miles on the road from the Potomac bridge. Lind F. Currie, a man of thirty-three, was in charge, and there were thirty children in the school ranging in ages from eight to sixteen. The men in the wagon hauled in the boxes of arms. Cook told Currie that the children could stay but Currie thought it better to send them home when he saw the schoolhouse being taken over by strange men.

Cook disappeared and reappeared several times that day and told the schoolmaster in a general way what was in progress. In the afternoon the firing became intense from Harper's Ferry, and Currie asked what it meant. Cook said, "Well, it simply means that these people down there are resisting our men and we are shooting them down." After one burst of gunfire, Cook turned to the two slaves and said, "There! Some more of your oppressors are gone!"

Currie asked, "With how many men did you commence the foray down there?" Cook did not give a direct answer. "I don't know how many men there are now. There may be five thousand or ten thousand for all I know." They would surely triumph. He talked vaguely of great assistance expected from up North, mentioning names such as Gerrit Smith and Frederick Douglass. Cook in delirium had lost contact with reality.

Evidently, in stocking with arms the schoolhouse, close to the bridge, and dispatching the three-man force to Hall's Rifle Works, Brown planned these as way-stations to arm the slaves, in the first case those coming down from places in Maryland such as Sharpsburg, Boonsboro, and Hagerstown; and in the latter case, those in Virginia coming down along the bank of the Shenandoah. But no slaves appeared to be armed.

Brown was disconcerted from nine o'clock in the morning to find so many guns firing at him from High Street and the hills in a town which he thought had no arms. After Dr. Starry had left for Charlestown, an armorer had pointed out a shed on a hill where some government guns were stored in case of an emergency or sudden flood, and so a number of Harper's Ferry citizens were now armed, but there was limited ammunition.

It was a peculiar situation. There were no fixed battle lines, and there was a great deal of informal traffic between the residents and the enemy. The action was taking place in a small compass, the armory being sixty yards from the bridge and the arsenal sixty yards from the armory gate. The foreign force had been plumped right into the center of the town. A hostage wanted to visit his home to say he was all right and Taylor escorted him there and back. The hostages had visitors. Daingerfield's wife and daughter visited him. He recounted: "We were treated kindly, but we were compelled to stay where we did not want to be." A hostage, Joseph Brewer, went back and forth asking the citizens for the sake of the hostages not to shoot.

The firing on both sides was aimless and desultory. Brown discussed with some hostages a proposal for a cease-fire on both sides, leaving him in possession of the armory, but this was dropped, probably because there was no opposite number to Brown in command on the other side with whom an agreement could be worked out.

The morning hours wore on without form or movement, Brown hoping for some sign or deliverance from Heaven, and his soldiers as confident as ever, relying on Brown. At 10 A.M., Patrick Higgins left the railroad office to go to a pump for water for the dying Hayward. William Thompson asked him for a drink and Higgins handed him the bucket. Thompson asked him to go to the bridge and give water to the other two guards, Oliver Brown and Dangerfield Newby. Oliver said, "Say, you're the buck who clouted me last night." "I guess so." "Well, you did a very unwise thing. It is only this bad leg which saved you," showing him a deep cut on his knee. Higgins said, "What's all this fuss about, anyway?" "Oh, it's a darky affair," said Oliver pointing to the grinning Newby. "I am one and here's another." Higgins: "I'm in a darky affair, too. That's to get water for a Negro you shot." Oliver: "All right. Go along. He brought it on himself by refusing to do what we told him," by which he probably meant Hayward's refusing to join up with them.

The Harper's Ferry men who had arms decided to divide into two groups to cross the Potomac and Shenandoah and take the exits to the bridges. At 11 A.M. the Jefferson Guards from Charlestown arrived near the town and so they took ranks in the larger force. The strategy mapped by Colonel John T. Gibson, of Charlestown, who had over-all command, was to draw a cordon around Brown and tighten it. They crossed the Potomac in small boats at a spot called Old Furnace, and then marched down the road beside the C. & O. canal. Brown spotted them across the river. "Here come our men," he said, thinking that they were a rescue army organized by Cook. Stevens had to let him down. "Captain, I'm afraid those aren't our men."

When they reached the bridge, the Guards charged it, advancing and shooting. Oliver Brown and William Thompson retreated in the face of the withering fire to the armory grounds. Dangerfield Newby retreated toward High Street.

George W. Turner, a forty-year-old gentleman farmer, a West Point graduate, had entered the town after hearing of the trouble and that his friend Colonel Washington was a prisoner. He was forty yards up High Street, saw Newby, and rested a gun on a fence to take aim. He was struck in the neck by a bullet fired by Newby and died instantly.

The honor of killing Newby was disputed by Jacob Bajeant and

Richard B. Washington, a kinsman of Colonel Washington. Instead of a bullet, a six-inch spike was driven into a gun-barrel and fired at Newby. Congressman Boteler said, "I saw his body while it was yet warm as it lay on the pavement in front of the arsenal yard, and I never saw on any battlefield a more hideous musket-wound than his, for his throat was literally cut from ear to ear by the six-inch spike."

From this point on, the excitement and fury of the people of Harper's Ferry boiled over. The proslave Frederick, Maryland, *Herald*, which detailed the indignities to which the bodies were subjected, said: "It may be thought there was cruelty and barbarity in this, but the state of the public mind had been frenzied by the outrages of these men, and being outlaws they were regarded as food for carrion bird and not as human creatures."

Newby's body was dragged up Shenandoah Street. The citizens spat on the body of the huge mulatto, kicked him, beat him with sticks and ran the sticks in the gaping wound, shouting obscenities at him. A local historian and witness that day, Joseph Barry, chronicled what happened next: "A hog came up, rooted around the spot and put its snout to the dead man's face. Suddenly the brute was seized with a panic and with bristles erect and drooping tail it scampered away as if for dear life. This display of sensibility did not deter others of the same species from crowding around the corpse and almost literally devouring it. This writer saw all this with his own eyes, and at the risk of further criticism he will remark that none of the good people of Harper's Ferry appeared to be at all squeamish about the quality or flavor of the pork that winter."

Brown had lost the Potomac bridge. The Jefferson Guards streamed into the town and occupied the arsenal. Hazlett and Osborn Anderson who had been guarding it escaped into Maryland. Apparently they hid in the brush along the Shenandoah until night, when they crept along the Potomac shore until they found a small boat in which they rowed across to the Maryland shore; then they took to their heels until they reached the Kennedy farm. The company under Captain Botts came down from Bolivar Heights and was augmented by some Harper's Ferry men. They seized the Shenandoah bridge on both sides, and so that was lost to Brown, too. Now there was only one escape route open, along the armory buildings and up the Potomac, if means could be found to cross it.

Billy Leeman, the twenty-year-old lad, became badly frightened. He decided to make a desperate run for his life. From the upper end of the armory yard, he tried to wade and swim across the Potomac. A volley of shots rang out. He was wounded, barely managed to reach a rock where he turned around, facing the Virginia shore, and held up his hands in surrender. G. A. Schoppert, a visitor in town from Richmond, waded the river, pistol in hand, as Leeman, petrified with fear, faced him. Within a few feet of him, Schoppert fired and shot his face off. Lying against the rock, Leeman was used as target practice, men wading out to him and setting him up in grotesque positions for the sport of the shooters. Finally, his riddled body fell off the rock and floated downstream.

Men took a position across from the Hall Rifle Works on the Shenandoah bank and started firing, while others marched on it from the town. Kagi went out the back way, walked on the roadbed of the Winchester and Potomac Railroad and then tried to wade across the river. When two-thirds of the way across, he was struck in the head and died instantly, falling into the river. Leary and Copeland also tried to wade across. Leary was hit when near a rock in the center of the river and fell on it, badly wounded. Copeland reached the rock and stood on it. James H. Holt of Harper's Ferry waded out to him, pistol in hand, and no doubt would have shot him, as Leeman was shot, had not the water entered the gun-barrel. He began using the pistol as a club and then took Copeland prisoner. When Copeland was dragged onto shore, many residents called for a lynching but, due mainly to Dr. Starry's efforts, he was saved for the law. Leary survived his terrible wound until midnight. He wrote messages to his family and said: "I am ready to die."

Cook looked from a height across the Potomac and saw his comrades in the armory yard becoming hemmed in on all sides, and saw men on High Street firing down on them. From a tree, half a mile away, Cook shot at them. Congressman Boteler said that a bullet whizzed by his ear which he was certain was fired by that fabulous marksman, Cook. Shots were returned across the river. One broke a limb of the tree on which Cook was hanging, and he fell twenty feet to the ground, ending his efforts to help the besieged force.

His position being near-desperate, Brown sent out a prisoner, Reason Cross, with William Thompson under a flag of truce to discuss a cease-fire. Brown thought he still had cards to play in his hand, the hostages who were at his mercy. The only result of this bid for peace was that Cross was freed and Thompson was taken prisoner to the Wager House. Brown tried again under a flag of truce, this time the emissaries being A. M. Kitzmiller, the acting superintendant of the armory, with Watson Brown and Stevens. Gentlemanly rules of war were totally scrapped. Watson Brown received a severe bullet wound in the pit of his stomach and staggered back to the engine-house. Stevens was also badly wounded in his neck and shoulder by two shots from the Galt house, and he was dragged as a prisoner to the Wager House.

A company of militia from Martinsburg under Captain E. G. Alburtis almost succeeded in ending the whole fray. They charged in from the west along the B. & O. railroad tracks. With quick presence of mind, Brown abandoned the watch-house part of the building facing west and retreated to the engine-house proper, selecting nine hostages whom he considered the most important, among them Colonel Washington, the Allstadts, father and son, Terence Byrne, the master armorer, Benjamin Mills, and the master machinist, A. M. Ball. Thirty of the prisoners were left to be freed by the Alburtis company.

Fontaine Beckham had been the B. & O. agent at Harper's Ferry for many years; he also was mayor of the town and a magistrate of Jefferson County. He was a man of nervous temperament and became even more excited when his beloved employee, Shephard Hayward, died at three in the afternoon. For some reason he decided to march unarmed to closer quarters with the enemy. He left the railroad office, crept around the watertower and peeked around it. Edwin Coppoc fired at him and he fell dead, struck in the right breast.

The news of this killing of a distinguished citizen who was unarmed raised the fury of the townspeople to its highest pitch. At the Wager House, young Harry Hunter, the son of the Charlestown lawyer Andrew Hunter and grandnephew of Beckham, wanted to kill William Thompson on the spot. "Mr. Beckham's life is worth ten thousand of these vile Abolitionists." The sister of the proprietor, Christine Fouke, shielded Thompson's body with her person Pocahontas-like as she flung her arms about him. She screamed, "For God's sake, don't. Let the law take its course." Hunter and his companions decided that this was not the right place for an execution and the best thing to do was to have a hanging party. They shoved Miss Fouke away and pushed Thompson outside.

During the trial of John Brown, under the examination of his father, who was special prosecutor, Harry Hunter testified without shame or apology about his cold-blooded murder of Thompson:

By the by, before we took him out of the room, I asked the question what he came here for; he said the only purpose was to free the slaves or die; then he begged, "Don't take my life, I am a prisoner," but I put my gun to him and he said, "You may kill me but it will be revenged; there are eighty thousand persons sworn to carry out this work." That was his last expression. We bore him out on the bridge with the purpose of hanging him. We had no rope and none could be found; it was a moment of wild excitement. Two of us raised our guns—which one was first I do not know—and pulled the trigger. Before he had reached the ground some four or five shots had been fired into his body. He fell on the railroad track, his back down to the earth and his face up. We then went back for the purpose of getting another one [Stevens] but he was sick or wounded and there were persons around him. We did this act with a purpose, thinking it right and justifiable under the circumstances, and fired and excited by the cowardly and savage manner in which Mr. Beckham's life had been taken.

According to a witness, Joseph Barry, Thompson was still alive when he fell through the railroad trestles to the bed of the river where he was showered with bullets. "For a day or two his body could be seen lying at the bottom of the river, with his ghastly face still showing what a fearful death agony he had experienced."

In a burst of gunfire, which followed the killing of Beckham, a bullet fired by a sniper in the armory yard struck Oliver Brown in his left side—a wound which like that of his older brother Watson was undoubtedly mortal. Brown accepted all these blows stoically. He fastened with ropes the large double doors of the engine-house to permit the folding-leaves which opened inward to be separated enough to give an aperture for shooting. He said to Phil, one of Allstadt's kidnapped slaves: "You're a pretty stout-looking fellow. Can't you strike holes through the wall for me?" He handed him mason's tools and Phil broke the wall to make four portholes. The other slaves threw away their pikes and did nothing. According to John Allstadt, two slept through the worst gunfire.

It was late afternoon. Samuel Strider, a gentleman farmer from the vicinity, walked to the engine-house with a white handkerchief tied to the ferrule of his umbrella. "Who commands this fortification?" he called out in his high-pitched nasal voice. The answer came from behind the doors, "Captain John Brown of Kansas." "Well, Captain John Brown of Kansas, I have been sent here by the authorities in command for you to surrender, and I do so in the name of the Commonwealth of Old Virginia, God bless her." "What terms do you offer?" "Terms? I heard nothing said about them. What terms do you want?" "I want to be allowed to take my men and prisoners across the bridge where I will release the prisoners unharmed provided no pursuit shall be made beyond that point." "Captain Brown, you will have to put that down in writing." "It's too dark to write." "Nonsense, don't tell me that an old soldier like you hasn't got the conveniences like pencil and paper." "All right."

A light was struck inside and after a while a note was handed out to Strider. It read:

Capt. John Brown answers:
In consideration of all my men, whether living or dead, or wounded, being soon safely in and delivered up to me at this point with all their arms and ammunition, we will then take our prisoners and cross the Potomac bridge a little beyond which we will set them at liberty; after which we can negotiate about the Government property as may be best. Also we require the delivery of our horse and harness at the hotel.

John Brown

Strider returned with this note to Captain Lawson Botts, who uttered an oath and said, "This is adding insult to injury. I'm in favor of storming the engine-house." Colonel Robert W. Baylor, who had a jurisdictional dispute that day with Colonel Gibson about final authority, decided that there would be no direct attack that day. It was getting dark. Besides, Brown was quoted as having said that he would put the hostages in front of him to receive the direct fire. Anyway, the men in the engine-house were as securely locked up as if they were in the county jail. Extra guards were posted around it to make sure that no one bolted as Leeman had done in the early afternoon.

A doughty warrior, Captain Thomas Sinn of the Frederick, Maryland, militia, disdaining any flag of truce, swaggered up to the fortress-door for a parley with Brown. At Brown's trial he testified about their conversation:

Brown complained that his men were shot down like dogs while bearing a flag of truce. I told him they must expect to be shot like dogs if they took up arms that way. Brown said he knew what he had to undergo when he came there. He had weighed the responsibility and would not shrink from it. He had had full possession of the town and could have massacred all the inhabitants had he thought proper to do so, but, as he had not, he considered himself entitled to some terms. He said he had knowingly shot no one who had not carried arms. I told him that Mayor Beckham had been killed and that I knew he was altogether unarmed. He seemed sorry to hear of his death, and said, "I fight only those who fight me."

This was all one of Brown's artful self-justifications. Brown had had no regard for a flag of truce at the battle of Black Jack in Kansas in 1856, and he had had no compunction about taking life if it served his cause. He would have soaked himself in blood at Harper's Ferry if it had helped his purpose. The basic contradiction in his tactics at Harper's Ferry was that it would have required mercilessness for him to conquer, and yet he wanted to appear to North and South as the merciful conqueror. Therefore he never put his hostages to any use, and they proved only an encumbrance. He had told Colonel Washington that his life would be worth no more than the lives of his men; he told the hostages that lacking breastworks he proposed to use them for that purpose; but yet at the end he was taking elaborate precautions to save their lives, warning them to stay out of the line of fire. At that stage there can be little doubt that he was weighing the consequences of his failure—and there was always the outside chance that he could exchange them for his escape.

Captain Sinn, after his talk with Brown, went back to the Wager House where he found a ruffian badgering the wounded Stevens. Sinn said, "Get out. If that man had a toy gun, you would jump out the window."

It was now night, a dismal, chilling night, with intermittent rain as it had rained intermittently through the day. High excitement mixed with a spirit of carnival reigned in the town. Militiamen were constantly streaming in, people were coming in from the countryside, newspaper correspondents were arriving. The saloons were jammed. The arsenal was open and anyone who wanted a gun could get it. Guns were constantly being fired into the air. Patrick Higgins recounted, "The people kept shouting and shouting at random, and howling."

At 11 P.M., twenty-four hours after John Brown crossed the Potomac bridge, Colonel Robert E. Lee with the United States Marines crossed over. What a change had been wrought in the space of a day in this drowsy, peaceful town! Lee was appalled by the scene, and his first order was to shut the saloons. Nonetheless, the ear-splitting din continued through the night.

In the engine-house, the dying Watson Brown scratched on a scrap

of paper: "Fight on, fight ever, you Hell houns of the Lower Re-
gions. Your day has come. Lower your black flag, shoot your dogs,
you Devil Hell and furies. Go in for Death."

Sometime during the night, Stewart Taylor standing near the
door-opening, was hit and fell noiselessly to the floor, dying as he
had predicted he would. The men of the original band unwounded in
the fortress were, besides Brown, Dauphin Thompson, Jeremiah
Anderson, Edwin Coppoc, and Shields Green. They had been without food and sleep for forty-two hours when midnight came, but
they indomitably manned the portholes, waiting for an attack. None
of Brown's men showed cowardice during the struggle. However,
the hostage Daingerfield heard Dauphin Thompson say to Brown,
"They say we are committing treason. I came only to free the slaves.
Is that so?" Brown answered gravely, "Yes. This is treason," and
Thompson said, "Then I don't want to fight."

"Men, are you awake?" Brown would ask from time to time. "Put
me out of my misery, Father," said Watson. "No, my son, I think
you will get well. If you die, you will die in a glorious cause." Oliver
pleaded, "Oh, God, let me die, let me die." He begged in his agony
to be shot. "Be quiet, son. If you must die, die like a man." Just before daybreak, Brown called, "Oliver, Oliver." There was no sound
or movement where he lay. "I guess he is dead," said the father.

Appraising the situation on his arrival, Colonel Lee decided to
postpone the storming of the engine-house until dawn since hostages
could not be distinguished from the enemy in the dark. He reported
to President Buchanan: "But for the fear of sacrificing the lives of
some of the gentlemen held by them as prisoners in a midnight assault, I should have ordered the attack at once."

At two o'clock in the morning, Lee had a conference with Lieutenant "Jeb" Stuart. At daybreak, Stuart was to advance to the door
and read a message to Brown asking for his surrender. If there was a
refusal to surrender, which Lee anticipated, Stuart was to give a
signal and a storming party would attack with bayonets, not using
guns in order to save the lives of the prisoners.

The message was as follows:

Headquarters, Harper's Ferry
October 18, 1859

Colonel Lee, United States army, commanding the troops sent by the
President of the United States to suppress the insurrection at this place,
demands the surrender of the persons in the armory buildings.

If they will peaceably surrender themselves and restore the pillaged property, they will be kept in safety to await the orders of the President. Colonel Lee represents to them in all frankness that it is impossible for them to escape; that the armory is surrounded on all sides by troops; and that if he is compelled to take them by force he cannot answer for their safety.

R. E. Lee
Colonel Commanding United States Troops

At 7 A.M. on Tuesday morning there were several thousand people assembled to watch the assault. Lee stood on an elevation forty yards away from the engine-house, protected by a pillar. Stuart went up to the doors. Brown opened them about four inches and placed his body against the aperture, a cocked rifle in his hand. Stuart said, "I know you, you are Osawatomie Brown. I met you in Kansas." The reply was, "Yes, I did my duty there." In the account he wrote to his mother from Fort Riley in Kansas on January 31, 1860, Stuart wrote: "I recognized old Osawatomie Brown who had given us so much trouble in Kansas. No one present but myself could have performed that service." It is a peculiar statement, since Brown had made no secret of his identity the day before.

The parley was a prolonged one. As Stuart described it: "He presented his propositions in every possible shape and with admirable tact, but they all amounted to this: that the only condition upon which he would surrender was that he and his party should be allowed to escape. Some of his prisoners begged me to ask Colonel Lee to come and see him. I told them that he would never accede to any terms but those he had offered, and as soon as I could tear myself away from their importunities, I left the door. . . ."

Stuart walked a distance away and waved his cap as a signal that the assault could begin. There had been a plan offered for breaking the wall between the watch-house and engine-house but a test made during the night determined that it was too thick to be broken through, and so only a frontal assault was feasible. Lee offered the honor of the assault to the volunteer-militia. A Colonel Shriver, of the Frederick militia, declined, saying, "These men of mine have wives and children at home. I will not expose them to such risks." Colonel Baylor also declined on behalf of the Virginia militia, saying, by report: "This is a duty belonging to the mercenaries who are paid for it." It was a sensible decision since it seemed certain that men would lose their lives, but it was a stain on the honor of the State of Virginia, in the eyes of many. O. Jennings Wise, the son of the governor, brought charges against Colonel Baylor in a military court of inquiry on the ground that he had given a "false, cowardly and insulting reason for not leading the attack on the engine-house when the service was offered to him by Colonel Lee."

Lee then turned to Lieutenant Israel Green and offered him the command of the storming party of twelve men. Green was the senior line officer of the Marines there; a Major W. W. Russell, who stood by Lieutenant Green, was a staff officer in the paymaster office. Green was a stocky, undersized man, but he had a world of grit. He doffed his hat respectfully and thanked Colonel Lee for the honor given to him.

The grim scene of impending death was given color by the elegant garb of the Marines. They wore dark-blue frock coats, skyblue trousers, chalk-white cross-belts, and French fatigue caps. On this chilly morning they put on sky-blue, single breasted overcoats, with capes similar to those worn in the Army.

Three Marines rushed forward with sledgehammers to break down the doors. A correspondent wrote that the "reverberations reached from the rocky sides of the mountains that rose in all their rugged majesty around us." But the ropes holding the doors withstood the blows. Then Green ordered that a ladder leaning against one of the shops be used as a battering ram. Three times the Marines ran the ladder against the doors, and on the third run the ropes broke apart and Green rushed in leading the charge.

There is a difference in the reports as to what happened next. According to one eyewitness, Green climbed to the top of one of the two fire engines right behind the doors, made a flying leap at Brown with his sword which caught in the buckle of Brown's belt and merely raised him from the ground, and then Green rained blows on Brown while he lay prostrate. Green's written account in 1883 indicates that he did strike Brown while he was down. As he entered, Colonel Washington said to him, "This is Osawatomie Brown," and pointed to him. "Quicker than thought, I brought my sabre down with all my strength upon his head. He was moving as the blow fell and I suppose I did not strike him where I intended for he received a deep sabre cut on the back of his neck. He fell senseless on his side, then rolled over on his back." Brown fired a shot from the rifle he held. "Instantly, as Brown fell, I gave him a sabre thrust in his left breast. The sword I carried was a light uniform weapon and either not having a point or striking something hard in Brown's accoutrements, it did not penetrate. The blade bent double."

At any rate, the essential fact was that because Green was wearing a dress sword he did not slash Brown to death on the spot. It was a fortuitous circumstance for abolitionism and the northern cause. Had the blade been sharper, John Brown would have been quickly forgotten.

In his letter to his mother, "Jeb" Stuart explained that he could have done things better. He was an Army officer and therefore could not command a storming party made up of Navy men. If he had been appointed, "it would have been an outrage to Lt. Green which would have rung through the Navy for twenty years." Green lamented to him afterward that his sword was so dull that it had spared Brown. "My sword in the Ordnance Office was like a razor so that if I had commanded the stormers, my sabre would have saved Virginia the expense of Brown's trial." As it was, "I feel that I did all that my position allowed me to do and for it I claim NOTHING, but if a bill passed the legislature of Virginia rewarding Green and not including me, I would feel exceedingly *mortified*. To reduce the thing to a nutshell, it is that Green was *ordered* to do what he did. I *voluntarily* left important business in Washington." Stuart, in fact, had contributed nothing.

Continuing with Green's story: "By that time, three or four of my men were inside. They came rushing in like tigers, as a storming assault is not a play-day sport. They bayoneted one man, skulking under the engine, and pinned another fellow up against the rear wall, both being killed instantly. I ordered the other men to spill no more blood. The other insurgents were at once taken under arrest and the contest ended. The whole fight had not lasted over three minutes."

A Marine, Luke Quinn, was killed, whether by Brown or by one of his men. Dauphin Thompson was bayoneted to death. Jeremiah Anderson was pinned against the wall, and in his death struggle he turned clear around like a cartwheel, so that he hung with his face down, a hideous sight. He lived for twenty minutes after he was dragged outside. Edwin Coppoc and Shields Green were taken unharmed, the former very calm, the latter very terror-stricken.

Porte Crayon was the pen name for David H. Strothers, an artist and correspondent for *Harper's Weekly*. He saw the engine-house assault, and then: "The dead and dying outlaws were dragged out onto the lawn amidst the howls and execrations of the people. It was a hideous and ghastly spectacle. Some stark and stiff with staring eyes and fallen jaws were the dead of yesterday, while others, struck with death wounds, writhed and wallowed in their blood."

An old farmer amused himself by aiming tobacco juice at Dauphin Thompson's wounds. Amid the horrors, Strothers saw a mountain beau with a girl on each arm who was disgusted with the lack of manners. "Gentlemen, please give room here. Can't you stand back and let the ladies see the corpses."

C. W. Tayleure, a reporter present for a Baltimore paper, was a South Carolinian but, as he wrote years later, to John Brown, Jr., "It is impossible not to feel respect for men who offer up their lives in support of their convictions." He gave Watson Brown a cup of water and made an improvised couch for him out of a bench with a pair of overalls for a pillow. "I remember how he looked, singularly handsome, even through the grime of his all-day struggles and the intense suffering which he must have endured. He was very calm and of a tone and look I can never forget. The look with which he searched my very heart I can never forget. I asked him, 'What brought you here?' He replied patiently, 'Duty, sir.' After a pause I again asked, 'Is it then your idea of duty to shoot men down on their hearth-stones for defending their rights?' He answered, 'I am dying. I cannot discuss the questions. I did my duty as I saw it.'"

Watson died at noon the next day. His body was given to the Winchester Medical School at Winchester, as were the bodies of Kagi and Jeremiah Anderson. Oliver Brown was buried with others on a bank of the Shenandoah two miles from Harper's Ferry. It was said that the Dangerfield Newby body was first deposited in the grave, face up, and then, in a symbolic gesture of contempt, Oliver was put face down and locked in the Negro's embrace.

The wounded commander-in-chief was carried to the paymaster's office which adjoined the engine-house in the armory yard. Stevens was also brought there from the Wager House. There were cries outside, "Lynch him!" and "The scaffold is going up!" Brown and Stevens, said Strothers, showed fear of being lynched.

Stuart spoke roughly to Brown and said: "That is the celebrated John Brown of Kansas notoriety, a man so infamous for his robberies and murders that if the people here knew his antecedents he would not be permitted to live five minutes."

Brown made no reply, turning glassy eyes from one person to another in silence. His face was grimed with blood and someone suggested that he be washed and the wounds on his scalp dressed. Stevens said: "Yes, it is a shame that a man like that should be so maltreated and neglected, with no surgeon near him and no one to pay him the least attention." Stuart shouted: "You son of a bitch! You had better keep silent! Your treatment is that of men who are midnight thieves and murderers, not of men taken in honorable warfare. If you came to make war, why didn't you bring a surgeon with you?"

Alexander R. Boteler entered the room and Brown knew that he was the congressman from Jefferson County. He saw the right side of Brown's head smeared with blood, "causing his grim and grizzly countenance to look like that of some aboriginal savage with his war paint on."

"Captain Brown, are you hurt anywhere except in your head?" "Yes, on my side." "What brought you here?" "To free your slaves." "How did you expect to accomplish it with the small force you brought with you?" "I expected help." "Where, whence and from whom did you expect help?" "Here and from elsewhere." "Did you expect to get assistance from whites here as well as from blacks?" "I did." "Then you have been disappointed in not getting it from either?" "Yes [in a mutter], I-have-been-disappointed."

Brown asked if he could write home, and Boteler said he was sure it could be arranged, adding, "Mr. Brown, we have women and children, too. Now, let me ask you. Is this failure of yours likely to be followed by similar attempts to create disaffection among our servants and bring upon us the horrors of a servile war?" Brown replied softly, "Only time will tell."

Major Russell, of the Marine detachment, whispered to Congressman Boteler that Brown was not as badly wounded as he appeared to be. When the room was temporarily emptied, he had sighted Brown rising to examine the wound on his side, but when he glimpsed Russell peering at him, he quickly slumped to the floor.

At noon, Governor Henry A. Wise arrived with Senator Mason, having taken the train from Richmond to Baltimore. Congressman Clement L. Vallandingham of Ohio also arrived. He had been in Baltimore on his way home when he heard the news and decided to change direction and go to Harper's Ferry. They were Brown's interrogators that afternoon in a long conversation in the paymaster's office.

Brown was asked if he wanted to talk and he said he was quite willing. Colonel Lee and Lieutenant Stuart were present and newspaper correspondents were in the crowd. Brown was quite collected, talking courteously and affably. After his terrible ordeal it was a remarkable exhibition of self-command. As a reporter said, "Among a desperate army of angry men, with the gallows staring him full in the face, he lay on the floor and, in reply to every question, gave answers that betokened the spirit that animated him." Brown was well aware of the fact that he was addressing a nation-wide audience, and he was never more skilled in artfulness and dissimulation.

This was the only questioning of Brown that ever took place. The following are significant excerpts from the transcript as it was run in the New York *Herald*:

Senator Mason. Can you tell us, who furnished money for your expedition?

Capt. Brown. I furnished most of it myself. I cannot implicate others. It is by my own folly that I have been taken. I could easily have saved myself from it if I had exercised my own better judgment, rather than yielded to my feelings. I should have gone away, but I had thirty odd prisoners, whose wives and daughters were in tears for their safety, and I felt for them. Besides, I wanted to allay the fears of those who believed we came here to burn and kill. For this reason I allowed the train to pass the bridge, and gave them full liberty to pass on. I did it only to spare the feelings of those passengers and their families, and to allay the apprehension that you had got here in your vicinity a band of men who had no regard for life and property, nor any feeling of humanity.

Senator M. But you killed some people passing along the streets quietly.

Capt. B. Well, sir, if there was anything of that kind done, it was without my knowledge. Your own citizens, who were my prisoners, will tell you that every possible means were taken to prevent it. I did not allow my men to fire, nor even to return a fire, when there was danger of killing those we regarded as innocent persons, if I could help it. They will tell you that we allowed ourselves to be fired at repeatedly, and did not return it.

A Bystander. That is not so. You killed an unarmed man at the corner of the house, over there (at the water tank) and another besides.

Capt. B. See here, my friend; it is useless to dispute or contradict the report of your own neighbors, who were my prisoners.

Senator M. If you would tell us who sent you here—who provided the means—that would be information of some value.

Capt. B. I will answer freely and faithfully about what concerns myself —I will answer any thing I can with honor, but not about others.

Mr. Vallandingham. Mr. Brown, who sent you here?

Capt. B. No man sent me here; it was my own prompting and that of my Maker, or that of the devil whichever you please to ascribe it to. I acknowledge no master in human form.

Mr. V. Did you get up the expedition yourself?

Capt. B. I did.

Mr. V. Did you get up this document called a constitution?

Capt. B. I did. They are a constitution and ordinances of my own contriving and getting up.

Mr. V. How long have you been engaged in this business?

Capt. B. From the breaking out of the difficulties in Kansas. Four of my sons had gone there to settle, and they induced me to go. I did not go there to settle, but because of the difficulties.

Senator M. How many are engaged in this movement? I ask these questions for your own safety.

Capt. B. Any questions that I can honorably answer, I will; not otherwise. So far as I am myself concerned, I have told every thing truthfully. I value my word, sir.

Senator M. What was your object in coming?

Capt. B. We came to free the slaves, and only that.

A Young Man (in the uniform of a volunteer company). How many men in all had you?

Capt. B. I came to Virginia with eighteen men besides myself.

Volunteer. What in the world did you suppose you could do here in Virginia with that amount of men?

Capt. B. Young man, I don't wish to discuss that question here.

Volunteer. You could not do any thing.

Capt. B. Well, perhaps your ideas and mine, on military subjects, would differ materially.

Senator M. How do you justify your acts?

Capt. B. I think, my friend, you are guilty of a great wrong against God and humanity—I say it without wishing to be offensive—and it would be perfectly right for any one to interfere with you so far as to free those you wilfully and wickedly hold in bondage. I do not say this insultingly.

Senator M. I understand that.

Capt. B. I think I did right, and that others will do right who interfere with you, at any time, and all times. I hold that the golden rule—"Do unto others as you would that others should do unto you"—applied to all who would help others to gain their liberty.

Lieutenant Stuart. But you don't believe in the Bible?

Capt. B. Certainly I do.

Mr. V. Where did your men come from? Did some of them come from Ohio?

Capt. B. Some of them.

Mr. V. From the Western Reserve, of course! None came from Southern Ohio?

Capt. B. O, yes. I believe one came from Steubenville, down not far from Wheeling.

Senator M. Did you consider this a military organization in this paper? (Showing a copy of John Brown's constitution and ordinance.) I have not yet read it.

Capt. B. I did in some measure. I wish you would give that paper your close attention.

Senator M. You considered yourself the commander-in-chief of this provisional military force?

Capt. B. I was chosen, agreeably to the ordinance of a certain document, commander-in-chief of that force.

Senator M. What wages did you offer?

Capt. B. None.

Lieut. S. "The wages of sin is death."

Capt. B. I would not have made such a remark to you, if you had been a prisoner and wounded, in my hands.

Senator M. Does this talking annoy you at all?

Capt. B. Not in the least.

Mr. V. When in Cleveland, did you attend the Fugitive Slave Law Convention there?

Capt. B. No. I was there about the time of the sitting of the court to try the Oberlin rescuers. I spoke there, publicly, on that subject. I spoke on the fugitive slave law, and my own rescue. Of course, so far as I had any influence at all, I was disposed to justify the Oberlin people for rescuing the slave, because I have myself forcibly taken slaves from bondage. I was concerned in taking eleven slaves from Missouri to Canada, last winter. . . .

A Bystander. Did you go out to Kansas under the auspices of the Emigrant Aid Society?

Capt. B. No, Sir; I went out under the auspices of John Brown, and nobody else.

Mr. V. Have you had any correspondence with parties at the North on the subject of this movement?

Capt. B. I have had no correspondence.

Bystander. Do you consider this a religious movement?

Capt. B. It is, in my opinion, the greatest service a man can render to his God.

Bystander. Do you consider yourself an instrument in the hands of Providence?

Capt. B. I do.

Bystander. Upon what principle do you justify your acts?

Capt. B. Upon the golden rule. I pity the poor in bondage that have none to help them. That is why I am here; it is not to gratify any personal animosity, or feeling of revenge, or vindictive spirit. It is my sympathy with the oppressed and the wronged, that are as good as you, and as precious in the sight of God.

Bystander. Certainly. But why take the slaves against their will?

Capt. B. I never did.

Bystander. Why did you do it secretly?

Capt. B. Because I thought that necessary to success, and for no other reason.

Bystander. And you think that honorable, do you? Have you read Gerrit Smith's last letter?

Capt. B. What letter do you mean?

Bystander. The New York *Herald* of yesterday, in speaking of this affair, mentions a letter in which he says, "that it is folly to attempt to strike the shackles off the slave by the force of moral suasion or legal agitation," and predicts that the next movement made in the direction of Negro emancipation will be an insurrection in the South.

Capt. B. I have not seen a New York *Herald* for some days past; but I presume, from your remarks about the gist of the letter, that I should concur with it. I agree with Mr. Smith, that moral suasion is hopeless. I don't think the people of the Slave States will ever consider the subject of slavery in its true light until some other argument is resorted to than moral suasion.

Mr. V. Did you expect a general rising of the slaves in case of your success?

Capt. B. No, sir; nor did I wish it. I expected to gather strength from time to time; then I could set them free.

Mr. V. Did you expect to hold possession here till then?

Capt. B. Well, probably I had quite a different idea. I do not know that I ought to reveal my plans. I am here a prisoner, and wounded, because I foolishly allowed myself to be so. You overrate your strength when you suppose I could have been taken if I had not allowed it. I was too tardy, after commencing the open attack, in delaying my movements through Monday night, and up to the time I was attacked by the government troops. It was all occasioned by my desire to spare the feelings of my prisoners and their families, and the community at large.

Mr. V. Did you not shoot a negro on the bridge, or did not some of your party?

Capt. B. I knew nothing of the shooting of the negro (Hayward).

Gov. Wise. Where did you get arms to obtain possession of the armory?

Capt. B. I bought them.

Gov. W. In what state?

Capt. B. That I would not state.

Gov. W. How many guns?

Capt. B. Two hundred Sharpe's rifles, and two hundred revolvers—
what is called the Massachusetts Arms Company's revolvers—a little
under the navy size.

A Reporter. I do not wish to annoy you; but if you have any thing
else you would like to say, I will report it.

Capt. B. I do not wish to converse any more; I have nothing to say. I
will only remark to these reporting gentlemen, that I claim to be here in
carrying out a measure I believe to be perfectly justifiable, and not to act
the part of an incendiary or ruffian; but, on the contrary, to aid those
suffering under a great wrong. I wish to say, furthermore, that you had
better—all you people of the South—prepare yourselves for a settlement
of this question. It must come up for settlement sooner than you are
prepared for it, and the sooner you commence that preparation the better
for you. You may dispose of me very easily. I am nearly disposed of now;
but this question is still to be settled—this negro question, I mean. The
end of that is not yet. These wounds were inflicted upon me—both the
sabre cut on my head, and the bayonet stabs in the different parts of my
body—some minutes after I had ceased fighting, and had consented to
surrender for the benefit of others, and not for my own benefit.

(Several persons vehemently denied this statement. Without noticing
the interruption, the old man continued.)

I believe the Major here (pointing to Lieut. Stuart) would not have
been alive but for me. I might have killed him just as easy as I could kill
a mosquito, when he came in; but I supposed that he came in only to
receive our surrender. There had been long and loud calls of surrender
from us—as loud as men could yell—but in the confusion and excitement I suppose we were not heard. I do not believe the major, or any
one else, wanted to butcher us after we had surrendered.

An Officer. Why did you not surrender before the attack?

Capt. B. I did not think it was my duty or interest to do so. We
assured our prisoners that we did not wish to harm them, and that they
should be set at liberty. I exercised my best judgment, not believing the
people would wantonly sacrifice their own fellow-citizens. When we
offered to let them go upon condition of being allowed to change our
position about a quarter of a mile, the prisoners agreed by vote among
themselves to pass across the bridge with us. We wanted them only as a
sort of guarantee for our own safety—that we should not be fired into.
We took them, in the first place, as hostages, and to keep them from
doing any harm. We did kill some men when defending ourselves; but I
saw no one fire except directly in self-defence. Our orders were strict
not to harm any one not in arms against us.

Gov. W. Well, Brown, suppose you had every nigger in the United States, what would you do with them?

Capt. B. (In a loud tone, and with emphasis.) Set them free, sir!

Gov. W. Your intention was to carry them off and free them?

Capt. B. Not at all.

Bystander. To set them free would sacrifice the life of every man in this community.

Capt. B. I do not think so.

Bystander. I know it. I think you are fanatical.

Capt. B. And I think you are fanatical. "Whom the gods would destroy, they first make mad"; and you are mad.

Gov. W. Was your only object to free the Negroes?

Capt. B. Absolutely our only object.

Bystander. But you went and took Col. Washington's silver and watch.

Capt. B. O, yes; we intended freely to have appropriated the property of slaveholders, to carry out our object. It was for that, and only that; and with no design to enrich ourselves with any plunder whatever.

Gov. W. Did you know Sherrod in Kansas? I understand you killed him.

Capt. B. I killed no man except in fair fight. I fought at Black Jack, and at Osawatomie; and if I killed any body, it was at one of those places.

Vallandingham was clearly trying to make political capital by tarring Congressman Joshua Giddings and other Ohio Abolitionists with the crime. This motivation may have affected the estimate, which was a "build-up," he gave of Brown after the interrogation: "It is in vain to underrate either the man or the conspiracy. Captain John Brown is as brave and resolute a man as ever headed an insurrection, and in a good cause and with a sufficient force would have been a consummate partisan commander. He has coolness, daring, persistency, the stoic faith and patience and a firmness of will and purpose unconquerable. He is the farthest possible removed from the ordinary ruffian, fanatic or madman. Certainly, it was one of the best planned and best executed conspiracies that ever failed."

Colonel Robert E. Lee was not similarly impressed. He concluded his report to the President: "The result proves that the plan was the attempt of a fanatic or madman."

Several years before, in 1850, when Brown founded the League of Gileadites in Springfield, he gave this advice to the Negroes: "After effecting a rescue, if you are assailed, go into the houses of your most prominent and influential white friends with your wives; and that will effectually fasten upon them the suspicion of being connected with you, and will compel them to make a common cause with you, whether they would otherwise live up to their professions or not. This would leave them no choice in the matter."

Brown's refusal, with a show of nobility, to implicate anybody else in the conspiracy was a device on his part to win sympathy. There can be little doubt that he had planned to involve all his backers. The Kennedy farm was already being ransacked while he was being questioned, and letters were found in a carpetbag. One from Gerrit Smith, signed "G.S.," enclosed $100. There were letters from Frederick Douglass and Hugh Forbes. Others of the Secret Six were referred to only by initials, but it was an easy matter from that point to identify them. Forbes, happy for the publicity, identified "G.S." and published his correspondence with Sanborn and Dr. Howe.

There is no evidence that the conspiracy had wider ramifications than those already described. Brown expected whites in that area who had an antipathy to slavery to join him, and in fact there was sufficient sentiment of this kind so that Harper's Ferry became part of the breakaway pro-Union state of West Virginia during the Civil War. Beyond that, we know of no reasonable expectation of aid on his part from any other source.

Several weeks later, the South was inflamed by the publication of a letter which purported to be a report written from Memphis, Tennessee, by an agent of Brown's in the South, reciting all the aid that was being mustered in his support, from slaveholders who were secretly sympathetic to emancipation. Thus: "Several of them told me they had gone so far as to procure arms for their slaves and instruct them in their proper use or how to act when the worst comes to the worst." A further excerpt read, that another man "said he could guarantee 1,000 armed slaves who would be ready to spring together at a moment's call and that as soon as operations were commenced with them that other slaves would flock to them by the thousands. I told him he hadn't ought to give too lose (sic) reins to his passions, to curb it until the proper time." The writer was amazed to find "so large a number of whites to aid us," and said, "The Southern people are easily gulled."

Sanborn and historian Albert Bushnell Hart examined this document and concluded in 1905 that it was a fake. It was signed by Lawrence Thatcher and sent to William Horner, who, as far as Sanborn knew, was a name not connected with Brown. It was mailed to Governor Wise by a man who signed himself "Traveller," who said that it had fallen out of a man's pocket on a train and he picked it up. Sanborn wrote to Professor Hart: "If 'Traveller' had been a proslavery man or a Northern Democrat, he would not have omitted his name but on the contrary he would have been eager to make himself known."

The mass of materiel that Brown had gathered up astounded the search-party at the Kennedy farm. He was obviously prepared for a long campaign. Beside the pikes, rifles, and revolvers with ammunition, he had a small cannon mounted on a swivel which could pour a quart of shot in any direction, ten kegs of gunpowder, sabers and bayonets, four large tents, blankets and extra clothing, surgical supplies, a couple of dozen picks and shovels, field-glasses, torches, and shrill boatswains' whistles which could be heard for a long distance.

The rifles and pistols were distributed to forty or fifty people around the neighborhood and the clothing was carried off. Lieutenant Green directed a Marine to throw the pikes out the window, and Green shouted to the spectators that they could have as many as they wanted. Few were interested, which was a great mistake money-wise, since their price soared later as souvenirs, so much so that fake pikes were being made and sold. A couple of hundred remained in the attic. When the Civil War broke out they were transported to the South, and in the last days a Texas cavalry unit which had no other weapons used the John Brown pikes as bayonets.

Around Monday midnight, Owen Brown, Cook, Tidd, Barclay Coppoc, Meriam, Hazlett, and Osborn Anderson had left the Kennedy farm and were now in full flight north to Pennsylvania.

The first reaction from the ardent friends of freedom in the North was one of embarrassment. They wanted to sweep John Brown under the rug as quickly as possible and forget about him. Horace Greeley said in the New York *Tribune* that the raid seemed "the work of a madman." The Cleveland *Leader*, located in an Abolitionist stronghold, said that "but for the loss of life attending the foray of the crazy Brown [it] would be positively ridiculous." Garrison in his *Liberator* dismissed it as "misguided, wild and apparently insane, though a disinterested and well-intentioned effort by insurrection." He added that if readers were interested they could find some "particulars" on the third page.

The raid would become progressively more plausible and more damaging to the prestige of the South. As soon as the first shock wave had passed, northern radicals at once discovered that it had great propaganda value. For years the South had been shouting to the Abolitionists, "If you feel so strongly about slavery, why do you stay in your safe roost up North and prattle? Why don't you come down here and do something about it? We have a rope ready for you." Well, nineteen men had accepted the challenge, and what had happened? The South had blenched with terror. Brown held a town of several thousand from a Sunday to Tuesday, it had called for aid from the surrounding countryside, thousands had poured in from Virginia and Maryland, from as far away as Baltimore. Still, they could not cope with this tiny force and so they had to call on United States troops to put it down.

There was ridicule poked at the South, as this ditty attests:

> There's a flutter in the Southland, a tremor in
>   the air,
> For the rice plains are invaded, the cotton fields
>   laid bare,
> And the cry of "Help" and "Treason" rings loud from
>   tongue and pen,
> John Brown has crossed the border with a host of
>   fifteen men.

Everywhere there were questions raised as to why Harper's Ferry had been unable to deal with dispatch with this "paltry" force. This is a letter written on November 17 by George A. Hall of St. Joseph, Missouri, to his sister, Mrs. Lydia Marmion of Harper's Ferry:

I am pleased to learn that the Harper's Ferry people did not act quite so disgracefully as was at first represented, though it does look badly that a town of near four thousand inhabitants, which would be at least seven hundred men, should have been held in subjugation for two days by twenty-two men headed by a man who, we have the best evidence to believe, is a coward. His only acts in Kansas Territory that had come to our knowledge were the assassination of unarmed families and the great skill in running off Negroes. Though his men were aged in fight, Brown was never seen except in running away.

In the United States Senate in early December, Senator Mason complained that so little sympathy had been extended to Virginia in the North. Senator Zachariah Chandler, of Michigan, responded with this taunt: "We do not understand a case like this. If seventeen generals from Virginia or North Carolina were to attack Springfield, I will guarantee, that, supposing there was not a man within five hundred miles, the women would bind them fast within thirty minutes, and would not demand any sympathy. . . . The papers tell us that Governor Wise compared the population of Harper's Ferry to sheep. That is slanderous. It is not true for I have never yet seen a flock of fifty or a hundred sheep in which there was not one warlike bell-wether."

The picture presented in the North was somewhat distorted. The truth was that Harper's Ferry was not a typical southern town. It was industrial, and filled with "foreigners" from the North—half the residents joined the Union cause in the Civil War. There were no guns held by the citizens and when some were found late Monday morning, just how many is undetermined, Brown held a fortified position and had forty or fifty hostages in his hands.

As for the militia from the environs—they responded immediately to the alarm and in great numbers. If they overreacted in numbers, that was pardonable in view of the terror generated by the unknown which magnified the size of the invading force. They charged and with alacrity they bottled up Brown from all directions, so that the invaders did not hold Harper's Ferry "in subjugation" beyond one o'clock on Monday afternoon. The militia postponed the *coup de grâce* because of indecision and the problem of the hostages. They willingly handed over the taking of the engine-house to United States troops since it seemed certain that there would be many casualties in storming a fort held by men with guns. Besides the Marines were trained for storming with bayonets, and the militia were not. Therefore, it was prudence, not cowardice. Virginians were not cowards, as the history of the Confederacy abundantly proved.

It was, however, an unfortunate set of circumstances for the South. Her vaunted valor did not shine and her insecurity complex about the institution of slavery was clearly visible.

The magnification of the Harper's Ferry raid as an event of American history and the magnification of John Brown as its martyr were largely due to the unwitting assistance of the remarkably mercurial Governor Henry A. Wise. The attitude of Lee was the sensible one from the standpoint of Virginia—to dismiss it as of little importance and to dismiss Brown as a crackpot, albeit a dangerous one. Wise chose to take a different tack. He made a huge bonfire of the event, inflamed and excited public opinion in Virginia and altogether inflated it to an importance that the North had not recognized on first glance. Moreover he exalted Brown as the agent of responsible

northern elements, not as a daft Don Quixote, which had been the
first impression. More than that, Wise did a great disservice to the
South by acting from then on as if the state of Virginia were under
siege from the North, advertising far and wide its insecurity complex. Altogether, Wise's conduct became as much an embarrassment
to intelligent southerners as Brown's action was initially to moderate
northerners.

What was his motivation? It has been suggested that he wanted to
dramatize the affair as an emergency and display his resourcefulness
in meeting it to enable him to grab the Democratic nomination for
President in 1860. It is more likely that he was genuinely excited
without much ulterior motive, particularly because the national spot-
light was on him.

Wise, then fifty-three years old, has been described as the last great
individualist in Virginia politics. Tall, lean, with piercing eyes, he was
a great chewer and swearer and talker—he could make a three-and-
a-half-hour speech and hold his audience spellbound with his wit and
eloquence. Histrionics, exaggeration, and bombast had been so much
practiced by him that it had become part of his political style. It was
said of him that he "rioted in the eccentricity of his genius." He was
known to be highly inflammable, "with a bump of combativeness."
In 1856 he had announced that if Frémont were elected President, he
would arm and equip fifty thousand men the next morning, ready for
revolution.

Lieutenant Stuart wrote his mother concerning Wise's conduct,
after he arrived in Harper's Ferry, that he certainly is a "queer genius." For some reason, Wise countermanded Lee's order and the
saloons were reopened. He made two long, wild harangues on Tuesday night, one before the Wager House and the other in the armory
grounds, denouncing the raid as instigated by northern Abolitionists
(in which he was in part right), and read as proof a letter of Gerrit
Smith's to Brown enclosing money.

Instead of minimizing the failure of Virginia's men to put Brown
in chains, he proclaimed it to the world. He told the residents of
Harper's Ferry to their face that they were "a flock of sheep." "I was
ready to weep when I heard the town was taken in ten minutes by
twelve men." He was obviously shaken with wounded pride when
he said in a speech in Richmond:

On Monday night the gallant and noble Virginian, Colonel Robert E.
Lee, worthy of any service on earth, arrived with his regular corps of

marines. He waited only for light. Then he tendered the assault in state pride to the Virginia volunteers who were there. Their feelings for the prisoners made them decline the risk of slaying their own friends and Lee could not delay a moment. His gallantry was mortified that the task was so easy. And now I say to you that I would have given my right arm to its shoulder for that feat to have been performed by the volunteers of Virginia on Monday before the marines arrived there.

This was indiscreet enough, but Wise went on to deliver a eulogy of Brown: "They are themselves mistaken who take him to be a madman. He is a bundle of the best nerves I ever saw, cut and thrust and bleeding and in bonds. He is a man of clear head, of courage, fortitude and simple ingenuousness. He is cool, collected and indomitable and it is but just to say of him that he was humane to his prisoners as attested to me by Colonel Washington and Mr. Mills and he inspired me with great trust in his integrity as a man of truth. He is a fanatic, vain and garrulous, but firm, truthful and intelligent."

Edmund Ruffin, a prominent editor-politician of Virginia, who kept a diary, confided to it that he was amazed by Wise's foolishness. As for himself: "It is impossible for me not to respect his thorough devotion to his bad course & the undaunted courage with which he sustained it through all lives & Hazards." But for Wise to make these remarks publicly was almost beyond belief. If a monument were erected to Brown in the North, it could carry these phrases in tribute to Brown. Moreover, Wise spoke nonsense. "He was 'humane to his prisoners' because his one chance for escape depended on it. When in Kansas he cut their throats before the eyes of their wives and mothers."

Brown was informed that he would be quickly put on trial in the Virginia courts. In 1850, Brown had said in his exhortation to the League of Gileadites: "The trial for life of one bold and to some extent successful man, for defending his rights in good earnest, would arouse more sympathy throughout the nation than the accumulated wrongs and sufferings of more than three millions of our submissive colored population."

A man with a great genius for self-justification would be given the forum to glow before the world. His words could be truly more effective than bullets. As James Redpath well put it, "He could afford the loss of his Sharp's rifles while he retained the faculty of speech—a rifle of far straighter sight and longer range."

Governor Wise ordered the Virginia militia to conduct Brown,

Stevens, Coppoc, and Shields Green to Charlestown for imprisonment
before trial. Wise was informed that there was considerable danger
that the militia might lynch them, and so he had to entrust this responsibility to the United States Marines under Lieutenant Green.
The Marines on Wednesday morning conveyed them by wagon to
the train and put them aboard. A large crowd shouted, "Lynch them!
Lynch them!" The governor answered in a loud voice, "That would
be cowardly now," and the train pulled out without molestation.

During the remaining six weeks of his life, Brown was not loath
to discuss the raid, except for the death of his sons, which he would
not discuss, but he never illuminated the reasons for the fiasco. He
had never been much given to retrospection and it was out of keeping
with his positive habits of thinking to retrace past failures. He took
full responsibility for the invasion of Harper's Ferry and expressed
no regret on that score. He accepted some killings of civilians as
inevitable.

His few regrets concerned the time factor. He told his counsel,
George H. Hoyt, that it was a mistake to have wasted time "chaffering" with the prisoners when he could have escaped to the hills
where he could not have been found. By "chaffering" he undoubtedly
included the time spent in ordering breakfasts for them and reassuring them as to their safety. If the reports were correct, no less
than three times he told visitors that it was a great mistake on his
part to have stopped the early morning train. He must have felt that
it was this train which gave the alarm to the outside world—in this
he erred, since Dr. Starry had sent the news to Charlestown and
Shepherdstown before then.

We may surmise that the paralysis of will, which descended on
him in the morning hours was lifted in the early afternoon, and that,
given an extra hour or two, having made a dramatic demonstration
in slave-land, Brown might have marched out of the steel trap before
it was sprung when he lost the bridges over the Potomac and
Shenandoah rivers.

CHAPTER NINE

Judgment in Virginia

SEVERAL WEEKS after the raid, on November 24, 1859, the New York *Independent* published this editorial:

For ourselves, we cannot resist the conviction that God has in view the overthrow of slavery in all the steps of this sad but most impressive event. No servile insurrection in the South, not even a combination among the slaves reaching throughout the states and a simultaneous uprising from the Potomac to the Gulf of Mexico and the Rio Grande could awaken such a sensation throughout the country as did the raid of John Brown into Virginia.

Men having no personal interest to serve were ready to make war upon slavery at the hazard of their own lives. This fact has commanded the attention of thousands who would have given but passing thought to negro insurrection, and has led them to inquire—what is the system that has provoked such an assault and what is the cause for which these brave and honest men are willing to die?

And now, as if on purpose that the lesson might not be lost, the Virginians have done everything to concentrate public attention upon the scene. The exaggerated dangers into which their own fears betrayed them, the movements of the Governor and their militia, the telegraphic rumors and alarms, the suspicion and vigilance manifested towards

strangers, all keep up the excitement until every newspaper in the land is
filled with it, and every reader made familiar with its details. The
indecent haste of the court to obtain a verdict of Guilty, the rude treatment of counsel from abroad, the disregard for the forms and proprieties
of law—all the infuriate zeal of the Slave-Power in contrast to the manly
demeanor and conscientious integrity of the prisoner, has excited universal discussion as to the principles of the case.

And what is this on trial before the great public of the United States?
What is it that is undergoing the scrutiny of thousands of eager eyes?
What is it that will be hung up on the gallows in the face of all men?

Not John Brown but Slavery. John Brown has already received the
verdict of the people as a brave and honest man. Gov. Wise himself has
told the world that he never saw such courage, truthfulness or sincerity
as he saw in that wounded man at Harper's Ferry. The letters of Brown,
his speeches to the court have convinced all that Gov. Wise read him
truly. Misguided as he was by his zeal for the oppressed, wild and unwar-
rantable as was his whole scheme for their emancipation, he yet stands
forth in his motive and his spirit and his intentions as the bravest, the
truest, the noblest man Virginia has seen since its race of Revolutionary
heroes passed away. It is impossible to hang such a man as to attach to
his name any of the obloquy of the gallows. For him it has no terrors
and it can inflict no reproach upon his memory.

Not John Brown but Slavery will be gibbeted when he hangs upon
the gallows. Slavery itself will receive the scorn and execration it has
invoked for him.

When John Brown is executed, it will be seen that he has done his
work more effectively than if he had succeeded in running off a few
hundred slaves. The terror by night that rules in every household on her
soil, drawing sleep from mothers and children, the anxieties and fears
that for months to come will burden her population, the spirit of revenge
—all these will make the cost of slavery to Virginia greater than she can
bear.

This remarkably perceptive statement, published a week and a day
before the execution, states well the grounds for the reasoned sympathy for John Brown that welled up in the North in the aftermath
of the raid. It was a delayed response which took shape after reflection on John Brown's motives and the conduct of the State of Virginia which tried and hung him.

The New York *Independent* was a radical Republican but not an
Abolitionist newspaper. Its initial reaction was that Brown was a
"lawless brigand" and was "mad." All journals except those that
found the raid infernally wicked, characterized it as mad. Some

southern papers ran out of adjectives. The New Orleans *Daily Picayune* termed it "crazy, ill-judged, incautious, (an act) of miserable fanatics hallucinated by some wild, incoherent ideas, impracticable as they were foolish and infamous."

In North and South there was to be a complete transformation in thinking. In a few days reference to Brown's craziness had disappeared as the raid was being seriously and soberly pondered. If Brown were crazy, then twenty or so men who were under his command were also crazy, almost an epidemic of the malady. Further doubts developed that this was, as the New York *Times* said on the first news, "the work of a single man, smarting under a sense of personal wrong and insanely seeking to avenge them upon the whole country."

On November 28, the Baltimore *Sun* said: "When the first intelligence of the Harper's Ferry outrage came upon the public, it was almost overwhelmingly regarded as the act of a mere crazy, old fool. People never dreamed that it was the fruit and matured result— rotten at maturity, it is true—of a long and deliberately prepared plan. As fact after fact came out, however, there seemed to be more in it than at first appeared. Day after day and week after week we have the cumulative evidence that John Brown is in fact the representative of a very large class of the people of the North."

The realization dawned, a rude shock to the South, that Brown was the spearhead of a well-backed northern conspiracy. Congressman Vallandingham's hunch after the first interrogation of Brown was correct. The first questionings grew out of the mammoth amount of money which had supported Brown. It had cost much to support this force through months of preparation. And then there was the arsenal of weapons. The two hundred Sharp's rifles alone had cost $5,000. Where did all this money come from? Then the letters in Brown's carpetbag at the Kennedy farm showed that he was connected with important persons. Gerrit Smith, the wealthy backer of abolitionism, had sent him $100. Frederick Douglass had sent him someone's gift of $10. There was a note found from Congressman Joshua R. Giddings to Brown that he would be away and not able to receive him at his home, but Brown was obviously on friendly terms with him.

Hugh Forbes confirmed the existence of the conspiracy. It was the "New England humanitarians" who had financed it, he said, and he published his letters of 1857 and 1858 to Sanborn and Dr. Howe.

He said that on his visit to the leading Republican, Senator Seward, in Washington he had indicated the scope of the conspiracy and that Seward cautioned him, "A man in my position ought not to know of such things."

The conspiracy was not only far-flung but had deep roots in time. Forbes had gone out to Iowa in July, 1857, to meet with Brown; Horace Greeley, he said, had escorted him to the railroad depot in New York and at parting had thrust $20 in his hand, asking that he keep him posted. Forbes's letter of May, 1858, to Dr. Howe described in some detail the argument he had with Brown out in Iowa about tactics to be used in stirring up the slave insurrection in the South, in which he persuaded Brown to abandon his plan for a direct invasion of the South, including a "dash at the Harper's Ferry manufactory," in favor of a plan for local slave stampedes on the Virginia and Maryland borders. Now Forbes said in the New York *Herald*: "These men ('New England humanitarians') who have plundered, betrayed and calumniated me ought to have felt the profoundest gratitude. They know they have wronged me and they hate me from that knowledge. Let them enjoy these feelings if they can."

The revelation that the outrage was the fruit of a diabolical Abolitionist conspiracy shook the South with anger. On November 1, the Charleston, South Carolina, *Mercury*, a leading organ, called for separation: "The great source of the evil is that we are under one government with these people, that by the Constitution they deem themselves responsible for the institution of slavery and therefore they seek to overthrow it. They do not plot insurrection for Brazil or Cuba. If we had a separate government of our own, the post office, all the avenues of intercourse, the police and military of the country, would be under our exclusive control. Abolitionism would die out in the North or its adherents would have to operate in the South as foreign emissaries."

The more moderate press, representing the bulk of opinion of the South, called on the North for a firm repudiation. The Richmond *Enquirer* said: "Let the people of the North weigh well their actions at the present moment—a crisis has arrived and the fate of the Union hangs as it were by a single thread which, if it can be preserved and strengthened, will require the united effort of all its friends, North and South." The Richmond *Whig* said: "We call on the Northern people to assemble in every town, village, country and neighborhood and unite before the country and the world in denunciation."

The press reaction in the North, particularly the lack of intersectional sympathy, became progressively more exasperating to the South. The attitude of the New York *Times* is illustrative. It was a middle-of-the-road, moderate Republican newspaper and initially it reassured the South, but it then turned critical and even caustic. At first, it was full of sentiments such as "The great mass of our people look on this with horror and execration," but in a few days it was wondering whether the raid was to be used "as the great engine for the sweeping away of all Southern toleration for moderate sentiments on the slavery question." Horace Greeley in the New York *Tribune*, after first branding Brown mad, then refused to condemn men who did not believe the axioms of the Declaration of Independence were "glittering generalities;" while he applauded the principle, he disapproved of the practicability of the raid. "They dared and died for what they felt the right though in a manner which seems to us fatally wrong." In a few days, Greeley had dropped all his reserve and was using the South as a punching bag.

The position of the New York *Herald*, though loud in sympathy, was even less comforting to the South. On the first news it reprinted Senator Seward's "irrepressible conflict" speech of the year before, said that John Brown was the fanatical tool of that philosophy, and "Seward is the arch-agitator who is responsible for the insurrection." The *Herald* was the leading Democratic organ, and it was determined to use the raid as propaganda against black Republicanism in the imminent November elections. When the conspiracy came to light, the *Herald*, far from reassuring the South, magnified the affair. In flaming editorials the *Herald* said that this was a conspiracy that included Seward, Senator Wilson, Greeley, Giddings, and Governor Chase, among other Republicans, and that Virginia should shift the prosecution of Brown to a federal court so that all the conspirators could be exposed. It was far graver than anyone realized thus far. Southern papers ran these alarmist editorials of the *Herald* as a northern confession of northern perfidy.

Many papers took the attitude that the raid was the inevitable occupational hazard of slaveholding, that if you choose to keep a powder magazine at your door, you have no one to blame but yourself since everyone knows that incendiaries are at large. The Albany *Evening Journal* said: "If a man builds his house on a volcano, it is not those who warn him of the danger who are to blame for its eruptions." The New York *Evening Post* said: "What a condition of society is that in which one-half the population constantly menaces the other half with civil war and murder—in which the leading classes go to sleep every night, carelessly, it may be, below the crater of a volcano, and in which the dangers do not lessen as in other societies with time, but grow with its growth, until an explosion becomes as inevitable as the eruptions of Etna or Vesuvius."

When the deeper significance of the John Brown raid made its imprint, it became difficult for a northern journal to condemn the raid on moral as distinct from policy grounds. The New York *Independent*, as we have seen, put it: "Men having no personal interest to serve were ready to make war upon Slavery at the hazard of their own lives." This was the essence, a clarion-call heard around the world—slavery was so odious that northern whites, most of them youths with their lives yet to live, were ready to give up their lives to strike a blow against slavery. Beside this truth which glowed incandescently bright, what case could be made for the South that would not look mean and insignificant?

The Abolitionist press now proclaimed its new Savior. Garrison in the *Liberator* said: "The picture of the Good Samaritan will live to all future ages, eulogized by Jesus as the model of human excellence for helping one whom he chanced to find in need. John Brown did more than that and emulated the beneficial Savior himself, for he went to seek those who were lost that he might save them."

The South had rejoiced that the slaves had been faithful to them and had turned their backs on Brown. Governor Wise said in a speech: "And this is the only consolation I have to offer you in this disgrace, that the faithful slaves refused to take up arms against their masters, and those who were taken by force from their happy homes, deserted their liberators as soon as they dared to make the attempt. Not a slave around was found faithless." (It was not published or known at the time that the Allstadt slave, Phil, who made the portholes for Brown in the engine-house, was suspected of sympathy, and was imprisoned in the Charlestown jail, where he died of fright or pneumonia.)

The northern press gagged at this picture of negro-contentment drawn by Wise. The New York *Times* said that it had learned that the slaves had not grasped that Brown had meant to free them but thought he had come to carry them off and "sell them in the South," their greatest fear, and "they held back not because they loved Virginia more but Louisiana less."

The New York *Independent* had found the hand of God in the unfolding events, designed to accomplish the overthrow of slavery. Rationalists must eschew a teleological view of history, that events are ordained by a predestined end. Yet, in this affair everything somehow seemed to conspire in one direction, to elevate John Brown to martyrdom and accentuate the sectionalism that would precipitate the great civil conflict.

Had Lieutenant Green's sword been a little sharper, that would have been the finale to Brown. Instead, Green inflicted wounds on him that did not entirely incapacitate him but were sufficient to arouse sympathy for him during his trial.

The next event, most unfortunate for the South, was that Governor Wise was unaccountably held up in Washington and then at the Relay House outside Baltimore so that he arrived at Harper's Ferry on October 17 after the engine-house had been stormed. Had he arrived earlier, he said explicitly in a letter of November 4 to Mayor Fernando Wood of New York City, he would have declared martial law on the spot and would have tried Brown and his accomplices immediately by court-martial. Had that happened, Brown would have been shot and quickly forgotten in the North. It was a mental lapse on Wise's part not to have declared martial law by telegraph from Richmond the day before. Brown did come to make war as commander-in-chief of a provisional government. The Baltimore *Sun* stated that such being the case, if he had been tried by court-martial, "No good ground for reproach would have existed."

Virginia newspapers demanded that summary treatment should be given the prisoners. The Richmond *Whig* said they were not entitled to the courtesies of war. "Immediate shooting or hanging without trial is the punishment they merit. In regard to these offenders, the just and safe principle is hang them first and try them afterward." The Fredericksburg *Herald* said: "Hang these villainous wretches, offenders against the public peace, without the benefit of clergy, and if there can be such a thing as sympathy for such wretches, let it be expended over their stiffened corpses. The wheel and the rack are not a whit too hard for them. Shooting is a mercy they should be denied. Hemp, do your duty!"

Governor Wise decided that, having arrived on the scene too late to declare martial law, he must protect Brown and his fellow-criminals from lynching and give them the protection of Virginia's laws. The legal machinery was then put in motion, but with such speed and disregard for the defendant's rights that it was to arouse widespread indignation through the North as a "judicial outrage."

Under a peculiar procedure in Virginia, a preliminary court trial had to be held and this examining court had to be convened within not less than five nor more than ten days from the date of the issuance of the warrant. The warrant was issued on October 20, and the examining court convened on the earliest date, October 25. As it happened, the semiannual term of the Circuit Court was now in session in Charlestown. Under Virginia law, an indictment for a felony had to be tried in the same term, unless good cause should be shown for a continuance. This was the excuse that Virginia gave for the celerity of Brown's trial, that the next session of the Circuit Court would not occur before the next May and presiding Judge Richard Parker was due at Winchester on November 14. As if John Brown was an ordinary criminal and the schedule and procedures were inflexible!

The rapidity was actually due to the request by Governor Wise that conviction be speedy with no nonsense about it, and special prosecutor Andrew Hunter wrote to Governor Wise: "The judge is for observing all the judicial decencies. So am I, but in double-quick time."

On the morning of October 25, Brown, Stevens, Coppoc, and Copeland were walked from the jail, which was a converted private dwelling, across the street to the courthouse and into a room filled with five hundred spectators. On the bench there were eight justices of the peace and examining magistrates. The New York *Herald* said of Brown that, although there were visible bruises on his body, "His confinement has not at all tamed the daring of his spirit." Stevens was hardly able to drag himself as far as the courthouse. Hunter reported to Governor Wise: "He will probably die of his wounds if we don't hang him promptly."

Several witnesses were heard and the examining tribunal decided to hold the defendants for trial. The prisoners were asked if they had counsel and they said they had none. The presiding judge said he would assign counsel. Brown rose and shouted, "Virginians! Virginians! I did not ask for quarter at the time I was taken. I did not ask that my life be spared. The governor of the Virginia tendered me his assurance that I should have a fair trial. But under no circumstances whatever will I be able to have a fair trial. If you seek my blood, you can have it any moment without the mockery of a trial. I have had no counsel. I have not been able to advise with anyone. My memory don't serve me, my health is insufficient though improving. I am ready for my fate. I do not ask a trial. I beg for no mockery of a trial, no insult, nothing but that which conscience gives or cowardice would drive you to practice. I have now little further to ask, other than that I may not be foolishly insulted as cowardly barbarians insult those who fall into their power."

Judge Parker assigned as counsel two members of the Virginia Bar, Charles J. Faulkner and Lawson Botts, and they represented Brown and Stevens during the preliminary examination without having conferred with their clients. Faulkner resented some remarks from Brown about this arrangement and he insisted on withdrawing, and so Thomas C. Green, the mayor of Charlestown, was appointed by Judge Parker to serve with Botts when the preliminary Court recommended at 2 P.M. that Brown and Stevens be held for trial.

Without any break whatever, the case against Brown and Stevens was presented to the grand jury that very afternoon while the prisoners were returned to the jail. The grand jury was in closed session until the next day. At noon, Wednesday, October 26, the grand jury said it was ready to report. Stevens was carried into the court on a mattress to hear the indictment, and Brown was carried in on a cot since he claimed he was too weak to rise. The New York *Tribune* said: "He is evidently not much injured but is determined to resist the pushing of the trial, by all means in his power."

Brown asked permission to speak, and it was granted. He stated: "I barely wish to say, as I have been promised a fair trial, that I am not in circumstances that enable me to attend a trial owing to my state of health. I have a severe wound in my back, or rather in one kidney, which enfeebles me very much. But I am doing well, and I only ask for a very short delay of my trial; I merely ask this so that, as the saying goes, 'the devil may have his due,' no more. I wish to say further that my hearing is impaired and rendered indistinct in consequence of wounds I have about my head. A very short delay would be all that I ask. I do not presume to ask more than a very short delay so that I may in some degree recover, be able at least to listen to my trial. If that should be allowed me, I should be very much obliged."

Prosecutor Hunter professed that he was astonished. "What does he mean by asking a delay for the purpose of having a fair trial? In a proper sense and its true sense in which it can be regarded by the court, it is a fair trial if it is in accord with the laws and safeguards guaranteed in the Commonwealth of Virginia. If the prisoner's idea of a fair trial is to have it shaped to produce a fairness in his conception outside of what our laws recognize, it becomes our duty to resist any attempt of this kind."

Judge Parker ruled that the prisoners must first hear the indictment and then there could be argument for delay. Brown and Stevens had to rise. The latter was so weak that he had to be held up by bailiffs and his breathing was so labored and stertorous that some feared he was dying on the spot.

The indictment was a long one. It was in four counts. The first was for treason, the second combined two separate charges, for conspiracy to induce slaves to rebel and for advising slaves to rebel, and the third and fourth counts were for murder. The New York *Tribune* said: "We doubt if the whole history of criminal jurisprudence can afford a single instance in which a prisoner has been put on trial at one and the same time upon such a multifarious collection of charges. Such a group of charges requires a very laborious preparation to meet them."

After the indictment was read, Judge Parker ordered the trial to be begun immediately. Brown was given no time at all to confer with the counsel who had been arbitrarily assigned to him by the Court. Brown would be tried first, Stevens later, that is, if Stevens was still alive.

Everything *appeared* correct, and the state of Virginia could boast that it was giving this foreign wretch a trial on an equality with one of its own citizens. The procedures established under the English common law were scrupulously observed; all of its safeguards were thrown around the defendant: Brown had two qualified counsel; the dignified Judge Parker with fitting gravity considered and ruled on all requests and objections made by defense counsel. But behind the façade this was a travesty of fair trial which was due to recoil on the South.

The arguments for delay were made after Hunter announced, "The Commonwealth elects to try John Brown first." Brown's counsel, Botts and Green, represented him fairly competently under the circumstances, as his northern counsel conceded when they took over the case; these Virginians could well afford to do so, since it was as certain that Brown would be condemned as that night follows day. Botts argued that Brown, who was the best judge of his condition, claimed he was physically unable to proceed with the trial. Counsel of his own choice would be present in two or three days. "It seems to be a reasonable request and I hope the Court will grant it." Green said he had had no time to confer with Brown or prepare any defense. "The letters for northern counsel have been sent off but not sufficient time had been afforded to receive answers." Botts then added that the excitement had been so great as to seem likely to deter northern counsel from coming. "But now that it is promised that the prisoners will have a fair and impartial trial, I presume they will come and take part in the case."

The argument against granting a delay of only two or three days in a capital case was stated by Hunter: "Able and intelligent counsel have been granted here and I apprehend there is little reason to expect the attendance of these gentlemen from the North who have been written for." Then this remarkable reason: "There is also a public duty upon us, within the forms of law and the principle of a fair trial, to avoid the introduction of anything likely to weaken our present position and give strength to our enemies abroad." Judge Parker agreed and said that a physician would testify about Brown's physical condition. "As for the expectation of further counsel," said Parker, "this does not constitute a sufficient cause for delay since there is no certainty about their coming. The brief period remaining before the close of the term of this Court renders it necessary to proceed as expeditiously as possible." A physician took the stand and gave his opinion that Brown was able to stand trial—and so it began.

There was no argument made for a change of venue since it would be obviously futile. Talesmen were examined for the jury. In this supercharged environment each man was asked, "Are you sure that you can try this case impartially from the evidence alone without reference to anything you have heard or seen of this transaction?" The answer was obviously "No," but everyone examined said "Yes," since everyone was eager to serve. A jury was quickly chosen.

The opening statements to the jury were made. Hunter discussed briefly the law of treason and the legal basis for state jurisdiction of cases of murder even within the federal establishment. "I ask only that the penalty be visited on the prisoner which the law demands, which reason demands, which our safety requires and which the laws of God and man approve." For the prisoner, Green said he had not had time to study the indictment, but it occurred to him that Brown could not be guilty of treason to Virginia since he was not a resident of Virginia. As for the charge of conspiracy for insurrection, it must be proved to have taken place in Virginia and not in Maryland or in the federal armory and likewise the charges of murder must be proven in areas not within the federal jurisdiction.

Witnesses were called by Hunter to establish the facts of the invasion and murders, including Colonel Washington, John Allstadt, and Colonel Gibson. They told their stories. He introduced into the record of the case the copy of the provisional constitution. He also incorporated copies of letters to Brown from Gerrit Smith and Congressman Giddings. (The Richmond *Whig* had just offered a reward of $10,000 for the body of Giddings, dead, or $5,000 for his head.) Hunter then closed the prosecution's case.

On Thursday morning, counsel Botts announced that he had received a telegram from Akron from one A. H. Lewis that insanity was rampant in Brown's family and that witnesses could be summoned from Ohio who could prove it. Brown was lying on a cot, as he would do for the rest of the trial. On hearing this, he struggled up to a sitting position and with excitement, waving a clenched fist, he said, "If the Court will allow me, I look upon it as a miserable artifice and pretext of those who ought to take a different course to me if they took any at all and I look at it with contempt more than otherwise. As I remarked to Mr. Green, insane persons, as far as my experience goes, have but little ability to judge of their own insanity, and if I am insane, of course, I should think that I know more than all the rest of the world. But I do not think so. I am perfectly unconscious of insanity and I reject so far as I am capable any attempt to interfere with me on that score."

The gallows would be far preferable to Brown to being locked up for life as a madman. Nonetheless, the question was shuttlecocked by opposing counsel as a ground for delay until Judge Parker ended the debate by saying there were no affidavits before the Court and so the case must proceed.

After the conclusion of the case for the Commonwealth, the case for Brown began. Everyone wondered what in the world could be presented in his defense, but the indomitable Brown had a plan. He had written instructions for his counsel:

We gave to numerous prisoners perfect liberty.
Get all their names.
We allowed numerous other prisoners to visit their families to quiet their fears.
Get all their names.

We allowed the conductor to pass his train over the bridge with all his passengers. I myself crossing the bridge with him and assuring all the passengers of their perfect safety.

Get that conductor's name and the names of the passengers, so far as may be.

We treated all our prisoners with the utmost kindness and humanity.

Get all their names, so far as may be.

Our orders, from the first and throughout, were that no unarmed persons should be injured under any circumstances whatever.

Prove that by ALL the prisoners.

We committed no destruction or waste of property.

Prove that.

Botts and Green complied with Brown's request and produced as many witnesses as were willing to come and were available on such short notice. When this line of questioning began, Hunter objected strongly: "What if a thousand witnesses told of the defendant's acts of kindness? This has no more to do with the case than the dead languages?" Brown's strategy, however, was sound from the standpoint of his hope of survival. He did not expect to influence the verdict in Virginia. Only massive pressure from the North could afterward save his neck, and it was vital to win maximum sympathy from that quarter.

Brown took a part, with the Court's permission, in drawing out witnesses, and seemed very alert. *Harper's Weekly* in its report said Brown was all trussed up, seemingly asleep, "but occasionally started up from his lair, grim and sudden, like a bridled wolf, interrupting the Court with short, snappish questions." He did manage to elicit testimony that he had been kind in his treatment of prisoners. Colonel Washington said, "In justice to Brown, I will say that he advised the prisoners to keep well under shelter and at no time did he threaten to massacre us or place us in front in case of assault."

Brown asked his counsel, for the purpose of contrast with his own kindness, to try to bring out the circumstances of the bestial killing of William Thompson. Hunter, after two references were made to it, said that the facts might not be such as he would approve, but he would reveal them fully. He then called his son, Harry, to the stand who told of his grisly murder of the prisoner after taking him from the Wager House to the bridge. Brown's sobs could be heard in the courtroom. It was a shameful story. Frederick Trevor Hill in his account of the trial in 1902 said: "At no time, perhaps, in the history of this country, would it have been possible for a man to repeat this story of such degraded ferocity in the presence of his father without a blush, and under no other conditions could a father have listened to such a confession without mental anguish and horror."

On Friday morning, the third day of the trial, George H. Hoyt, a twenty-one-year-old lawyer from Athol, Massachusetts, entered the courtroom and announced that he had been hired as a counsel for Brown. He looked even younger than his actual age, and Hunter was suspicious. He wrote to Governor Wise: "A beardless boy came in last night as Brown's counsel. I think he is a spy."

Hunter happened to have hit the nail on the head. Hoyt had been hired by John Le Barnes, a lawyer of Boston, to go to Charlestown, pretend to be acting as counsel but to report any message Brown wanted to send to Boston, and communicate "an accurate and detailed account of the military situation in Charlestown, the number and distribution of troops, the location and defenses of the jail, the approaches to the town and jail, the opportunities of a sudden attack and the means of retreat." Hunter insisted that Hoyt must show proof that he was a member of the Massachusetts bar, which Hoyt, though a bona fide lawyer, could not do. However, Judge Parker saw no harm in giving Brown northern counsel, and so Hoyt was sworn in. He took no part in the day's proceedings.

During the day, the defense continued to present its case based on Brown's humanity during the raid. In the late afternoon, a list of more witnesses was called, none of whom was present.

Brown was lying quietly on his cot, being fanned by Hoyt. To the amazement of all, he jumped to his feet. "May it please the Court. I discover that notwithstanding all the assurances I have received of a fair trial, nothing like a fair trial is to be given me. I gave the names, as soon as I could get them, of the persons I wished to have called as witnesses and was assured they would be subpoenaed. But it appears that they have not been subpoenaed, as far as I can learn. Now I ask, if I am to have anything at all deserving the name and shadow of a fair trial, that this proceeding be deferred until tomorrow morning, for I have no counsel, as I before stated, in whom I can rely. I am in hopes counsel may arrive who will attend to seeing that I get the witnesses who are necessary for my defense. I have nobody to do any errands for my money was all taken when I was sacked and stabbed and I have not a dime. I had two hundred and fifty or sixty dollars in gold and silver taken from my pocket. I have not had all the witnesses subpoenaed. They are not here. I ask at least until tomorrow morning to have something done."

Messrs. Botts and Green in tones of sorrow said that since Mr. Brown had expressed his lack of confidence in them in the presence of the jury they could no longer represent him. And so, the stripling Hoyt, who had come as a spy, was confounded to find that the defense of Brown rested on his frail shoulders. He told Judge Parker that he could not see how he could proceed that afternoon. He had not slept that previous night since he had been traveling and he had not read the indictment. He knew that a Judge Daniel R. Tilden of Ohio was on the way and would be in court the next morning.

Judge Parker adjourned the case until the next day. The greater excitement was that John Cook, who had been apprehended in Pennsylvania, was on the way to Charlestown and would be arraigned that very night.

Hoyt conferred with Brown. He wrote to Le Barnes: "It certainly was most fortunate for Brown that I was here when he dismissed Botts and Green. In justice to the others, I must say their management of the case was as good for Brown as the circumstances of their position permitted." Of Brown he said: "I confess I do not know what most to admire, the thorough honest and admirable qualities of the brave, old soldier or the uncontaminated simplicity of the man. John Brown is an astonishing character. The people here generally admit and applaud his conscientiousness, honor and bravery." Of Stevens who was in the same cell as Brown, he said, "He bears his sufferings with silent fortitude, never complaining. He is a splendid-looking young fellow, such black and penetrating eyes, such an expansive brow, such a grand chest and looks!"

That night, young Hoyt worked over the case with Botts until he fell asleep in his chair from exhaustion. However, additional counsel had arrived by the following morning, experienced lawyers, Samuel Chilton, of Washington, who had been sent through the agency of John A. Andrew of Boston, and Hiram Griswold, of Cleveland, who had been sent by Judge Tilden. In a letter which Brown had written on October 20 to Judge Thomas Russell of Boston asking for counsel, he shrewdly wrote, "Do not send an ultra Abolitionist," and these men fitted the bill. But they had no time for preparation. At the beginning of the Saturday session, Judge Parker again refused a delay, saying that the term of the court remaining was quite short.

Hoyt continued the line of questioning designed to establish
Brown's forebearance, and then closed the case for the defense. The
remainder of the trial was given over to summations of facts and
arguments about the law, not only before the judge but also before
the jury because in Virginia the jury decided questions of law as well
as of fact. Chilton submitted a motion to the judge that the prosecution should be forced to elect among the different charges since there
was a conflict between charges that the prisoner took part in insurrection and treason and that he instigated them. Parker said that the
only remedy was to move for an arrest of judgment if there was a
conviction.

Every effort was made by the defense to protract the trial on this
Saturday afternoon. Brown, "the crafty, old fiend," as Hunter described him in a letter to Wise, claimed he was too weak to listen to
the case. Chilton and Griswold insisted that they needed time to look
up Virginia law, that in justice to Brown a little time should be allowed in a case so extraordinary in its aspects as this one.

Hunter said that there was no reason for delay and the case could
be completed by midnight. According to the New York *Herald*
report, these were the reasons he gave: "The unfortunate prisoner
is responsible for his own act in dismissing his faithful, skilful, able
and serious counsel on yesterday afternoon. He would simply say
that not only were the jurors kept away from their families by these
delays, but there could not be a female in this county who, whether
with good cause or not, was not trembling with anxiety and apprehension." Defense counsel Chilton replied, "In a trial for life or death
we should not be too precipitate." Judge Parker decided that the case
should go over until Monday morning after a haggle about the time
the defense would require for their speeches, which they agreed
would be no more than two hours and a half. The judge told Hunter
at the bench he was doing so "to avoid all further cavil at our proceedings." Hunter wrote Governor Wise, "Brown did not require to
be carried back to jail that evening. He walked back."

The legal arguments on Monday indicated that there might have
been an extensive lawyers' donnybrook in another time and place.
There were jurisdictional complications in the prosecution's case,
since Brown, except for the time that he had escorted the train across
the bridge, spent all his time in the armory grounds under federal
jurisdiction, and the conspiracy had been hatched not in Virginia but
in Maryland or northern states. Chilton claimed that there could be

no treason since Brown owed no allegiance to Virginia. Hunter answered, "True, he occupied a farm five miles off in Maryland but not for the legitimate purpose of establishing his domicile there. No, for the nefarious and hellish purpose of rallying forces and establishing himself at Harper's Ferry as the starting point of a new government. Let the word treason mean breach of trust and did he not breach the trust which as a citizen he is invested when within our borders? Citizens of Virginia are those who come here to be residents and when he planted his feet at Harper's Ferry he came there to reside permanently."

Chilton claimed there was no conspiracy in Virginia since there could be no conspiracy if the slaves did not join in. Hunter replied, "The law says the prisoner is equally guilty whether insurrection is made or not. Advice may be given by actions as well as by words. When you put pikes in the hands of the slaves and have their masters captive, this is advice to the slaves to rebel and punishable by death." Brown's lawyers said the provisional constitution was an "imaginary government for a debating society . . . a wild and chimerical production." Hunter answered, "Whatever it was, whether tragical, or farcical or ridiculous, as Brown's counsel presented it, his conduct showed, if his declarations were insufficient, that it was not alone for the purpose of carrying off slaves that he came there. His Provisional Government was a real thing and not a debating society, and in holding office under it and exercising its functions, he was clearly guilty of treason."

Defense counsel Griswold claimed as to the charge of murder that the only murder which occurred where Brown had a physical presence, that of Luke Quinn, was on federal premises and even there the murder was not premeditated since he was only resisting federal authority. Hunter did not deem that worthy of answer.

The case went to the jury at 1:45 in the afternoon. Three-quarters of an hour later the jury returned with its verdict, guilty on all three counts. Brown merely adjusted his blanket and rolled over in his cot. *Harper's Weekly* in its report of November 12 said that when the verdict was rendered Brown was picking his teeth with a pin. "Well, well, a truce to philosophy! Here in all probability is the end of old John Brown, saint or sinner, martyr or murderer, famous or infamous." The writer was grateful for one thing: "He has blown up the whole magazine of Abolition hypocrisies. Pray God, there may not be a cracker or squib remaining unburned."

There was not the slightest sound in the courtroom when the

verdict was announced. Brown's lawyers made a motion for arrest of judgment because of the undue multiplicity of charges in the indictment. Judge Parker said he would rule on Wednesday. He explained later that he had intended to rule that very day but a jury to try Edwin Coppoc was already seated, and he felt that he should wait until that trial was completed because the identical objection might be made. Brown was carried out, and the spectators as usual had to wait for a time before the exits were opened for them.

Judge Parker's delay of a day gave Brown the opportunity to prepare a splendid speech. After Parker overruled the motion for arrest of judgment November 2, Brown was asked if he had anything to say before sentence was passed. He rose and said:

I have, may it please the Court, a few words to say.

In the first place, I deny everything but what I have all along admitted: of a design on my part to free slaves. I intended certainly to have made a clean thing of that matter, as I did last winter, when I went into Missouri and there took slaves without the snapping of a gun on either side, moving them through the country, and finally leaving them in Canada. I designed to have done the same thing again on a larger scale. That was all I intended. I never did intend murder, or treason, or the destruction of property, or to excite or incite slaves to rebellion, or to make insurrection.

I have another objection, and that is that it is unjust that I should suffer such a penalty. Had I interfered in the manner which I admit, and which I admit has been fairly proved—for I admire the truthfulness and candor of the greater portion of the witnesses who have testified in this case—had I so interfered in behalf of the rich, the powerful, the intelligent, the so-called great, or in behalf of any of their friends, either father, mother, brother, sister, wife or children, or any of that class, and suffered and sacrificed what I have in this interference, it would have been all right. Every man in this Court would have deemed it an act worthy of reward rather than punishment.

This Court acknowledges, too, as I suppose, the validity of the law of God. I see a book kissed, which I suppose to be the Bible, or at least the New Testament, which teaches me that all things whatsoever I would that men should do to me, I should do even so to them. It teaches me, further, to remember them that are in bonds as bound with them. I endeavored to act up to that instruction. I say I am yet too young to understand that God is any respecter of persons. I believe that to have interfered as·I have done, as I have always freely admitted I have done, in behalf of His despised poor, I did no wrong, but right. Now, if it is deemed necessary that I should forfeit my life for the furtherance of the ends of justice, and mingle my blood further with the blood of my children and with the blood of millions in this slave country whose rights are disregarded by wicked, cruel, and unjust enactments, I say, let it be done.

Let me say one word further. I feel entirely satisfied with the treatment I have received on my trial. Considering all the circumstances, it has been more generous than I expected. But I feel no consciousness of guilt. I have stated from the first what was my intention, and what was not. I never had any design against the liberty of any person, nor any disposition to commit treason or incite slaves to rebel or make any general insurrection. I never encouraged any man to do so, but always discouraged any idea of that kind.

Let me say, also, in regard to the statements made by some of those who were connected with me, I hear it has been stated by some of them that I have induced them to join me. But the contrary is true. I do not say this to injure them, but as regretting their weakness. Not one but joined me of his own accord, and the greater part at their own expense. A number of them I never saw, and never had a word of conversation with, till the day they came to me, and that was for the purpose I have stated.

Now, I have done.

In the funeral services for Abraham Lincoln at Boston, Ralph Waldo Emerson said that his speech at Gettysburg could not easily be surpassed by words on any other recorded occasion and could be compared only to John Brown's speech to the Court. The Lawrence, Kansas, *Republican* said, "For sublimity and solemn appeal, it has not been excelled since Paul spoke before King Agrippa." Brown's speech was recognized in the North as masterful, even among those who had been cool to him. The New York *Times* said while it was not convinced as to his logic, "Brown's speech classifies him at once and in a class by himself. He is a fanatic *sui generis*. He is simply John Brown of Kansas, a man logical after the narrow fashion of the Puritan individualist, a law unto himself. . . . Every thoughtful, dispassionate person must recognize, whether in the North or South, in his demeanour, in the language and ideas of this stout, old fanatic the stuff of which the great heroes of mankind are made—simplicity, absolute faith in his own ideas, a religious earnestness of purpose and the great courage of a man consciously honest of will."

It was entirely beside the point that the speech was a lie from beginning to end. Robert Penn Warren has rightly said, "It was so thin

that it should not have deceived a child, but it deceived a generation."
Brown always had a contempt for the credulity of the public, for
their "greedy swallowing everywhere of what I have told," and he
was sure that this would be swallowed, as it was. In the extremely
polarized, emotionalized atmosphere of the time, his arguments nowhere received critical examination.

It was a lie that he had run off slaves from Missouri "without the
snapping of a gun." David Cruise was murdered. How could he say
that he did not intend bloodshed in Virginia when he brought with
him hundreds of guns and attacked the government arsenal to get
more? How could he reconcile his statement that he did not intend
insurrection when he brought along for enactment copies of his
provisional constitution and brought along pikes to arm the slaves? It
is true that some of his men joined him voluntarily but the greater
number were energetically recruited by him and inculcated by him
with his sense of mission.

Prosecutor Hunter comprehended and set forth during the trial the
essence of Brown's plan for "mighty conquest," to create a larger
and larger territory by servile insurrection for the operation of his
provisional government. After the trial, the whole subject seems to
have been dropped. Brown even retreated from the position he took
in his speech to the Court on November 2. In a letter of November 22
to Hunter he adverted to a seeming "confliction" of his speech with a
statement to Governor Wise in his interrogation after capture at
Harper's Ferry that he did not intend to run off slaves but only to
free them. He said that was correct, and in his speech to the Court he
spoke too hastily. "I intended to convey this idea, that it was my object to place the slaves in a condition to defend their liberties, if they
would, without any bloodshed, but not that I intended to run them
out of the slaves states." This made even less sense.

After Brown finished talking, Judge Parker sentenced him to be
hung on December 2.

Governor Wise's obtuseness in dealing with northern public opinion was little short of incredible. He opened the gates for the rabid
foes of slavery to picture Brown as the wounded, old eagle, forced
to go on trial only a week and a day after his capture, so weak that he
had to lie prostrate in the courtroom, not permitted to choose his
own counsel but assigned slave-counsel by the slave-court, put on
trial immediately on the same day as the indictment, so that he had

no opportunity, as his slave-counsel readily admitted, to prepare any defense.

Brown, of course, was guilty of murder, and if he had had a hundred lawyers and a hundred days to prepare a defense it would have made no difference. "The prisoners in fact have no defense," Horace Greeley wrote in the New York *Tribune* when Brown was arraigned, and the New York *Independent* said, "By his acts his life is forfeit." In a later day, Professor Von Holst said, "The forms were sinned against but in the main justice was done. He who undertakes such a game stakes his life. Brown had forfeited his life, and that, not only according to the laws of Virginia, for in every state where the death penalty existed he would necessarily have been condemned for a similar crime."

Moreover, there was some excuse for speed. The northern historian James F. Rhodes wrote: "The public sentiment of the community called for a speedy trial and with newspapers and people demanding summary vengeance by lynch-law, the authorities were right to take prompt action." The Negro educator W. E. B. DuBois conceded: "The trial was a difficult experience. To defend the good name of the state, Virginia had to restrain the violent blood-vengeance of men whose kin had been killed in the raid and who had sworn that no prisoner should escape the extreme penalty."

But was such infuriate haste required? Very little was required to give the semblance of a fair trial. Could not Virginia have afforded to give Brown two or three days to study the indictment and to procure his own counsel? Brown in all probability was faking when he insisted on hearing the trial from his cot. It appears, however, that he received no medical attention. Why did not Virginia, in order to assuage public opinion in the North, gave him adequate medical assistance and then publish a full report on his wounds? Then, too, the reasons that Hunter gave for pushing the case to a swift conclusion, as he did on Saturday afternoon, sounded insulting and positively silly to the northern public—that the jury had spent enough time away from their families and that every female in the county was trembling with anxiety.

There was an outcry in the North against this violation of fundamental legal rights established in the English common law. John A. Andrew of Boston said that in all his legal experience he had never encountered anything like it. In a recent case of kidnapping in Massachusetts, the Court gave defense counsel a two-month delay, after arraignment, just to file a plea. The Lawrence, Kansas, *Republican*

said that the proceedings could find a parallel only in the bloody records of the Inquisition. "We defy an instance to be shown in a
civilized community where a prisoner has been forced to trial for
his life when so disabled from his ghastly wounds as to be unable
even to sit up during the proceedings and compelled to be carried to
the judgment hall upon a litter."

The New York *Times*, which had previously been conciliatory,
issued a blast on November 1:

> We are sorry to be obliged to say that the course which has been thus
> far followed has, on the whole, tended to create an unwholesome reaction
> in the prisoner's favor. In the first place, it was a most unusual and
> uncalled-for thing to insist on the arraignment and trial of a wounded
> man, actually unable to stand upright in the dock. No one in such a
> condition of body as Old Brown ought to be tried for his life except
> before a drum-head court martial. It is no easy matter for a person
> accused in a capital case to arrange his defense in perfect health and vigor.
> It is all but impossible that a man with sabre cuts on his head and bayonet
> thrusts in his body should be equal to the exigencies of such a situation.
>
> Moreover, Brown had another good reason for claiming delay. He
> had no time to procure counsel. To allege that the Court had assigned
> counsel and that he ought to be satisfied with the gentlemen so designated
> is simply a cruel mockery alike of law and a dying man. The very excite-
> ment out of doors which is put forward as a reason for hurrying the
> trial was still a better reason for Brown's refusal to be defended by any
> members of the Virginia bar. How could he be asked to believe, after all
> he heard in court, that any Virginia lawyer, however capable or honor-
> able, could so far divest himself of the passions of which his friends and
> neighbors were shaken as to defend him, as a man in such a dreadful
> plight ought to be defended, with heart and soul, zealously, even
> enthusiastically?

The trampling on Brown's rights gave the fiery Abolitionists the
very opening they craved. On November 2, Wendell Phillips, in a
sermon at the Plymouth Church in Brooklyn, entitled "Lessons of the
Hour," said amidst wild applause: "Virginia today is only an insurrection. I mean exactly what I say. She is a pirate ship. John Brown
sails with letters of marque from God and justice against every pirate
he meets. He has twice as much right to hang Governor Wise as
Governor Wise has to hang him. I am speaking of the case as God
sees it without cringing to the corrupt morals of the Nineteenth century. Virginia has proved by her own haste that she has no government—the same haste that the pirate ship shows when it tries a man on
the deck and then runs him up the yard-arm."

On November 5, the Richmond *Enquirer* said: "What means the applause that greeted the treason of Wendell Phillips in Brooklyn? What in the world do we understand from such an exhibition of approbation? Is this the government of two peoples as different in our sentiments of right and wrong as we are in our institutions?"

"Where is John Cook?" was the big question after the capture of Brown. He was that detested figure in war, the spy, and was erroneously elevated to an importance he did not really have, as the chief lieutenant of Brown. Governor Wise offered a reward of $1,100 for his capture. A search of his home in Harper's Ferry showed that he had broadcast to all his friends in the North that he was about to launch the glorious enterprise to free the slaves of the South. There were letters and even poems discovered, that had been sent to him in encouragement. Thus, one letter said, "Press on nobly! By your instrumentality, millions may have the pleasure of singing the song of liberty."

The search for him was concentrated around Chambersburg because his wife and child were at Mrs. Ritner's boarding house there. His teen-age wife was hysterical on the news of the raid, but when she heard that Cook had escaped from there, she said with relief, "He's safe. He escaped a dozen times in Kansas."

At Carlisle, Pennsylvania, forty miles from Chambersburg, a man was arrested on October 22 when he sought food, whom the authorities believed was Cook. He claimed his name was William H. Harrison. The sheriff notified Richmond and asked that a requisition be sent for Cook, and the requisition was mailed. Then the description was read more closely in Richmond and it was apparent that this man was not Cook but answered to the description of Albert Hazlett, who had escaped from Harper's Ferry on October 17, and so another requisition was mailed for him.

On October 26, Cook emerged out of the woods at the Mount Alto Iron Works, eight miles from Chambersburg, and told one David Brombaugh that he was a hunter who had got lost and he asked for food. While he was eating at his home, Brombaugh went for help and met Daniel Logan and a friend and told them he was certain he had Cook. Cook was taken by surprise in Brombaugh's home. On the way to Chambersburg he said to Logan, "Why are you arresting me? Are you a proslave man or are you interested in the reward?" Logan said it was the latter. Cook laughed and said, "If that's the case, this can be settled. My family is rich and I can give you much more than $1,100." But Cook was taken before a judge in Chambersburg and ordered held to await extradition.

At the jail there was a conference between Logan, the sheriff and a lawyer who had been hired by Cook, A. K. McClure. There was no proslave sentiment in Chambersburg, and Logan had now changed his mind and wanted to see Cook released, perhaps because of the money Cook promised. The men agreed that since the requisition would not come for two days from Richmond they would arrange an escape that would look credible, on the next day. Cook was so informed and was happy about it.

But the next day before noon, the sheriff came in great excitement to McClure's office, and said, "Cook is gone!" What had happened was that the sheriff in Carlisle had heard of Cook's arrest. He had in hand the requisition for Cook that, because of the error in identity, had been sent him and he came in early morning with the requisition to the Chambersburg jail, whisked Cook off to a United States commissioner, received a telegram from Pennsylvania's Governor Packer approving the extradition, and Cook was on his way back to Charlestown. It was a freak mischance that had prevented Cook from becoming a free man. Hazlett accompanied Cook back to Virginia.

The first man tried after Brown was Edwin Coppoc, and he was convicted in a day. There was short shrift given to the Negroes, John Copeland, and Shields Green, who were given snapshot trials. The Negroes were defended by a Boston lawyer, George Sennott, who contended that a Negro with no rights under its laws could not be guilty of treason to Virginia. Hunter and Judge Parker agreed, and so they were convicted on the two other charges, murder and insurrection.

Cook was tried next amid great excitement since he was so well known in the local area. He had the best legal help Indiana could furnish. His brother-in-law, Governor Ashbel P. Willard, sat beside him during his trial. Cook's main counsel was Daniel W. Voorhees, United States Attorney for Indiana, who was to become a distinguished United States senator. He pictured Cook as Brown's helpless pawn in an eloquent plea that reduced many to tears. He had great praise for Virginia, which "has thrown around a band of deluded men who invaded her soil with treason and murder all the safeguards of her constitution and laws and placed them on an equality with her own citizens." In spite of the eloquence, tears, and bouquet to Virginia, the jury promptly returned a verdict of guilty. The Baltimore *Sun* reported: "Cook said he was willing to be shot but always had a great repugnance to hanging."

These four trials were over by November 9, a week after Brown had been sentenced. All were sentenced to be hung. Hazlett's trial was held up because he insisted that he had never been in Harper's Ferry, that it was a case of mistaken identity and his name was William Harrison. His comrades cooperated by addressing him as Mr. Harrison. Stevens was to be prosecuted by federal authorities and not by Virginia, Hunter announced in the courtroom on November 7. On December 15, President Buchanan inquired when Stevens would be turned over; on December 18, Governor Wise instructed Hunter to advise the President that Stevens would be tried by Virginia, after all. "I am convinced that there is a political design in trying now to have him tried before the Federal courts." Why had Wise changed his mind? It is believed that he planned originally to move Stevens' trial to a federal court in order to get the goods on the men whom Hunter termed "the higher and wickeder game" in the conspiracy, but he saw no need for it when the United States Senate on December 14 appointed the Mason Committee to investigate the Harper's Ferry raid. Three of the five members would be proslave senators.

On the most surface consideration, it seems puzzling that all the men should have been tried not in federal but in state courts, and that no appeal should have been taken to a federal court. As it was, the only appeal was to the Virginia Court of Appeals for a writ of error based on the contention that the indictment was unfair since it contained a multiplicity and conflict of allegations. This was denied on November 19 by the higher court, which said that an indictment could embrace in separate counts several crimes from the same act.

Most of the action took place in the federal armory grounds and the engine-house was taken by federal troops. Colonel Lee, in his message to Brown, conveyed by Lieutenant Stuart, stated that Brown and his men would "await the orders of the President." The Baltimore *Sun* on October 22 indicated that the federal courts would take over and said that the United States attorney for Western Virginia was in conference with President Buchanan. Then it announced: "Virginia trials, and the sending of the prisoners to Charlestown is believed to be a concession to Governor Wise."

Legal experts have attributed this to the atrophy of federal power at the time. George Caskie addressing the Virginia State Bar Association in 1909 said: "Were this occurrence to take place today, it would hardly be doubted that the jurisdiction of the whole matter would be taken by United States courts." The importance of such a shift of authority would have been that Brown would have obtained a change of venue, which would have made his trial appear to the North a good deal fairer.

All of John Brown's men bore themselves with fortitude until the end. Cook wrote a confession that aroused Brown's ire and contempt, and he was called a Judas. There does not seem to be anything damaging in it, though his sketch of the development of the conspiracy might have been used to refute Brown's bizarre contention in his speech to the Court that his men joined of their own volition and he planned only to run off some slaves from Virginia. Cook confirmed that Sanborn, Howe, the Reverend Mr. Parker, Stearns, and Gerrit Smith were the financial angels.

And what of the Secret Six, the fine gentlemen who furnished the guns and money, who "whooped" Brown on to death, and were not called on to fire a shot. This was the one phase in the affair that gave the South a laugh. These men did not have the grace or courage to remain in their northern havens but ran as if their lives were in peril.

Mr. Sanborn, the young, soul-burning idealist, was the first to flee. Immediately on the news of Harper's Ferry he consulted John A. Andrew for legal advice as to whether he might be extradited and tried. Andrew said off-the-cuff, "Yes," and Sanborn in panic took the first boat for Portland, Maine. From there he wrote to Higginson: "According to advice of good friends and my own deliberate judgment I am going to try change of air for my old complaint." He could be reached through a Frederick Stanley in Quebec.

Dr. Howe and Stearns followed him to Canada on October 25, although Andrew had changed his mind about the law and said they could not be tried in Massachusetts or "carried to any other state." They remained in Canada until after Brown's execution on December 2.

Stearns said nothing while Howe was full of words. Instantly, on the news, he tried to mobilize legal counsel for Brown. "No stone must be left unturned to save his life & the country the disgrace of his execution." When he saw his peril, his thoughts turned to himself. He told Higginson: "It is true that I ought to have expected an onslaught *somewhere*, but the point is that I did not expect anything like what happened, anything more than a stampede." While he was in Canada, on November 14, a "card" from him was published in Boston: "That event was unforeseen and unexpected by me, nor does all my previous knowledge of John Brown enable me to reconcile it with his characteristic prudence and his reluctance to shed blood or excite servile insurrection. It is still to me a mystery and a marvel." To the Reverend Mr. Parker, in Rome, he wrote that his flight would at least "draw attention to the infamous act by which southern slaveholders can throw the lasso over northern citizens when they are wanted for wicked purposes."

The New Orleans *Daily Picayune* found Dr. Howe's conduct uproariously funny: "At the indistinct vision of a possible rope for himself, the chant of glorification to the hero subsides suddenly to a feeble quaver and the eulogist of another man's treason absconds." Higginson, too, was disgusted by his backtracking statement in his "card" and wrote Howe, "since language was first invented to conceal thoughts, there has been no more skilful combination of words."

It is interesting that Howe and Sanborn gave diametrically different reasons for fleeing. Sanborn said it was "very important that the really small extent of our movement should be concealed and its reach and character exaggerated." Howe, on the other hand, said that everything must be done to show that "John Brown was not the agent or even the ally of others but an individual acting upon his own responsibility." He believed "that every manifestation at the time of public sympathy for him and his acts lessens the chances of his escape."

To inquiries from the press, Gerrit Smith said he found it hard to place John Brown. Perhaps it was that man to whom he had given someone's note for $300 three years ago for the free Kansas cause—the note had been uncollectible and so he furnished him recently $100 of his own cash to wind up his Kansas work. Smith was frantically trying to bury the evidence. He sent his son-in-law to Boston to get and destroy his letters to Sanborn regarding Brown and then to John Brown, Jr.'s, home in Ohio on the same mission. He shipped off the tutor in his home, Edwin Morton, who knew all, on an indefinitely long trip to Europe.

As the storm built up, Smith became more fear-ridden. His warm letter to Brown, found at the Kennedy farm, addressed in the first person became more difficult to explain. It was not consistent with his claim that he hardly knew the man. Then the nation was stunned by the news that Gerrit Smith was an inmate of the New York State Asylum for the Insane at Utica. This was a safe haven. The New York *Herald* gave a report about him in the asylum: "He recognized his friends. He grasped them frantically by the hand and told them they saw him for the last time, that he was a poor wretch not fit to live, that he had not a friend on earth." Governor Wise announced that he did not intend to try to extradite Smith, that if anyone should smuggle Smith to him he would read him a moral lecture and send him home. After a stay of several weeks, Smith emerged from the asylum. He was too enfeebled in health, he told the press, to discuss the matter of John Brown further.

His biographer, Ralph V. Harlow, wrote: "His Abolitionism consisted entirely of talk and spending money. None of these things, talk, spending money or the Underground Railroad called for real courage, the kind of courage necessary to act or face the consequences of action."

The Reverend Mr. Parker was safe in Rome. Higginson would not flee. Benét put it: "Only the tough, swart-minded Higginson/ Kept a grim decency, would not deny." Higginson's name, however, for some reason did not crop up in 1859. His connection became known only in early 1860 when Richard Realf told the Mason Committee that a Worcester clergyman named Higginson was a Brown backer and the Committee took no action on the information.

Higginson was disgusted by the conduct of Sanborn, who had returned from Canada after Ralph Waldo Emerson assured him that there was no legal process against him. Sanborn was imploring Higginson to burn all his letters as he had burned Higginson's (which he had not done). The bewildered boy, Francis Meriam, who had escaped from the Kennedy farm, came to Concord to see Sanborn and get his advice. This fellow Meriam must be insane, said Sanborn, to come here and implicate me in that damned Harper's Ferry mess. Sanborn sent Thoreau in his stead, who met Meriam under the name of Lockwood and put him on the first train out of Concord, instructing him to go to Canada and stay there.

Higginson addressed Sanborn: "Sanborn, is there no such thing as *honor* among confederates? . . . Can your moral sense be so sophisticated to justify holding one's tongue in the face of this lying—and lying under the meanest of circumstances—to save ourselves from all share in even the reprobation of society when the nobler man whom we have provoked on to danger is the scapegoat of that reprobation—& the gallows too?"

Frederick Douglass was also in flight, to Canada and then to England. He left behind a letter to a Rochester newspaper in which he said, "I have always been more distinguished for running than fighting, and by the Harper's Ferry insurrection test, I am most miserably deficient in courage." He disputed Cook's statement in his confession that Douglass had promised Brown to participate but failed him through cowardice. "I am ever ready to write, speak, publish, organize, combine and even to conspire against slavery when there is a reasonable hope for success." He would explain later why he had not joined Brown, "the noble old hero whose right hand has shaken the foundations of the American Union and whose ghost will haunt the bed-chambers of all the born and unborn slaveholders of Virginia." The Baltimore *Sun* said it was printing the letter "as a curiosity, a rare specimen of craven impudence."

There was great rejoicing in the ranks of abolitionism that a martyr had arrived, the symbol, the living personification of suffering needed by the cause.

From Rome, the Reverend Mr. Parker wrote: "Brown will die, I think, like a martyr and also like a saint. His noble demeanor, his unflinching bravery, his gentleness, his calm, religious trust in God and his words of truth and soberness cannot fail to make a profound impression on Northern men, yes, on Southern men." He thought that the Six had made a good investment. "I do not think the money wasted nor the lives thrown away. None of the Christian martyrs died in vain."

Wrote the Reverend Mr. Higginson: "I don't feel sure that his acquittal or rescue would do half as much good as being executed, so strong is the personal sympathy with him. We have done what we could for him by sending him counsel & in other ways that must be nameless."

The great fear agitating the sympathizers for Brown, said the Boston *Herald* bluntly on November 5, was that the execution might be postponed or the sentence commuted to life imprisonment. They passionately wanted the martyr. "They languish for the blood of a victim. The New England Anti-Slavery Society wants a sensation. The old *émeutes* have become stale."

They had lost interest in the fate of the man as such. They yearned for the drama to be fulfilled in a spectacular funeral pyre after which the hero would be lifted to Valhalla. Reverend Henry Ward Beecher, in a sermon of October 30, said, "Let no man pray that Brown be spared. Let Virginia make him a martyr. His soul was noble, his work miserable. But a cord and gibbet will redeem all that and round up Brown's failure with a heroic success."

The New York *Herald* published on its front page a story that on the margin of this sermon in a newspaper, Brown had written, "Good." Brown denied this to his wife when he saw her.

They had to be sure that Brown came through for them, and so the letters came to buck up his spirit. Thaddeus Hyatt wrote him: "Your courage, my brother, challenges the admiration of men! Your faith, the admiration of angels! Be steadfast to the end!"

Higginson conceived the idea of a good spectacle to dramatize the martyrdom. The suffering widow-to-be must travel to Charlestown to see Brown in his cell. The only anguish that Brown ever displayed throughout his imprisonment was about this projected visit. He did not want to see his wife. George Hoyt wrote to Mrs. Brown: "Mr. Brown fears your presence will undo the firm composure of his mind and so agitate him as to unman or unfit him for the last great sacrifice." Brown wrote his wife, giving the reasons for her staying at home, and they were cogent ones. She would be a "gazing-stock" in transit, might be insulted, any comfort of such a meeting would be more than offset by the pain of final separation, and, moreover, she should save her scanty means. "There is little more of the romantic about helping poor widows and their children than there is about trying to relieve poor 'niggers.'" A letter to Higginson begged him to keep her away, saying that he was cheerful until he heard she was on the way. "Her presence here would deepen my affliction a thousand fold."

To Higginson, Brown's feelings were a secondary matter. He had traveled to North Elba himself to get her. He wrote Mrs. Brown after her husband's conviction that the chances were that the sentence would be commuted to life imprisonment, because "they cannot afford to give the North any martyrs to talk about." It is probable that Higginson at North Elba used this argument and that her trip would whip up sympathy for Brown. She consented. In Boston he held a levee for her, in which she was showered with presents, money, and kisses. She reached Baltimore on the way to Harper's Ferry on November 8.

Higginson received a telegraph message from George Sennott in Charlestown: "Mr. Brown says for gods sake don't let Mrs. Brown come. Send her word by telegraph wherever she is." Higginson was puzzled. Something might have happened. "It can hardly be a matter of *sentiment* on his part." Her visit to Brown was cancelled, but it was only a postponement.

That John Brown was going to be a martyr was plain, even to the Brown-hating New York *Herald*: "In France they set up a naked courtesan as Goddess of Liberty. Thus they plan the apotheosis of John Brown. His gallows will be the emblem and symbol of nigger redemption and bits of the rope with which he will be hanged will be sold in little pieces and venerated like pieces of the true Cross. He will be regarded as the second Savior. His words and acts will become a new Gospel."

If John Brown would thereby be made an Abolitionist martyr, why should Virginia hang him? Why should she gratify the wishes of her most bitter foes and arm them with a powerful weapon? "The blood of the martyrs is the seed of the church."

Organs in the North which bitterly denounced Brown's act pointed out this clear, cold logic to Governor Wise. *Harper's Weekly* said: "We have no advice to offer Gov. Wise on this point. If he be the man we take him for, he needs none. Certain it is that the hanging of Brown would strengthen as the pardon of Brown would discredit the Northern Abolitionists." The New York *Journal of Commerce* said: "To hang a fanatic is to make a martyr of him and fledge another brood of the same sort. Better send these creatures to the penitentiary and make miserable felons of them." The New York *Times* said: "Brown has forfeited his life. But we can tell the South that Brown on the scaffold will do more damage and involve them in far more peril than a hundred Browns at large in the Northern states."

Thoughtful persons in the South raised their voices to express the same thought. Virginians wrote to Governor Wise in this vein. The Frankfurt, Kentucky, *Yeoman* was the first southern newspaper to urge commutation of the sentence: "It would place the South upon a vantage ground in the eyes of the whole world and show that the spirit of Legree does not pervade our people, that conscious of the rectitude and humanity of our institutions we can afford to be magnanimous to the very Barabbas of our enemies. . . . If Old John Brown is executed, there will be the thousands to dip their handkerchiefs in his blood, relics of the martyr will be paraded through the North, pilgrimages will be made to his grave and we shall not be surprised to hear of miracles wrought there as at the tomb of Thomas à Becket."

The Berryville, Virginia, *Clarke Journal* said: "But now the deed is done and blood has been shed in return, and a few are fugitives and outcasts and the rest are in chains and dungeons. How much more can a generous, magnanimous people ask? How will it appear in the eyes of the world to ask more—even to the last drop of their blood? We must remember that but a small part of the Christian and civilized world are on our side in regard to Slavery."

It was a tragedy of history that these pleas, that the South not play straight into the hands of its worst enemies and inflame sectional passions, came before a man of extremely limited capacity and no vision. Governor Wise, as his letters and speeches showed, was totally unable to grasp, as Higginson and Parker so readily did, that Brown was relatively unimportant as an individual, that this was an affair of state in which Brown was a pawn in the big game, a handle to be used in the national contest over slavery. Wise's turgid sentences and his ponderous thoughts, which wound about in long circles, boiled down basically to the equivalent of, "It's a fine state of affairs when Virginia can't hang criminals in her own borders without outsiders butting in," and "No one is going to push *me* around." He wrote to Hunter on November 6: "I wish you to understand, confidentially, that I will not pardon or reprieve one man *now* after the letters I have rec'd from the North." Personal pique governed the decision affecting the nation. The Boston *Herald* claimed that there was an organized campaign among Abolitionists to write letters to Wise abusing him, knowing that this would be certain, Wise being the man he was, to extinguish any possibility that he might spare Brown's life.

Wise's pronouncements were full of *non-sequiturs*. Thus in a message to the state legislature on December 5, three days after Brown was hanged, he said: "Indeed, if the miserable convicts were the only conspirators against our peace and safety, we might have forgiven their offences. . . . But an entire social and sectional sympathy has incited their crimes and now rises in rebellion and insurrection to the height of sustaining and justifying their enormity." Does this make sense? If Brown and his men were merely tools for others there was every reason not to punish them. Then he said it would have been more martyrdom to have imprisoned Brown since he would have been the object of constant attention. "His state of health would have been heralded weekly, as from a palace, visitors would have come affectedly reverent etc." But Brown could have been shut up in some inaccessible dungeon and the attention of the North would have turned to different things.

Wise's imagination was not lacking when it came to concocting terrors besetting Virginia, as we shall see, but he had no constructive imagination in using the opportunities he had in hand for matching craft with craft. There was the matter of Brown's alleged insanity. After the trial, nineteen affidavits were presented to Wise, almost all from his friends in the Ohio Western Reserve. Wise wrote a letter to the superintendant of the State Lunatic Asylum at Staunton, Dr. Stribling, instructing him to go to Charlestown and examine Brown. "If the prisoner is insane, he ought to be cured and if not insane the fact ought to be vouched in the most reliable form, now that it is questioned under oath and by counsel since conviction." On the back of this letter there is a later notation by Wise, "Countermanded on reflection." To the state legislature Wise explained that he had talked often to Brown, and "I know he was sane and remarkably sane, if quick and clear perception, if assumed rational premises and consecutive reasoning from them, if cautious tact in avoiding disclosures and in covering conclusions and inferences, if memory and conception and practical common sense and if composure and self-possession are evidence of a sound state of mind."

This is a formidable array of criteria but it is irrelevant to the main issue, which was not whether Brown was truly mad but whether it would have served Virginia's purpose to declare him mad. Wise could have scored a tour de force. He could have held up execution and submitted to a jury the question of Brown's insanity. Brown would probably have tried to prove that he and his venture were sound. In any event he would have appeared ridiculous and abolitionism would have been sadly embarrassed. The Abolitionists were worried that something along this line would happen. To the Plymouth Church, Wendell Phillips joked, saying, "It is hard to tell who is mad. The world says one man's mad, John Brown says the same of the Governor. I appeal from Philip drunk to Philip sober." It was no laughing matter. Wise lifted this concern from their minds.

In justice to Wise, it must be said that a commutation of sentence in a conviction for insurrection would have required the consent of the legislature, and this would have been difficult to obtain. Public opinion in Virginia was strongly for Brown's hanging and hang the consequences. The Richmond *Whig* said: "Though it convert the whole Northern people without an exception into furious, armed abolition invaders, *yet Old Brown will be hung*! That is the stern and irreversible decree, not only of the authorities of Virginia but of the PEOPLE of Virginia without a dissenting voice." Of the *Clarke Journal* editorial, the Richmond *Enquirer* said that the owner must have been bought by northern gold or subverted by northern intrigue, that he should be fined and imprisoned and the incendiary sheet suppressed.

Outside Virginia, in the Deep South, sentiment was more virulent for no compromise. The hotheaded southern temper which was to play a large part in promoting the great cataclysm of 1861 was much in evidence. The New Orleans *Daily Picayune* dealt cavalierly with the martyr argument: "We are not persuaded that it is going to carry the whole North in a whirlwind of fury into the ranks of political Abolitionism. If there were any such peril, we would treat it as the sign of the state of the Northern mind so perverse on Southern subjects as to be hopelessly incurable and proof that there is no longer any possibility to live with them on terms of unity."

As the day of execution approached, the magnanimity of spirit which Brown claimed as his motivation became increasingly impressive and persuasive. This was due not only to his demeanor and words in the court but in the letters he wrote from prison, which were widely published in the northern press. He was amazingly prolific. Said Thoreau, "To omit his other behaviour, see what a work this comparatively unread and unlettered man wrote within six weeks! He wrote in prison not a 'History of the World' like Raleigh, but an American book which I think will live longer than that." Brown's oneness with God and as the activator of God's purpose was the role that suited him best and in which he was more successful than as the warrior. The power and pathos of his words were tremendously moving. Even Sheriff James W. Campbell in Charlestown prison, who read them before their mailing, brushed tears from his eyes. It was typical of Governor Wise's thorough bungling that, while he took elaborate pains to ensure that Brown should make no speech from the scaffold, he did not prevent him from delivering carefully prepared speeches from his prison cell.

James Redpath, who was feverishly writing a book about Brown which he hoped would have a big market (provided the untoward event did not occur that Brown's life would be spared), said in the Boston *Atlas & Daily Bee*: "Living he acted bravely, dying he will teach us courage . . . no greater compliment could be paid to Brown than his execution by Virginia." There is every indication that Brown was willing to forego the "compliment." He told George Hoyt that he had been in tighter fixes than this one. His spirited defense at the trial, his instruction that no "ultra Abolitionist" be sent him as counsel, his claim that he intended only to run off slaves which he watered down to an intention only to enable slaves to defend themselves, all add up to the strong inference that he wanted to live. But if martyrdom was to be thrust on him, Brown would meet it as a true martyr should.

Brown's unflinching courage and even joy in facing death were exalted in the northern press, which riled the southern press no end— as if he had a monopoly on it! The New Orleans *Daily Picayune* said: "If we are to make heroes of all who look death firmly in the face, the list of felons will give us a long roll." The Baltimore *Exchange* said that for the honors given Brown for heroism, "the Southern men have themselves in a great measure to thank. They have magnified unduly the importance of Brown and they have themselves praised his fortitude and courage. How idle it is to talk of Old Brown's courage as if there had never been before him many a poor wretch, condemned to death for sheep-stealing or shop-lifting, who has not shown as much fortitude as he!"

He was imprisoned in the same cell with Stevens, who was slowly recovering from his wounds. His feet were manacled and he was watched constantly by guards who had instructions to kill him instantly if there was an attempt made to free him. His chief jailer, John Avis, was as considerate as he could be under the circumstances. Brown was on friendly terms with his guards and asked them to refrain from profanity in his presence. There was little talk with Stevens, while he wrote and read constantly. He was buried in thought, smiled little, and showed emotion only by some facial twitching when he read letters from his family. Books were supplied by friends; the sheriff removed the pasteboard covers fearing that they might enclose fine steel saws. He read Gibbon, Carlyle on the French Revolution, but mostly a book about Toussaint L'Ouverture. A guard, William Fellows, who later supplied these details, said that

Brown told him he ranked Toussaint with Socrates, Luther, and John Hampden as one of the world's greatest men.

He was allowed two visitors a day. Some were not of his own choice. Governor Wise visited him and asked whether he had any special thing he wanted to say, or any confidential request. "When we parted he cordially gave me his blessing, wishing me every return for the attentions to him as a prisoner." Militiamen were admitted in groups to gaze at the prize, caged exhibit. Samuel C. Pomeroy of Kansas, the official of the Emigrant Aid Society, asked him if a rescue should be attempted, to which Brown replied, "I am worth now infinitely more to die than to live." Rescue was out of the question. He knew that he would be shot down like a dog instantly. Judge Thomas Russell and his wife came from Boston. G. W. Brown in his *Herald of Freedom*, in Lawrence, Kansas, was "ventilating" Brown's activities in Kansas and was excoriating him for the Pottawatomie murders, which were being discussed in the press. Russell asked him about them and Brown repeated the bland lie that he was not there at the time. Henry Clay Pate came to gloat, and they had an angry exchange. Pate in his pamphlet published after the execution said they discussed not only the battle of Black Jack, but Brown made some reference to the Pottawatomie murders, muttering that the victims were "peaceable men."

He had no clergyman visitors since he would not pray with southern ministers. To the Reverend Mr. McFarland of Wooster, Ohio: "There are no ministers of *Christ* here. These ministers who profess to be Christian and hold slaves or advocate slavery, I cannot abide them. My knees will not bend in prayer with them while their hands are stained with the blood of souls."

For the rest of the time, Brown wrote letters.

"I have been whipped, as the saying goes, but I am sure I can recover all the lost capital occasioned by that disaster by only hanging a few moments by the neck, and I feel quite determined to make the utmost possible out of a defeat. I am daily and hourly striving to gather up what little I may from the wreck." So Brown wrote to his wife on November 11. To a Miss Stearns of Springfield he wrote: "Success is in general the standard of all merit. I have passed my time quite cheerfully, still trusting that neither my life nor my death will prove a total loss."

In those last days, Brown was still battling with that haunting nemesis from his early years, failure, and in his last gasp he was trying to expunge the stigma of failure from the balance sheet of his entire life. He could fight now only with his words. His letters were purposefully beamed to the large public audience, since they were being reprinted in northern papers and would live on after him. Philosophically, he reconciled himself in a peculiar sense to the belief that he had lived a full span of years. He would have been sixty on May 9 of the following year, he wrote Reverend Luther Humphrey. "I have never since I can remember required a great amount of sleep so that I can conclude that I have already enjoyed full an average number of waking hours with those who reach the 'three score years and ten.' "

He used religious imagery very skillfully, associating himself with Christ and revered figures in Christian theology. To his wife and children: "I beg of you all meekly and quietly to submit to this, not feeling yourselves in the least degraded on this account. Remember, dear wife and children all, that Jesus of Nazareth suffered a most excruciating death on the cross as a felon and under the most aggravating circumstances. Think also of the prophets and apostles and Christians of former days and be reconciled." To a Quaker, E.B., of Rhode Island: "You know that Christ once armed Peter. So also, in my case, I think he put a sword into my hand and there continued it, so long as he saw best, and then kindly took it from me. I mean when I first went to Kansas. I wish you would know with what cheerfulness I am now wielding the 'Sword of the Spirit' on the right hand and the left. I bless God that it proves 'mighty to the pulling down of strongholds.' " To the Reverend Mr. McFarland: "I think I feel as happy as Paul did when he lay in prison. He knew if they killed him it would greatly advance the cause of Christ. That was the reason he rejoiced so. On the same ground I do rejoice, yea, and will rejoice."

His only crime was that he had gone forth to help the oppressed in bonds. To Thomas M. Musgrave: "They cannot imprison or chain or hang the soul. I go joyfully in behalf of millions that have no rights that the great and glorious Christian Republic is bound to respect. Strange change in morals, political as well as Christian, since 1776. I look forward to other changes in God's good time, believing that 'the fashion of this world passeth' away." To the Reverend Mr. McFarland: "Let them hang me. I have no regret for the transaction for which I am condemned. I went against the laws of men, it is true, but whether it be right to obey God or men, judge ye. Christ told me to remember them that were in bonds as bound with them. My conscience bade me do that. I tried to do it, but failed. Therefore I have no regret on that score. I have no sorrow either as to the result, only for my poor wife and children."

To the very end he felt certain that he had been selected by God as his instrument. To the Reverend Mr. Humphrey: "For many years I have felt a strong impression that God has given me power and faculties, unworthy as I was, that he intended to use for a similar purpose. This most unmerited honor he has seen fit to bestow. . . . The scaffold has few terrors for me. God has often covered my head in the day of battle and granted me many times deliverances that were almost so miraculous that I can scarce realize their truth, and now when it seems quite certain that he intends to use me in a different way, shall I not most cheerfully go?" God's good plan could not be discerned by men, and was probably infinitely better than his own. To the Reverend H. L. Vaill: "Had Samson kept to his determination of not telling Delilah where his great strength lay, he would probably have never overturned the house."

He was fortunate that unlike the mass of men he could die for a cause. On November 22 he wrote to his younger children: "I have been confined over a month with a good opportunity to look the whole thing as 'fair in the face' as I am capable of doing, and I now feel grateful that I am counted in the least degree worthy to suffer for the truth." Five days later he wrote to his sisters Mary and Martha: "I feel astonished that one so rude and unworthy as I should ever be suffered to have a place anyhow or anywhere among the least of all who when they come to die (as all must) were permitted to pay the debt of nature in defence of the right of God's eternal truth . . . it is even so I am now shedding tears but they are no longer tears of grief or sorrow. I trust I have nearly DONE with those. I am weeping for *joy*."

(Charles Eliot Norton in the *Atlantic Monthly* for March, 1860, said that Brown truly belonged to the class of Scottish Covenanters, pointing out that one of them, before being hanged in Grassmarket in Edinburgh in 1684, expressed exactly the same thought. "Suffering is a gift not given to everyone, and I desire to bless God's name with my whole heart and soul that He has counted such a poor thing as I worthy of the gift of suffering.")

Brown repeatedly invoked the plight of the suffering. To his wife and children: "May God Almighty 'comfort all your hearts and soon wipe away all tears from your eyes.' To Him be endless praise. Think too of the crushed millions who have no comforters. I charge you never (in all your trials) to forget the griefs of the poor that cry and have none to help them." In his farewell to Mrs. George L. Stearns: "I have asked to be spared from having any mock or hypocritical prayers over me when I am publicly murdered and that my only attendants be poor, little, dirty, bareheaded and barefooted slave boys and girls led by some old, grey headed slave mother."

An ugly side of this self-righteousness must be borne in mind. As the weeks went by, the people of the North who wept over these letters tended to forget that the hands of this man, who was the self-appointed coadjutor of the Lord, were imbrued with much innocent blood. Five men had been killed by the invading force at Harper's Ferry. Brown came there armed for slaughter, even if Governor Wise painted it unduly crimson when he said that Brown had "whetted knives of butchery for our mothers, sisters, daughters and babes." While Brown was awaiting execution, he received this letter from a poor woman bereaved in a night of savagery on the banks of Pottawatomie Creek in May, 1856. She was illiterate and this was written for her:

> Chattanooga, Tennessee
> Nov. 20th, 1859

John Brown:—Sir,—Altho' vengence is not mine I confess that I do feel gratified, to hear that you were stopped in your fiendish career at Harper's Ferry, with the loss of your two sons, you can now appreciate my distress in Kansas, when you then & there entered my house at midnight and arrested my Husband and two boys, and took them out of the yard and in cold blood shot them dead in my hearing, you cant say you done it to free slaves, we had none and never expected to own one, but has only made me a poor disconsolate widow with helpless children, while I feel for your folly I do hope & trust that you will meet your just reward. O how it pained my heart to hear the dying groans of my Husband & children, if this scrawl gives you any consolation you are welcome to it.

> Mahala Doyle.

N.B. My son John Doyle whose life I beged of you is now grown up and is very desirous to be at Charlestown on the day of your execution, would certainly be there if his means would permit it that he might adjust the rope around your neck if Gov. Wise would permit it.

> M. Doyle.

Charlestown was like a fort besieged, fearing that an attempt might be made from the North to rescue Brown and the other prisoners. There were as many as three thousand militia troops from all over Virginia quartered there at one time, camped in schools, churches, in the courthouse, even using the graveyard for washing and cooking, parading back and forth. They were in colorful uniforms, many of their own choosing. The Winchester Continentals wore buckskin clothes like the Continentals of 1776.

It was a dreadful commotion. Rumors were rife that northern bands were already on the march. One Smith Crane, a native of Charlestown who had just returned from Kansas, related that he overheard a conversation in Ohio that a gang of Kansas desperadoes were about to invade; the next day Hunter got a telegraph message from Cleveland that a thousand men were arming there. All such reports were dutifully telegraphed by Hunter to Governor Wise, who became progressively more terrified. On November 19, Colonel J. Lucius Davis telegraphed to Wise from Charlestown: "Send me 500 men armed and equipped instanter. A large body are approaching from Wheeling armed with pikes and revolvers." Wise replied: "Be cautious. Commit no mistakes tonight. Men will march tomorrow morning." Four hundred men from Richmond and Petersburg, accompanied by Wise, boarded a train the next day. A New York *Herald* correspondent reported that the scene at the railroad depot was unlike any other he had witnessed except that at a Paris station in April when troops left for the Italian front line in the Franco–Austrian war of 1859. There were ten thousand people from all over the county mobbing the station as flowers and tears bade the men farewell. When they reached Charlestown there was no use for them and so they were sent back to Richmond, but then the excitable governor recalled most of them.

In his report to the legislature after the execution, Wise said: "I did not remove the prisoners further into the interior because I was determined to show no apprehension of a rescue, and if the jail of Jefferson [County] had been on the line of the State, they would have been kept there to show they could be kept anywhere we chose." But seemingly, Wise was almost out of his mind with panic. He appealed to President Buchanan for intervention, saying "a conspiracy of formidable extent in means and numbers is formed in Ohio, Pennsylvania, New York and other states to rescue John Brown and his associates . . . places in Maryland, Ohio and Pennsylvania have been occupied as depots and rendezvous by these desperadoes." He called on Buchanan to "take steps to preserve peace between the states." Buchanan replied that he did not have the facts to verify these charges, that he could not conceive of such "atrocious wickedness," Virginia was "abundantly able and willing to carry her own laws into execution. . . . were I thus to act, it would be a palpable invasion of state sovereignty and as a precedent might prove highly dangerous." However, he would dispatch three companies of artillery from Fort Monroe to Harper's Ferry, and Colonel Robert E. Lee returned there on November 30 in command of these companies.

Wise wrote to Governor Chase of Ohio that he expected him to cooperate faithfully with Virginia authorities "to preserve the peace of coterminous borders. Necessity may compel us to pursue invaders of our jurisdiction into yours. If so, you may be assured it will be done in no disrespect to the sovereignty of your state."

Some haystacks were burned in the vicinity of Charlestown, and Wise wrote to Hunter: "Information from every quarter leads to the conviction that there is an organized plan to harass our whole slave-border at every point. *Day* is the *very* time to commit arson with the best chance against detection. No light shines, nor smoke shows in daylight before the flame is off & up past putting out. I tell you those Devils are trained in all the Indian arts of predatory war."

What was termed the "excitement in Virginia" became a source of increasing merriment in the North. It was reported in the press that Governor Packer of Pennsylvania had offered troops to protect Governor Wise—which Virginia denied. It was reported that Governor Grist of South Carolina had offered him troops—which Virginia denied.

A letter to the New York *Herald*, unsigned, from Weston, Lewis County, Virginia read: "Virginia is disgraced! If the people of Virginia had the power, they would let Old Brown go free, if he would promise not to say anything about it." The Charleston, South Carolina, *Mercury*, on November 29, in an editorial captioned, "The Farce in Virginia," said:

From 500 invaders in possession of Harper's Ferry to 1,000 negroes carried off to the mountains of Pennsylvania, from the further invasions and threats of invasion, the arsons and fears of arsons, the panics and cessations of panics, the marches and counter marches, down to the final climax of military aid offered by Governor Grist of South Carolina to the governor of Virginia for the purpose of making certain the hanging of Old Brown—it is a tissue of disgrace, exaggeration and invention sufficient to stir the gall of any Southerner who has regard for the dignity and respectability of the Southern people. It seems as though the men who hold the telegraph wires had joined together to make us an object of mockery and ridicule to the world.

The New York *Herald* reported an alarm in Charlestown, beating of drums and assembling of troops. A hostile encampment of moving men had been spotted on a distant mountain. When the telescope was applied, it was seen to be only the branches of pine trees waving in the wind. Elijah Avey recalled that one night in Charlestown at eleven o'clock a picket stationed on the railroad track saw something approaching. He called out, "Halt," but it continued to advance. He fired, and found he had shot a cow. Nonetheless, word was passed along that the northerners were opening the attack. "The pickets were called in, the long roll was sounded by muffled drums, the shrill piping of fifes was heard, the rattle and clatter of arms and the tramp! tramp! of 3,000 soldiers disturbed the quiet of the night. Cannons were planted all around the jail, the soldiers formed a hollow square around the building and remained drawn up in a line of battle until daylight."

Americans love to feast on the practical joke, and partisans of Brown, reading of Wise's jitters, determined to make the most of it. The letters poured in. A typical letter of November 23 from Chicago said that the writer dared not give his name. "I take the liberty to inform you it is true. There are two or three thousand (2000 or 3000) being raised in certain parts of Ohio, which will be joined by at least (one thousand two hundred) 1200 from this place and vicinity. You may think this is written to cause alarm on your part and fear for the Abolitionists, but if you are wise you will give heed to what is written." Some letters stated vaguely that five thousand men had set out from Philadelphia and nine thousand men from Detroit. Others had detail. "T.A.B.," from Zanesville, Ohio, informed Governor Wise that he saw "between 30 & 36 men, all armed with Colts Six Shooters & a species of home made Bowie knife, well calculated to do Exicution," who were about to cross the Ohio River and join up with two hundred and seventy-five others, and would be in Harper's Ferry on December 1. Wise sent these letters on to Hunter, who put them into two piles, "Contemptible Nonsense" or "Consider."

Many letters warned of awful consequences for Wise. This one came from New York: "My most esteemed friend—if you know what is best for you, you would release Old John Brown forthwith.

I am a friend of yours and a warm friend of Old Virginia and would not like to see her cities, towns and villages laid waste by the ruthless hand of the Lovers of Freedom, but I tell you as a friend as sure as Old Brown is hung there comes a tug of war. Now take my advice and let the Modern Moses go or the Immaculate God of Armies will visit you with a mighty visitation as he has done such as you in days gone by. One word more & I have done. Until Old Brown is hung, then Virginia shall and will be sunk into Oblivion."

A letter mailed in a yellow envelope from New York said that the writer had by accident overheard a plan: "A box of fancy soap is to be impregnated with the WONARA, an Indian poison and presented to your family for use. Now, sir, the slightest quantity absorbed in a mere erosion of the skin will be fatal." Wise noted on this letter, "Such hoax put poison in peoples' mind!"

A "Friend" wrote Wise from Worcester: "Being a friend of your noble, Godlike, your peculiar institution, I feel it my duty to inform you of a plot already matured too hideous and Satanic in its nature for a Christian people to tolerate. It is proposed that a Balloon shall ascend from the Southern part of Ohio on the day of execution and taking the easterly current at high altitude and pass directly over the field of execution, and while in that position to cast over a large number of deadly shells, which on reaching the earth will explode with terrible destruction to all who may be in the way. It is also proposed to carry several barrels of NITRIC acid and pour the same on the heads of all who may be near the fatal spot which will surely blind and injure many persons. It will be the principal aim to throw a shell that may burst near you, Excellency. Take Warning."

There is a memo by Governor Wise, which he probably wrote later, about the letters he received: "They do, however, splendidly illustrate the passion on the part of obscure individuals to have a finger in the pot of public events and therein perhaps lies their chief significance."

Some cogitation was going on in Boston about the possibility of a rescue of Brown. The Boston lawyer, John Le Barnes, had dispatched young George Hoyt to Brown's side in the trial for the special purpose of espionage as to escape possibilities. Hoyt reported, "If you hear anything about such an attempt, for Heaven's sake do not *fail to restrain the enterprise*." Even if Brown managed somehow to be extricated from jail, it would do no good since the countryside was thick with troops.

Nonetheless, Le Barnes persisted. He presented a plan to Higginson. Higginson had originally thought that Brown could make his best contribution to the cause by dying manfully, but now he toyed with rescue plans. The "daredevil" aspect of it appealed to the man who had tried some years before to rescue the fugitive slaves Thomas Sims and Anthony Burns. Moreover, it would complete the ignominy of Virginia in its farcical state of terror if Brown were actually saved from the fiery furnace.

The first plan had only some ostensible connection with saving Brown's life, since Higginson must have realized that Brown probably would be executed even if it were successful. The plan called for nothing less than the kidnapping of Governor Wise in Richmond and demanding Brown's freedom as ransom. This would really terrify the South. Wise would be shanghaied to a tug in the harbor. Le Barnes lined up a tug and its captain who said his tug with eighteen knots an hour could easily outrun the gunboat in the harbor which could make only thirteen knots. The project would cost $10,000 to $15,000. Le Barnes was not too sure about the plan and said, "Success would be brilliant—defeat fatally inglorious." It was abandoned.

The next plan was for an overland rescue by a group of German lovers of liberty who had settled in New York after the revolution of 1848. A group of "a hundred or more" would join up with a force from Ohio headed by John Brown, Jr., and descend on Charlestown. Le Barnes told Higginson, "They are confident, strange as it may seem to us—of success." However, George Hoyt who visited the Western Reserve of Ohio reported that there was nothing stirring. Again, there was the question of money, since the Germans demanded $100 apiece as compensation and also protection for their families in case they failed to return. Le Barnes from New York wrote: "The men are ready. They ask for funds. It is for you in Boston to say 'go' or 'stay.'" It could cost from $2,000 to $3,000.

Sanborn replied promptly, "Object abandoned." Had Sanborn ever seriously contemplated a fund-raising campaign among fellow-Abolitionists, so many of whom were convinced that it was better that Brown should die, or were Sanborn and Higginson more concerned with the balm to their conscience? As the slight fever to do something subsided, the two wearied intellectuals of Boston closed the book on the living Brown as Sanborn heaved a sigh and dashed off a note to Higginson: "So I suppose we must give up all hope of saving our old friend."

CHAPTER TEN

His Soul Went Marching On

PROCLAMATION

In pursuance of instructions from the Governor of Virginia, notice is hereby given:

That, as heretofore, particularly from now until after Friday next, the 2nd of December, STRANGERS found within the county of Jefferson and counties adjacent, having no known or satisfactory account of themselves will be at once arrested.

That on, and for a proper period before that day STRANGERS, and especially parties approaching under the pretext of being present at the execution of John Brown, whether by railroad or otherwise, will be met by the military and turned back or arrested, without regard to the amount of force that may be required.

No women or children will be allowed to come near to the place of execution.

Wm. B. Taliaferro
Major-General in Command

November 26, 1859

❦

Citizens are urged to remain in their houses tonight, tomorrow night and Friday night. Their presence in the streets may be dangerous to themselves and will interfere with the efforts and orders of those in authority to maintain the public peace.

Thomas C. Green, Major

❦

November 30, 1859

The emergency security precautions that were clamped down on the Charlestown area, comparable to those in a state of war, were in response to orders from the panicky Governor Wise, who was now convinced that the plan of the rescuers was not to invade the South en masse but to infiltrate singly or by twos and threes into Charlestown. To Major-General Taliaferro he instructed, "Keep full guard on the line of frontier from Martinsburg to Harper's Ferry on the day of 2nd Dec. Warn the inhabitants to arm and keep guard and patrol on that day and for days beforehand. These orders are necessary to prevent seizure of hostages. Warn the inhabitants to stay away and especially to keep the women and children at home. Prevent all strangers and especially all parties of strangers from proceeding to Charlestown on 2nd Dec. To this end, station a guard at Harper's Ferry sufficient to control crowds on the cars from East and West. . . . If you err, err on the side of precautions." To Hunter he warned of the nefarious plans afoot. "They come *one by one, two by two,* in *open* day and make you stare that the thing be attempted. But on the days of execution what is become of the borders? Have you tho't of that? 5 to 10,000 people flock into Chastown & leave the homesteads unguarded! What then but most burnings to take place? To prevent this you must get all the papers in Jeff, Berk: & Fredk & Morgan & Hampton: to beg the people to stay at home and keep guard. Again a promiscuous crowd of women & children would hinder troops terribly if an emeute of rescue be made. . . ."

Hunter communicated with the presidents of the railroads. President Garrett of the Baltimore and Ohio Railroad wrote Governor Wise that no tickets would be sold to anyone for Harper's Ferry destination unless he received a certificate of approval from an authorized officer of the road. To Hunter he said, "If they seize the trains we have given instructions to the engineers to run the train down the first embankment they come to." President Felton of the Philadelphia Railroad said no excursion tickets for groups would be sold from New York to Baltimore. "We have ordered an extra guard to protect and repair the telegraph wires during the days of the execution." All those who came not by rail, but overland into Charlestown or Harper's Ferry and were not properly vouched for or did not come on business would land in the guardhouse.

Alexander M. Ross, the Abolitionist friend of Brown's who was in Richmond at the time of the raid, made an attempt to go to Charlestown to see Brown before execution, but got no farther than Harper's Ferry. He returned to Richmond and obtained an interview with Governor Wise who lashed him in a fury. "I am *wise* enough to understand your object in wishing to go to Charlestown, and I dare you to go. If you attempt it I will have you shot. It is such men as you who have urged Brown to make his crazy attack. I would like to hang a dozen of you leading Abolitionists." He handed him a document: "The bearer is hereby ordered to leave the state of Virginia within 24 hours."

Mrs. Brown, after having been turned back on November 9 in Baltimore in her intended visit to her husband, did not return to North Elba but stayed in Perth Amboy, New Jersey, at the home of the Abolitionist Mrs. Rebecca Spring, and with the J. Miller McKims, also ardent Abolitionists, in Philadelphia. Mrs. Brown insisted in a letter to her husband that she wanted to see him for one last time. He acquiesced reluctantly, if she would come at the end of November. "If you feel sure you can endure the trials and the shock which will be unavoidable, I should be glad to see you once more; but when I think of you being insulted on the road, and perhaps while here, and of only seeing your wretchedness made complete, I shrink from it."

She wrote to Governor Wise asking for the remains of her two sons and her husband "for decent and tender interment among their kindred." He sent her a kind letter with an order on Major-General Taliaferro for the delivery of the mortal remains of her husband to her or her agent at Harper's Ferry. "Would to God that 'public considerations could avert his doom,' for the Omniscient knows that I take not the slightest pleasure in the execution of any whom the laws condemn."

On November 30, the authorities were unprepared when Mrs. Brown arrived at Harper's Ferry, accompanied by Mr. and Mrs. McKim and Hector Tyndale, a lawyer of Philadelphia, and requested that she be allowed to proceed directly to Charlestown to visit her husband. The wires hummed for twenty-four hours. Major-General Taliaferro telegraphed Richmond, and the answer came back: "Detain Mrs. Brown at Harper's Ferry until further orders with the lady and two gentlemen who accompany her and watch them." While waiting, Mrs. Brown asked for the remains of her sons Watson and Oliver. She was told that they were too badly decomposed to be identified. She was not told that Watson's body had been sent to the medical college at Winchester. She had a brief interview with Colonel Robert E. Lee, stationed there, the content of which is unknown.

On the afternoon of the next day, she was advised that she could proceed without her companions to Charlestown, and she went there by carriage under a guard of a sergeant and eight soldiers. James M. Ashley, a newly elected congressman from Ohio, was in Charlestown in a vain attempt to see Brown and described the scene on her arrival at 5 P.M. This lone woman was treated as if she were a formidable enemy. There had been two brass cannon facing the jail but now three more were added. Eight hundred to a thousand men with glittering bayonets, pistols, and swords formed a hollow square in front of it.

After a cursory search of her person by Mrs. Avis, the wife of the jailer, she entered the cell where husband and wife embraced. Stevens had been moved to another cell for the visit. According to Avis, the conversation was something like this: "My dear husband, it is a hard fate." "Well, well, cheer up, cheer up, Mary. We must all bear it in the best manner we can. I believe it is all for the best." "Our poor children—God help them," and Brown said, "Those that are dead to this world are angels in another. To those still living, tell them their father died without a single regret for the course he has pursued."

He urged that his body, with those of Oliver and Watson and the two Thompson boys, be burned all together on a wood fire, the ashes collected in a box and carried to North Elba for burial. She would not hear of it, and added that she believed Virginia authorities would not give their consent. They talked about some business matters and they had a brief dinner; she was supplied with fork and knife but he had to use his fingers. Then Major-General Taliaferro entered the room and said that she must depart. According to

Andrew Hunter the only testiness that Brown displayed during his entire confinement was when Taliaferro refused his request that his wife be allowed to spend the night with him. This is hard to credit. It is likely that Brown was greatly relieved when she left. She reached Harper's Ferry physically and emotionally exhausted at 9 P.M.

Charlestown was jammed with people on this, the eve of the execution. The John Brown affair was a milestone in the history of American journalism. Never before had so many writers and artists come from so far to cover an event. Carter's Hotel was the caravansery where they were all kept under military durance.

The cadets of the Virginia Military Institute had been called for guard duty, and they were under the command of a man with severe and vigilant mien, Professor Thomas J. Jackson, later to be famous as "Stonewall" Jackson. The Richmond Greys were bivouacked in the courtroom where Brown had been convicted, their guns stacked there, and the benches as their beds. One of them was destined to play the leading role in another drama of martyrdom. The New York *Tribune* in its correspondence from Edwin H. House, said: "In the ranks of Company F from Richmond are O. Jennings Wise, the Governor's son, and a younger brother of Edwin Booth, the tragedian. The latter, we are told, left the theatre immediately after a performance and hastened to join his company."

Brown slept peacefully his last night on earth. To Judge D. R. Tilden of Cleveland he wrote: "I fancy myself entirely composed and that my sleep in particular is as sweet as that of a healthy, joyous little infant. I pray God that He will grant me a continuance of the same calm but delightful dream until I know of those realities which eyes have not seen and which ears have not heard."

December 2 was a mild and lovely day. Crosby S. Noyes for the Washington *Star* in his news report said, "The day opens beautifully. The Eastern sky upon which the doomed man has an outlook from his cell window is gilded with all the colors of the rainbow, the air is deliciously soft and balmy and all nature, to anyone less hard and stony than the prisoner, has an inviting aspect to make parting from earth more than usually bitter."

He had risen early as usual and was hard at work. He finished a project that he had undertaken a few days before, to mark the passages of the Bible that had most influenced him. Twenty years afterward, Reverend Abner C. Hopkins of Virginia gave his personal opinion to an English author: "The very copy of the Bible owned and used by him in jail has been before me. Its passages touching 'oppression' etc., are heavily and frequently pencilled, but no pencil mark distinguishes or emphasizes a single passage that is distinctly Christian. He was religious but not Christian. Religion was the crutch on which his fanaticism rested."

In a letter to his wife, bidding her another farewell, and "bee of good cheer," he enclosed the following:

To be inscribed on the old family Monument at North Elba.
Oliver Brown born—— 1839 was killed at Harpers ferry Va Nov 17th 1859. Watson Brown, born—— 1835 was wounded at Harpers ferry Nov 17th and died Nov 19th 1859.
(My wife can) supply blank dates to above.
John Brown born May 9th 1800 was executed at Charlestown, Va, December 2d 1859.

There were errors in it. Despite his outward composure, Brown might have been inwardly agitated. His sons perished in October and not in November, and Oliver died on the eighteenth and not the seventeenth day of that month.

He called Hunter to his cell, and asked him to prepare his will. Hunter told him that no strict legal form was necessary. He could dispose of his personal property by a holographic will written by his own pen and Hunter would tell him how to write it. Brown replied, "Yes, but I am so busy answering my correspondence of yesterday and this being the day of my execution of judgment, I haven't time and will be obliged to you if you will write it." Hunter drew up a will leaving all his personal property in Virginia and Maryland, which Brown claimed included the $260 or so in gold taken from his person on capture, to his wife. Brown appointed Sheriff Campbell the executor and he left to Campbell and John Avis each by a codicil a Sharp's rifle, but, if not available, to each a pistol. Hunter and Avis attested the will as witnesses.

The testamentary situation was complicated by the fact, of which Hunter was probably aware, that this was a supplementary will since Brown had made a will the previous day in his own hand disposing of personal property. He made bequests to his children: to Jason his silver watch, to Owen his "double Spry or opera glass," to Salmon $50, to Ruth his old Bible with the family record, and to John Jr. his surveyor's compass and other surveyor's tools. Gifts of Bibles for his kin was an important provision of his will: "I give each of my sons and each of other daughters in law; as good a copy of the Bible as can be purchased at some Book store in New York or Boston at a cost of Five Dollars each. I give to each of my Grand Children that may be living when my Father's Estate is settled; as good a copy of

the Bible as can be purchased (as above) at a cost of $3, Three Dollars each. All the Bibles to be purchased at one and the same time for Cash on best terms." Very handsome Bibles could be purchased at those prices.

All the property at North Elba, real and personal, was already in his wife's name. However, Brown had an expectancy of several hundred dollars remaining unpaid to him from his father's estate of which he could dispose. Owen Brown had died in Ohio in May, 1856, leaving a quite substantial estate worth $7,625 of which his son John Brown and his heirs would receive in all about $950. To the executor of his father's estate, H. C. Thompson of Summit County, Ohio, he had written four days before to pay over any money beyond what he had already received to his brother Jeremiah "to be by him disposed of as by me directed." Hence this will. He willed $50 each to creditors of the distant past, including $50 to George Kellogg, the agent of the New England Woolen Company, whose check to him of $2,800 way back in 1839 he had embezzled to his own uses. The sum remaining from his father's estate after specific bequests was to be divided equally beween his wife, children, and the widows of Watson and Oliver.

It was 10:30 A.M. with little time before his execution scheduled for eleven o'clock, and so he made haste to complete preparations for his departure. He finished his last letter, one of thanks to Lora Case, undoubtedly a woman but whom he addressed as a male. It is reproduced on the preceding page by courtesy of the Ohio Historical Society. His hand was as firm and his expression as compelling as ever. He asked if he could bid good-bye to the other prisoners who all, with the exception of his cellmate, Stevens, were on the second floor, and this permission was granted by Avis.

He first spoke to Cook reproachfully. He could not forgive him for his confession. "You have made statements that were not true." Cook asked, "What?" "In saying that I sent you to Harper's Ferry." Cook replied, "Did you not tell Stewart Taylor and myself to go to Harper's Ferry and report to you?" "You know I opposed it in Cleveland." Cook bowed his head and said, "I am sorry, Captain, but I have a different recollection."

To Coppoc, who was in the same cell with Cook, he said, "You have also made false statements but I am glad that you have corrected them." He gave him a quarter, saying he had no further use for money. He apologized for being unable to repay the $40 he had borrowed. He shook hands with both Cook and Coppoc and said, "Farewell."

Copeland and Shields Green were in the same cell. He reproved Copeland, saying that he objected to statements he had made about the leadership of his beloved lieutenant, Kagi, who commanded the small party at the Hall Rifle Works. Copeland said, "There can be no harm in it, Captain, since Kagi is dead." Brown answered, "You only gain the contempt of mankind by making false statements." He shook the hand of Copeland and Green warmly and gave each man a quarter. "If you must die, die like men," were his parting words. Hazlett was in an adjoining cell. Brown denied that he had ever set eyes on him before and ignored him. Hazlett was continuing to conduct his defense on the ground that he had never been in the Harper's Ferry raid.

After returning to the ground floor, he said to Stevens, "I am here to bid you farewell as the others." Stevens: "I feel in my soul, Captain, that you are going to a better world." Brown: "Yes, yes, but stand up like a man. No flinching now. Farewell, farewell."

He distributed his books among the guards. As he left the jail building he thrust this statement into the hand of a guard, a prophecy, the apocalyptic vision of the Civil War. (See below.)

Brown left the building with Avis on one side, Sheriff Campbell on the other, his arms bound to his sides. He wore a suit of black cassimere which had been given him new about three weeks before, a slouch hat turned up in front, a colored cotton shirt, gray wool un-

dershirt which was visible since his shirt was uncollared, white woolen stockings, and red-figured carpet slippers. He was tightly surrounded by a bodyguard of the Petersburg Greys which opened ranks to permit him to climb into a furniture wagon for the trip of a third of a mile to the execution ground.

His seat in the wagon was his coffin, which did not seem to bother him. He looked up at the sun which shone with great splendor, he scanned the landscape—fertile, undulating fields with the winding Shenandoah at the foot of the rising Blue Ridge—and he murmured something like, "This is very beautiful country." The gay-colored uniforms of the soldiers, the sparkle of guns and bayonets was an impressive spectacle to blend in with the beauty of the landscape.

Since seven in the morning, carpenters had been busy erecting the scaffold with lumber which had been stored in an enclosure of the new Baptist church. The rope had been on public display for three days—several southern states competed for the honor of furnishing it, with Kentucky hemp winning out, cotton not being strong enough. The authorities were intent on minimizing the number of future props for the martyr-veneration which they knew was inevitable, and Hunter said in a later year, "We chose an elevated place just out of town where there wasn't a tree or anything else to serve as a landmark. There isn't a man living who can say where John Brown was hung except myself."

Brown fairly leaped from the wagon and quickly climbed the steps. Hunter's one regret in the whole affair was that, "As he ascended the gallows, be bowed to me very politely. I was looking in another direction. If I had seen him, I certainly would have returned the bow." On the scaffold, there was no interruption before proceeding to the main business. The white hood with an aperture for the rope was immediately put over his head and his ankles were tied. As the rope was being adjusted, he said, according to Avis, "Be quick," and according to Hunter, "I hope that I won't be kept waiting any longer than necessary."

He was kept waiting for twelve to fifteen minutes, which was not an act of deliberate cruelty but was necessitated by Governor Wise's orders. To prevent him from making any speech the hood was put on quickly, and the governor instructed that two concentric squares be made about him to prevent rescue. It required up to fifteen minutes for the military, which consisted of about a thousand men to form two octagons about the scaffold. Beyond the octagons, there were cavalry and squads of sentinel soldiers as far as the eye could see. The nearest civilian onlooker, not invited to the proceedings, was on a roof a quarter of a mile away.

The press had been stationed a healthy distance away from the scaffold two hours before. Crosby S. Noyes wrote for the Washington *Star*: "We believe that it was the unanimous verdict of the Fourth Estate that the reason assigned, that John Brown might say something and the press report it, was too childishly puerile to do credit to the Executive of Virginia."

During this long interval, while Brown knew his life might be snuffed out at any moment, he stood frozen like a statue. Not a tremor or quiver was discernible to any spectator. Professor Thomas J. Jackson of the Virginia Military Institute wrote his wife that evening: "He behaved with unflinching firmness. . . . I was much impressed with the thought that before me stood a man in the full vigor of health who must in a few moments be in eternity. I sent up the petition that he might be saved, awful was the thought that he might in a few moments receive the sentence, 'Depart ye wicked into everlasting fire.' I hope that he was prepared to die but I am very doubtful —he wouldn't have a minister with him."

A witness, Edmund Ruffin, the Virginian, noted in his diary that day: "His movements & manner gave no evidence of being either terrified or concerned & he went through what was required of him apparently with as little agitation as if he had been the willing assistant instead of the victim. . . . The villain whose life has been forfeited possessed but one virtue (if it should be called that). This is physical or animal courage or the most complete fearlessness of & insensibility to danger & death. In this quality he seems to have had few equals."

Finally the trap was sprung. The awful silence was broken by Colonel J. T. L. Preston mounted in front of the scaffold: "So perish all such enemies of Virginia! All such enemies of the Union! All such enemies of the human race!" After the body had been hanging twenty-five minutes, it was examined by a physician who gave his opinion that life had been extinguished. After forty minutes, this was confirmed by a group of physicians and the body was cut down and put in the coffin.

Ruffin set down in his diary: "The return of the corpse to the jail was accompanied by the same numerous escort of several uniformed companies. This was the only part of the ceremonies & conduct which I think was decidedly objectionable. It seemed like offering evidence of respect & honorable attention to the atrocious criminal."

The inevitable mythology and fictionizing of John Brown began almost simultaneously with his execution. On December 5, there appeared in the New York *Tribune* with a Harper's Ferry dateline a story that Brown on leaving the jail had leaned over and kissed the baby of a slave mother. This did not happen and moreover could not have happened. Brown had been tightly enclosed by militia; there

were no civilians in sight on the street, since they were kept away by
the soldiery. It was an invention of a highly imaginative reporter, Edwin H. "Ned" House, who, Sanborn believed, was also the author of
the phoney letter from Brown's secret southern agent who signed
himself, "Lawrence Thatcher."

This fable was credited, since people in every age will believe what
they wish to believe. In the New York *Independent* of December 22,
there appeared a poem by John Greenleaf Whittier, entitled, "John
Brown of Osawatomie." It gained wide circulation.

> John Brown of Osawatomie
>   Spake on his dying day,
> I will not have to shrive my soul
>   A priest in Slavery's pay.
> But let some poor slave-mother
>   Whom I have striven to free
> With her children, from the gallow-stairs,
>   Put up a prayer for me.
>
> John Brown of Osawatomie,
>   They led him out to die,
> When lo, a poor slave-mother
>   With her little child pressed nigh.
> Then the bold, blue eyes grew tender,
>   And the old, hard face grew mild,
> And he stooped between the jeering ranks,
>   And kissed the negro's child.

Redpath in his 1860 book on Brown, which for years was the
standard authority, not only included the kissing episode but added
another fancy touch: "As he passed along, a black woman with a
child in her arms ejaculated, 'God bless you, old man; I wish I could
help you, but I cannot.' He heard her, and as he looked at her, a tear
stood in his eye." In 1863 there was a Currier & Ives colored lithograph, depicting John Brown on the way to the gallows, looking
with compassion on a slave mother and child, and some symbolism
was injected by the artist, such as the figure of blindfolded Justice
with her scales and fragments of her broken arm lying at her feet.
Two decades later, there was a painting by Thomas Hovenden, "Last
Moments of John Brown," which showed the kissing amid detail
which was almost entirely inaccurate.

Then there were the statements, all fictional, attributed to Brown,

such as "I did not think Governor Wise considered me that important," referring to the large number of militia; "I do not think the
civilians should have been kept away"; and a conversation in the
wagon carrying him to the gallows in which the undertaker said,
"Mr. Brown, you seem to be the most cheerful man here today," to
which Brown responded, "That is so, and I have good reason to be."

As soon as Brown's body was cut down, the carpenters took apart
the scaffold and hauled off the lumber. Joseph Barry, the local historian of Harper's Ferry, whom we have previously cited, said, "The
gallows on which Brown was hung must have been a vast fabric
and the rope used must have been as long as the Equinoctial Line, or
else both had some miraculous powers of reproduction. . . . The
writer saw pieces of wood and fragments of rope purporting to have
formed parts of them, enough to build and rig a large man-of-war."
Confederate and then Union troops occupied Jefferson County until
1866, and every soldier, said Barry, had what he believed to be a true
fragment. The truth was that the rope was burned. As for the lumber
used for the scaffold, it was owned and stored away by a Charlestown carpenter named David Cockerell. Just before he left to join
the Confederate Army, he used it to build a porch for his home and
it was painted so that it looked like a part of the original structure.
The fragments of the scaffold that were sold were as genuine as the
"John Brown pikes" turned out by local blacksmiths.

Brown's body was delivered to his wife at Harper's Ferry at 6 P.M.
on the day of execution. Professor Jackson wrote his wife that Mrs.
Brown opened the coffin when she received it and, again, when it was
put on the train for Baltimore, for fear "that there should be an
imposition." The train bearing the wife and the coffin reached Philadelphia the following day at noon. At the station at Broad and Price
streets there was a large crowd and much excitement. A telegraph
message had been sent ahead from Baltimore that there should be a
wagon to take the body to an undertaker for embalming, and a
delegation of fifty from the Shiloh Baptist Colored Church came to
the station to serve as an escort. They could not gain admittance and
stationed themselves across the street.

The mayor arrived with a large body of police. He had a conference with Mrs. Brown and her friends in the baggagecar and told her
that in view of the divided and excited state of public opinion in
Philadelphia, the coffin could not be unloaded in that city. A strate-

gem was resorted to. A long tool box wrapped in deerskin was conveyed carefully to a wagon on the shoulders of six policemen and
driven to the antislavery offices, followed by a mob of black people
in a frenzy. Then, after the station was cleared, the real coffin was
driven out in a furniture car to the Walnut Street wharf for the trip
by boat to New York City.

Late that Saturday evening, the body was in New York and taken
to the funeral parlor of McGraw and Taylor on the Bowery. Mrs.
Brown did not want her husband to be interred in a Virginia coffin
and a northern one was supplied. We have a letter from an employee
of the funeral home, Louisa Williamson, to her brother Jedidiah of
December 6: "Dozens. . . . I never had such illustrious guests, the
very *biggest bugs* and no mistake. I never saw a finer looking man of
his age. His countenance seemed as if asleep and just real enough to
look like life." Strangely, on arrival the body was still warm, he was
black in the face, "but the ice soon restored his looks and he went to
his bereaved family the better for his stay at McGraw and Taylor.
. . . He must have known if he was not *monomaniac* on the subject
that he was sure to fail." There was a long line of persons who subjected the body to close and critical examination at the funeral home,
so many that the New York *Herald* commented, "Henceforth, let no
one say that the Vampyre is in fiction."

On Monday, at two in the afternoon, the funeral party reached
Troy and stayed overnight at the American House, where Brown
had always taken lodging. The next morning they were in Rutland,
Vermont, then on to Vergennes and across Lake Champlain by boat.
The funeral service was held on the afternoon of Thursday, December 8, at North Elba. The open grave was opposite a great boulder
near his farmhouse.

There were four grieving widows at the funeral: Mrs. Brown, and
the wives of Oliver Brown, Watson Brown, and William Thompson. The funeral oration was delivered by Wendell Phillips. He compared the "marvelous old man" with Joseph Warren at Bunker Hill,
a death that many had considered a useless sacrifice, but symbolized
the overthrow of British rule. Brown "has abolished slavery in Virginia. . . . History will date Virginia Emancipation from Harper's
Ferry. True, the slave is still there. So, when the tempest uproots a
pine on your hills it looks green for months—a year or two. Still, it is
timber, not a tree. John Brown has loosened the roots of the slave
system. It only breathes—it does not live hereafter."

The Reverend Joshua D. B. Young of Burlington, Vermont, prayed and intoned the words of the Apostle Paul: "I have fought the good fight. I have finished my course. I have kept the faith. Henceforth there is laid up for me a cross of righteousness which the Lord, the righteous judge, shall give me." As the body was lowered into the grave, the family of a black neighbor, Lyman Epps, sang a hymn.

In 1882 it was published that a Dr. J. J. Johnson of Martinsville, Indiana, had possession of a skeleton that he was sure was that of Watson Brown. Johnson was a surgeon for the Twenty-Seventh Regiment of Indiana Volunteers in the Civil War, and during the sweep of the Shenandoah Valley under General Banks in 1862 he gained possession of a skeleton at the medical museum at Winchester which he was told was that of John Brown's son Watson. He had used it for years to teach anatomy in Indiana. John Brown, Jr., came from his home in Put-in-Bay, Ohio, to examine it and confirmed that it was the skeleton of Watson. With Dr. Johnson's permission it was buried at North Elba in a service attended by Mrs. Brown.

In 1899, Dr. Thomas Featherstonaugh of Washington, D.C., a John Brown enthusiast, with the permission of Virginia authorities, collected the remains of Oliver Brown, William Leeman, William and Dauphin Thompson, Dangerfield Newby, and Lewis Leary, put them in a trunk, and transported them to North Elba for burial. The remains of Aaron Stevens were also transported there from Perth Amboy, where he had been buried by Mrs. Rebecca Spring. Thus the remains of John Brown today lie surrounded by those of his gallant comrades at Harper's Ferry. Kagi's body, which was shipped to Winchester along with that of Watson Brown, is unaccounted for to this day.

The spirit of John Brown imbued the brave men who went to the gallows at Charlestown without the least "flinching." On Friday, December 16, four men were hanged, John Cook, Edwin Coppoc, John Copeland, and Shields Green.

Coppoc's thorough honestness and idealism made a profound impression. Governor Wise had a conversation with him, and said, "You look too honest a man to be found in a band of robbers," to which Coppoc responded, "But, Governor, we look on you as the robber." There were many petitions to the governor to show mercy to this youth. Wise, himself, noted on a petition, "This man's petition for Coppoc coincides with my own view, that he is the only one entitled to the least mercy. Whether he is, is questionable." Clemency for Coppoc was broached to members of the state legislature but was droppped after a hostile reception.

Three days before his execution, Coppoc wrote his uncle that he was ready to die. "Thank God, the principles of the cause in which we were engaged will not die with me and my comrades. They will spread wider and wider and gather strength with each hour that passes. The voice of truth will echo through our land, bringing conviction to the erring and adding numbers to that glorious army which follows its banner. The cause of everlasting truth and justice will go on to conquer until our land shall rest under the banner of freedom."

Coppoc and his cellmate, Cook, made an attempt to escape which was unsuccessful. They got two knives, one slipped to them by Shields Green and another borrowed from a guard to cut a lemon and not returned. They pulled a screw from the bedstead to use for digging. In the dark, they loosened a plank on the side of the cell and took out bricks from the jail wall, some of which they put in their bed and others were left loose. They made an aperture wide enough to crawl through. Everything was in readiness on the night of December 14 when a confederate, a comrade from Kansas who had enlisted in the Virginia militia for the purpose, Charles Lenhart, would be on sentry duty in the prison yard. However, Cook would not go. His sister, Mrs. Ashbel Willard, had visited him that day and had been so affected that she was spending the night in Charlestown. Cook was afraid that the escape might, if successful, reflect on her. So they postponed it and Lenhart waited that night in vain. The next night they made their way into the yard, and climbed up the prison wall, but since Lenhart was not on guard they were detected by a sentry and they were soon back into a well-guarded cell to wait their deaths the next morning.

The Negro, John Copeland, wrote to his brother at Oberlin on December 10: "It was a sense of the wrongs we have suffered that prompted the noble but unfortunate Captain John Brown and his associates to attempt to give freedom to a small number at least of those who are now held by cruel and unjust laws and by no less cruel and unjust men. And now, my dear brother, could I die in a more noble cause? Could I die in a manner and for a cause which would induce true and honest men more to honor me and the angels more readily to receive me to the happy home of everlasting joy above?"

Unlike the execution of Brown, Governor Wise permitted civilians to watch the executions on December 16, and there was a large crowd on hand, many coming from Harper's Ferry to see Cook on the gallows. There were two trap doors on the scaffold and Cook and Coppoc were hung side by side, followed by Copeland and Green. Cook showed some emotion on the scaffold after a minister read a prayer, resting his head on an elbow. After the hoods were put on, Cook called out, "Ed, let me feel your hand," and John Avis guided their hands together so that they could clasp. Copeland and Green died bravely next. On his way to the gallows, Copeland shouted, "If I am dying for freedom I could not die for a better cause. I had rather die than be a slave!"

After Governor Wise had decided that Stevens should not be tried by a federal tribunal, Stevens was tried in the next term of the Circuit Court and convicted. Albert Hazlett was also convicted, the testimony of an eyewitness at Harper's Ferry overcoming his protestations that he was not a participant in the raid.

There was a good deal of public interest manifested in Stevens. A southerner was quoted: "If Old John Brown had not been such a remarkable man, that fellow Stevens would have attracted the admiration of the whole country." The Charleston *Free Press* said on the day of his execution: "It is impossible not to look on Stevens' manly form and his eye flashing with intellectual fire and not feel something akin to sorrow for his untimely fate."

In the Kansas State Historical Society there is Stevens' first letter to his sister Aimee after the raid, written in early 1860: "I had a very hard time of it for about four or five weeks, but I am as well now as ever—except my face is paralyzed on one side, which prevents me from laughing on that side." Aimee and his sweetheart, Miss Jennie Dunbar, of Cherry Valley, Ohio, visited him often in his cell. He seemed to be in good spirits and sang with them and sang alone, but on the next to last day he whispered to John Avis, "Get them away as soon as you can. I can't bear this much longer."

He was executed on March 16, 1860. With him on the gallows was Hazlett, who, the day before his execution, wrote to Mrs. Rebecca Spring: "I am willing to die in the cause of liberty, if I had ten thousand lives I would willingly lay them all down for the same cause."

The Richmond Medical College had asked for the bodies, "if the transfer will not exceed the cost of $5 each," and Wise had originally ordered the transfer, telling Hunter, "Any who are hung should not have burial in Virginia." Then he consented to allowing the bodies to be claimed by relatives or friends, but he stipulated that no body of a Negro would be given up by Virginia unless a white person petitioned for it.

Frederick B. Sanborn, the esthete who was John Brown's financial promoter and who was to parade and capitalize on his friendship with Brown for the rest of his life, sat quivering with fear in Concord after he had returned from Canada in November. When the United States Senate set up the Mason Committee in January, 1860, to investigate Harper's Ferry, he scooted off again in panic to Canada. In his letters to Higginson, which he asked him to burn, he begged him constantly to say nothing. "There are a thousand better ways of spending a year in warfare against Slavery than by lying in a Washington prison. . . . Some of us are so fond of charging bayonets that for fault of any enemy we rush upon our friends . . . do not tell what you know to the enemies of the cause, I implore you."

After his fears were allayed, he returned again to teach school at Concord. He received a summons from the Mason Committee to testify but refused, on the ground that he might be seized in Maryland and the committee could not assure his personal safety—after all, Senator Sumner was not safe from attack on the floor of the United States Senate. Sanborn was determined not to budge from Massachusetts.

On the night of April 3, there was a rap on the door of Sanborn's house and he answered it. A man was asking for alms and Sanborn admitted him, but then four other men followed in on his heels. A Boston constable, Silas Carleton, read a warrant from the United States Senate for Sanborn's arrest. They handcuffed him and tried to drag him to a closed carriage outside. His sister, Sarah, rushed out screaming. One of the neighbors ran to a judge living nearby, Rockwood Hoar, who quickly filled out a writ, a "proper blank for the great writ of personal replevin." Alarm bells were ringing. Sanborn put up fierce resistance, clinging to the doorpost and porch railings. Wriggling and kicking, Sanborn was shoved almost inside the carriage when sister Sarah pulled the beard of one man so hard that in pain he had to let go of Sanborn, then a woman neighbor whipped the horse and so the carriage took off without Sanborn. The arresting party refused to heed Judge Hoar's writ but a posse comitatus, hastily formed of Concord citizens, protected Sanborn. Thus ended the second battle of Concord and Sanborn was saved from the awful fate of having to disclose publicly his relationship with John Brown.

Higginson for some reason was not summoned to testify before the Mason Committee, to his chagrin since he was anxious to testify. So much so that Governor Wise received a letter, signed "Friend of Order," stating that Messrs. Sanborn of Concord and Higginson of Worcester "can explain the whole of Brown's plot," and Sanborn in 1909 accused Higginson of having written this letter in a disguised hand; Worthington Ford, president of the Massachusetts Historical Society, examined the letter and concluded that Higginson actually did write it. Higginson felt that he was not called because the southerners on the Mason Committee were intimidated by his refusal to run to Canada.

George L. Stearns accepted the summons from the Mason Committee and testified on February 24, 1860, in Washington. He disowned any knowledge of Brown's intent to make a foray into Virginia. Yes, he had given him money in the spring of 1859. "Well, my object in giving him the money was because I considered that as long as Kansas was not a free state, John Brown might be a useful man there. That was one object. Another was a very high personal respect for him. Knowing that the man had an idea that he was engaged in a work that I believed to be a righteous one, I gave him money to enable him to live or do whatever he thought was right."

He admitted that John Brown, Jr., had visited his home in Medford in August, two months before the raid. Had they discussed any plans of John Brown? No, indeed. "I was particularly struck by the fact that he inquired about some bas-reliefs that I had put on the wall. He looked at the garden and picked one or two flowers and asked that he might take them home to his wife. I told him he might take as many as he chose. In a few minutes I found that he was holding them up and contrasting the colors, what not a man in five hundred would do. I was struck particularly with the natural love he showed not only for art but for nature. That was all that occurred at that time."

Stearns had the spunk to make a ringing affirmation of faith in Brown. When asked if he disapproved of the raid, he said, "I should have disapproved of it if I had known of it, but I have since changed my opinion. I believe John Brown to be the representative man of this century as Washington was of the last—the Harper's Ferry raid and the capacity shown by the Italians for self-government the great events of this century. One will free Europe and the other America."

Dr. Howe, when he testified, lied most blandly. Yes, John Brown, Jr., had visited him in Boston in August, but he was not aware of what was the object of his visit, except as a social call. He was shown the letter to Brown found at the Kennedy farm signed, "Doctor," stating, "I am beginning the investment with $50. . . ." There was no date on this letter, and Howe said that as far as he could recall this letter was in connection with money he gave Brown for work in Kansas or toward the purchase in 1857 of the farmland for his family in North Elba. There was no committee counsel as in modern congressional investigations, and the senators floundered around. Sanborn later wrote, with only little exaggeration, that the questions were "so unskilfully framed that they [the witnesses] could without literal falsehood, answer as they did."

As for Gerrit Smith, he claimed he was too sick and weak to testify and he was not summoned. In time, Smith brainwashed himself into believing that he never had an active part in the Harper's Ferry affair and ever afterward he denied that his connection with Brown was more than casual. An 1878 biography by Octavius B. Frothingham discussed the psychological mechanism of drawing the blinds. "On emerging from the mental obscuration at Utica, the whole scheme or tissue of schemes had vanished and become visionary. It was a dream, a mass of recollections, tumultuous and indistinct. . . . The man of business repelled the association with the visionary and tried to persuade himself that he had taken no part in operations that were so easily disconcerted. He set himself to the task of making the shadowy recollections more shadowy still, and reducing his terms of alliance with the audacious conspirator to sentiments of personal sympathy and admiration."

In assessing the impact of the John Brown raid on the course of history, we must first make the observation that may be needless at this point, that it was at the time a sensation of sensations. There were no headlines in that day but the newspapers filled their lead columns day after day with the story. Of the feeling in the South, the Charleston, South Carolina, *Mercury* said: "The public mind rolled and tossed 'like the storm-whipped billows of an enraged sea.'" Of the feeling in the North, Charles Eliot Norton of the *Atlantic Monthly* wrote an English friend: "I have seen nothing like it. We get up excitements easily enough, but this was different. The heart of the people was fairly reached and an impression has been made upon it which will be permanent and produce results long hence."

James Buchanan, after his Presidency, spent the Civil War years writing a documented account to vindicate his Administration, published in 1867 under the title of *Mr. Buchanan's Administration on the Eve of The Rebellion*, and in a chapter, "Republican Fanaticism as a Cause of the Civil War," he said this:

In the already excited condition of public feeling throughout the South, the raid of John Brown made a deeper impression on the Southern mind against the Union than all former events. Considered merely as the isolated act of a desperate fanatic, it would have had no lasting effect. It was the enthusiastic and permanent approbation of the object of his expedition by the Abolitionists of the North which spread alarm and apprehension throughout the South.

At first, the southern press was pleased by the uniform condemnation in the North of Brown. The New Orleans *Daily Picayune* said: "There is encouragement in the fact that conservatism of the North is more deeply aroused than it has been during any of the preceding struggles." But the admiration elicited by Brown, even from those condemning the raid, changed complacency to alarm. Southerners could not grasp or condone the distinction made by the moderate New York *Times*, when it said: "While our people do unquestionably respect the *personal* qualities of sincerity, conscientiousness and courage which Brown has displayed, not one in a hundred of them has the slightest sympathy with his invasion or fails to brand it as a high crime against Virginia, the peace of the community and the dictates of conscience and common-sense." In the eyes of the South, if the raid was wicked, then John Brown must be wicked, and the distinction between character and deed must melt into invisibility, as it did, in fact, when John A. Andrew of Massachusetts proclaimed, "Whatever may be thought of John Brown's acts, *John Brown himself was right.*"

The New Orleans *Daily Picayune*, which had first been so pleased by the conservatism of the North, was in a rage by the day of Brown's execution: "Crime has become godliness and criminals red from the slaughter of the innocent are exalted to eminence beside the Divine Teacher of the Gospel of Peace." Abolitionism could be taken lightly as long as it was sickly sentimentality, but now with the exaltation of Brown it seemed inevitable that gangsters would be financed and sent forth in increasing numbers to assault the institutions of the South. The black Republicans were hypocrites in their profession of peace. "'Art thou in health, my brother?' quoth the innocent Joab, and then he smote him under the fifth rib."

Such expressions of dismay and apprehension were abundant among thoughtful southerners. Take the diary of Edmund Ruffin. On November 10, he wrote of the northern papers: "All these shades of opinion concur in one general spirit, which is that the people of the North, even embracing many who have been deemed most our friends, are more or less enemies of the South as well as of negro slavery & do not entirely condemn the attempt to incite insurrection of the slaves with all the unspeakable atrocities & horrors which would attend even their partial success in establishing their freedom." On November 18: "It is astonishing to me that there should be so general an aroused sympathy among the people of the North for the late atrocious conspiracy & outbreak and for the villains engaged thereon. . . . The Northern friends of the South are few and timid. This must open the eyes of the people of the South who have heretofore trusted the justice and forebearance of the majority of the Northern people." On November 24: "Many people hitherto conservative say something must be done, separation is admitted by others as the coming result."

The Raleigh, North Carolina, *Register* was one of the two or three papers in the South classed as Whig. On October 14 before the raid it had an article teeming with regard for the Union. By November 10, its lead editorial showed a sharp revulsion of feeling: "The outbreak at Harper's Ferry and the disclosures consequent thereon, the dangerous character of public sentiment in the North as manifested by the tone of the press and pulpit, lead unerringly to the conclusion that the election of a Black Republican to the Presidency is probable, and we must infer that it would be the signal for immediate secession of the South from the Union. . . . Not content with fighting the South with the ballot-box, the enemies of the South have resorted to the cartridge-box. . . . To suppose that the states of the South would submit to see one of these aiders and abettors of treason, murder and robbery placed at the head of and invested with the immense powers and patronage of the great government, to see him placed in the commander-in-chiefship of the army and navy, invested with the control of armories, with the national treasury within his grasp and all the national property under the control of himself and his partisans, is to suppose that the South has run madder than

Old Brown himself is alleged to be and to suppose what will never occur. No! The South will never submit to the election of Seward or any other Sectional Republican."

In January, in the United States Senate, Robert Toombs of Georgia declaimed, "Never permit the federal government to pass into the hands of the Black Republican party! It has already declared war on you and your institutions. Defend yourself! The enemy is at your door!"

It had always been something of a puzzle what motivated secession of the southern states on Lincoln's election, since the Republican party, as Lincoln himself said explicitly in his inaugural address, lacked the numbers in Congress to take any action diminishing the strength of slavery. The traumatic effect of the John Brown raid furnishes a key. The South did not believe that slavery could be maintained in the face of a hostile federal establishment. One could argue about the circumstances until one was blue in the face, but the fact remained that the John Brown raid was finally quelled by federal troops. Moreover, without federal authority to pursue and capture invaders who came across state lines and authority to recover fugitive slaves, how could the South cope with a series of incursions following the Harper's Ferry pattern? The Raleigh *Register* voiced the opinion of the South—*Never*.

To a friend, the great political scientist of Columbia University, Francis Lieber, wrote: "Brown died like a man and Virginia fretted like an old woman. . . . The deed was irrational but it will be historical. Virginia has come out of it damaged, I think. She has forced upon mankind the idea that slavery must be, in her opinion, but a rickety thing."

The South shouted loudly the fealty of its slaves, protested the use of the term "insurrection" for the event at Harper's Ferry, saying it was a misnomer since no slaves joined in. Yet, the behavior pattern of the South before and even more so after the execution convinced many observers in the North that, if the pattern was not entirely neurotic, it was a clear sign that the South lived in mortal dread of a slave insurrection, and more than that, the power structure built on slavery rested on a very queasy foundation, insofar as enjoying the support of the entire white population.

During November, the southern correspondents of the New York *Herald* reported arrests made of those who uttered anything sympathetic to Brown or unfavorable to the peculiar institution. In

Richmond, a gentleman was mobbed in a tavern when he presented a Massachusetts banknote for drinks. The excitement mounted after the execution, and on December 5 the Charleston, South Carolina, *Mercury* said that there was danger in individual action, and so it advocated some French Revolutionary apparatus for dealing with traitors in their midst: "There is danger that injustice will be done to innocent individuals by the irresponsible and disorganized bodies who by their voluntary acts are working to secure the safety of the people of the South. We beg leave to suggest that they had better be carried on by a regular system of organization. Let a Committee of Public Safety composed of the older and more discreet men be formed in every district, county or precinct in the South for the purpose of considering and judging all suspicious persons and in order that they may be detected and apprehended let Committees of Vigilance be appointed in every district, county and precinct."

There was a popular song in the South, "Old John Brown; a song for every Southern man." It is significant that instead of gloating about the fiasco, it ended up as a plea to the slaves to be obedient. Here are the first and last stanzas.

> Now all you Southern people, just listen to my song,
>   It's about the Harper's Ferry affair, it's not very long,
> To please you all, I do my best, I sing it in every town
>   And while I'm in Richmond, I'll tell you about Old Brown.
>
> CHORUS: Old, Old Brown, Old, Old Brown,
>   That will never pay,
>   Trying to come away down South
>   And run the niggers away.
>
> Now, all you Southern darkies, a word to you I'll say,
>   Always mind your masters and never run away,
> And don't mind those Northern agents, they tell you all a lie,
>   They get you to the North and starve you till you die.

Virginia banned mail delivery of the New York *Tribune* as an Abolitionist sheet. Virginia's attorney-general, John Randolph Tucker, gave an opinion that state law overrode federal law: "If there be a conflict between the postal regulation of Congress and the laws of Virginia, it is because the former has transcended the true constitutional limits and has trenched upon the reserved rights of the states."

A wave of the "Great Fear" prevailed after the publication of the phoney Lawrence Thatcher letter. Volunteer companies of cavalry and unmounted companies were springing up everywhere. The Richmond *Enquirer* said, "Let the 'higher law' of Abolitionism be met by the 'higher law' of self-preservation." Drummers and business agents of northern firms for their safety had to evacuate the South and flocked into Washington. C. Vann Woodward in his essay on Brown gives examples of the mob spirit which pounced on victims ranging from aged eccentrics and itinerant piano-tuners to substantial citizens. A sixty-year-old minister in Texas made a criticism of slavery in a sermon and was given sixty lashes. A New England mechanic was driven out of a village in Georgia because he had a clean shirt wrapped in a New York newspaper which contained a sermon by Reverend Henry Ward Beecher. Four months after Harper's Ferry, a man was lynched in South Carolina as "one of Brown's associates."

There is no doubt but that the specter raised by Brown was used by the ruling class to stamp out dissidence among nonslaveholders and poor-whites and to steam-roller public opinion into monolithic support of slavery. Thus the Mississippi *Free Trader* warned: "If Brown had succeeded, out of the ashes of our fair Republic would have risen another Santo Domingo, our soil would have reeked with human gore," and Albert Gallatin Brown pointed out to the poor of Mississippi that they would fare worse if that would happen. "The rich will flee the country. They will see the danger afar off and will prepare to meet it. . . . But the poor who are doomed to toil, they will have no time to watch the storm or mark the coming. The poor will have to bear its fury. They alone will be left to await whatever fate betides them."

There is one final observation, an important one when we recall that it was Virginia's adherence that made the Confederacy a viable force in 1861. The Charleston *Mercury* said that it rejoiced that "like a slap in the face," Virginia had been roused from its hesitant neutrality. Indeed, in the John Brown affair Virginia had found brotherhood with the other slave states.

Through the weeks before the execution of Brown, there were meetings in the North held in his honor. There was a notable meeting at the Tremont Temple at Boston on November 18, addressed by Ralph Waldo Emerson, which raised $500 for Mrs. Brown and her family. There were many prayer meetings. This is a notice of one at Somersworth, Massachusetts, on November 4: "TREASON! ALL TRUE CHRISTIANS who believe in Immortality through Jesus

Christ alone are requested to pray for Captain John Brown, who is now under sentence of death and is to be hung next month for righteousness sake and doing justly with his fellow-men, his country and his God."

On the day of the execution, Justin Morgan of West Springfield, Massachusetts, wrote Governor Wise: "As I write the bells far and wide toll the Martyrdom of John Brown, congregations of men and women meet and unite in solemn prayer—business is hushed. The entire community is awaiting, solemnly awaiting, the hour when they shall feel it is all over. Governor Wise—can you imagine what an awakening will take place in another hour? Be ready to meet God and John Brown at any moment."

There were many such assemblies to do honor to John Brown on the day. In Concord, while bells tolled, there was a meeting attended by all the Concord intellectuals. Mr. Sanborn, acting as bard, composed a dirge for the occasion:

> Today behind Potomac's wave
>   Beneath Virginia's sky,
> They slay the man who loved the slaves,
>   And dared for him to die.
>
> Great Washington's indignant shade,
>   Forever urged him on,
> He heard from Monticello's glade,
>   The voice of Jefferson.
>
> But chiefly in the Hebrew page
>   He read Jehovah's law,
> And there from youth to hoary age,
>   Obeyed with love and awe.

Louisa May Alcott wrote in her journal: "The execution of Saint John the Just took place on the second. A meeting at the hall and all Concord was there. Emerson, Thoreau, Father [Bronson Alcott] and Sanborn spoke. All were full of reverence and admiration for the martyr."

Among notable meetings in the East was the one at Albany, New York, which went on through the afternoon and evening while a hundred guns were fired, and in Syracuse the City Hall was packed for three hours of speeches.

It was in Ohio's Western Reserve where the demonstrations were greatest. In Akron, banks, business houses and the Court of Common

Pleas were closed. In Cleveland, there was a streamer across Superior Street, "I cannot better serve the cause I love than to die for it." There were memorial meetings not only for Brown but also individual memorial meetings later for John Cook, Edwin Coppoc, and the Negroes, John Copeland and Shields Green, and a fund-raising meeting for the widows of all the executed men.

The historian and his reader can err in putting undue emphasis on these manifestations of grief for the fate of John Brown. There were the Abolitionists, the idealists, the transcendentalists and sundry other intellectuals, the excited young extremists, and a hodgepodge of others running through all strata of northern society who were so moved by the spirit of the man that they embraced his purpose. Nonetheless, the majority sentiment in the North did not approve of John Brown's deed.

In the *Atlantic Monthly* for March, 1860, in a review of Redpath's book on Brown, Charles Eliot Norton said that an unbiased biography was needed "for that much larger class—the mass of the Northern community—whose timidity had been startled at his rash attempt, whose sympathy had been more or less awakened by his bearing and his death, who were and are in a painful state of perplexity in the endeavour to reconcile their abhorrence or at least their disapproval of his attack in Virginia with the sense of the admirable qualities he displayed."

The plain import of the John Brown raid was discord, disunion, and even civil war; the majority of the people wanted accommodation, union, and peace. Abraham Lincoln spoke in Leavenworth, Kansas, on the night of the execution, and said of the event, "We cannot object, even though he agreed with us in thinking slavery wrong. That cannot excuse violence, bloodshed and treason." Besides practicing the trade of politics, Lincoln was a great believer in the democratic process to achieve change; he might well be termed a "law and order" man. Even in Massachusetts, with its strong antislavery movement, sentiment was in the majority anti-Brown. A resolution on the day of execution to adjourn in honor of Brown was defeated in the Massachusetts legislature, by a slim vote in the Senate but by an overwhelming margin in the lower house, the General Court. Edward Everett, the famed Boston orator, said, "When I contemplate the horrors that would have ensued had the tragedy upon which the curtain rose at Harper's Ferry been acted out, through all its scenes of fire and sword, of lust and murder, by rapine and desolation to the final catastrophe, I am filled with emotions to which no words can do justice."

The Reverend Joshua D. B. Young, who officiated at the burial service in North Elba, later said, "Going to the burial of John Brown, I left Burlington a respected and beloved pastor. I returned to find myself in disgrace, an exile in the place of my residence, and little better than a social outcast." Some of the clergy was prominent in the exaltation of Brown. There was, for example, the Reverend George B. Cheever of the Church of the Pilgrims of New York City, who said *inter alia*, "Forcible redemption, even by insurrection, would be a blessing since the slaveholders' souls might be saved, but continuing in this guilt they must be shut out from Heaven, so that John Brown was in reality their greatest, kindest friend." The majority of the clergy, however, were silent. William S. Rollins, who made a study of the religious press at the time, found that of forty-six journals, nine condemned the action of Brown, four abhorred the action but admired Brown, three did not make their position clear, one passed no judgment, and twenty-nine ignored it entirely.

Grand Union meetings in various cities drew crowds larger than the pro-John Brown meetings. The call for the meeting in New York City on December 18 at the Academy of Music was signed by virtually every business firm of any size, and read in part: "The mass of the citizens of the great metropolis were horrified that any man could be found in the Northern states possessing so much temerity and reckless disregard of the peace and well-being of the nation as to organize an armed expedition, the success of which would be attended with widespread murder, rapine and arson and the substitution of anarchy for constitutional government."

It was not until the Civil War that the extremist John Brown won the heart of the North, a logical development since war is the extremist method of human persuasion. The shift in sentiment was described in a letter written by John Wilkes Booth to his brother-in-law, John S. Clark, in 1864: "When I aided in the capture and execution of John Brown, I was proud of my little share in the transaction, for I deemed it my duty and that I was helping our common country to perform an act of justice. But what was a crime in poor John Brown is now considered (by themselves) as the greatest-only virtue of the whole Republican party. Strange transmigration! Vice to become a *virtue*, simply because *more* indulge in it."

While the John Brown raid did not accomplish a revolution in thinking in the North, there was an increase in the number of those who thought militantly, who accepted the dynamic of action. In his funeral oration at the North Elba burial service, Wendell Phillips said, "How vast the change in men's hearts. Insurrection was a harsh, horrible word to millions a month ago." After Brown's execution, there was a meeting at the Tremont Temple at which Garrison spoke. He read Brown's plea to the Court and asked the audience how many nonresistants there were in the audience. Only a single voice spoke out. Garrison then announced that he was abandoning his policy of nonviolence. He had tried in the past to effect Abolition by peaceful methods. "Yet, as a peace man, I am prepared to say, 'Success to every slave insurrection in the South and in every slave country.' And I do not see how I compromise or stain my peace professions in making that declaration. Whenever there is a contest between the oppressed and the oppressor, God knows my heart must be with the oppressed and always against the oppressor. . . . Rather than see men wearing their chains in cowardly and servile spirit, I would, as an advocate of peace, much rather see them breaking the head of the tyrant with their chains. Give me, as a non-resistant, Bunker Hill and Lexington and Concord rather than the cowardice and servility of a Southern slaveholder."

The attack on slavery in the South itself, as distinct from banning it in the territories, had been hitherto in the realm of polemics. Now, with bloody confrontation no longer a theory but a fact, the possibility of force as an expedient first crossed the threshhold of consciousness of many in the North. This affirmative type of thinking is illustrated in a letter of Mrs. Sarah Everett of Lawrence, Kansas, of January 18, 1860: "I don't like to have him stigmatized as misguided. It would not grate more horribly on my feelings to hear Moses called misguided because he failed to enter into the promised land. It's of no use to Christians to pray that the bondsmen's chains be loosed unless they are determined to arise in the strength of the Lord and undo them and let the oppressed go free. How in the name of commonsense do Christians propose to do away with this enormous sin if not with John Brown's methods? You know very well and everybody knows that southern slaveholders will not allow any kind of Christian teaching, only the Christianity of devils, and how is the great Southern heart to be reached but by God's monsters of vengeance?"

Yet, because radical sentiment was in the minority in the North, the Republican party shuddered that the Democrats would tar them with John Brown. Dr. Charles H. Ray, an editor of the *Chicago Press and Tribune*, wrote a friend: "We are damnably exercised here about the effect of Brown's wretched fiasco upon the moral health of the Republican party. The old idiot! the quicker they hang him and get him out of the way, the better." Speaking at Cooper Union in New York City on February 27, 1860, Lincoln said, addressing the South, "You charge that we stir up insurrections among your slaves. We deny it. And what is your proof? Harper's Ferry? John Brown was no Republican and you have failed to implicate a single Republican in his Harper's Ferry enterprise." Two days later, in the United States Senate, Senator Seward, who had been abroad at the time of the Brown affair, sought to sever the Republican party from any responsibility for it. Brown's action was one of "sedition and treason . . . under a delirium." On the other hand, "the method we have adopted of appealing to the reason and judgment of the people to be pronounced by suffrage is the only one by which free government can be maintained anywhere."

Lincoln repeatedly disassociated himself from John Brown before he assumed the Presidency, and there is no indication that he thought more favorably about him for the rest of his days. Lincoln's train passed through Hudson, Ohio, in February, 1861, on his way to Washington and the inauguration. There was a large crowd to hear the President-elect talk from the rear platform and it was expected that some reference would be made to the fact that he was in John Brown's home town. Lincoln, however, had only a few words of greeting and said that, since it was evident that he spoke hoarsely, the people would forgive him if he said no more. The spirit of John Brown was what he least needed to invoke in those days of fearful crisis with the Union splitting apart.

We can sum up by saying that there was a galvanization of Abolitionist sentiment in the North, and a swing by many to the more radical position on slavery, though it was not in scope equal by any means to the movement that took place in the South in the opposite direction. Yet, the split in opinion about Brown as an individual, apart from the deed, seemed so sharp and bitter that to many observers it was a portent that the conflict between North and South might indeed be "irrepressible." As the New York *Herald* sonorously expressed it, "the gathering and marshalling of thunderclouds from the horizon to the zenith, which threaten to explode in a fearful tempest when they meet the dark, lowering masses charged with electricity coming from the opposite heaven."

In Rome, the Reverend Theodore Parker eagerly devoured all the press reports mailed to him about the Brown affair, and had no doubt that Armaggedon was inevitable and close at hand. "All the great characters of humanity have been writ in blood. It is plain now that our pilgrimage must lead through a Red Sea wherein many a Pharoah will go under and perish."

John Brown would not perish, although his corporal form disappeared.

Wrote the Reverend Mr. Parker: "No American has died in this century whose chance of earthly immortality is worth half as much as John Brown's. The ex-governors of Massachusetts are half-forgotten before they are wholly dead; rhetoricians and sophists are remembered while they are talking. But a man who crowns a noble life with such a glorious act as John Brown's at Harper's Ferry is not forgotten. The red martyr must be a precious one."

"Poor old man" said Governor Salmon B. Chase. He was "misled . . . rash . . . criminal." And yet Chase predicted we have seen "a tragedy which will supply themes for novelists and poets for centuries. Men will condemn his act and pity his fate forever."

The minds and hearts of men had been stirred in far-off places, all over the globe. Victor Hugo, an exile in the English Channel island of Guernsey, wrote a letter to the London *Star* pleading that Virginia extend mercy to John Brown. "Such things cannot be done with impunity in the face of the civilized world. The universal conscience of humanity is an everwatchful eye. Yes, let America know and ponder it well. There is something more terrible than Cain slaying Abel. It is Washington slaying Spartacus." After the news was received of the execution, Hugo drew his famous sketch of Brown on the gallows, a vague form hanging from a gibbet, and he inscribed it, *"Pro Christo sicut Christus"* ("For Christ just as Christ").

Garibaldi and Hugo could pay no greater compliment to Abraham Lincoln than to rate him with Brown. On hearing the news of the Emancipation Proclamation in 1863, Garibaldi hailed Lincoln as "the heir of the aspirations of Christ and John Brown." On the news of Lincoln's assassination, Hugo wrote, "Let not America weep for Lincoln. This martyr has his place between John Brown and Jesus Christ as the third redeemer of humanity."

It was in the town of Concord that Franklin B. Sanborn worked to raise the money and provide the arms to make possible the Harper's Ferry raid and it was in this same Concord that its distinguished intellectuals, Henry D. Thoreau and Ralph Waldo Emerson, initiated the apotheosis of Brown. Thoreau was the first American of note to make a public utterance in favor of Brown. He announced that on Sunday evening, October 30, he would speak in the vestry of the Old Parish Church in Concord on the character of John Brown. The county Republican committee and the antislavery committee sent him word that it was premature and inadvisable. He replied, "I did not send to you for advice but to announce that I would speak." He spoke again at Worcester, in Concord on the day of the execution, and an address written by him was read at an assemblage honoring Brown at the gravesite at North Elba on July 4, 1860. William Ellery Channing said, "Thoreau worshipped a hero in a mortal disguise . . . his pulses thrilled and his hands involuntarily clenched together at the mention of Captain Brown."

Among the hyperbolic statements by Thoreau were these: speaking of Brown's career, there was "nothing so miraculous in history." "He could not be tried by his peers because his peers did not exist." "Some eighteen hundred years ago Christ was crucified. This morning perchance John Brown was hung. These are the two ends of a chain, not without links." Thoreau hailed Brown, "as a transcendentalist above all," and, in fact, his unstinted praise "transcended" the violent means Brown had used because Thoreau approved the end. "I shall not be forward to think him mistaken in his method who quickest succeeds to liberate the slave. I speak for the slave when I say that I prefer the philanthropy of Captain Brown to that philanthropy that neither shoots me nor liberates me."

Emerson spoke about Brown four times: in a lecture on "Courage," in Boston on November 8; at the Tremont Temple meeting on November 18 in Boston; on the execution day at Concord; and at Salem on January 6 of the next year. His most noted declaration was in the lecture on "Courage," in which he referred to Brown as "that new saint, than whom none purer or more brave was ever led by love of men into conflict and death—the new saint awaiting his martyrdom, and who, if he shall suffer, will make the gallows glorious like the cross."

Both Thoreau and Emerson made the appreciation of Brown a sign of moral superiority and a reflection of one's own excellence. Said Thoreau, "When a noble deed is done, who is likely to appreciate it? They who are noble themselves. I was not surprised that certain of my neighbors spoke of John Brown as an ordinary felon, for who are they? They have either much flesh or much office or much coarseness of some kind. They are not ethereal in their nature in any sense. The dark qualities predominate. Several of them are decidedly pachydermatous." Said Emerson, "All gentlemen, of course, are on his side. I do not mean by 'gentlemen' people of scented hair and perfumed handkerchiefs but men of gentle behavior, generosity, 'fulfilled with all nobleness,' who like the Cid give the outcast leper a share of their bed, like the dying Sidney, pass the cup of cold water to the wounded soldier who needs it more."

The words of Thoreau and Emerson gave powerful impetus to the canonization of Brown. Emerson, however, was by no means as enthusiastic or convinced as was Thoreau. Concerning Harper's Ferry, he noted in his journal: "He is a true hero but he lost his head there," and ten years later, when he revised his essays for publication in a new edition, he eliminated the reference to Brown from his essay on "Courage."

Up to this time in our history, George Washington had been the great American hero, but now many argued that he deserved second place. Reverend Moncure D. Conway sermonized in this vein on December 4 at the First Congregational Church in Cincinnati. Brown was certainly greater, he said, than Frederick the Great whose sword he wore in the engine-house. "Now let us turn to the next heir of the sword, the Father of our Country. Nowhere, with more reverence than here, shall be spoken the name of Washington. Yet, what was the cause for which he so bravely fought? Why, King George had touched the *pocket* of New England. That was it, a few shillings tax more than was right brought about the American Revolution. Also, Washington had the sympathy of the two leading powers of the world, Prussia and France, and the self-interest of every soldier was concerned. But this man, armed only with his faith, marches on to a certain death, marches over the dead bodies of his sons to the scaffold, laying his all upon the altar of the just God."

Portraits of Brown were on sale and were widely displayed. At the Tremont Temple on November 18, Emerson said, "I am glad to see that this sudden interest in the hero of Harper's Ferry has produced an extreme curiosity in all parts of the Republic. Every anecdote is eagerly sought. . . ." A week before the execution there was a book on the market by Robert M. DeWitt of a hundred pages costing twenty-five cents. *The Life, Trial and Conviction of Capt. John Brown of Kansas* consisted mostly of a verbatim report of the trial, and had engravings of Brown and his associates. The major opus was a four-hundred-page book by James Redpath which was on the market in the second week of January, *The Public Life of Captain John Brown*. It included Brown's own autobiography of his youth, and also had an essay by Higginson about his visit to the North Elba household. The book was endorsed by Mrs. Brown and she received a share of the profits.

"I have written the book because I could not resist it," said Redpath. The subject had a further cogent appeal to him. It was as he anticipated a tremendous commercial success. Priced at a dollar, it sold at least 40,000 copies. On the basis of the population of the North, that would be comparable to a sale of over 350,000 copies today. Redpath was truly a journalistic genius since he turned it out in only three or four weeks, and the book is remarkably coherent and vivid. He did a good deal of fictionizing, as previously noted, but it was to be the standard work until Sanborn published his biography in 1885. There were books published in 1860 about Brown in Edinburgh, Paris, and Berlin. In France, where the Goddess Liberty has a special appeal, the title of the book by Pierre Vesinier was, *Le Martyr de la Liberté des Nègres; ou, John Brown, le Christ des Noirs*.

A play, *Ossawattomie Brown*, by Mrs. J. C. Swayze, opened at the Old Bowery Theatre in New York on December 16. It was an old-fashioned melodrama in which Mrs. Swayze showed an imaginative turn of mind. Brown loses not only his son Frederick in Kansas but also another son named Lewis. The murders on the Pottawatomie are carried out by his enemies in order to "frame" him. Distraught by his persecutions in Kansas, he falls an easy prey to the machinations of the master-mind, Mr. Cook, who sends him to Harper's Ferry to die. The play was designed to appeal to those who disapproved as well as those who approved of Harper's Ferry, and had a long run of sixteen weeks.

"Permit me to write the songs of a people and you may make its laws."

> John Brown's body lies a-moldering in the grave,
> John Brown's body lies a-moldering in the grave,
> John Brown's body lies a-moldering in the grave,
> His soul's marching on!

Glory, Hally, Hallelujah! Glory, Hally, Hallelujah!
Glory, Hally, Hallelujah!
His soul's marching on!

The three other stanzas in the original song of 1861 were:

He's gone to be a soldier in the army of the Lord, etc.
His soul's marching on!

John Brown's knapsack is strapped on his back, etc.
His soul's marching on!

His pet lambs will meet him on the way, etc.
They go marching on!

There was a dispute in the 1880s about the history of the song, some saying that it had originated before the Civil War in ribald verses deriding John Brown. George Kimball, in the *New England Magazine* for December, 1889, recounted how he saw it born. Speculation that it was sung prior to the war, he said, was "utterly groundless." On April 17, 1861, he became a member of a Massachusetts militia, the Second Battalion of Infantry, called The Tigers, which was ordered to Fort Warren in Boston harbor. There was much work to be done. The fortress was in wretched condition and there were huge piles of earth, brick, and stone encumbering the parade grounds. There were many good singers in the company and they sang to work off their weariness. One of the songs that was popular was a Methodist hymn, "Say, Brothers, Will You Meet Us?" which had a broad, swinging rhythm. Ditties, many of nonsensical doggerel, were sung to this tune.

One of the leading figures in the funmaking was a jovial Scotchman named John Brown. If he appeared a few minutes late, the working squad would josh him, "This can't be John Brown; why, John Brown is dead." Some wag added, "Yes, poor, old John Brown is dead. His body lies a-moldering in the grave." Some doggerel on this style was sung to the Methodist tune. Then someone added the line, "His soul is marching on," and the meaning was clearly shifted to the historical John Brown since it was recognized that the combination of words and melody was an inspired one.

The Twelfth Massachusetts Regiment, named the Webster regiment, came to the fort to drill and the song spread among the men like wildfire. One Sunday evening, to great applause, it was sung in a dress parade while the regimental band played it. On July 18, 1861, the Webster Regiment visited Boston for a grand field day and review on Boston Common and, while marching up State Street, every man in the long line joined in singing it heartily.

The next month the regiment left Boston for the front, and when they marched on Broadway in New York City the crowds were electrified by the song. The New York *Independent* of August 29 had this editorial:

> Who would have dreamed, a year and a half since, that a thousand men in the streets of New York would be heard singing reverentially and enthusiastically in praise of John Brown. Such a scene was witnessed on Saturday evening last. Seldom if ever has New York witnessed such a sight or heard such a strain. No military hero of the present war has thus been honored. No statesman has thus loosed the tongues of a thousand men to chant his patriotism.
>
> It was a notable fact that while the regiment united as with one voice in singing this song, thousands of private citizens, young and old, on the sidewalks, in crowded doorways and windows, joined in the chorus. The music was in itself impressive and many an eye was wet with tears.

The obscure Scotchman, John Brown, who occasioned the birth of the song, found a watery grave at Front Royal, Virginia, on June 6, 1862, thus joining hands with the celebrated John Brown in having given his life for the cause. Their song was by far the most popular one in the Union Army and the soldiers composed a thousand stanzas or more. Oliver Wendell Holmes wrote:

> All through the conflict, up and down
> Marched Uncle Tom and Old John Brown,
> One ghost, one form ideal; . . .

It girdled the globe. It was sung in the streets of London while our Civil War was going on. Prussian soldiers were heard chanting it when they invaded France in 1870. It was adapted to their revolutionary cause by the Irish Fenians. In the mountains of Macedonia, guerrillas fighting the Greek government sang it.

We have testimony as to the universality of the appeal of his story in a revolt in the deep recesses of Africa in 1915 against British colonial rule which was inspired by John Brown. It is related in a 1968 book, *Strike A Blow and Die*, a manuscript recently discovered which was written by an ill-educated native black, George Simeon Mwase, telling of the uprising in Nyasaland led by John Chilembwe, who assembled the tribal chiefs and told them "about one, a Mr. John Brown of America, who after losing his hope in succeeding the request in writing to the authorities concerned in regard to slave trading, he determinate to strike a blow and lose his own life." Chilembwe assured them that, "This case stands the same," and, "Let us then strike a blow and die for our blood will surely mean something at last." The revolt was futile and ended in the execution by the British authorities of Chilembwe and the ringleaders.

The hero-worship rolled on in America after the Civil War, although it had to compete with the growing Abraham Lincoln mythology. There was by no means one voice about him. In most responsible quarters in the South, he was never regarded as anything but a blackguard. There was the sharp anti-Brown reaction in Kansas. There were backbiters in New England, most prominent of whom was Eli Thayer, who in an envenomed campaign against the Brown canonization spoke in this vein: "All his fame as a hero and martyr rests upon his lies and those of his biographers. If we admit his sanity, we must regard him either as a felon or fiend."

The Haymarket Affair, the bomb thrown in Haymarket Square in Chicago on May 4, 1886, during a labor riot, which resulted in the hanging of four anarchists who probably had nothing to do with the throwing of the bomb, and then the scare because of the spread of Socialist doctrine in the United States roused some to the danger that the John Brown doctrine bore to established institutions. There were evidently subversives in America who looked on the system of capitalism with the same abhorrence that John Brown felt for the yoke of slavery, and who regarded industrial slavery as unjustifiable as was chattel slavery. What if such persons, following the example of John Brown and acting in response to the dictate of their own conscience took it on themselves to wreck the bastions of capitalism—such as a raid on Pittsburgh to seize the steel mills and liquidate the steel millionaires?

Thayer assailed Brown as the "Prince of Anarchists," and the Brown legend was indeed invoked in the anarchist movement. Then, too, the Socialist leader, Eugene V. Debs, who also had a burning conviction of right versus wrong, cherished Brown as his great hero. In 1910, Theodore Roosevelt in an article in *Outlook* magazine, while praising Brown as an individual expressed his reservations about his social philosophy. "The experience of John Brown illustrates the evil of the revolutionary short-cut to ultimate good ends. The liberty of the slave was desirable, but it was not to be brought about by slave insurrection. The better distribution of property is desirable, but it is not to be brought about by the anarchic form of Socialism which would destroy and uproot capital and tend to destroy our present wealth."

Brown has had a place in Marxist propaganda, but leftists have had no monopoly; for example, rightists who support the doctrine of the "preventive war" might well cite him for precedent. In fact, it was the champion of conservatism in America, Senator Barry Goldwater, who proclaimed a Brown-like philosophy at the Republican National Convention of 1964, after he was nominated for President: "Extremism in the defense of liberty is no vice . . . moderation in the pursuit of justice is no virtue." This same Goldwater was strongly condemnatory of actions in the streets by the black militants and sympathetic white activists who felt, in accordance with their concept of the "higher law," that extremism for attaining justice for Negroes was not wrong.

"John Brown in American Literature" was the subject of a Ph.D. thesis by Joy K. Talbert at the University of Kansas in 1941. She compiled a list of 58 novels, 11 short stories, 245 poems, and 31 plays. A compilation up to the present day would show an expanded number in each category. "Men cannot imprison or chain or hang the soul," wrote John Brown in prison before his execution and his spirit did. march on. Thus Carl Sandburg wrote fittingly in his "Osawatomie":

> They hauled him into jail,
> They sneered at him and spat on him,
> And he wrecked their jails,
> Singing, "God damn your jails."
> And when he was most in jail,
> > Crummy among the crazy in the dark,
> > Then he was most out of jail.
>
> They laid hands on him and he was a goner,
> > They hammered him to pieces and he stood up,
> They buried him and he walked out of the grave, by God,
> > Asking again, where did that blood come from?

After the death of her husband, Mrs. Brown stayed continuously on her North Elba farm, her means augmented considerably by the funds contributed by sympathizers and some part of the profit from the Redpath book. Higginson had been much piqued by her refusal to permit Brown to be buried in Boston which would be a martyr's shrine within reasonable distance and suitable transportation facilities. Higginson suggested Mt. Auburn cemetery in Cambridge. How many pilgrims would make the long trek to the Adirondacks? Mrs. Brown would not yield and make this final contribution to the cause and Higginson, in a peeve, discouraged any futher fund-raising for the Brown family. Sanborn put the Brown girls, Annie and Sarah, tuition-free into his Concord school where they did not remain long. George L. Stearns, who met them there, said, "They were good girls but with dreary expressions, as if their lives had been hard and joyless."

In 1865, Annie went south to Virginia to teach in a school for freed black children. Francis H. Pierpont was governor of the loyal state of Virginia at Wheeling, in western Virginia, which moved to Alexandria in June, 1863, and then to Richmond after it fell to Union forces in 1865. He had an interesting story to tell. He met former Governor Wise in Richmond in 1866, and Wise told him that he had gone down to his farm in Princess Anne County. "Very soon I found John Brown's daughter teaching school in my mansion house and they would not permit me to go into the house." Pierpont found this greatly amusing. "In less than seven years since you hanged John Brown for his attempt at Harper's Ferry, a Negro school is being taught in your mansion house, taught by his daughter, and you are a fugitive, not permitted to enter it."

Wise meditated, and then, as he walked off, he muttered, "John Brown was a great man, sir. John Brown was a hero."

From time to time honors were paid to the surviving Browns. In 1874, Victor Hugo presented a gold medal to Mrs. Brown, the money for which had been raised by public contribution in France. Hugo continued his veneration of Brown and, in *Les Miserables*, Volume V, Hugo commented, "*Pour nous qui préfère le martyr au succès, John Brown est plus grand que Washington.*"

All the Browns steadfastly refused to capitalize on their family relationship and intimate knowledge of John Brown. They refused all offers to publish books or articles or receive fees for lectures. John Brown, Jr., in declining one such offer for a lecture said, "I cannot consistently do it because it looks so much like making money out of my father that I feel that it would impair my own sense of self-respect."

The engine-house at Harper's Ferry was bought by a group of speculators, taken apart, and then reassembled at the Chicago

World's Fair in 1893 where it was exhibited as John Brown's Fort. There was a great deal of pressure exercised on Ruth Thompson through Sanborn to take a job as ticket-seller at the Fort, but though in great financial need she refused. After the fair, the building was repurchased and set up on a farm on the Shenandoah, two miles from Harper's Ferry. Later it changed hands again and was located at Storer College at Harper's Ferry, a Negro college founded there in 1867. Again it was moved in the town and today, a great tourist attraction, it stands near the Shenandoah Bank, not far from the Potomac bridge which Brown crossed on the night of October 16, 1859, but closer to the arsenal site than to the armory. In all these transplantations and relayings of bricks it may not be the same building since it is probable that the dimensions of the original structure have altered and, indeed, some of the bricks may have been lost.

In 1870, the North Elba farm was sold to the John Brown Associaton, and Mrs. Brown lived with one or another of her children until her death in 1884. In 1896 the farm was sold to New York State which preserved the farm as an historic site. Owen Brown died in 1889, John Brown, Jr., in 1895, Ruth Thompson in 1905, and Sarah Brown in 1906. Jason Brown died in Pasadena, California, in 1910. His great passion in life had been flying machines and he had made his first model in 1876, explaining that the religious teachings of his father had made him think since he was six years old of the angels of heaven and that man might like them acquire wings. Salmon Brown died in Portland, Oregon, in 1919. He had been bedridden for two years; one day there was a report of a gunshot and he was found dead in his bed. The last survivor of the children of John Brown, Annie Brown Adams, died in California in 1926.

At a later time, in paying tribute to John Brown, Thomas Wentworth Higginson said that he had been the most eloquent of the Abolitionists, since he had spoken with the eloquence of a life. Speaking at Harper's Ferry in May, 1881, on the fourteenth anniversary of the founding of Storer College, Frederick B. Douglass said: "His zeal in the cause of my race was far greater than mine. It was as a burning sun to a taper light. I could live for the slave but he could die for him."

A martyr by definition is one who voluntarily, that is, by an act of his own volition, suffers death as the penalty for carrying out or refusing to renounce his religion or principle. The term is often loosely or inappropriately applied. In a certain sense, Abraham Lincoln was a martyr in freedom's cause since the commander-in-chief fell victim of that great armed conflict. Other American Presidents who have been assassinated while performing their official duties and were illogical victims of madmen—James A. Garfield, William McKinley, and John F. Kennedy—have each been described as a martyred President, but however poignant the tragedy or deep the sense of loss, they do not seem to qualify under the narrow meaning. On the other hand, Reverend Martin Luther King who, in a flash of pre-science soon before his assassination, said in a sermon that while he wanted like other human beings to live a long life, he was aware that in consequence of his beliefs he might live a short one, was justly termed a martyr to his cause.

The Christians who in the time of the Caesars or the English Tudors sought to emulate Christ and lovingly wore the crown of thorns as they went to their deaths were fitting cases, and martyrdom has been frequent in religions other than Christianity. It is interesting that so much of the John Brown martyrdom glorified in literature has been patterned on the Christ story. In Carl Sandburg's poem, "Osawatomie," he sounded overtly the "He was despised and rejected" theme, and the resurrection theme.

Intense moral conviction about a cause can repose in saintly quiescence. Brown's activism flowed from ordinary human drives. There was his great will to command and his intense egotism powered by the conviction that he had been singled out by the Lord as his instrument. Undoubtedly the enormous drive owed much to an overcompensation for the continuous frustrations and failures of his first fifty-five years. Beneath the harsh and isolate exterior, there was a good deal of introspection and personal philosophy. There was his fatalism, expressed to visitors to his cell while awaiting execution, that all this was ordained thousands of years before the world was born, just as he had told James Townsley that night before the massacre on the Pottawatomie that it had been ordained from the beginning of eternity that he make an example of the victims.

Following his formal interrogation by Governor Wise, Senator Mason, and Congressman Vallandingham at Harper's Ferry, Brown had a short colloquy with the governor, and there is a striking passage. Governor Wise said that he had been reddened with blood and should think upon eternity. Brown answered, "Governor, I have from all appearances not more than fifteen or twenty years the start of you in the journey to that eternity of which you kindly warn me. There is an eternity behind and an eternity before, and the little speck in the center, however long, is but comparatively a minute. The difference between your tenure and mine is trifling and I want to therefore tell you to be prepared. I am prepared."

The life to live or the life to give? The question is as deep and impenetrable as is the mystery of life itself. Brown had preferred to take the risk involved in his foray and, if he failed, to go out in a blaze of glory. In his thinking, whether he died then or later, in the natural course, was the difference of a fraction of "a little speck in the center."

Our life seems to have been given us by nature's law on condition of sustaining it as long as possible. The great mass crawl meaninglessly across the stage and sink into oblivion. The few who are strong enough to sacrifice days of their lives, to break the bonds of self in order to seek a mystic unity with all humanity, have faith that they thereby reach beyond the grave to victory. And who is there to say with certainty that they are mistaken in that faith?

Bibliography

THE BIOGRAPHIES of John Brown mentioned in the Introduction are as follows: *The Public Life of Captain John Brown* by James Redpath (1860), see the review by Charles E. Norton in the *Atlantic Monthly* for March 1860; *The Life and Letters of John Brown, Liberator of Kansas and Martyr of Virginia* by Franklin B. Sanborn (1885); *John Brown and His Men with Some Account of the Roads They Travelled to Reach Harper's Ferry* by Richard J. Hinton (1894); *John Brown* by W. E. Burghardt Du Bois (1909); *John Brown, a Biography Fifty Years After*, by Oswald Garrison Villard (1910), see the reviews of the Sanborn and Villard books by John T. Morse in the *Atlantic Monthly* for February 1886 and November 1910 respectively; *John Brown: The Making of a Martyr* by Robert Penn Warren (1929). A scholarly semi-biography is *John Brown and the Legend of Eighteen Fifty-Six* by James C. Malin (1942). There are other biographies of lesser note by William E. Connelley (1900), David Karsner (1934), and Jeannette Nolan (1950). A subsidized attack on his reputation was made in *John Brown, Soldier of Fortune* by Hill Peebles Wilson (1918).

There are extended treatments of John Brown in *Abraham Lincoln, a History* by John C. Nicolay and John Hay (1890); *History of the United States* by James F. Rhodes, volume II (1904); *The Emergence of Lincoln* by Allan Nevins, volume II (1950); *John Brown's Private War* by C. Vann Woodward in the book *America in Crisis* edited by Daniel Aaron (1952). Gamaliel Bradford has an interesting psychological study in his book *Damaged Souls* (1923).

The letters of John Brown are seemingly endless in number and are bricks with which one can almost construct the edifice of his life. Sanborn in his 1385 book has the most complete collection (with corrected spelling) but he acknowledged that he missed his purpose of printing them all by a wide mark. I have encountered additional ones in all collections I have consulted. Beyond the Brown letters, the narratives, interviews, and undated newspaper clippings in the Boyd B. Stutler collection which have been used cannot be specifically identified. Additional sources on various subjects will be listed in this bibliography.

In Chapter I, James Foreman, who worked for John Brown in Pennsylvania around 1830, wrote a full letter to James Redpath about his recollections of his employer and George B. Delameter likewise supplied vivid memories. For this phase of his life, see the pamphlet *The Pennsylvania Career of John Brown* by William R. Lingo (1926) and also *John Brown, Pennsylvania Citizen* by Ernest C. Miller (1952). Mary Land has an excellent study, "John Brown's Ohio Environment," in the *Ohio State Archaeological and Historical Quarterly* for January 1948. John Brown, Jr., and Ruth Brown Thompson furnished recollections of their father to Sanborn who incorporated them into his book. Salmon Brown in his last years often reminisced. See *Outlook* for January 25, 1913, and the *American Magazine* for January 1917. John Brown's abortive plan to settle in Virginia is discussed in "John Brown and the Oberlin Lands" by Boyd B. Stutler in *West Virginia History* for April 1951.

For the North Elba experience, see "John Brown in the Adirondacks" by Albert Shaw in the *Review of Reviews* for September 1896; a description of the site is in *The New York Times* of October 20, 1929, and "The Grave Where John Brown Sleeps" by Ed Eastman in *American Agriculturist*, September 19, 1959. Richard Henry Dana, Jr., related his encounter there in "How We Met John Brown" in *Atlantic Monthly* for July 1871. For the Springfield experience, see "John Brown in Springfield" by Harry A. Wright in *New England Magazine*, May 1894; the meeting of Frederick L. Douglass with Brown in Springfield in Douglass's autobiography (1882) and the biography of Douglass by Philip S. Foner (1964); Aaron Erickson's tale of Brown's failure in the wool business is in the affidavit regarding Brown's insanity submitted to Governor Wise of Virginia in the Library of Congress. Wendell Phillips Garrison discussed the evolution of Brown's consciousness on the slavery question in "The Preludes of Harper's Ferry" in the *Andover Review* for December 1890.

The struggle for the control of Kansas waged by North and South was the subject of books from the earliest date. In 1856, the correspondent of the New York *Tribune*, William A. Phillips, published his *The Conquest of Kansas by Missouri and Her Allies*. The next year in England there appeared a book by the correspondent of the London *Times*, Thomas H. Gladstone, *Kansas; or Squatter Life and Border Warfare in the Far West*. Sara T. L. Robinson, the wife of the prominent free-state leader, wrote an 1856 book *Kansas; Its Interior and Exterior Life*. *The Kansas Conflict* by her husband, Charles Robinson, did not appear until 1898. Eli Thayer glorified his own role in *A History of the Kansas Crusade* (1889). Since James H. Lane was a suicide in 1866, he did not live long enough to explain how he had saved Kansas, but a biography by John Speer in 1898 *Life of Gen. James H. Lane* performed the task for him. A report in depth is *History of the State of Kansas* by A. T. Andreas (1883) and also *Kansas: The Prelude to the War for the Union* by Leverett W. Spring (1885). Recently we have a book by Alice Nichols, *Bleeding Kansas* (1964). *Cheerful Yesterdays* by Thomas Wentworth Higginson (1898) looks at Bleeding Kansas through the eyes of a proper Bostonian.

A vitriolic attack on John Brown was mounted by George Washington Brown in his *The Rescue of Kansas from Slavery, with False Claims Corrected* (1902). Some participants in the Kansas fighting gave accounts which are none too reliable. Among those who claimed they fought with Brown, see *With John Brown in Kansas* by Edward P. Bridgman collaborating with Luke F. Parsons (1915), and *John Brown, the Hero* by Jonathan W. Winkley (1905).

Turning to articles on Kansas, see "Bleeding Kansas and the Pottawatomie Murders" by M. W. Quaife in *Mississippi Valley Historical Review* for March 1920 and "John Brown and Sons in Kansas Territory" in the *Indiana Magazine of History* of June 1935. John Brown, Jr., made an interesting statement about the massacre in the Cleveland *Leader* of November 29, 1883. For the roles of Theodore Weiner and August Bondi, see "Some Jewish Associates of John Brown" by Leon Huhner in *Magazine of History* for September 1908. Henry Clay Pate gave his version of the battle of Black Jack in his 1859 pamphlet entitled "John Brown as Viewed by H. Clay Pate."

The earliest literary attack on John Brown's reputation was made by David N. Utter, after the Townsley confession, in "John Brown of Osawatomie," published in the *North American Review* of November 1883. He grinds the same ax in his review of Sanborn's biography in the *Dial* for October 1885. A highly favorable viewpoint on John Brown was rendered by Kansas United States Senator John J. Ingalls, replying to Utter, in the *North American Review* for February 1884, "John Brown's Place in History." The correspondent W. A. Phillips told of his talks with John Brown on three different occasions in Kansas in *Atlantic Monthly* for December 1879. *Newsweek* magazine for July 7, 1941, discusses the argument over the John Steuart Curry murals in the Kansas State capitol building. For a neglected phase of the Kansas struggle, the crusade from the South, see "The Buford Expedition to Kansas" by Walter L. Fleming in *American Historical Review* for October 1900.

There are several recent worthy books on the antislavery movement: *The Crusade Against Slavery* by Louis Filler (1960); *The Crusade for Freedom in America* by Dwight L. Dumond (1961); *From Slavery to Freedom, a History of American Negroes* by John Hope Franklin (1956). For Boston leadership in the Abolitionist movement, see *The Bold Brahmins, New England's War Against Slavery 1831–1863* by Lawrence Lader (1961). Also see *On Freedom's Altar: The Martyr Complex in the Abolition Movement* (1952) by Hazel Catherine Wolf.

The Road to Harpers Ferry by J. C. Furnas (1959) is concerned in most part with the activities of the Secret Six of Boston and has good personality sketches. Sanborn discoursed on his relationship with John Brown in his *Recollections of Seventy Years* (1909). Higginson did so in his *Cheerful Yes-*

terdays (1898). There is a rewarding biography of Higginson of 1968, *Strange Enthusiasm*, by Tilden G. Edelstein. Sanborn wrote of his friend, Dr. Howe, in *The Philanthropist* (1891). Julia Ward Howe wrote of her husband in her *Reminiscences* (1900) and there is a good 1956 biography by Harold Schwarz entitled *Samuel Gridley Howe, Social Reformer*. Theodore Parker was the subject of biographies by Octavius B. Frothingham (1874) and by Henry Steele Commager (1936). For Gerrit Smith, see the biographies by Frothingham in 1878 and by Ralph V. Harlow in 1939. *The Life and Public Services of George Luther Stearns* was written by his son, Frank P. Stearns (1907).

Turning to articles on Brown's Boston sponsorship: Sanborn described his first meeting with the hero in "John Brown in Massachusetts" in *Atlantic Monthly* for April 1872 and then wrote "John Brown and His Friends" in the same publication in July 1872. He discussed two of his colleagues in "Gerrit Smith and John Brown" in the *Critic* for October 1905 and "Theodore Parker and John Brown" in *Outlook* for December 4, 1909. Frank P. Stearns was the author of "John Brown and His Eastern Friends" in the *New England Magazine* for July 1, 1910. See Zita Dyson's article "Gerrit Smith's Efforts in Behalf of the Negroes" in *Journal of Negro History* for October 1918. For Brown's first meeting with the great Concord intellectuals, see "Emerson, Thoreau and John Brown" by Gilman M. Ostrander in *Mississippi Valley Historical Review* for March 1953.

There are some useful articles on John Brown while in the West in 1857–58. Soon after Richard Realf's death there was an article about him in *Lippincott's* for May 1879 and in July 1903, "An Overlooked American Shelley" by John Ward Stimson in *Arena Magazine*. John Brown's interesting sojourn among the Quakers is the subject of a number of articles: "John Brown and His Iowa Friends" by B. F. Gue in *Midland Monthly* for February 1897; "A Woman's Recollection of John Brown's Stay in Springdale" by Mrs. E. S. Butler in *Midland Monthly* for November 1898 and "John Brown—They Had a Concern" by Jeannette Mather Lord in *West Virginia History* for April 1959.

For the Chatham convention in Canada in the spring of 1858, see the book by Hermann E. Von Holst entitled *John Brown*, which discusses this subject in the early pages. The best source is the article "John Brown in Canada" by James C. Hamilton in *Canadian Magazine* for December 1894. See also "From Chatham to Harper's Ferry" by Fred Landon in *Canadian Magazine* for October 1919 and by the same author "The John Brown Raid" in *Journal of Negro History* for April 1921.

The description of the Hamelton massacre in Chapter Six is based in the most part on literature prepared by the Kansas State Historical Society for the Marais des Cygnes Massacre Memorial Park in Linn County. For John Brown's raid into Missouri, see the article in the *Missouri Historical Review* for October 1931 and the article in the St. Louis *Globe-Democrat* for April 5, 1888, which contains the account of Rufus Cruise. Dramatic events in the flight from Kansas to safety are told in these sources: "The Battle of the Spurs" in *Kansas Magazine* for October 1872; for the cold-shoulder treatment in Tabor, the Reverend John Todd recounted it in "John Brown's Last Visit to Tabor" in *Annals of Iowa* for April 1898; for the reception in hospitable Grinnell, see the book by Josiah B. Grinnell entitled *Men and Events of Forty Years.*

For the sojourn in Cleveland by the John Brown party on the return from Kansas, see "John Henry Kagi in Ohio" in the *Ohio State Archaeological and Historical Quarterly* for July 1925. For John Brown's last days in Boston, *Letters and Recollections of John Murray Forbes*, edited by Sarah Forbes Hughes (1899). Benjamin F. Gue related how he and his brother David sent the letter to Secretary of War Floyd exposing the plot in *Review of Reviews* for March 1897.

The primary source material for the account of the Harper's Ferry raid is the testimony in the hearings of 1860 before the Mason Committee of the United States Senate, *United States Reports*, 36th Congress, 1st Session, Number 278. In addition to the testimony of participants such as hostages and residents of the area, the hearings also investigated the background of the raid, including correspondence of Brown and the conspirators and testimony of individuals involved such as Richard Realf and William F. M. Arny.

Two books of recent years are *The Raid: A Biography of Harper's Ferry* by Lawrence Greene (1953) and *Thunder at Harper's Ferry* by Allan Keller (1958). Joseph Barry was a resident of Harper's Ferry at the time and his account is in his book *The Strange Story of Harper's Ferry* (1903) which was originally a pamphlet of 1873 by Josephus Junior entitled *Annals of Harper's Ferry*. Osborn P. Anderson, one of the John Brown's men, made good his escape from Harper's Ferry to Canada, and gave his account in *A Voice From Harper's Ferry* (1873), a combination of the factual and fictional. Elijah Avey was then a youth living in Charlestown and contributed *The Capture and Execution of John Brown* (1906); Alexander M. Ross, a friend of Brown, was then in Richmond, see his *Memoirs of a Reformer* (1893); Lieutenant J. E. B. Stuart described the raid in detail in a letter to his mother from Fort Riley in Kansas on January 31, 1860; see *Life and Campaigns of J. E. B. Stuart* by H. B. McClellan (1885); for the role of a famous southerner in taking Brown captive, see volume II of *R. E. Lee* by Douglas S. Freeman (1934).

There is a profusion of purported eyewitness accounts in newspapers and articles, but on examination most merely recite the published accounts of the affair. Some have historical importance. Alexander R. Boteler, the Congressman from Jefferson County, was there and gave an informed story in "Recollections of the John Brown Raid" in *Century* for July 1883. John E. P. Daingerfield was one of the hostages taken by Brown; see his "John Brown at Harper's Ferry" in *Century* for June 1885. Lieutenant Israel Green led the Marine storming party and he has an important story to tell in "The Capture of John Brown" in *North American Review* in December 1885. David H. Strothers, known as Porte Crayon, was in the paymaster's office when the captured Brown was carried there and related the scene in "Last Hours of the John Brown Raid" in *Virginia Magazine* for April 1905 (it was not published fully at the time in *Harper's Weekly* by whom he was employed).

Newspapers of the time have been used by the author for the assessment of the state of public opinion in North and South at the time of the news of the

raid, and newspaper accounts have also been used for the testimony at the
trial of John Brown and his comrades. The New York *Herald* had the best
reporting of the trials. Frederick Trevor Hill as part of a series "Decisive
Battles of the Law" recounted the trial of John Brown in *Harper's Weekly*
for July 1906. In his 1953 book, *Fair Trial*, in which he analyzed American
trials from Anne Hutchison to Alger Hiss, Professor Richard B. Morris declared that John Brown had received an unfair trial. In reply to the criticism
of Professor Von Holst in the same vein, General Marcus J. Wright defended
the trial's fairness in *American Historical Association Papers*, volume IV (1890).
The presiding judge, Richard Parker, retrospected about the trial in the St.
Louis *Globe-Democrat* of April 8, 1888, and the prosecutor Andrew Hunter
gave his thoughts in *Southern History Association Publications*, volume I,
1897. A valuable discussion is "Legal Phases of the Trial of John Brown" by
Daniel C. Draper in *West Virginia History* for January 1940. For the trial
and execution of Edwin Coppoc, see the article about him by Charles C.
Galbreath in the *Ohio State Archaeological and Historical Quarterly* for
October 1921. For the role of Governor Henry A. Wise of Virginia, see the
biography by his grandson, Barton H. Wise (1899). F. Alexander McClure
gave the details concerning the apprehension of John Cook in Chambersburg
and his extradition to Virginia in his book *Recollections of Half a Century*
(1902).

For details on John Brown's conduct in imprisonment, see the article in the
New York *Sun* for February 13, 1898, entitled "Saw John Brown Hanged"
by Colonel William Fellows. In connection with Brown's will that he made
before execution, the mimeographed pamphlet, "Owen Brown's Estate," published by Edwin W. Brouse in 1952 explains the money that his son John
had in expectancy to bequeath. There seem to be as many fictional accounts
of the hanging as there are of the Harper's Ferry raid. "Stonewall" Jackson
was there and for his impressions, see his life written by his widow Mary
Anna Jackson in 1892. For other authentic eyewitness reports, see Murat
Halstead in the *Independent* for December 1, 1898, and a recently discovered
report by David H. Strothers, the correspondent for *Harper's Weekly*, which
was unpublished until it appeared in *American Heritage* for February 1955.
For a discussion of the origin and spread of the kissing episode myth, see
"The John Brown Legend in Pictures" by James C. Malin in *Kansas His-
torical Quarterly* for November 1939. Reverend Joshua Young described the
funeral of John Brown and how he was treated afterward as a pariah by his
parishioners in *New England Magazine* for April 1904. A. W. Macy described
the later recovery of the remains of Watson Brown in the *Independent* for
June 20, 1895, and then we have "The Final Burial of the Followers of John
Brown" by Dr. Thomas Featherstonaugh in *New England Magazine* for
April 1901. "Owen Brown's Escape from Harper's Ferry" appeared in *Atlantic
Monthly* for March 1874 by Ralph Keeler.

Last we have the materials on the aftermath and repercussions of the event.
The best source for the immediate impact, although grossly exaggerating the
sympathy for Brown, is the book *Echoes of Harper's Ferry* by James Redpath
(1860). A more balanced judgment was made by C. E. Norton in the *Atlantic*

Monthly for March 1860. For the attitude of the religious press in the North, see the article by William S. Rollins in the *Ohio State Archaeological and Historical Quarterly* for April 1952. The Reverend Theodore Parker's feelings were given in his letters to Francis Jackson of Boston and published in 1860. For other reactions, see the autobiography of Moncure D. Conway (1904) and letters of Sarah Everett in *Kansas Historical Quarterly* for November 1939. The diatribes of Eli Thayer under the heading "Felon or Saint" appeared in the New York *Tribune* for October 8 and November 19, 1887. Victor Hugo's letter on John Brown with a hostile reply by Mrs. Ann S. Stephens was published in 1860. For the apotheosis abroad, see "Abraham Lincoln and John Brown: a Parallel" by Boyd B. Stutler in *Civil War History* for September 1962. John Michael Ray in "Rhode Island's Reaction to John Brown's Raid," in *Rhode Island History* for October 1961, finds that Rhode Island was not much enthused. The origin of the John Brown song is discussed by Samantha Whipple Shoup in the *Independent* for July 21, 1910, and by George Kimball in *New England Magazine* for December 1889. The final subject is the effect of the John Brown raid in precipitating the Civil War. The opinion of President James Buchanan that it did have an important effect is contained in his *Mr. Buchanan's Administration on the Eve of the Rebellion* (1866). There are discussions of the impact of the raid in these books: *Antislavery Origins of the Civil War* by Dwight L. Dumond (1939); *The Coming of the Civil War* by Avery Craven (1942); *The Disruption of the American Democracy* by Roy Nichols (1948).

Index

Index